From Oratory to Scholarship

FROM ORATORY TO SCHOLARSHIP

Two Centuries of Talks on the American Revolution Given Before the Society of the Cincinnati in the State of New Jersey

Compiled by
Denis B. Woodfield, D.Phil.
John W. Gareis, M.D.
and John Saunders, PH.D.

With an Introduction by
Vincent C. De Baun, PH.D.

1783

Published by
THE SOCIETY OF THE CINCINNATI
IN THE STATE OF NEW JERSEY
2008

The senior editor of this volume is Denis Buchanan Woodfield (D. Phil., Oxford University); the associate editor is John Van Dyke Saunders (Ph.D., University of Florida); the illustrations were chosen and captioned and the Appendix was written by John William Gareis (M.D., University of Maryland); and the introduction was written by Vincent Claud De Baun (Ph.D., Rutgers University).

Library of Congress Control Number: 2008923039
ISBN: 978-0-615-19637-4

Manufactured in the United States of America

Book jacket and interior design by Max Crandall

Distributed by the University of Virginia Press

CONTENTS

Illustrations

(Illustrations appear between pages 144 and 145)

Preface

The Society of the Cincinnati in the State of New Jersey has existed since June 11, 1783, when General Elias Dayton convened an organizational meeting in Elizabeth-town (as it was then known) of the officers of the New Jersey Line (as General Dayton referred to them) for the purpose of considering the Institution of The Society of the Cincinnati. We are told in the minutes of the meeting of 11 June, 1783, of the Society: "After some time spent thereon, they *resolved unanimously* to become members and subscribed the institution accordingly." The new Society then adjourned to meet at Princeton the following September 22. See *The Society of the Cincinnati in the State of New Jersey* Trenton, N.J., The John L. Murphy Publishing Company, Printers, 1898, p. 29.

Although 1783 is universally accepted as the year of formation of our One Society of Friends, it is interesting to note that the first of the series of *Toasts*, which have been transcribed and printed for the first time as the Appendix to this volume, is clearly dated from internal evidence at 1782. This new evidence proves that the officers of the New Jersey Line Regiments held at least one meeting during the previous year, and that this meeting was formal enough to warrant the drinking of a number of previously conceived and recorded toasts.

The extensive records of our New Jersey Society are preserved in the Library of the Society of the Cincinnati at Anderson House, together with a number of other historical artifacts relating to New Jersey. Our legal seal dates from our earliest days and is still used by our Society. It was described by President Joseph Bloomfield (see illustration 22) on July 4, 1809, as follows:

The Seal of the Society in the State of New Jersey.

Extract from the report of President Joseph Bloomfield, made to the Society at Elizabethtown July 4, 1809

The Principal figure Cincinnatus. The Time, when his Country no longer needed his exertions in Arms.

His Sword and Shield, ornamented with an Eagle, are thrown aside, to which he is pointing, with one hand and with the other taking hold of the Plough; intimating that he has given up his high Military Employments; become a private citizen, and devoted himself to the pursuits of Agriculture.

On a scroll, above Cincinnatus, is inscribed the "Reward of Virtue," "Virtutis Premium;" ornamented with Roses, as Emblematical of the Beauty and fragrance of Virtuous Actions which like the fragrance of the Rose remains after death.

A fortified City and Harbour, with an Ancient Galley in view; distant mountains, with a rising Sun.

One hundred years later, our Society published a book in a dark maroon binding in a very limited edition entitled:

Excerpts of the Proceedings of the Society of the Cincinnati in the State of New Jersey from May 13th, 1783, to July 4th, 1906.

Also a Summary of the Treasurer's Account with the original members.

At the head of this title page is a hand-colored die-sunk image of the Society of the Cincinnati Eagle, about seven-eighths inches wide by about one inch high. Engraved inside the center of the image is the legend:

Societas.Cincinnatorum.Instituta. ***A.D.*** **1783.**

Below the representation of Cincinnatus is the motto ESTO PERPETUA in block capitals on a plain (no ribbon) background. An enlarged reproduction is shown in this volume as illustration 1. On the next page is the statement: Copyright, 1908, by W.T.B.S Imlay for the Society of the Cincinnati in the State of New Jersey.

Use of this ESTA PERPETUA motto is similar to its use in the Virginia Eagle of 1906, image number 63, in *The Insignia of the Society of the Cincinnati* by Minor Myers Jr., where the motto is used on a ribbon. This motto does not appear distinctly in any of the other eagle medals illustrated by Dr. Myers. Close examination of our 1908 New Jersey Eagle clearly indicates, however, that it was designed as a die for stationery and not as a medal to be worn. The design of the arrows clutched in one of the eagle's talons, as well as the design of some of the foliage, is so delicate that it could not have been reproduced as a free-standing medal. Jack D. Warren Jr., executive director of Anderson House, states that several stationery dies of Cincinnati Eagles exist in the Anderson House collections, but that our New Jersey variant has not yet been found.

Our most spectacular treasure is probably the Flag of the Society of the Cincinnati in the State of New Jersey, which dates from about 1838 and currently hangs on the third floor of Anderson House. It is a silk flag, painted on both sides by the well-known sign painter, artisan, and artist John Archibald Woodside (1781–1852). A resident of Philadelphia, Woodside was a member of the Artist's Fund Society and exhibited at the Pennsylvania Academy between 1817 and 1836.

The front of the flag features a scene with three Roman senators presenting a sword to Cincinnatus, with a bald eagle with outstretched wings clutching a shield. In the right quadrant, behind Cincinnatus, is a log cabin with his wife standing in the doorway. The words "OMNIA RELINQUIT SERVARE REMPUBLICAM" are evident.

The verso features a central scene with Cincinnatus standing next to a hand plow in a plowed field and holding a pitchfork. Overhead is an archangel blowing a horn and holding a gilt wreath and banner with the words "VIRTUTIS PREMIUM" over the head of Cincinnatus.

The minutes of the New Jersey Society meeting in 1838 note that a sum had been spent for a "Standard of the Society." The flag was rediscovered in the attic of Anderson House in 1971, and the New Jersey Society preserved and mounted it shortly thereafter. It has been on display at Anderson House since that time and is shown as illustration 2 in this book.

Individual members of our One Society of Friends also have family treasures that are illustrated in this book.

Horace Pease Phillips Jr., of Fullerton, California, has provided copies of two such documents. One is the original commission appointing his great-great-great-grandfather Jonathan Phillips, a second lieutenant in Captain Brearly's Company of the Second Battalion of the New Jersey Troops, signed *By Order of Congress, John Hancock, President,* and dated November 20, 1775 (see illustration 3).

The other document is the original certificate of membership in the New Jersey Society of the Cincinnati of his great-great-grandfather, Horatio Gates Phillips, signed: *Joseph Bloomfield, President,* and *Andrew Hunter, Secretary,* January 7, 1809. Note that it is sealed with our Society's legal seal (as described earlier), which proves this seal to be at least two centuries old (see illustration 4).

As Dr. Vincent De Baun explains in the Introduction to this book, the tradition of an oration read at the annual meeting goes back to the earliest days of our Society. Many of these orations have been preserved very carefully in our archives at Anderson House. The earliest example still existing, dated July 4, 1789, and given by Major General (of Militia) Frederick Frelinghuysen, an Honorary Member admitted 1783, is printed for the first time in this volume as Oration 1. The earliest orations exist only as manuscripts, and even then sometimes only as rough drafts of the original text, while later orations often survive in printed form as pamphlets. In the minutes of our Society's 1869 Annual Meeting, it is reported that

> *The President called the attention of the Society to the fact that the day [July 4th] was no longer observed as in former times by reading of the Declaration of Independence and an oration, and expressed a wish that some action might be had to restore a custom so appropriate to the celebration of the day.*

Surviving copies of orations in our files indicate that this custom was indeed reinstated, and numerous examples are preserved for the next half-century.

A modern set of files resulted from the new series of History Prizes, which was approved in 1979. President Ross Maghan Jr. carefully preserved the texts of these lectures whenever possible, and from these later texts came the inspiration for this volume. Following is a list of the winners of our New Jersey Cincinnati History Prize since its inception:

1980	*Richard McCormick*	*1994*	*Clement Price*
1981	*Larry Gerlach*	*1995*	*James Kirby Martin*
1982	*Carl Prince*	*1996*	*David Cohen/Louis Presti*
1983	*Donald Sinclair*	*1997*	*Herbert C. Kraft*
1984	*Mark Lender*	*1998*	*Richard Waldron*
1985	*Peter Wacker*	*1999*	*Garry Stone*
1986	*Eugene Sheridan*	*2000*	*Charles Cummings*
1987	*John Murrin*	*2001*	*Marc Mappen*
1988	*John O'Connor*	*2002*	*Karl J. Niederer*
1989	*Mary Murrin*	*2003*	*Brendan McConville*
1990	*Thomas Slaughter*	*2004*	*Harry Ward*
1991	*Carla Mulford*	*2005*	*David H. Fisher*
1992	*Bernard Bush*	*2006*	*Bruce Chadwick*
1993	*David Fowler*	*2007*	*Evan Thomas*

Finally, for those readers who wish to find more reminiscences and original diaries of Revolutionary War veterans from New Jersey whose orations are published here, the following sources are recommended:

The diary of Major Joseph Bloomfield, which has been published as *Citizen Soldier: The Revolutionary War Journal of Joseph Bloomfield*, edited by Mark E. Lender and James Kirby Martin, Newark, *New Jersey Historical Society*, 1982. Joseph Bloomfield was an officer in the Third New Jersey Regiment from 1776 to 1778. A native of Woodbridge, New Jersey, he was later mayor of Burlington and served as governor of New Jersey from 1801 to 1812. His Revolutionary War service took him from Fort Stanwix to Fort Ticonderoga in New York, to the battle of Brandywine in Pennsylvania, and to Monmouth and elsewhere in his native state.

A Journal kept during an Expedition to Canada in 1776 by Ebenezer Elmer, printed in the *Proceedings of the New Jersey Historical Society* for 1847 and 1848, with an addendum of *Lost Pages* printed in 1925. Elmer was a lieutenant in the Third New Jersey Line under Colonel Elias Dayton and later became Surgeon of the Second Regiment. He died October 21, 1843, aged 91 years—the last surviving officer of the New Jersey Line of the Revolutionary Army. The original journal is in the research library at the New Jersey Historical Society in Newark, New Jersey.

The *Journal* of Brigadier General Elias Dayton still exists. Some of it is preserved with the New Jersey Historical Society and was published in its *Proceedings*, but the rest is dispersed in several other locations. Dayton was an original member, admitted 1783, and served as the first president of our Society, 1783–1807. The text is quite interesting and deserves to be better known.

Finally, I wish to record my and my co-compilers' indebtedness to Ellen McCallister Clark, the library director of the Society of the Cincinnati at Anderson House, without whose help this book could not have been written. Ellen always knows exactly where to find any piece of material relating to our Society, and she usually can suggest additional relevant material that the rest of us did not know even existed. She has shown infinite patience in answering all our questions and is a tremendous resource to all the members of our One Society of Friends. Our most sincere thanks and appreciation are due to Ellen for all her invaluable help, suggestions, comments, and general assistance.

—Denis B. Woodfield, D.Phil. (Oxon)
Treasurer, The Society of the Cincinnati in the State of New Jersey

FROM ORATORY TO SCHOLARSHIP

INTRODUCTION

Vincent C. De Baun

GLORY RECOLLECTED

Since 1783, members of the Society of the Cincinnati in the State of New Jersey have gathered in twice-yearly meetings. In the beginning, the Original Members (a title always capitalized) were officers who had served in the Continental Line under George Washington in the War for Independence; when peace was declared, they had formed this special organization to dedicate themselves to preserving the ideals that had driven the Revolution and given energy and direction to a new nation.

As the Original Members departed, they were succeeded by their sons or grandsons down the generations, or when direct lines had died out, by nephews or other collateral descendants. We who are current members honor their memory: "Let us now praise famous men."

At almost every meeting since 1783, a speaker has addressed the members. These addresses have gone under a number of names—orations, papers, presentations, speeches, remarks, and so on. Seen *seriatim,* changing steadily as the nation has changed, they represent a unique picture of the way the Revolution has been imaged and understood. In the beginning, we have what are, in effect, extended arias of ringing praise for Washington and the heroes of the war (with many side excursions to assail the British), mixed with references to ancient history and Scripture and exhortations to the listeners to lead Christian lives.

Then, starting at about the time of the Civil War, the papers become much shorter, take on occasional light humorous touches, and deal less with the full flow of the Revolution than with specific episodes in the war. The change is understandable when we realize that those who had served in the war itself—those who had been at Quebec or Brandywine or Yorktown—had all passed from the scene, as had almost all the generation that had followed, who might have heard stories of the long struggle directly from those who had endured it. (The last remaining Original Member of the Society, Ebenezer Elmer, had died in 1843, at the patriarchal age of 91; remarkably, his son, Lucius Quintius Cincinnatus Elmer, survived until 1883, dying at 90, long after the rest of the second generation had departed.) The newer presentations include ventures into original historical and/or genealogical research, and the voices become simpler and less declamatory, as though the speakers had taken cues from the more naturalistic styles of American contemporaries such as Twain or Howells, or even popular English authors such as Dickens or Trollope.

The changes begun in the Civil War years kept evolving into the twentieth century. The foundations and mission of the Society are freshly explored. The combat experiences of members' propositi are historically reconstructed, so that they become individual personalities. Little-known clashes like the British assault on Egg Harbor are brought to light. But alas, from the era just before the First World War through mid-century, the energy seems to fade and the papers become thin and perfunctory; none will be offered in this collection. Then, with the 1960s, there is a different touch as at least one speaker ventures into irony and we feel an edge of defensiveness about New Jersey itself.

A distinct shift was now in the wind. A committee of the Society under the leadership of the late Craig Colgate Jr., then president, determined to seek out and reward (with a financial grant) scholars whose work has constituted "distinguished achievement in promoting the knowledge, understanding, and appreciation of the history of the State of New Jersey in its early years." Since 1980, such scholars—usually professors holding endowed chairs at major universities, sometimes officers of historical associations or museums—have been identified in a search coordinated by Ross Warne Maghan Jr. and invited to address the members.

By and large, their papers are different from those of earlier years. The tone is clearly more intellectual than emotional, but the style is crisp—blessedly free of acadamese and any detectable tendency (yet) to deconstructionism. Interestingly, although the speakers have been recognized for outstanding work on aspects of New Jersey history, most have chosen to explore broader themes such as the personalities and standards of the Founding Fathers, or the compromises, both practical and philosophical, that lie behind the Articles of Confederation and the Constitution. Other speakers, of course, have concentrated, as expected, on comparatively neglected aspects of Jersey history that reflect back on the larger story.

This current phase of reflecting on the Revolution—at least in its spoken (and then printed) form to the Society—clearly still has a long way to run. What phase may develop in future years remains to be seen.

The Early Years: The Image of Washington

Fellow-Citizens. For decades, that term was part of the salutation of every speech delivered to the Society. It was a declaration of sorts: You and I are not mere residents or settlers, much less are we *subjects*. We are *citizens*. Not since ancient days, when a man might say in the fullness of proud security, *civis Romanus sum,* could a more important title be held. We are owners in part, the speakers said, of an independent nation shaped in struggle and blood from a new land.

Inevitably these orations (we'll come back to that word in a moment) rehearsed the drama of the winning of that independence. In varying sequences, the stories were told of Lexington and Concord and Bunker's Hill, Trenton and Princeton, Brandywine and Germantown and Valley Forge, and on to Monmouth and Charleston and finally Yorktown. Some narratives even reached back beyond Braddock and the disaster at Fort Duquesne in the French and Indian War.

Through all these accounts, the great figure of Washington looms. To the admiring speakers in those early years, he is an exemplar of "matchless fortitude and perseverance"; when mutiny threatens at the end of the war, the officers are guided "by the experience, wisdom, and rational conduct of their beloved Commander, their father and long tried friend"; he is "bold and intrepid" and marked by powers of "reasoning and persuasion . . . affectionately beloved . . . unboundedly respected." When he is called upon to lead his comrades in a now almost forgotten episode in American history, the near-clash with Napoleonic France in 1797, he is seen as "hero, patriot, Christian," for he dares "to put his immortal reputation once more to hazard, unsheathe his glittering sword, and decorate his hoary head with the high-plumed beaver."

In these early addresses to the Society, Washington's leadership inspires the Founders, who see that they must steer past the shoals of the Articles of Confederation to reach the safe harbor of the Constitution, carefully formed on its "principle of checks and balances." (The now-familiar phrase appears several times.) As though the subject still needed explanation, the framework of government is oddly—and not entirely correctly—outlined. Beyond the general power of Congress to make laws, the House is described as having "the exclusive right to declare War . . . [and to hold] the purse strings," while the Senate has "the exclusive right of assenting to Treaties . . . [and] approving the publick functionaries nominated by the President," who in turn is "vested with those powers . . . necessary to carry the laws into execution" while appointing ambassadors and "commanding the Armies and Navies of the United States." Over all preside the ultimate "Courts of Justice . . . with permanent salaries, during good behavior." The fascinating possibility of delinquency from good behavior is not explored.

Throughout these happy descriptions of a sturdily balanced republic runs a thread of concern that personal ambitions and party rivalries could tumble the infant government. Washington had been deeply troubled by this thought, and it is a recurring theme in his correspondence and his Farewell Address (1796), for he had seen the flowering of the bitter enmities of the Jeffersonians and the Hamiltonians. He would surely have approved the New Jersey speakers who warned that "party spirit is the bane of free republics" and that

> *no administration of the federal government, . . . supposing it be both virtuous and able, can long succeed with honor or success, opposed . . . by a persevering and powerful opposition, aided by the press, availing themselves of talent and riches, watching and exposing the errors, difficulties, and even misfortunes of the ruling party.*[1]

Washington's prescience has been borne out amply over the centuries, of course, and seldom more so than for the past half century, during both Democratic and Republican administrations. Elias Boudinot, speaking to the Society on July 4, 1793, hardly more than four years after Washington's first inauguration, at first seems innocently hopeful when he declares that

> *the highest officers of our government are but the first servants of the people. . . . They have therefore a just claim to a fair and candid experiment of the plans they form, and the laws they enact for the public weal. Too much should not be expected from them; they are but men . . . and of like infirmities with ourselves; they are likely to err, though exercising the purest motives and best abilities.*

[1] *Joseph J. Ellis, in* American Sphinx: The Character of Thomas Jefferson. *Random House, Vintage (paperback) edition, 1998, p. 144, explains that in America's early years, "the term 'party,' and the very idea for which it stood, had yet to achieve any measure of respectability. A 'party,' as the term was commonly understood, was nothing more than a 'faction,' meaning an organized minority whose very purpose was to undercut the public will, usually by devious and corrupt means."*

But he then sounds a prophetic note:

> *Mistaken and wicked men . . . are often laboring with indefatigable zeal, which sometimes proves but too successful, to sour minds, and derange the best-formed systems. Plausible pretensions, censorious insinuations are always at hand to transfer the deadly poison of jealousy, by which the best citizens may for a time be deceived.*

For a long period, well into the nineteenth century, these orations were part of a ceremonial pattern. Members of the Society gathered at some convenient place and then, wearing their official ribbons, marched somberly with a military escort, to a church—usually Presbyterian, sometimes Methodist—to hear a reading of the Declaration of Independence and then an address which, according to official minutes, was to have "the purpose of inculcating those principles which form the basis [of the Society], as of tracing the causes of the American Revolution, and which attended and preceded that vast event, and showing the influence which it has had and probably will have on the morals, religion, and politics of the Society in general."

It is pleasing to know that after this solemnity, the members repaired to a nearby hall for a hearty meal with an amplitude of wine and spirits.

The Early Years: Classical Forms and Scripture

Orations is the right word. It is a word likely to make a modern reader or listener wince, perhaps bringing to mind unhappy memories of struggles to translate Cicero in second-year Latin, or even worse, bloviations of the "I have decided to become a candidate for president because . . . " stripe.

By our standards, the addresses were indeed fearfully long. Almost all the early speakers must have talked for well over an hour, and in 1835, Aaron Ogden Dayton even longer, in his *Eulogy on La Fayette*, although the printed version of his encomium tells us that "such portions of it were delivered as time would allow." (The text does not specify.) It should be remembered that length of this order was the standard of the era. In Parliament, Edmund Burke, one of America's few defenders in pre-Revolutionary days, often spoke for several hours at a stretch; as late as 1863 at Gettysburg, Edward Everett spoke floridly for a full two hours, and when Lincoln followed with his quiet statement of less than five minutes—now considered one of the glories of American literature—many listeners thought it a mean effort and unworthy of the moment.

The orations were usually described in the minutes as "very eloquent and truly patriotic" or "very pathetic" or "excellent and appropriate," and the speakers were requested to submit a copy for permanent inclusion in the Society's records. Some were printed. Others, but not all, survive in original manuscript form, often in flowing script on fragile paper, and are preserved in the temperature- and humidity-controlled archives of the Society of the Cincinnati at Anderson House in Washington, D.C.

Almost all of the early orations employed classical conventions and classical allusions, usually interwoven with quotations from Scripture. Parallel structures abound. Thus, with the coming of the war, "[the fields of the country] were to be crimsoned with the best blood of its sons . . . its fruitful plains were to be ravished . . . the frame of society was to be shattered . . . the sources of wealth and happiness were to be dried up . . . brother was to come into conflict with brother." At the time of the crisis with Napoleonic France, when Washington's leadership was called for once again, "Was it not enough, that thou [Washington] didst conduct [the nation] to independence. . . . Was it not enough, that thou didst spend the prime and vigor of thy life. . . . Was it not enough, that in thee the sublime virtues."

Students of rhetoric will also recognize the classical manner in various forays into Homeric simile and metaphor: Washington in crisis was "immovable as a rock upon which the raging tempest beats in vain," and Parisian mobs during the Terror in their "thousands upon thousands in dense mass extended as far as the eye could see, raging and roaring like an angry ocean," while Lafayette stood alone in the Assembly "in the very jaws of these bloodhounds."

Likewise, abstractions are called into being. With the coming of peace, we have the unwittingly risible image of "Anarchy & Discord . . . flapping their retiring wings," and there are evocations reminiscent of chants from a Greek chorus: "Ye American sages! . . . Ye American warriors! . . . Ye venerable divines! . . . Ye fair daughters of Columbia!" and so on.

Ancient history and mythology formed a background to almost all of the early addresses. The speakers clearly took it for granted that their listeners would understand references to "Fabian" tactics, while most modern readers—like this one—would need an explanation: namely, that the Roman general Quintus Fabius Maximus Cunctator (d. 203 B.C.) had perfected a technique of repeated unexpected attacks and quick withdrawals that avoided defeat in a head-on confrontation while simultaneously exhausting Hannibal's powerful invaders. The listeners knew that in the early years of the war, Washington had been sneered at as a timid Fabius; critics sniped at him and urged direct clashes with the British, either because they overestimated American strength or suffered from a vanity-driven longing for heroism and fame. (Possibly the hot heads saw themselves in the role of the Spartans at Thermopylae, who are mentioned reverentially in several early addresses.)

The audience presumably also understood, without explanation, how fearful Greek anxieties could change to joy after victory at Marathon (490 B.C.), when a small Athenian army defeated a much larger Persian force, and how that sequence paralleled the desperate retreat across New Jersey, reversed at last by the brilliant strikes at Trenton and Princeton.

Folded into the flow of the orations are Scriptural allusions, often adapted rather than directly quoted, that tell us something of the minds of the listeners. The Americans who freed themselves from Britain are likened to the Israelites liberated from Egypt. With the end of the war, America becomes a peaceful land where now every man might take his rest "under his vine and under his fig tree" (*I Kings,* 4:25);[2] thus we may "eat our bread with gladness and drink our wine with a merry heart" (*Ecclesiastes* 9:7). America is David "with a sling and the stories of a brook" and Britain is Goliath (*I Samuel,* 17). When soldiers at the end of the war were refused their just pay, "You asked for wine and they gave you a stone" (*Matthew,* 7:9). The women of New Jersey are urged to bid their children practice "whatsoever things are true, whatsoever things are honest, whatsoever things are just" (*Philippians,* 4:8). The Stuart kings Charles II and James II are the demons Belial and Moloch. And so on.

Ebenezer Elmer's oration of July 4, 1812 is worth some particular attention. Unfortunately, it begins with a parade of heavy paragraphs of tortured formality, as though he felt that only the most complex and elegant sentences could suit the occasion; but then he does find a readable rhythm. (The opening high flown style will be a disappointment to readers of his remarkable wartime journal, published in segments in the quarterly of the New Jersey Historical Society from 1846 to 1848, with an additional previously lost segment in 1925. It is the work of a somewhat priggish young man, but it is lively, alert, and full of details of day-to-day life in a regiment of the Continental Line and peppered with many shrewd observations and touches of gossip. It is utterly unlike the oration's stiff exercise in declamation.)

The intense religiosity is immediately striking; but Elmer was not a minister. Rather, he was a successful physician who had given up his practice to serve in state government and been a member of the U.S. Congress, of Jeffersonian

---

[2] *This image was a favorite of Washington's. For example, interested readers might see, among others, his letters of June 18, 1788 to Lafayette, or of June 25, 1797 to Rufus King.*

persuasion, from 1801 to 1807. Nevertheless, he calls upon all American citizens, blessed as they are with liberty in a democratic society, to be "penetrated with lively gratitude with that Devine Being from whom descendeth every good and perfect gift," for "the throne of the unchangeable deity is at all times accessible by every individual and nation who by piety and virtue are made fit objects of his benedictions." His spiritual earnestness and his sincerity are woven throughout the address. Like his contemporaries, he uses Scripture for his metaphors; thus, when he asks if "pure patriotism and disinterred love of country have motivated political decisions," he wonders, "who can say I have hitherto washed my hand in innocence" (*Psalm* 25:6), and then he admonishes possible critics, "let him who is without sin cast the first stone" (*John* 8:7).

In seeking the wellspring of his religious conviction, we may surmise that his family had been swept up in the impassioned revival commonly called the "Great Awakening" that had burned through the colonies in roughly 1720 to 1750. The Mid-Atlantic region had been especially affected, as itinerant preachers gathered vast crowds in meadows or town squares and harangued them in a spirit of evangelical Calvinism. Emotions ran high, often bordering on hysteria, and converts were many. It is curious to reflect that while many Americans became, in effect, ardently "born again," others—Washington, Jefferson, Franklin come to mind—were Rationalists or Deists who apparently never sought a relationship with Jesus as a personal Savior but contented themselves with acknowledging the existence of a Creator who, having endowed humankind with the right to life, liberty, and the pursuit of happiness, merited a sober reverence and devotion, but of a very private kind.

Elmer's sense of the abiding presence of God is evident as—leading finally to his references to the War of 1812, for which his audience must have been waiting. He recounts ominous events of the year just passed, even while declaring that he and his informed listeners are "no longer influences by . . . superstitious forebodings":

- He describes the "burning sphere," the "fierce fiery form" of the comet that had flashed across the sky in December 1811 for several nights and had astonished and terrified people everywhere. (It was a phenomenon of such weird incandescent brilliance that it is mentioned in Tolstoy's *War and Peace* as a portent of horrors to come.)

- On December 16, 1811, a massive earthquake had struck New Madrid, Missouri, and then been followed by a series of other shuddering quakes (now known to seismologists as the New Madrid Sequence) that continued for five months. The earth split and emitted foul odors, volcanoes of sand erupted in meadows, and at one point the mighty Mississippi actually flowed backward as tides roiled and huge pieces of riverbank crashed into the stream.

- On December 26, 1811, a fire broke out in a theater in Richmond, Virginia, horribly burning to death 72 patrons—including, in Elmer's words, "the wise sage, the hoary-headed father, the tender and palpitating mother, the spritely and heroic youth, and the gay, captivating virgin."

Elmer sees these direful events against a background of war and mass murder in the world (or at least the world as he knew it.) Civil war rages, he says, in "the Spanish American provinces," and "a brother's hand has been deeply tinctured with a brother's blood . . . [in Mexico and Paraguay, Peru and Caracas.]" In keeping with his generation's instinct to refer to ancient models, he compares these battlefields to Pharsalia (48 B.C.) and Philippi (42 B.C.). Even worse, in Europe "two great belligerents continue to cast about firebrands, arrows, and death . . . slaughtering thousands and spreading death and destruction." One of these belligerents, of course, is Britain. Now, because of its "injury . . . and persevering obstinacy," Americans are "called upon by the constituted authority of our country to defend that independence and those privileges with our arms which we obtained by them."

It is worth noting that Elmer does not specify Britain's offenses, such as the suppression of trade or the impressments of seamen that we all learned about in school, but rather he takes the occasion to warn that the fierce desire of our enemies is "that our citizens [will] not coalesce under a government sufficiently energetic as to secure the prosperity and preserve the internal peace of society." Basically, in their envy, "the Sovereignties of Europe are averse to the prosperity of these States," and "they estimate our loss as their gain—our fall their rise—our shame their triumph."

Typically, he sees the looming war as a form of divine retribution for our sins: "We have, my friends, all of us, offended the majesty of heaven, and the sword of our foe, it seems, is to be lifted up for our chastisement." We can survive the crisis and return to the calm joys of prosperity and peace only, first, by "repentance of our personal and national crimes," and then by following the paths of "reason and the cool suggestions of deliberative wisdom."

Above all, in the manner of so many other contemporary speakers to the Society, he urges that we renounce "party spirit, for that is almost universally a spirit of intolerance and violence." To illustrate "the indulgence of discontent and envy," and "the fatal effects of jealous, fretful . . . temper on a nation," he offers as a peculiar example the Biblical history of the Jews, at least as he interprets it. He tells of the Israelites, who, after being freed from Egyptian bondage through "the many miracles [that had been] wrought for their deliverance," had let themselves fall under the sway of "artful men," forgotten their gratitude to Moses, and "rebelled against the institutions of their lawgiver." They accused him of "peculation and knavery" and of seeking to make himself a prince, and many were prepared to stone him.

Then with the passing of generations, after "reputed wise men had sadly defaced and corrupted the Institutions of Moses," the Jews succumbed to "the artifice and influence of the Scribes and Pharisees, who boasted much of their intelligence and purity" until at last "with the same temper and increased malignity" they sought the death of Jesus and rejoiced in the Crucifixion.

Elmer's lesson to his audience: The Jews had given in to poisonous party spirit promoted by "artful men" who made much of their "intelligence and purity." Thus: "From this awful example we ought to take warning lest we incur the same Judgments which lighted upon them."

Modern readers may find this passage somewhat discomfiting, as bordering on anti-Semitism. But it was very much in the cultural spirit of his time, and his contemporaries very probably nodded their heads sagely. They must have liked what they heard, and how it was expressed. Elmer was invited to address the Society three times (1803, 1812, 1822).

Myth, as in the earlier mentions of Thermopylae and Marathon, tended to be of a martial or at least heroic mold. When British oppressions finally drive the Americans to full revolt, "the Gordian Knot is cut." When the former colonies become states within the new nation, "like the infant Hercules [they] seem to spring from the cradle in all the maturity of vigour and power." Washington is a new Horatius, the legendary hero at the legendary bridge in the 6th century B.C., rallying his troops to heroic sacrifice. Oddly, though, Joseph Walter Scott, who drew the Washington-as-Horatius figure in 1846, has Horatius speak in rather flat prose: "Behold the roof under which you drew your first breath . . . " and so on. One wonders if he knew Macaulay's stirring verse version, which had been published four years before and was already immensely popular. It was well on its way to becoming a memory assignment for generations of schoolchildren—at least until it became politically incorrect:

> For how can man die better
> Than facing fearful odds
> For the ashes of his fathers,
> And the temples of his gods? (St. 27)

Literature had its innings, too. There were lines from such as Milton (*Paradise Lost*—more on this later), Pope ("Verses Left by Mr. Pope"), Thomson ("The Seasons"), and Dwight ("Columbia"), but Shakespeare was the clear favorite. Peter Kean, in 1823, recalling that officers were denied their just pay at the end of the war, quotes *King Lear* (I,iv)—"Ingratitude, thou marble-hearted fiend"—and then, neatly reversing the point of Marc Antony's famous lines in *Julius Caesar* (III,ii), says of the sacrifice of the patriots, "The good that men do lives after them." Aaron Ogden Dayton, comparing Lafayette to Brutus at the end of his eulogy (1835), also echoes Marc Antony: "He was the noblest Roman of them all . . . the elements so mix'd in him that Nature might stand up and say to all the world—'This was a man' " (*Julius Caesar*, V,v). Earlier, describing the blood-crazed pitiless mobs in Paris during the Terror, he takes Marc Antony's "O judgment, thou art fled to brutish beasts, and men have lost their reason!" (III,ii) and, like Kean, shifts the focus, so that it is compassion, not judgment, that is "fled to brutish beasts."

Elias Boudinot (1810) also uses Shakespeare, but here a problem arises. He writes of governments in the old world that have collapsed and disappeared. Then, from Prospero's lovely melancholy lines in *The Tempest* (IV,i) that begin "Our revels now are ended" and conclude, in most public readings, "We are such stuff as dreams are made on," he compares their legacy only with the fragment "the baseless fabrick of a vision" and closes with the thought that they have left "scarcely a *wreck* behind. " (Emphasis supplied.) The original manuscript in his hand clearly shows *wreck*. A slip of the pen, or an intentional use of the word? Most scholars believe that Prospero's word was *rack* (a thin wisp of cloud) or *wrack* (a dried fringe of foam and seaweed on the shore), but certain not *wreck*. Perhaps this is academic niggling.

As for *Paradise Lost*, Dayton's eulogy on Lafayette held an unintentionally comic moment. To describe the Founders pondering the immense responsibility of issuing the Declaration of Independence he uses the quote: "deep on their front engraven/ Deliberation sat and public care" (Book II, 11. 302–3). Dayton, a graduate of Princeton, must have been much taken by the grim tension of those lines but quite forgot their application: Milton is describing Satan and his senior devils in Hell, plotting revenge after being expelled from Heaven. Thus, there stand the likenesses of Jefferson and Satan, side by side.

This raises a question that could be worthy of academic research. How knowledgeable were the audiences who heard these addresses? Certainly they knew Scripture. They were regular churchgoers, and every family had a Bible, often a handsomely bound volume especially mentioned among bequests. But how many had seen Shakespeare's plays or read them in print? How many had read Milton?

The Middle Years: From the Civil War to Vietnam

In 1859, humorous moments bubbled up for the first time. The Reverend Dr. John Hall, reflecting positively on America's variety of religions, points out that after all, Queen Victoria contrives somehow to be "a Presbyterian at Balmoral and an Episcopalian at Windsor, and I suppose, as a grandmother, a Lutheran at Berlin. " Later in the same address, picturing Cincinnatus preparing to go to war, Hall puns gently that "the good man" might be concerned that while he is gone his "little fields must remain unsown," but one may also wonder if his wife "thought that she had sewing enough of her own to do."

A note of passing interest to students of phraseology: In referring to the years that have passed since the signing of the Declaration of Independence, Hall uses the formulation "fourscore and three years ago."

In any event, Hall gives us the last touch of levity for some while. With war in the offing and then bloodily in force—New Jersey would lose more than 6,000 men in the conflict—the immediate crisis swept all before it, and apparently the custom of regular patriotic addresses fell away. The minutes in 1869 tell us that the president of the Society was concerned that Independence Day "was no longer observed as in former times by reading the Declaration of Independence and an oration, and expressed a wish that some action might be had to restore a custom so appropriate."

So talks to the Society resume, but of a rather different kind. Gone were the surging passionate declamations by ministers who often equated the struggles of the Revolution with the struggles to live a Christian life. The new addresses covered a variety of topics and in their printed versions were no longer described as "orations." For a brief period around the turn of the century, a group of much shorter pieces called "historical papers," substantially the outgrowth of research by Society members themselves, and mostly 20 to 30 minutes in length, appeared in a series of pamphlets.

For instance, Dr. Timothy Matlack Cheesman and Dr. Hughes Dayton write accounts of their propositi that are appealingly human in detail and try to picture events as they actually occurred, so that their intrinsic drama is present without oratorical flourishes. Cheesman's paper (1898) on the campaign in Canada tells of troops at Montreal who are not the unflinchingly patriotic heroes of legend but who sleep at their posts "with impunity" and who try to wangle discharges by pretending illness (e.g., by "swallowing tobacco to bring on obstinate vomiting"). Likewise, certain officers are foolishly reckless, launching an unauthorized attack that results in forty-five men being taken prisoner and causes Generals Montgomery, Schuyler, and Washington "great anxiety, illustrating, as it did, the insubordination that existed." The paper ends with a brief description of the death of Captain Jacob Cheesman during an assault on Quebec, December 31, 1775, in a driving snowstorm.

Similarly, Hughes Dayton's (1901) paper on the life of his great-great-great-grandfather, Brigadier General Elias Dayton, is written in simple declarative sentences without recourse to high theater. It differs from the Cheesman work in that it outlines the general's genealogy and early career, including his service in the French and Indian War, and quotes at length from his journals and letters, with their original free-wheeling spelling and punctuation, or lack thereof. In a letter from Yorktown on October 12, 1781, to his son (whom he addresses as "Sir"), he writes of a report that "Ld. Cornwallis has got into a cave to be out of the way of our shells, both shells and shot we are informed by deserters do great execution." Later, the letter goes on:

> *I am very sorry to hear that your Mama continues so much indisposed but hope by proper assistance she may be recovered. . . .*
>
> *And now my dear son take the advice of a fond father it may be the last you will ever receive from him. Attend to your Studies & prepair yourself to be usefull to your fellow men and if possible an ornament to the Society in which you live. Above all I pray you to do justice love mercy and to walk humbly with your God, & then I am sure happiness will attend you through all eternity.*
>
> *The drums are just going to beat to parade for the march to the trenches. So fare well and God bless you—remember me most effectionately to your dear brothers & sisters. The drum beats to arms.*

From the same period (1898), William S. Stryker gives us a valuable description of "The Affair at Egg Harbor" in October 1778. This little-known engagement, which took place at a bay and inlet that are just north of what is now Atlantic City, was one of the many comparatively small clashes that helped determine the course of the war but are only passingly mentioned in major histories. Stryker's work is substantially original in going to primary documents rather than secondary sources; indeed, in appendices he includes six extended official reports, one American, the others British. He also gives diagrams that are useful in tracing the course of the action.

The story is amusing in that British accounts described the Americans as "skulking banditti" and "virulent rebels" and "a piratical crew. " It is less amusing in British justification for the massacre of prisoners: "It being a night attack, little quarter could, of course, be given," and in any case "Mr. Pulaski has, in public orders, lately directed no quarter should be given"—an order "unworthy of a gentleman." (This charge of dishonor against Pulaski, originating with a deserter, was false.)

Note that Pulaski, seen as a mere revolutionist in an unrecognized army, is referred to as "Mr." In keeping with British practice at the time, he is denied either his military title as general or his aristocratic title as count. It is also interesting—typically, in official dispatches—that the British "numbered . . . [the American] dead about fifty," while claiming for themselves "[not] a man lost" and just one soldier wounded by a bayonet in the leg. The Americans, on the other hand, estimated their own loss "dead, wounded, and missing about twenty-five or thirty," while "that of the enemy appears to be much more considerable." No wonder casualty estimates for the war remain such a guessing game.

Another very useful original paper of the time was Dr. Luther Foster Halsey's "The Revolutionary Worthies of the Medical Staff," delivered to the Society in 1890. It is an extended report on individual physicians, who, without any models to guide them, played a major role in developing medical services to the army and then struggled with problems of hospital administration—establishing and staffing medical centers; and obtaining funding from a reluctant Congress. When funding did come, devalued Continental currency almost always lagged the crucial needs. To add to the executive stress, professional conflicts grew out of strained human egos and ambitions that lay very near the surface: hospital surgeons and regimental surgeons, usually men of professional vanity, often wrestled for supremacy.

Of course as before, the turn of the century continued to be marked by discourses on Washington and on the foundation and purposes of the Society. Stryker's picture of Washington (1897) is one of almost unrelieved praise, beyond a glancing reference to "the disastrous battle of Long Island," and the text quotes admiring American and French observers, almost all of whom mention the general's height (more than six feet) and remark on his "calm dignity . . . the severity of his countenance and the majestic gracefulness of his deportment," "his dignity and grandeur," "his candour, sincerity, affability, and simplicity," and so on.

In the same period, William Pennington's several presentations to the Society (1897, 1909, 1911) are of a new character, correctly seeing that worrisome changes were gathering. Attendance at meetings had sagged, and by 1909, the papers "written and read by a member upon some revolutionary subject" had ceased publication "[despite] the pleasure they gave those present." He even sees signs of decay in the fact that Fourth of July banquets have been replaced by "buffet lunches such as our ancestors would have considered almost a breach of propriety." Pennington's anxieties (other than those about the enjoyment of banquets) seem to have been borne out by the placid and unremarkable character of Society activities in the years ahead. The members continued to meet semi-annually, conducted their business *proforma*, and made regular contributions to good causes but somehow failed to produce or attract addresses that could be said to reconsider the Revolution in original or interesting ways.

Why there should have been such a long quiescent stretch in the life of the Society—at least in terms of intellectual stimulation—might require the analysis of a social historian. It was, after all, a hectic period that encompassed World War I; the boom years of the 1920s, with the overlay of the Jazz Age and/or the Flapper Age; the Great Depression and FDR; World War II; Auden's Age of Anxiety and/or Galbraith's Age of Affluence, and so on, leading finally to the uproar (some might say chaos) of the demands for sexual freedom and civil rights and protests against the Vietnam War in the 1960s.

A renewed approach to the Revolution came from an unexpected source. In 1968, author, historian, essayist, and journalist John T. Cunningham—not a member of the Society—addressed a triennial meeting of the Society at Morristown in sharp but humorous terms. His title, "George Washington Stayed Awake Here," may need some explanation. For some years, country inns up and down the East Coast had advertised (dubiously) that "George Washington Slept Here," and in 1940, there had even been a successful Broadway comedy with that title by Kauffman and Hart.

Cunningham opens with the jape that for too many modern Americans, Washington had apparently existed "as an excuse for an annual clearing of surplus merchandise on his birthday"; he then points out that the general had to have stayed keenly awake in New Jersey because ONE-THIRD OF THE ENTIRE WAR (Cunningham's capitals) took place there—indeed, that the central belt of the state, positioned as it is between New York City and Philadelphia, properly has been called "the cockpit" of the war; the army fought with superb bravery but was never far from the risk of total annihilation, especially during the viciously cold winter of 1779 to 1780. In this lively talk, Cunningham reminds us that "history is a matter of human beings who once lived. . . . We forget that people of two centuries ago laughed and lived and loved; these things were not invented in the twentieth century."

In calling for "a rebirth of American patriotism," he also warns us, "We do not honor bold ancestors by becoming timid descendants. We do not preserve the past by demeaning the present." That is a good thought to keep for those who have an intimate link with New Jersey—object of too many snide jokes by late-night TV comics and seen by too many mostly as the home of Tony Soprano.

A final note on Cunningham's talk: It was given in late May 1968. Earlier in the decade, John F. Kennedy and Malcolm X had been assassinated. In April of that year, Martin Luther King Jr. had been assassinated. Soon Robert F. Kennedy would be assassinated. Within months, the Democratic National Convention in Chicago would take place amid rioting in the streets outside. In the immediate years that followed, the Watergate fiasco would boil over, Richard Nixon would resign in disgrace, the United States would withdraw from Vietnam after more than 50,000 troops had died, and the economy would be battered by inflation, recession, and two oil crises. It was not a good period for continuing prideful and thoughtful consideration of the Revolution, even though 1976 marked the 200th anniversary of the Declaration of Independence.

At Present: Scholars' Light and Shadow

This introduction has already described how, beginning in 1980, fresh views of the Revolution and its origins and outcomes and unusual aspects began to be part of the regular addresses to the New Jersey Society. Most of these were the contributions of professional scholars being recognized for distinguished achievement in research and publication, but individual members also were motivated to delve into history and report their findings. (See, for example, this author's 1982 review of the so-called New Jersey "Red Book" of 1908, which summarized minutes of Society meetings since its founding; Lt. Colonel William H. Forman Jr.'s 2002 biographical account of his propositus, Brigadier General David Forman, which provides an especially interesting comparison with Hughes Dayton's sketch of his propositus, Brigadier General Elias Dayton, exactly one hundred years before; and "New Jersey Men in the Continental Artillery," by William B. Brown III in 2006, which is both a valuable contribution to genealogical research and an interesting sidelight on the relationship of artillery units to other combat troops.)

It is striking that although almost all the invited speakers were being honored for their work in the early history of New Jersey, most chose to dwell on political and social issues in the nation at large. An exception is Peter O. Wacker's (1983) study of damage claims made to the state following the war. This intriguing melding of geography and cultural history looks at such homely matters as the breed of barnyard fowls or the design of Jersey fences to draw conclusions about the folk who lived in certain areas, and the recompense they requested from the state legislature for stolen or ruined property. Generously, claims were to be considered not only for damage caused by the contending armies, but also by marauders intent mostly on pillaging or on wanton destruction aimed at settling old scores. Harry M. Ward, in his (2004) essay on "The Refugee War," touches on the latter—the savage elements of civil conflict in which the indiscriminate attacks of guerilla raiders were a kind of terrorism.

In a more civilized realm, but one with its own intensities, most of the other Cincinnati Prize speakers have dwelt rather on the often painful compromises of the Articles of Confederation and the Constitution that gave birth to problems that plague us still. True, Carl E. Prince's (1982) thoughtful study of Governor William Livingston does confine itself to a New Jersey topic, but even there we are drawn to consider the perpetually vexing broad questions of class distinctions and equal rights. Prince tells us that Livingston, a patrician of great wealth and property, began his long service (he was governor from 1776 to 1790) as "cold, austere [and] private," but he learned, as he traveled his state, "to shed his inherited prejudices against the great mass of middling, anonymous Jerseymen" and "to respect and admire" their solid virtues.

Contrast this with Mary R. Murrin's (1989) picture of Edward Rutledge of South Carolina, who during debate over the forming of the Articles of Confederation said of his Yankee opponents, "I dread their low Cunning, and those leveling Principles, which Men without Character and Fortune in general Possess, which are so captivating to the lower class of Mankind."

Indeed, both Murrin and John E. O'Connor (1988) describe how America's groping toward a Constitution meant finding a way "to institutionalize an idea that all had heard enunciated on many occasions but that no society had ever been able to convert into concrete and routine principles—the sovereignty of the people" (O'Connor). As Murrin points out, the delegates succeeded in Philadelphia "not because they all became angels but because they abandoned a form of government hand-cuffed by jealousies and local prejudices and started over." At the end, the supreme touch of political genius came when the power of central government was balanced by the individual protections in the Bill of Rights. Thus, James Madison could write:

> *Is it not the glory of the people of America, that whilst they have paid a decent regard to the opinions of former times and other nations, they have not suffered a blind veneration for antiquity. . . . Happily for America, happily we trust for the whole human race. . . . [T]hey accomplished a revolution which has no parallel in human society: They reared the fabrics of governments which have no model on the face of the globe.*

Richard P. McCormick (1980) and Larry R. Gerlach (1981), the first two speakers in the current Cincinnati Prize series, give us sensitive analyses of the emotions and personal standards that drove the Framers. Yes, it is true that deeply felt passions often threatened to overwhelm the cool seeking of a "Middle Way." Fierce enmities divided Hamiltonians and Jeffersonians, and Jefferson and John Adams became for a time bitterly estranged. Thomas Paine went so far as to accuse Washington of being "treacherous in private friendships . . . and a hypocrite in public life." These remain for us deeply troubling aspects of our national history until we realize that, as McCormick tells us, "It was their very commitment to republicanism . . . that made these patriots so passionate. . . . Paradoxically, it was because they shared the same basic faith."

From another perspective, Gerlach adds that whatever the intense differences among the Framers, it was conscience that drove their decisions. Honor could be realized only "by adhering to a code of ethical conduct that merited approval in one's own mind as well as in the eyes of contemporaries. There was no distinction between ethical private and public behavior. The one was impossible without the other." True fame would be reached only "in recognition by peers and posterity for deeds performed in the public interest."

A final note to close this introduction: Even today, we debate the question of the immutability of the Constitution. Is it a perpetual model, unchangeable and forever fixed? Or is it an evolving document, living and flowering? Gerlach offers two interesting quotations. The first is from Thomas Paine: We must "refresh our patriotism by reference to first principles. It is by tracing things to their origins that we learn to understand them and that it is by keeping that line and that origin always in view that we never forget them."

On the other hand, Thomas Jefferson wrote that we must not look at constitutions "with sanctimonious reverence . . . too sacred to be touched," but as human progress advances "and manners and opinions change with the change of circumstances, institutions must advance also."

There is an odd comfort for us in knowing that some arguments never die. *Plus ça change,* and all that.

For more than 200 years, speakers to the Society of the Cincinnati in the State of New Jersey have been reflecting on our Revolution and writing its story. Style has altered, of course, since the early days. Declamation and oratorical ornament have given way over the generations to calm observation, reflective questioning—even affectionate humor. We find today's scholars teaching us that research and academic analysis may have changed the angle of our views, but other things have not changed—pride, for example—pride not in ourselves, but in what we have been given. And gratitude has not changed, but only grown deeper—gratitude to those who in courage and passion and brilliant political insight gave us our nation. In return, we give abiding thanks. E. B. White has said it well: "To hold America in one's thoughts is like holding a love letter in one's hand."

∽ ONE ∼

AN ORATION

Major General the Hon. Frederick Frelinghuysen, 1789

The Honorable Frederick Frelinghuysen, 1753–1804 (Honorary Member, admitted 1783), was educated at Princeton College and was graduated in 1770. He achieved a Master of Arts degree in 1773. Frelinghuysen was First Major in Colonel Charles Stewart's Battalion of Minute Men, February 15, 1776. He was Captain, Eastern Company of Artillery, New Jersey State Troops, March 1, 1776. He was promoted to Colonel, First Battalion, Somerset County, New Jersey Militia, February 28, 1777. As such, Frelinghuysen took part in the Battle of Monmouth, June 28, 1778. He was later promoted to Major-General of Militia of New Jersey. He was a member of the Continental Congress, 1778–1779, and later a trustee of Princeton College, 1802–1804. As an Honorary Member, he is not represented in the Society today (see illustration 5).

An Oration
delivered before the Society of the Cincinnati of New Jersey, in consequence of their request, at Trenton, on the 4th day of July 1789

This is the day, the day of universal joy for the inhabitants of this western world. The anniversary of American Independence once more dawns on us, and it dawns with unusual brightness. The hostile desolating bands have not only left our shores, and hushed the noise of wars; our freedom & emancipation from foreign bondage, the noble objects of the bloody conflict, are not only happily effected, not only have we gained a name and station among the empires of the world, but to crown the summit of our wishes, Anarchy & Discord are flapping their retiring wings, and all the blessings of a free and efficacious government lie in the pleasing prospect now before us.

If other nations of the world have had cause to commemorate events by which their civil privileges have been enlarged, or their oppression diminished; if other nations have thought it necessary, by public festivals and splendid shews, to preserve in their memory, and to perpetuate to the knowledge of their posterity, the deliverances of their country from threatened ruin, or its elevation to superior happiness; Americans, above all other people, have reason to commemorate the event of which this day is the anniversary, with the most exalted joy, with the most cheerful festivity, and with the most unbounded gratitude to the supreme ruler of the universe. History has nothing to parallel our situation, humanity can reach no farther. Permit me therefore, my countrymen, to bespeak your indulgence to this, in discharge of the task assigned me, I take up a small part of this auspicious day, in making a few observations on the American Revolution. A subject too extensive for my feeble abilities, the greatest human abilities are inadequate to discuss it with propriety. A people extending from New Hampshire to Georgia, these millions of souls, but yesterday doomed to servitude, are emancipated and free. The empire of oppression is broken; America is independent. Welcome, thrice welcome, glorious day, whose return reminds us of the dignity of our situation! Hail blessed Epocha! Which has raised human nature from disgrace, has enlarged the empire of reason, and promises blessings, heretofore unheard of, to the present generation and to millions yet unborn.

It is a revolution, my countrymen, great in itself, and highly important in its consequences, both to these United States and to the world at large.

confederation, was at length universally acknowledged. They knew, they now felt, they were freemen. The glorious political truth, that all power is derived from the people and that they have a right to take the necessary measures for the preservation of that liberty to which they are entitled by the laws of nature, and of nature's God, was never before so happily applied. Delegates were appointed to consider the important subject of a federal government. The result of their deliberations was fairly submitted to the free and unbiased discussion of the American people; and, as pleasing to relate! After having exercised a power never before granted to the children of men, the constitution framed by their delegates was honourably adopted. A constitution securing the great and valuable rights of the people, firmly confederating these extensive and populous States, and calculated to draw forth the resources of this great empire on principles of equality and justice. By this great event the glorious fabric of American happiness has been completed, and we may now rejoice in the idea that the blood of the martyrs who died in the sacred cause of freedom was not spilt in vain.

Thus great, my countrymen, is the American Revolution in itself. Let us, for a few moments, view it in its consequences to these United States, and also to human society at large. And here the consciousness of the subject overwhelms description. The eloquence of angels is necessary to manage the majestic topic. Let us humbly, then, attempt a few traits of the glorious picture.

The freedom and independence of an immense territory, inhabited by a brave and hardy race of men, are the first fruits of the important struggle. The mind of man can hardly take in the comprehensive and novel idea. Petty republics have heretofore enjoyed, and still enjoy, a species of liberty. Placed below the envy of their neighbors, or perhaps necessary to be supported in the scale of politics, they have preserved it by this precarious tenure. America is a continent of freemen. Here millions are already in the full possession of the blessings of genuine liberty; and from her happy situation, the fertility and extent of her cultivated and uncultivated lands, she promises to extend the incomparable boon to additional millions & millions & millions.

Peace, the great harbinger of all earthly blessings, promises long to be the portion of this happy land. Unconnected with the politics of foreign nations, united at home by a firm and equal government, war and the rumors of war shall no more disturb our repose; but contented with Sovereigns of our own extensive and exuberant country, we shall naturally betake ourselves to the cultivation of those arts which are calculated to make us a great & happy people. The farmer, the merchant and the mechanic will, with united efforts, promote our wealth; cheerful industry shall smile on every side, whilst temperance and frugality shall produce the fruits of its labor. Learning shall flourish, and continually add to the number of worthies devoting themselves to the commendable task of preserving, improving and enlarging the blessings gained by the wisdom of our councils and the valor of our armies. Religion too unrestrained by the secular arm, and unawed by earthly power, shall here bless her victories, and whilst enjoying the highest temporal felicity, teach them to prepare for the fruition of more exalted bliss, of pleasures which are to last for evermore.

This revolution hath also enlarged the bonds of human society, and like the intermarriages in families, promoted a useful connection between parties before totally separated. Had America remained dependant on Great Britain, these extensive States, now so happily united by the ties of interest and affection, enjoying one firm and uniform government, calculated to support, improve and defend the whole and every part, would have been so many different colonies kept by the arts of their transatlantic sovereign in perpetual broils and ferment to render them a more easy prey to the tyranny of himself and his minions. But this is not all, they would moreover have been, if not enemies, strangers to the rest of mankind. Instead of those beneficial alliances already formed, and which may be hereafter formed, royal mandates from Great Britain prohibiting all intercourse with them, would have constituted the records of our connections with the nations of the eastern continents. We should have been strangers, oh France, to thy generous benevolence, to this elegance of thought and manners, strangers to thee, Great La Fayette, thou enthusiast in freedom's cause—the soldier's boast and pride—the soldier's friend.

Another effect of the American Revolution is that it hath fixed, in the minds of the people, such a love of freedom, as must eventually preserve the important blessing. We naturally prize at a great rate what hath cost much in the attainment. The perilous struggle for American deliverance from bondage, the precious treasure & the more precious blood which has been sacrificed to accomplish it, have deservedly increased its value in the estimation of all her sons, and, no doubt, will keep them on a constant watch against every encroachment on their rights and privileges. Nay, such is the spirit of liberty which actuates the bosom of every American, that if, during its continuance, any man, entrusted with power, should attempt a measure leading to subjugate this country, he will but have risen to fall despicably low. Beware then ye present and ye future rulers of this extensive empire, that ye sport not with the liberties of your constituents, nor rouse the indignation of a people determined to be free. To use the language of the enlightened Pliny, "remember it is Athens you approach, remember it is Lacedemon you govern."

But the greatest and most beneficial effect of the American Revolution is that it hath taught mankind to revere the cause of freedom. When the nations of the old world beheld these thirteen colonies, without arms, ammunition, or discipline engaging in a war with Great Britain, then in the zenith of her glory, claiming to herself the empire of the seas, and deeming her armies invincible, they called it madness, and the more humane pitied our folly: when they saw them nobly struggling and sometimes conquering the veteran armies of this cruel foe, gaining fresh vigour in difficulties, and rising superior to the most dreadful defeats, they viewed them with silent amazement. But when they saw the God of armies, after having smiled upon their daring efforts, and frequently interposed by the most extraordinary providences in their favour, at last granting to their unexampled performance and unshaken firmness the noble objects of the contest, the freedom and independence of their country, they added esteem to their admiration, and we literally became the wonder of the gazing world. That warmth for freedom, which was here kindled into a perfect flame, could not be here confined. By wind and by water it hath crossed the wide Atlantic, and if we may judge of future events from the effects it hath already produced, the enraptured mind is pleased with the delightful idea, that it will, ere long, disenthrall the world, that tyranny will be driven from its strongest holds, and universal liberty bless the globe.

But I cannot enlarge. Those, my countrymen, are the happy consequences of this great revolution, consequences which must fill the mind of every American with raptures untasted by the unfortunate sons and daughters of bondage; with pleasures more refined than ever tyrant or tyrant's friend enjoyed. And, what is sufficient to increase that pleasure to the highest degree of ecstasy, these happy consequences promise to be perpetual. Our local situation will protect us from hostile attacks from abroad, the glorious fruits which we have reaped from our former union at home, will preserve us from all fatal dissensions among the States confederated, the natural disposition of the people will guard us against all encroachments on our freedom; and, to crown our satisfaction with this pleasing subject, the former and frequent interpositions of the divine providence, in our favor, must presage to every contemplative mind, that the omnipresent ruler of the universe hath not interfered in vain with his blessings on our arduous struggle for freedom and independence.

Rejoice then, ye Americans all, of every age, sex and condition, of every occupation & employment!

Ye *American Sages*, who, in our councils, have aided in this transcendent work, rejoice, both ye who have laid the firm foundation, and ye who have planned the magnificent superstructure!

Ye *American warriors* of every description, rejoice! Heaven hath at last stamped a value upon a *soldier's* name. Ye have not fought to make an addition to the sable list of tyrants; ye have not bled to increase the number of slaves; ye have reared a fabric of freedom the most glorious the world hath ever beheld: view it with raptures, and shout for joy; rejoice that a nation of freemen is born; rejoice that ye are its fathers!

Ye *venerable divines* and all ye friends of religion, rejoice! The liberty of conscience is one of the cornerstones of this glorious building. No slavish shackles can here be framed for the human soul. The demon, Persecution, with all its instruments of torture, is forever banished from our happy climes. Already have charity and liberality of sentiment taken place of bigotry and superstition among the different worshippers of the deity. The pure religion used undefiled will now recommend itself by its own native excellency, under the fostering and protecting care of the rulers of this extensive empire.

Ye *friends of learning,* rejoice! Lo! The sun of science hath risen on this western world, and already shines with refulgent splendour. Its rays will brighten its light increase until the perfect day. Statesmen we have who do honour to human society; in every art, in every science, we can boast of men who do honour to human nature. Republics are favorable to the muses. Large is the harvest and many laborers will be wanted. Take courage then, ye American youth, let a noble emulation fire your breasts. Believe me; the Philips will leave enough for the Alexander. Tread with pleasure in the paths of science; and for your encouragement, remember that a *Madison*, a *Paterson,* and a *Hamilton* were once the tender pupils of an Academy.

Ye *American matrons,* rejoice! Exult in the idea that you are the wives of freemen, the mothers of sovereigns.

Ye *fair daughters of Columbia!* Your charms would be lost on slaves. For heroes ye raise triumphal arches, for freemen ye throw your flowers.

Ye *American farmers,* rejoice. Your flocks and your herds are all your own. Ye are sovereigns of the fertile hills, and still more fertile vales. From well-fought fields we have gained our freedom; from well-tilled fields, we will gain both wealth and importance.

Ye *American merchants,* rejoice. The world is all before you. Hoist now the sail, and let the streamers float upon the wanton breezes. Spread your canvas to the inviting winds, and by a well-directed and extensive commerce, enrich yourselves and repay the farmer's toils.

Ye *American tradesmen and mechanics,* view your increasing consequence in this great republic, and rejoice! Long have you suffered by your country's folly; their eyes are opened, and pleasing is the prospect now before you.

But why do I confine myself to the inhabitants of this western world? Ye distant isles, ye distant nations, rejoice! Ye who groan under the hard yoke of bondage and never tasted the sweets of freedom! Lo! Here is an asylum for all the oppressed: our harbours, our cities invite you; our fertile fields invite you. Here you may enjoy the blessings of a free and happy government, plenty shall deck your boards, you shall sit in the pleasant shades of your own orchards, and there shall be no tyrant or tyrant's slave to make you afraid. But ye cannot come—learn then the sacred flame of freedom. Learn from us the important lesson, that men determined to be free, cannot be conquered. The God of armies will befriend their sacred cause and command the very elements to conspire for their deliverance. Let, therefore, the American story be rehearsed in the ears of your children, let them relate it to their children, and their children to another generation. Sound in their ears the name of *Washington:* for then argument will be needless. And now hasten, O Time! on thy rapid wings, the happy hour, when kings shall be taught that they rule for the people, and when all who govern shall know and feel this sacred truth, that liberty is the birth right of man.

Ye *departed ghosts* of heroes who nobly died in your country's cause! If aught you know of what passeth on earth, come, join with us in the joys of this happy hour. Great is the boon you have purchased with your blood, and great is your glory. It shall survive the patriot's tear gratefully dropped to your dear remembrance, it shall survive the wreck of matter and the fall of worlds.

Ye *angelic hosts,* who as revelation informs us, take delight in the works of your great creation for the happiness of men, deign to embellish the rejoicings of this auspicious day, by the junction of your harmonious views, and vouchsafe an additional *hallelujah* on American freedom. But I forbear. Let us my countrymen, who are the immediate partakers of the blessings resulting from this great revolution, rejoice with an exceeding great joy. And whilst we eat our bread with gladness and drink our wine with a merry heart, let us seriously reflect on the importance of our perfect conduct to the fate of future unnumbered generations, and let us practice those duties which alone can preserve the precious deposit of freedom pure and uncorrupted. Let virtue be the characteristic of every American, and let us unanimously subscribe to the sacred truth, that vice degradeth a people, and that righteousness alone can exalt a nation. So doing, peace shall attend, not only our days, but also those of our well-instructed posterity. Riches, and honors, and blessings of every kind shall constantly await us, and when we have finished our course of patriotism here, that virtue, which alone can recommend us to the divine benediction as a people, will also ensure to us, as individuals, the joys of a happy immortality hereafter.

But I should indeed be wanting in my duty on this pleasing occasion, and do injustice to my own feelings, if I suffered my oration to conclude without particularly addressing myself to you, gentlemen of the Cincinnati. I know not how to express the rapturous emotions of my esteem which possesses my breast, when I turn myself to those, who have been active instruments in effecting the glorious revolution I have humbly attempted to describe. I trust I need not use the language of persuasion to induce you to rejoice on the anniversary of American independence. Your Country is in full possession of the object of its wishes. You have attained the prize for which you so nobly contended. Mortifying indeed it must have been to every patriotic soldier, to behold America, after its happy emancipation, as it were oppressed with the weight of the hard earned blessing, and without the means adequate to preserve it; but surely equal might be their satisfaction, when by the smiles of indulgent heaven, the dark clouds of anarchy and discord are so happily dissipated by the blessed rays of government. If, however, your cares and difficulties since your retirement to the peaceful shades of private life, if the marks of ingratitude in your emancipated country to its military survivors have in any degree interrupted that flow of joy naturally arising on the contemplation of so glorious an event of which you made so great a part, then, gentlemen, think of the years of the war, recollect your toils and sufferings, bring back to your imagination the bitter hardships of the eight years conflict—the summer's heat—the winter's cold—the days ye thirsted, and the nights ye hungered—the painful wounds—the loathsome dungeons: add to these the blood of brothers slain whilst nobly struggling for their country's freedom; and having dropped the tributary tear to their blessed memory, you cannot but rejoice in the idea that, neither you have suffered, nor they bled, in vain. It is even glorious in great attempts to fail. What then must be the glory of America's patriot army, who have nobly succeeded in the greatest accomplishment ever made, the liberation of a continent from thralldom. Let the breath of the malignant, let the envious tongue endeavor to blast the reputation of those who have procured peace, liberty, and safety for their country. Let them gratify their narrow souls by charging the American army, when forming, from the purest motives, an amicable association, at the close of the brilliant contest, with design dangerous to the freedom of that country, the love of which nerved their arms with desperation, and enabled them to brave unparalleled dangers and difficulties unutterable. Another still greater revolution must happen before malice and envy will be banished from the world. The applause, the gratitude, the confidence of the great and good, is all your own, it is all you want. In one word: America is free; Washington lives and rules. It is enough! Rejoice then, and again rejoice in your country's happiness. And may that happiness be perpetual; may it be transmitted from generation to generation, until human governments shall be no more, and until the immediate exercise of all power shall be placed in the hands of the *Mighty Creator* and *Prince of Peace.*

∽ TWO ∾

AN ORATION

Elias Boudinot, 1793

Elias Boudinot was born in Philadelphia May 2, 1740; he was admitted to the bar in New Jersey and practiced his profession in that state. He was appointed Colonel and Commissary General of Prisoners, May 15, 1777, a position that he resigned May 11, 1778, when he was chosen a member of the Continental Congress from New Jersey. He served in that body from 1778 to 1779 and from 1781 to 1784 and was president of Congress from November 4, 1782 to November 3, 1783. As president, he signed the treaty of peace with Great Britain. After the Revolution, he served as a member of Congress from New Jersey from 1789 to 1795, when he was appointed Director of the Mint, where he served until 1805, when he resigned and removed his residence to Burlington, New Jersey, where he died October 24, 1821.

In 1772, Boudinot was chosen a Trustee of the College of New Jersey, at Princeton, retaining his place on the board until his death; in 1780, Yale College conferred upon him the degree of Doctor of Laws.

At a meeting of the Society of the Cincinnati in the State of New Jersey, held at Princeton, September 23, 1783, "His Excellency Elias Boudinot, Esqr. President of Congress" was elected an honorary member. He evidently took great interest in the Society as he attended its meetings with regularity and was chosen one of its delegates to the General Society in 1785, 1786, 1788, 1791, 1792, 1793, 1795, 1796, 1811, 1812, 1814, and 1815 (see illustration 6).

At its July 4, 1793 meeting, the Society adopted the following:

> *Resolved that the thanks of this Society be given to the Honble. Elias Boudinot, Esqr. Doctor of Laws, for his excellent and well adapted Oration, delivered this day in celebration of the Anniversary of the Independence of the United States of America, and that he be desired to furnish the Society with a copy thereof to be deposited in their Archives.*

and at the July 4, 1810 meeting, the following was adopted:

> *Resolved that the thanks of this Society be presented to Doctr. Boudinot, the venerable and much respected Orator of the day, for his very appropriate, instructive and excellent Oration, and that he be requested to give a copy to be placed in the Archives of the Society as a precious Legacy.*

An Oration
delivered at Elizabeth Town, New Jersey, agreeably to a resolution of the State Society of Cincinnati on the Seventeenth Anniversary of the Independence of America

Gentlemen, Brethren and Fellow-Citizens—

Having devoutly paid the sacrifice of prayer to that Almighty Being, by whose favor and mercy this day is peculiarly dedicated to the commemoration of events which fill our minds with joy and gladness, it now becomes me, in obedience to the resolutions of our Society, to aim at a further improvement of this festival, by leading your reflections to the contemplation of those special privileges which attend the happy and important situation you now enjoy among the Nations of the Earth.

Is there any necessity, fellow-citizens, to spend your time in attempting to convince you of the policy and propriety of setting apart this Anniversary for the purpose of remembering, with gratitude, the unexampled event of our political salvation?

The cordial testimony you have borne to this institution, for seventeen years past, supersedes the necessity of an attempt of this kind; and, indeed if this had been the first instance of our commemorating the day, the practice of all nations, and of all ages, would have given a sanction to the measure.

The history of the world, as well sacred as profane, bears witness to the use and importance of setting apart a day as a memorial of great events, whether of a religious or political nature.

No sooner had the great Creator of the Heavens and the earth finished his almighty work, and pronounced all very good, but he set apart (not an anniversary, or one day in a year, but) one day in seven, for the commemoration of his inimitable power in producing all things out of nothing.

The deliverance of the children of Israel from a state of bondage to an unreasonable tyrant, was perpetuated by the Paschal Lamb, and enjoining it on their posterity as an annual festival for ever, with a "remember this day, in which ye came out of Egypt, out of the house of bondage."

The resurrection of the Savior of mankind is commemorated by keeping the first day of the week, not only as a certain memorial of his first coming in a state of humiliation, but the positive evidence of his future coming in glory.

Let us then, my friends and fellow-citizens, unite all our endeavors this day to remember with reverential gratitude to our supreme Benefactor, all the wonderful things he has done for us, in our miraculous deliverance from a second Egypt—another house of bondage.

> *And thou shalt show thy son on this day; saying, this day is kept as a day of joy and gladness, because of the great things the Lord hath done for us, when we were delivered from the threatening power of an invading foe. And it shall be a sign unto thee, upon thine hand, and for a memorial between thine eyes, that the law of the Lord may be in thy mouth, for with a strong hand hast thou been delivered from thine enemies: Thou shalt therefore keep this ordinance, in its season, from year to year, for ever.*

When great events are to be produced in this our world, great exertions generally become necessary; men are therefore usually raised up, with talents and powers peculiarly adapted to the purposes intended by Providence, who

the service, benefit, and best good of the whole and not for their oppression or destruction.[1]

It is our duty then, as a people acting on principles of universal application, to convince mankind of the truth and practicability of them, by carrying them into actual exercise, for the happiness of our fellow men, without suffering them to be perverted to oppression or licentiousness.

The eyes of the nations of the earth are fast opening, and the inhabitants of this globe, notwithstanding it is 3000 years since the promulgation of that invaluable precept "thou shalt love thy neighbor as thyself," are but just beginning to discover their brotherhood to each other, and that all men, however different with regard to nation or color, have an essential interest in each other's welfare.

Let it then be our peculiar constant care, and vigilant attention, to inculcate this sacred principle, and to hand it down to posterity, improved by every generous and liberal practice, that while we are rejoicing in our own political and religious privileges, we may with pleasure contemplate the happy period when all the nations of the earth shall join in the triumph of this day, and one universal anthem of praise, shall arise to the Universal Creator, in return for the general joy.

Another essential ingredient in the happiness we enjoy as a nation, and which arises from the principles of our revolution, is the right that every people have to govern themselves in such a manner as they judge best calculated for the common benefit.

It is a principle interwoven with our constitution, and not one of the least blessings purchased by that glorious struggle, to the commemoration of which this day is specially devoted, that every man has a natural right to be governed by laws of his own making, either in person or by his representative; and that no authority ought justly to be exercised over him, that is not derived from the people, of whom he is one.

This, fellow-citizens! is a most important practicable principle, first carried into complete execution by the United States of America.

I tremble for the event, while I glory in the subject.

To you, ye citizens of America! do the inhabitants of the earth, look with eager attention, for the success of a measure on which their happiness and prosperity so manifestly depend.

---

[1] *Lactinus, lib. 5, cap, 14, fol. 501, speaking of the universal equality of mankind, says:*—Equitatem dic—secum ceteris coequandi, quam Cicero aequabilitatem voceat—Deus enim qui bonimes generat et inspirit omnes equos, id est, pares esse voluit; candem conditionem vivendi omnibus posuit—Omnes ad sapientiam genuit; omnibus immortalitatem spopondit—Nemo apud Deum servus est, nemo Dominus.

To use the words of a famous foreigner "You are become the hope of human nature, and ought to become its great example. The asylum opened in your land for the oppressed of all nations, must console the earth."

On your virtue, patriotism, integrity and submission to the laws of your own making, and the government of your own choice; do the hopes of men rest with prayers and supplications for a happy issue.

Be not therefore careless, indolent, or inattentive in the exercise of any right of citizenship. Let no duty, however small or seemingly of little importance, be neglected by you.

Ever keep in mind that it is parts that form the whole, and fractions constitute the unit. Good government generally begins in the family, and if the moral character of a people once degenerate, their political character must soon follow.

A friendly consideration of our fellow-citizens, who by our free choice become the public servants, and manage the affairs of our common country, is but a reasonable return for their diligence and care in our service.

The most enlightened and zealous of our public servants, can do little without the exertions of private citizens to perfect what they do but form, as it were in embryo. The highest officers of our government, are but the first servants of the people, and always in their power; they have therefore a just claim to a fair and candid experiment of the plans they form, and the laws they enact for the public weal. Too much should not be expected from them; they are but men and of like passions, and of like infirmities with ourselves; they are liable to err, though exercising the purest motives and best abilities required for the purpose.

Times and circumstances may change, and accidents intervene to disappoint the wisest measures. Mistaken and wicked men (who cannot live but in troubled waters) are often laboring with indefatigable zeal, which sometimes proves but too successful, to sour minds, and derange the best-formed systems. Plausible pretensions, censorious insinuations are always at hand to transfer the deadly poison of jealousy, by which the best citizens may for a time be deceived.

These considerations should lead to an attentive solicitude to keep the pure, unadulterated principles of our constitution always in view; to be religiously careful in our choice of all public officers; and as they are again in our power at very short periods, lend not too easily a patient ear to every invidious insinuation or improbable story, but prudently mark the effects of their public measure, and judge of the tree by its fruits.

I do not wish to discourage a constant and lively attention to the conduct of our rulers. A prudent suspicion of our public measures is a great security to a republican government; but a line should be drawn between a careful and critical examination into the principles and effects of regular systems, after a fair and candid trial and a captious, discontented and censorious temper, which leads to find fault with every proposition in which we have not an immediate hand; and raise obstacles to rational plans of government without waiting a fair experiment. It is generally characteristic of this disposition, to find fault without proposing a better plan for consideration.

We should not forget that our country is large and our fellow-citizens of different manners, interests and habits. That our laws, to be right, must be equal and general; of course, the differing interests must be combined, and brotherly conciliation and forbearance continually exercised, if we will judge with propriety of those measures that respect a nation at large.

While we thus enjoy, as a community, the blessings of the social compact in its purity, and are all endeavoring to secure the valuable privileges, purchased by the blood of thousands of our brethren, who fell in the dreadful conflict; let us also be careful to encourage and promote a liberality and benevolence of mind, toward those whom they have left behind, and whose unhappy fate it has been to bear a heavier proportion of the expensive purchase, in the loss of husbands, parents or children, perhaps their only support and hope in life.

Mankind, considered as brethren, should be dear to each other; but fellow-citizens, who have together braved the common danger—who have fought side by side—who have mingled their blood together, as it were in one rich stream—who have labored and toiled with united efforts to accomplish the same glorious end, must surely be more than brethren—it is a union cemented by blood.

I can no longer deny myself the felicity, my beloved friends and fellow-citizens, members of a society founded in these humane and benevolent principles, of addressing myself more particularly to you on a DAY which in so peculiar a manner, shines with increasing luster on you, refreshing and brightening your hard-earned laurels, by renewing the honorable reward of your laborious services, in the gratitude of your rejoicing fellow-citizens.

Methinks I behold you on the victorious banks of Hudson, bowed down with the fatigues of an active campaign and the sufferings of an inclement winter, receiving the welcome news of approaching peace, and your country's political salvation, with all that joy of heart and serenity of mind that became citizens, who flew to their arms, merely at their country's call, in a time of common danger.

The war-worn soldiers, reduced to the calamities of a seven years' arduous service, now solemnly pause and reflect on the peculiarity of their critical situation. The ravages of war had been extended through a country dearer to them than life, and thereby prevented that ample provision in service, or reasonable recompense on their return to private life, that prudence required and gratitude powerfully dictated.

They thought that the distresses of the army had before been brought to a point, "that they had borne all that men could bear; their property expended—their private resources at an end—their friends wearied out and disgusted with incessant applications." But another trial, severer than all still awaits them. They are now to be disbanded, and a separation to take place, more distressing than every former scene! Till now the severe conflict was unseen or unattended to. Poverty, and the gratitude of their country, are their only reward.

True, they are to return to their friends and fellow citizens with blessings on their heads. The general liberty and independence are now secured—but yet want and dire distress stare many in the face. They are to return to wives and children, long used to dependence on the cold hand of charity, in hopes of a sure support from the success of the common cause, when their husband, father or child returned glorious from the field of conquest. Alas! these flattering hopes now are no more.

Their country's exhausted treasury cannot yield them even the hard-earned pittance of a soldier's pay. Being urged on one hand by the subtle poison of inflammatory, violent and artful addresses, under the specious mark of pretended friendship (the last expiring effort of a conquered for)—warned on the other hand by the experience, wisdom and rational conduct of their beloved Commander, their father and long tried friend—they solemnly deliberate.

Some guardian angel, perhaps the happy genius of America, ever attendant on the subject of her care, raises the drooping head, wipes the indignant falling tear from the hardy soldier's eye, and suggests the happy expedient!

Brotherly affection produces brotherly relief—the victorious bands unite together—they despise the infamous idea—they refuse to listen to the Siren's song—they form the social tie—they cast in the remaining fragment of their scanty pay, and instead of seizing their arms, and demanding their right by menace and violence, they refuse

> *to lessen the dignity or sully the glory they had hitherto maintained. They determine to give one more proof of unexampled patriotism and patient virtue, rising superior to the pressure of their complicated sufferings, and thereby afford an occasion to posterity to say, had that day been wanting, the world had not seen the last stage of political perfection, to which human nature is capable of attaining.*

The glorious certainty of peace, purchased by their sufferings and perseverance, now rouses the patriotic fire. They again rejoice in the event; they unite in a firm indissoluble bond,

> *gratefully to commemorate the event which gave independence to America—to inculcate to latest ages, the duty of laying down in peace, arms assumed for public defence in war—to continue their mutual friendship, which commenced under the pressure of common danger, and to effectuate every act of beneficence, dictated by a spirit of brotherly kindness to any of their number and their families, who might unfortunately be under the necessity of receiving them*

and by this unanimous act, establish this sacred truth, "that the glory of soldiers cannot be completed without acting well the part of citizens."

This, gentlemen, is your origin as a Society—the source from whence you sprang, and this day we are carrying on the work first begun in these social principles.

With a heart filled with unfeigned gratitude to the Author of all our mercies, and overflowing with the most affectionate friendship towards you, suffer me to congratulate you on this Seventeenth Anniversary of our happy Independence. Long! long! even to the remotest ages, may the citizens of this rising empire enjoy the triumphs of this day; may they never forget the invaluable price which it cost, as well as the great purposes for which it was instituted, and may a frequent recurrence to the first principles of our constitution, on this anniversary, be a constant source of security and permanence to the rising fabric! May the rights of men and the purity of a free, energetic and independent government, be continually cherished and promoted by every Son of Cincinnatus! May the remembrance of those worthy heroes, once our beloved companions, who lives they did not hold dear, when required for their country's safety, animate us to preserve inviolate what they purchased at so high a rate! May we, by the uniform conduct of good citizens, and generous faithful friends, show ourselves worthy of such valuable connections!

Long, long may you live to enjoy the reward of your labors, in the exercise of the duties of this honorable anniversary; and after a long life of service to your country, usefulness to your society, and happiness to yourselves, may you leave your generation in the full enjoyment of peace and a sound constitution, justified by experience, for the example of which, nations yet unborn shall rise up and call you blessed!

And now my respected audience, we appeal to your candor and generosity; you have heard our origin—you have known our conduct—our society is designed for the benefit and happiness of mankind—we have no secrets—we claim no separate privileges—we ask no independent immunities—we are embarked in one common cause with you—we glory in one perfect political equality, all we wish for is the pleasure of renewing ancient friendships—of the mutual remembrance of past labors and sufferings—the liberal exercise of that celestial principle charity, and one common interest with you, in the security of our liberty, property and independence.

We profess to be a band of brethren, united to our fellow-citizens by every tie of interest, gratitude and love. Let us then go hand in hand with you, in looking forward to the happy state of our country, during a long succession of ages yet to come.

We are encouraged in this animating hope, by the numerous advantages arising to us, in a peculiar manner, from the happy resolution we commemorate this day; they are conspicuous in every quarter to which the view can be directed.

If we turn our attention to the strong hope of every community, the rising generation, the world has yet enjoyed nothing equal to their advantages and future prospects.

The road to honors, riches, usefulness and fame, in this happy country, is open equally to all. The equality of citizens in its true sense, must raise the most lively hopes, prompt the noblest exertions and secure a certainty of success to all who shall excel in the service of their country, without respect of persons.

The meanest citizen of America educates his beloved child with a well-founded hope, that if he should become equal to the task, he may rationally aspire to the command of our armies, a place in the cabinet or even to the filling of the presidential chair: he stands on equal ground, in regard to the first honors of the state, with the richest of his fellow-citizens.

The child of the poorest laborer, by enjoying the means of education (afforded in almost every corner of this happy land) is trained up for, and is encouraged to look forward to a share in the legislation of the Union, or of a particular state, with as much confidence as the noblest subject of an established monarchy.

This is a peculiar happiness of our highly favored republic, among the nations of the earth, proceeding from the successful revolution in which we this day rejoice.

Suffer me, fair daughters of New Jersey, to call on you also, in a special manner, to add your invigorating smiles to the mirth and festivity of this day. Our happiness can be but half completed, if you refuse to crown the whole with your kind approbation.

Have you not at all times, and do you not still continue to participate deeply in the multiplied blessings of our common country? Raised from the humiliating state of your sex in most other countries, you also breathe the sacred air of Freedom, and nobly unite your exertions for the general good.

The Rights of Women are no longer strange sounds to an American ear; they are now heard as familiar terms in every part of the United States; and I devoutly hope that the day is not far distant when we shall find them dignifying, in a distinguishing code, the jurisprudence of the several States of the Union.

But in your domestic character, do you not also enjoy the most delightful contemplations, arising from the Revolution of Seventeen Hundred and Seventy-Six?

Can you look on the children of your tenderest care, and reflect on the cheerful prospects opening upon them through life, without feeling the most lively emotions of gratitude for the inestimable privileges conferred on the citizens of America?—Are not your resolutions strengthened, and your endeavors redoubled, to furnish them with every qualification, both mental and personal, for the future service of a country thus rendered dear to you?

But your share of the joy of this day does not rise from a single source. To whom are we more indebted for the origin of our present happiness, than to your delicate and discerning sex. In vain did Columbus, our great founder and discoverer, after settling the principles of his sound philosophy, apply to the wise men of his country—in vain did he solicit, in strains of the most suppliant humiliation, the different thrones of Europe, where kings considered themselves as God's vice-regents here below. Despised by the ignorant—traduced by the malevolent—condemned by the great—laughed at by pretended philosophers—and trifled with by the arrogance of ministers, and their hirelings; all his hopes, and those of a New World, had at last sunk in despair, and we, this Day, might have mingled our fate with the slaves of the Old World, had not the penetrating wisdom and persevering magnanimity of the fair, but undaunted Isabella, the ornament of your sex, and the jealousy of ours, saved this Western World from the oblivion of more than five thousand years. Did they employ the excess of useful treasure in this happy adventure?—No!—After the refusal of her husband—despising the appendages of brilliant royalty, when compared with the general good of mankind, her enlarged mind, incapable of being confined by the shackles of the age, found a resource in her costly Jewels, which she freely offered as a pledge, to accomplish the glorious discovery of the Four Quarters of the Globe!

To your sex, then, ladies, we are obliged to yield the palm. Had this great event depended altogether on our sex, it is not easy to guess what our united fate had been at this moment. Instead of our present agreeable employment, we might have been hewers of wood, and drawers of water to some mighty Pharaoh, whose tender mercies would have been cruelty. Your right then, my Fair Auditors, to a large portion of the general joy must be acknowledged to be of a superior kind.

Do you, my worthy fellow-citizens of every description, wish for more lasting matter of pleasure and satisfaction in the contemplating the great events brought to your minds this day?—Extend, then, your views to a distant period of future time. Look forward a few years, and behold our extended forests (now a pathless wilderness) converted into fruitful fields and busy towns. Take into view the pleasing shores of our immense lakes, united to the Atlantic States by a thousand winding canals, and beautified with rising cities, crowded with innumerable, peaceful fleets, transporting the rich produce from one coast to another.

Add to all this, what must most please every humane and benevolent mind, the ample provision thus made by the God of all flesh, for the reception of the Nations of the Earth, flying from the tyranny and oppression of the despots of the Old World,[2] and say, if the prophecies of ancient times are not hastening to a fulfillment, when this wilderness shall blossom as a rose—the Heathen be given to the Great Redeemer as his inheritance, and these uttermost parts of the earth for his possession.

Who knows but the country for which we have fought and bled, may hereafter become a theatre of greater events than yet have been known to mankind.

May these invigorating prospects lead us to the exercise of every virtue, religious, moral and political. May we be roused to a circumspect conduct—to an exact obedience to the laws of our own making—to the preservation of the spirit and principles of our truly invaluable constitution—to respect and

[2] *Providence, that if the late Revolution had not taken place, and America had still continued under the dominion of Great Britain, the unhappy sufferers in the cause of Freedom, both in Europe and the West Indies, would not now have had a spot on the globe, to which they could, with propriety and safety, have retired, in case of a failure of their exertions in favor of Universal Liberty. Neither can any European nation afford to complete an asylum, as the United States, for the opposition, in case they should finally be driven from a country, which might conceive itself essentially injured by their hostile conduct in the day of her distress.*

attention to magistrates of our own choice; and, finally, by our example as well as precept, add to the real happiness of our fellow-men, and the particular glory of our common country.

And may these great principles, in the end, become instrumental in bringing about that happy state of the world, when, from every human breast, joined by the grand chorus of the skies, shall arise with the profoundest reverence, that divinely celestial anthem of universal praise—"Glory to God in the highest—Peace on earth—Good will towards men."

THREE

AN ORATION

James Giles, 1800

Lieutenant James Giles, ?–1825 (Original Member, admitted 1783), was a lieutenant in the Second Regiment, Continental Artillery, and was appointed Adjutant on January 1, 1781. He was also a Brigadier-General in the New Jersey Militia. Giles was originally a member of the New York Society and transferred to the New Jersey Society on July 4, 1789. He was Clerk of Cumberland County, New Jersey, in 1789, 1790, and 1794. James Giles is currently represented by James Oscar Nixon V of Dunedin, Florida (see illustration 7).

An Oration delivered at Trenton, New-Jersey,
agreeably to a resolution of the State Society of Cincinnati,
on the fourth day of July 1800.
Being the twenty-fourth anniversary of the Independence of America

Brethren and Fellow-Citizens,

The anniversary of that event, which gave birth to an empire, and liberty to millions, has again returned to witness our smiles and receive our salutations.

Assembled, as usual, for mutual congratulation, and the preservation of an attachment formed and fostered in the rugged fields of hardship, privation and danger, happy should we be if no adverse circumstance had occurred to damp their joy and mar the pleasure of this festive day. But the sorrowful event, which has bathed our nation in tears, clothed our temples in sack cloth, and caused the "harp and the viol" to cease in our land, so peculiarly interests us that we can neither pass it over in silence, nor think of it, but with the deepest regret, and most melancholy reflections.

By this afflictive dispensation of Providence, the duty assigned to me is rendered unusually difficult. I feel myself wholly incompetent to the performance. To omit altogether, or but slightly touch a subject so interesting to us all, might justly be considered a disrespectful inattention. To confer the merited reward of praise upon our late incomparable Chief, is a tribute peculiarly due from those who enjoyed the full blaze of his virtues, and were admiring witnesses of his military skill and prowess. But what prospect of success can I have in attempting to reach, with my feeble powers, the sublimity of a theme, upon which the treasures of genius and learning have already in vain been exhausted? How much must my hopes be humbled when I consider also, that on this very floor, an eulogium has been pronounced on the virtues of our own **Washington**, by a Gentleman as deservedly celebrated for his eloquence, as his genius and science.

To your indulgence therefore, I commend myself, while (in the discharge of the duty with which I am honoured) I add my little tribute of praise to the universal encomiums, with which our illustrious Cincinnatus, the glory and the ornament of our nation, has so deservedly been extolled by his affectionate and mourning countrymen, and by the admiring world.

Long before the period in which we had the honour of serving under this accomplished Chieftain, the germ of his military genius shot forth, and grew with surprising luxuriancy. Having applied himself with laudable industry to the attainment of those branches of science which were within the reach of his opportunities, he brought into action, with rapid succession, the admirable powers with which the Author of nature had endowed him. Employed in an embassy, while yet a youth, which required the prudence and experience of age, and the fortitude, bravery and perseverance of a veteran, he executed it with honour to himself and satisfaction to the government.

In the war that succeeded, the fields of Braddock, and the banks of the Monongahela saw the intrepidity of his soul, and the vast resources of his mind. Dismal was the scene, when amidst the horrid yells, and the unerring savage discharges of a savage foe, the veterans of Europe, commanded by an officer old in fame, with death-like dismay, fell the restless victims of error and pride. In the height of this carnage, and when the despair became general, behold young Washington assume the command—lead his Virginians on to the charge—check for a moment the progress of the triumphant victors, and thus cover the retreat of the few surviving, and dispirited vanquished. The fame of this brilliant action resounded through America, and Britain herself crowned with laurels his brow.

The character he established by this bold and intrepid conduct, progressed with rapidity in both worlds, till the hardships of the service, and the vicissitudes of the climate impaired his health, and compelled him to retire from the martial field. Cultivating the arts of peace, filling with honour and intelligence the offices of Legislator and Magistrate, Mount Vernon was the peaceful retreat of the Hero, till the nation, in whose service he had so nobly fought, became unjust and oppressive to her children.

Summoned, at this period, to head the Armies of America in defense of her rights—see the distinguished patriot, with unexampled modesty, but with genuine magnanimity, clothe himself in armour, and hasten to serve where hostilities had commenced. Tho' possessed of an immense estate, and rich in domestic felicity, he nobly resolved to risk both, with life itself, to prevent the least diminution of that liberty which nature had given, and the most solemn contracts had confirmed to his countrymen.

The immense difficulties he had to encounter in the organization of his army, their ignorance of the military art, their repugnance to discipline, the almost total want of well-informed and experienced officers, skillful engineers, arms, ammunition, and other military apparatus; neither shook the firmness of his mind, nor caused him for a moment to repent of his undertaking. Possessing the unbounded love and confidence of his companions in arms, which his justice, humanity, courage and skill had inspired, he checked the progress of an enemy as superior in numbers, as in experience, discipline and stores. But, tho' he conquered, he did not exult. With a modesty and humility, such as a Nelson has since displayed, he ascribed his successes to the God of armies, and neither spoke disrespectfully nor contemptibly of his vanquished enemy. As he was not elated with success, neither was he dismayed with disaster. Who of us that saw him, during that succession of defeats which darkened the campaign of '76, can say, that despair ever sat on his brow, or that his fortitude ever forsook him. Oppressed with accumulated misfortunes, dejection would for a moment be visible; but quickly recovering his wonted firmness, he would rise superior to every calamity, and diffuse the rays of hope to all parts of his reduced and dispirited army.

When the foe, flushed with victory, believed the contest decided, when every heart palpitated with terror, and every countenance indicated despair, then did his vast military powers and his undaunted valour shine with "triumphant brightness."

Majestic, and ever memorable stream! [the Delaware River—Ed.] Thou didst witness his consummate skill and invincible greatness of soul, when contending with thy adverse waves, he forced a passage—surprised—routed—and captivated an army—dispirited the enemy—dispelled the gloom of his countrymen, and gave a new direction to the current of affairs! Glorious was the moment! Never was the tide of misfortune so rapidly turned with such incompetent means.

Following up his successes with vigour and promptitude, he soon compelled the enemy to abandon the greater part of their conquests, concentrate their forces, and confine themselves to their strongholds.

In the succeeding campaigns, tho' always encompassed with difficulties; badly supplied with money, clothes, provisions and ammunition for his troops; and constantly inferior to his enemy in numbers, he suffered them to gain no material advantages, and often attacked them with considerable success. At length, baffled by his precautions, weakened by his surprises, wearied by his perseverance—in fine, subdued by his superior prudence and valor, Great Britain was compelled to relinquish the contest, and to allow us the name and the rank of a nation.

It was at this interesting moment, the virtues of Washington gave additional luster to the rays of his glory. Impelled by their sufferings, necessities and sense of hard treatment, his companions in arms, on the eve of dispersion, were meditating a redress of their own grievances. To this they were especially excited by a masterly address, calculated to inflame their already irritated minds, and precipitate them into measures, both ruinous to their country and destructive to their fame. To counteract the effects of this ingenious, but dangerous performance; to quell a spirit of disorder, which was almost justified by the cause; to prevent the effusion of kindred-blood; and to preserve the matchless reputation of his suffering and heroic arms, interested every spring of sensibility within him, and put to its severest trial the vast force of his wisdom, his influence and authority. He happily succeeded. The reasoning and persuasion of a Chief, so affectionately beloved, so unboundedly respected, and the extreme distress he discovered on the occasion, operated like magic on the minds of his officers, soothed their resentments, and induced them to relinquish such rash and precipitate measures, and trust for redress to the honour and gratitude of their country.

The world has paid homage to the singular integrity, which resisted such means and prospects of aggrandizement—to the unexampled magnanimity, which resigned, with reluctance, the charms of power, and the splendour of military scenes—and to the generosity, which refused the most remote compensation for eight years' toil, responsibility and danger. Posterity will admire such pre-eminent patriotism, and the name of our Hero will be pronounced with veneration and applause, when the nation which he established, like the empires that have existed, will have run its destined course, and be no more.

With what affection, and regret, he bid us farewell, while the Hudson shall flow, and while memory exists, cannot be forgotten. Can we think of that solemn, that pathetic scene, my brethren, but with reflections, and "emotions too big for utterance"?

The dignity, and sensibility, with which he resigned his commission; and the gratitude and respect, with which Congress acknowledged his services, will constitute of the brightest and sublimest pages in the history of our Country.

With a reputation as pure as it was splendid, our Cincinnatus bid adieu to the cares and labours of public employment, and sought, in the shades of Mount Vernon, and in rural amusements, the repose and retirement which he had left with reluctance.

If the virtues and services of Washington had terminated here, the fabrick of his glory would have exhibited a unity, magnificence, and symmetry unrivalled in ancient or modern times. But it was reserved for this illustrious man to give to the world as great an example of consummate wisdom, and uprightness in the government of a nation, as he had given of heroism and talents in establishing its independence.

The period that succeeded the contest for liberty displayed the imbecility of our first national government. While united by a danger common to all, the several States complied, in some degree, with the requisitions of Congress. But when danger was removed, they disregarded a power that had not the means of compulsion. Hence anarchy, want of credit and national degradation prevailed. To remedy these evils, which had become prominent and alarming, a Convention was proposed. The Father of his Country was called from his retirement to aid by his wisdom in preserving the nation. Among stars of the first magnitude in our western hemisphere, he shone with acknowledged superiority, and presided of course. This dignified Council, as venerated for their patriotism as celebrated for their talents and wisdom, produced, as the first of their labours and deliberations, our present admirable system of government. When it was ratified by the States, and a Chief Magistrate was to be chosen, all eyes and hearts were concentrated on Washington. Such a union of wishes, it would have seemed criminal to resist. Yielding therefore to duty, other than to choice, he a second time embarked on the fluctuating sea of popular opinion, and consented to risk his immense and deserved reputation among the dangers of an inexperienced and highly responsible station. With a diffidence and modesty as genuine as unusual, he acknowledged his incompetency for so elevated and difficult an office, and threw himself upon the indulgence of his country-men for the errors he might unintentionally commit in the course of his administration. How well he succeeded in wielding the scepter of government, the world will bear witness. The improvements and increase of our agriculture, the magnitude and extent of our commerce and navigation, the restoration and establishment of our public credit, the rising glory of our navy, and the general prosperity which the face of the country displays are illustrious monuments of the wisdom and rectitude of that system of policy which he adopted and invariably pursued.

When the term of his office approached to a close, he fondly hoped that his affectionate country-men would consent to his retirement from so arduous and perplexing a station, and therefore had prepared his valedictory address. God-like mortal! How justly didst thou estimate the vanity of human greatness? How little were the charms of an elevation, almost as splendid as a throne, to thy well-ordered mind! Compared with thee, how incredibly do the Alexanders and Caesars of the world sink in our admiration!

The period when he contemplated this retirement from office was big with events. The rival powers of Europe, with whom our commercial relations were intimate and extensive, were engaged in a war unusually vindictive, and threatened to involve us in the vortex of their fury. To counteract their designs, and preserve us from a calamity so dreadful, required the wisdom and influence of Washington. Notwithstanding, therefore, his repugnance to a repetition of his presidential labours, at the earnest solicitation of his fellow citizens, he consented once more to take the helm of affairs, and sacrifice his wishes and repose for the welfare of his country.

Arduous was the duty. The popular opinion was in favor of France. The aid her Monarch had afforded us in our struggle for independence, and the kindred name of republic which her revolutionists had falsely assumed, very naturally gave her an interest in the public affections. She had strengthened this predilection by her insidious conduct. While she openly disavowed all wish or intention of involving us in her quarrels, she was secretly encouraging a faction among us, with the direct view of making us a party in the war. Great Britain, always tenacious of her dignity and interest, and jealous of our rising greatness, saw this partiality towards her enemy with secret resentment, and resolved to revenge it by the capture of our vessels. To defeat the machinations of France, without giving her a plausible pretext for offence; to restrain the active preference for her cause, which too many of our Citizens discovered; and to induce the British to desist from their aggressions and make restitution of the property they had wrongfully wrested from us, was the Herculean task he had to perform. His penetrating mind at once saw the conduct proper to be pursued, and he resolved to pursue it with vigour and firmness. Tho' the partisans of France, thwarted in their views, heaped on his venerable head the bitterest reproaches of disappointed ambition, and ascribed his measures to the basest motives, yet he remained immovable as a rock, upon which the raging tempest beats in vain. Convinced that it was just, and would promote the happiness of his country, to preserve a strict neutrality with the belligerent powers, he smiled at the ineffectual threats and invectives of factious citizens, and adhered to his purposes with invincible firmness.

If the plans he pursued had not the desired effect, it must be ascribed to the injustice and cupidity of the French government, and to the base efforts of domestic enemies. So far as wisdom, justice and rectitude can prevail against treachery, violence, and insatiable ambition, so far were his measures crowned with success.

As wise in the cabinet, as he had been skilful and brave in the field, this august personage, thus conducted our national barque, during an eight year voyage through the stormy sea of political discord, and finally resigned it, unimpaired, and in good order, to the direction of his successor. Neither the charms of pre-eminence and power, the caresses and solicitations of his country-men, nor the approbation and applauses of the world, could prevail on him to defer any longer his meditated retirement from public cares. His delightful Vernon, and his much-loved family, again, therefore, received their long-absent Lord, encircled with all the honours, and accompanied with all the affection, which a grateful people could bestow.

Enjoying the repose of domestic and rural life, and the pleasures of agricultural pursuits, he flattered himself with the hope that no inauspicious circumstance would again summon him to the theatre of public service, or disturb the tranquility in which he desired to spend the remainder of his days. How vain were his hopes! How illusive his wishes! The power which was meditating the subjugation of the world, disappointed in its views with respect to this country, displayed its revenge by a war upon our commerce. Our remonstrances were unheard—our attempts at reconciliation were treated with insult. The spirit of America at length was roused. The patriots of our country resolved to repel insult with insult, force with force. While the Hero of independence could wield a sword, or mount a horse, in no other Chief could his country-men confide.

Washington must command us! was the universal cry. When the "war worn soldier" received the information, indignant at the wrongs his country had suffered from the common disturbers and plunderers of mankind, he immediately resolved to put his immortal reputation once more to hazard, unsheathe his glittering sword, and decorate his hoary head with the high-plumed beaver.

August patriot, and hero! Methinks I see thee now, clad in thy well-remembered military array, bending with years, but full of martial vigour, and ready to hasten to whatever part the dangers of thy country should call.

Was it not enough, that thou didst conduct her to independence, rescue her from anarchy and contempt, and elevate her to order and respectability? Was it not enough, that thou didst spend the prime and vigour of thy life in these more than human services, and without accepting any other compensation or reward than the pleasure of doing good, and the gratitude of thy fellow-citizens? Was it not enough, that in thee the sublime virtues of Hero, patriot, Christian, shone with a luster exceeding all former example! No—this last act was wanting as the "apex to the pyramid" of thy unparalleled glory. Other celebrated Statesmen and Generals have consented, after retirement, to accept of more elevated stations; but it was reserved for thee alone to give the world an example of real humility and genuine patriotism, in declining the most dignified office in the gift of thy country, and afterwards, when its welfare required it, in condescending to accept of a subordinate appointment.

Hardly had he entered upon this important duty, when a messenger from Heaven announced his recall. As, by this last act, he had given the final polish to the vast fabrick of his glory, and had finished his legation on earth; he cheerfully obeyed the summons, and ascended, with the plaudits of Heaven, to the throne of his Almighty Sovereign, to render an account of his embassy, and receive the reward of a "good and faithful servant."

To him, how blessed was this removal; but to us, how inexpressibly painful and inauspicious! We, my brethren, have lost a Father and Friend who was peculiarly endeared to us by his affectionate regard, and by his parental care of us in the hour of danger. We have lost the head and ornament of our Society. Ah! who can supply his place? Where shall we find the mortal worthy to succeed our Washington? The world cannot produce him. My fellow citizens, we have lost the delivered of our country, the founder of our federate republic, the glory and boast of America. We may wish, but we cannot reasonably expect ever to see his equal. Depressing consideration!

But tho' we cannot retrieve our loss, yet we must neither repine nor sink under it. We should endeavor (since we can no more have recourse to his personal advice and assistance) to profit of the lessons he has left us; especially of those contained in his incomplete valedictory address. Like Abel, tho' "dead he yet speaketh." He tells us (and on this national day it is especially proper to inculcate his advice) that in our union, and attachment to the government, consist our strength and safety—that party spirit is the bane of free republics—that "religion and morals are indispensable supports to political prosperity"—that the "general diffusion of knowledge" is of "primary importance" in a nation, whose government is supported by "public opinion"—and that "passionate attachments" to one, and "inveterate antipathies" against another "foreign nation" ought to be discouraged, as productive of fatal evils. At no time has the consideration of these truths been more necessary than at the present. The spirit of party has already made an alarming progress among us, under the specious pretext of preserving liberty. And if, through the insidious attempts and unweaned exertions of its leaders, a majority of the people should be so far deluded, as to unite in the demolition of our Constitution, that Palladium of our liberty, a total dissolution of the Confederacy would be the inevitable consequence. Two or more mighty States would arise out of the mighty mass of ruins, which would become the sport of European politics, and be played off against each other to their mutual injury, if not total destruction.

To prevent so dreadful a calamity, let us rally round the government, as the rock of our political safety. Let us not sit still, as idle spectators, of the ruin that so evidently menaces our country; but use all the lawful means in our power to preserve unimpaired our independence, and our excellent Constitution. To offset this important object, let us, my fellow citizens, pay a sacred regard to the counsel of our late incomparable military and civil Chief. Let us encourage the promotion and extension of religion and morals, not only by our influence, but also by our example. Let us be active in the institution and execution of plans for the diffusion of knowledge, especially of just political sentiments. Let us avoid all undue attachment to, or antipathy against, foreign nations; and with vigilance, moderation, and firmness endeavor to detect and expose the fallacies, and counteract the schemes of the enemies of our federal government.

And in the inculcation of these duties, may I not with great propriety call on you, my fair friends, to aid with your influence in giving it effect. The ladies of Trenton, immortalized by the taste and elegance with which they displayed their gratitude and respect to the Father of their country, will surely omit nothing in their power to give energy to his advice, and preserve for their children the blessings of a good government.

Impressed with the importance of these duties, let us, in conjunction with our own exertions, look up unto the omnipotent Source of all good; humbly hoping that He will not suffer so fair and beautiful an essay towards political happiness to be blasted in its origin, by the rude and pestilential breath of an unprincipled faction.—And may the infinitely wise and beneficent Sovereign of the universe, in this most critical conjuncture, be the gracious director of all our ways, and the unerring counselor of all our counsels; may He plenteously transfuse a spirit of wisdom, fortitude, and unanimity throughout this wide extended empire; and may His good Providence ever be the guardian of our public rights and privileges.

FOUR

An Oration

Elias Boudinot, 1810

Elias Boudinot was born in Philadelphia May, 2, 1740; he was admitted to the bar in New Jersey and practiced his profession in that state. He was appointed Colonel and Commissary General of Prisoners, May, 15, 1777, a position that he resigned May 11, 1778, when he was chosen a member of the Continental Congress from New Jersey. He served in that body from 1778 to 1779 and from 1781 to 1784 and was president of Congress from November 4, 1782 to November 3, 1783. As president, he signed the treaty of peace with Great Britain. After the Revolution, he served as a member of Congress from New Jersey from 1789 to 1795, when he was appointed Director of the Mint, where he served until 1805, when he resigned and removed his residence to Burlington, New Jersey, where he died October 24, 1821.

In 1772, Boudinot was chosen a Trustee of the College of New Jersey, at Princeton, retaining his place on the board until his death; in 1780, Yale College conferred upon him the degree of Doctor of Laws.

At a meeting of the Society of the Cincinnati in the State of New Jersey, held at Princeton, September 23, 1783, "His Excellency Elias Boudinot, Esqr. President of Congress" was elected an honorary member. He evidently took great interest in the Society as he attended its meetings with regularity and was chosen one of its delegates to the General Society in 1785, 1786, 1788, 1791, 1792, 1793, 1795, 1796, 1811, 1812, 1814, and 1815 (see illustration 6).

At its July 4, 1793 meeting, the Society adopted the following:

> *Resolved that the thanks of this Society be given to the Honble. Elias Boudinot, Esqr. Doctor of Laws, for this excellent and well adapted Oration, delivered this day in celebration of the Anniversary of the Independence of the United States of America, and that he be desired to furnish the Society with a copy thereof to be deposited in their Archives.*

and at the July 4, 1810, meeting the following was adopted:

> *Resolved that the thanks of this Society be presented to Doctr. Boudinot, the venerable and much respected Orator of the day, for his very appropriate, instructive and excellent Oration, and that he be requested to give a copy to be placed in the Archives of the Society as a precious Legacy.*

An Oration delivered before the Society of the Cincinnati of New Jersey at Trenton, New Jersey, July 4, 1810, during the Annual Meeting of this Society

Brethren and fellow citizens:

Our grateful acknowledgments having been rendered to Almighty God, for indulging us with another publick commemoration of the great epic in the annuals of time, the anniversary of American Independence, our existing rules as a society, have established the laudable custom of presenting a publick address, previous to entering on the ordinary business of the day.

The intent of this regulation is obvious. Popular discourses on the principles of our revolution, and upon the means of perpetuating its blessings, are well calculated to preserve and enhance their purity of value. And if this be their effect upon the ordinary occasions, how impressive and useful might those become, delivered on a day which first dawned upon our independence.

So many excellent men have preceded me, from year to year in this service, and have so exhausted general subjects, that it is a difficult task to form a plan of address, worthy the attention of so respectable an audience, without requiring a repetition of what has passed on former occasions.

The happy circumstances of our country were almost twenty years past, although but just rising from the horrors of a sanguinary contest for our liberties, and the devastation of war's political confusion, might be thought more than insufficient to afford matter of pleasing gratulation for free men and philanthropists. But our political horizon has become of late, rather cloudy and dark. The lightening flash around us, and the hollow thunders are heard at no great distance. This cannot but make a contemplative mind thoughtful, and fearing for the ark of his political safety, to be looking out for some well-tried means to disperse the storm, or to direct the stroke when it comes and lead it aside, so as to pass it off harmless and inoffensive.

This ought to be the business of every good citizen who has leisure of penetration to examine principles, to compare causes and effects, to enquire into the relative situation of interest to our country, with those of the old world; and particularly to attend to the policy of conduct of the nations with whom we have to do. Amongst the most approved means of security: to be ever watchful and on our guard, to foresee approaching events, and be always prepared for the worst, without confusion or disorder, are not among the least of many that might be named; at the same time by performing well, all the duties of men and Christians, to avoid giving offense to any.

To be able to accomplish so desirable an end, it will be worthwhile again to look back to the origins of our government; for without often doing this, the rising generation on whom the past important events relative to our political existence, have not made so deep impressions; are apt to forget or overlook, the true principles of our constitution, and by a careless inattentive conduct, sap its foundations without seeing or fearing the consequences.

Advanced to that period of life, when the busy passions are at rest, and few hopes or fears remain, but for invaluable friends—a beloved country—and an immortal destiny beyond the grave; suffer me to claim (upon this occasion) the common privilege of years, that of stating important facts, giving opinions and leaving advice on a few interesting topics, which appears to me worthy of your most serious or dispassionate consideration. This shall at least be sincere and if long experience and close observation confer any particular value on human sentiments, I may justly hope for and claim from my fellow citizens, respectful attention.

That the people of the thirteen united colonies on their separation from the mother country, were in some measure reduced almost to a state of nature, had the power of self government in their own hands, and were truly in a state of complete democracy, is a truth I will not controvert. But they had too much experience of the nature of government in general; and were possessed of too great a share of sound common sense and prudence, to suppose they could carry on a contest with so mighty a nation, as their parent state and preserve peace among themselves, without a well-organized and more energetic and competent form of government. A time of war of defensive opposition to a powerful invader, was wholly improper to form constitutions of a permanent nature. Those of the different colonies under their former head, were in general made the outlines of a temporary government, but adapted rather more to the present circumstances of each state; while a general superintendence was admitted, by common consent, to be vested in the congress of the United States.

But only establishment of our independence and on being numbered among the nations of the Earth, it was soon found that the time was come for forming an obligatory united and permanent government, to extend over the immense territory gained by this arduous contest.

The citizens of the state, were now in peace. The noise of war was no longer heard in our land. Every man set under his own vine and under his own fig tree and there were none to make him afraid. Good sense and sound policy prevailed. The people throughout the union, instead of claiming all power as centering in themselves to be exercised in their own persons, thereby forming a perfect democracy, which is much better calculated to destroy than to carry on a government, wisely chose representatives, with power to meet together and deliberately form a constitution of government, to be submitted to each state for their consideration of adoption in their several legislatures.

The members of this convention, the real pride by glory of the United States, were chosen with enlightened understandings, patriotick independence of great wisdom. Here were no violent parties; no preferences for selfish or interested purposes, no contest for the loaves or fishes, or struggles for power by authority. Some of the best men in each state were sent, and a more enlightened and competent assembly seldom ever met before. They came together with sincere dispositions to perform their duties with judgment and by exercising the most conciliatory tempers, to consult the best interest of the union.

They were fully sensible of the prevalence of both natural and moral evil in America as well as in other parts of the world. And although in the infancy of our Nation we were not so far advanced in them, as older Nations, yet we were hastening with rapid strides to a state of Manhood in this respect, and they well knew that the same causes, would generally produce the same effects.—They were not so weak as to suppose the nature of Man was better here, than in Europe or Asia; but that equal checks and balances were a requisite, by which the human passion, habits, and natural selfishness of individuals should be controlled, prevented, or overcome.

Whilst despotic power, on the one hand, was to be avoided as the terror of every free American; so on the other hand, was wild fanaticism; arising from the tumultuous assemblies of the people at large, as equally destructive to peace of happiness of mankind.

When they sought for example from the old world, by which they might be taught knowledge, arising from long experience, they were unable to find a government founded on the true and essential principles of civil liberty. If they looked to the East all was despotic rule, arbitrary power, anarchy or confusion. If to the West either monarchy, aristocracy or simple democracy were the scourge of that portion of the globe, the kingdom of Great Britain excepted.

From her we had descended. She had made trial of a mixed government, partaking of unequal parts of each form. She had met with greater success than had been the fate of any other People. From her experience we informed our first ideas of improvement and were thus led to endeavor to seek a still more pure and perfect system, better adapted to our habits and wishes.

The Convention became convinced after full discussion and deliberate consideration that a form of government, either Democratic, Aristocratic, or Monarchical, separately considered was but another name for the same Tyranny in a different shape. They therefore wisely concluded that something before unknown in the experience of Nations, formed from a more happy combination of the most approved principles of all three forms, but with greater restraints and more simple and effective checks applicable to our particular circumstances as a people, was a great object that should engage their united consideration and pursuit.

Their deliberations ended in recommending a Constitution to the people of the United States, formed with consummate wisdom. And as far as human prudence could go, calculated to raise the United States to the pinnacle of human glory, provided its principles and provisions should be religiously and inviolably adhered to and practiced.

It was adopted by the legislatures of the different states, after a most scrupulous and critical investigation, and immediately carried into execution, with a joyful acclamation of high approbation of that people, who had thus voluntarily and with general consent, yielded up their rights of Authority as individuals, for a mutual apposition of united protection and defense.

The government proposed by this Constitution was before unknown to mankind. Nothing exactly similar had ever appeared. It was entirely *sui generis*. It consisted of the most valuable parts of all three of the forms aforementioned; but it was neither of them by itself considered, not all three united together.

A fair and equal representation of the people to be governed, formed the essential basis of the whole fabric. While the People, retained the right of choosing their Representatives, for different terms of service, without restraint, who were to constitute a general Legislature for the union and to make those laws which were to become with the Constitution the only sovereigns of the United States; they gave up their other rights of the state of nature and virtually pledged subjugation to those laws.

Convinced that too frequent elections would tend to anarchy or disorder; and the long service of the elected would promote a love of power, if not despotism, the Convention agreed on a happy mean, by restricting the service of the Representative in one House to two years and to prevent the Nation from ever being totally without permanence in the Legislature they gave a term of six years to the Senate; at the same time obliging a third part to go out every two years, by which wise provision, tho' continually changing every two years, yet there always remained a permanent majority, acquainted with the business of the state.

While the most numerous House had the exclusive right to declare War, and in some measure by holding the purse strings eventually the power of initiating peace also; the Senate had the exclusive right of assenting to Treaties—of trying all impeachments of publick officers by the other House, as the highest Court of Judicature of the Nation—an equal voice in the enacting of all laws, with the exclusive right of approving of the publick functionaries nominated by the President.

The President was to be appointed by Electors chosen by the people, and while he was vested with those powers of monarchy which were necessary to carry the laws into execution, such as making all treaties with foreign Nations, the appointment of ambassadors with the consent of the Senate—the final approbation of all laws enacted by Congress, the nomination and appointment, (with the consent of the Senate) of all officers of government but with the sole power of removing them—the commanding the Armies and Navies of the United States, the pardoning of all offenders, except in the case of impeachment. He is restricted to a political existence of but four years and exposed, equally with every other officer of government, to the impeachment of the most numerous House of Congress in case of maladministration.

Had the Constitution of laws when made been left to the executive administration, all the security of the citizens against arbitrary power, would have been in vain.

The wisdom of the Convention, therefore, led them to attend to every avenue of danger. They prudently provided Courts of Justice, to be established by Congress, with permanent salaries, during good behavior; but their nomination and appointment, as afore said, were left wholly to the President.

Thus was your government formed on the principle of checks and balances, prompting the most glorious success as far as human wisdom and foresight could go. In this manner was the present political Constitution of your country formed and established comprising many independent States, with various conflicting interests. Its face was the express and explicit compact of the people upon the acknowledged principles of justice and well-regulated liberty; and from the experience we have hitherto had of its efficient effects it demands from every citizen of the United States the most profound reverence and esteem.

But as all earthly things are transitory and uncertain, so even the perfection of this beautiful fabric at last depends on the virtue and faithfulness of the individual citizen to his own best interest, to his pledged truth and honor, in performing the duty obligatory upon him, in the nomination and election of his representatives.

Without the utmost care and the most impartial and disinterested execution of this trust, vain are all the restraints and provision of this invaluable instrument. If this should fail to accomplish the great purposes attended by it, in their practical extent, the world's last hope from republican institutions will expire.

The *social contract,* which despots despised as much as they were hated, and which even the friends of man only pictured as a dream of perfection, too precious to be realized, is now reduced to *fact* and *experiment.*

Instead of undefined prerogatives or their licentious meetings of the people at large, we have a *written charter* approved and ratified by the solemn acceptance of the States and People. The last work of our *Washington* united with the *states men and heroes,* who accomplished the revolution we now celebrate.

We are committed by the ties of a grateful respect, by our obligation to humanity itself, by an oath before God, and by our best interest of the rights of posterity, to maintain and execute it, *as it is* in the way and manner it prescribes.

On you then my fellow citizens still depends the main spring of our government. For although you have given up your natural right to govern yourself and have promised submission and obedience to those laws of Congress, made according to the Constitution, as the only sovereign power of your country, yet you have retained that essential part, without the due exercise of which, all the rest is but a dead letter.

You may boast of your liberty. You may value yourselves on a Constitution, establishing a government of departments, executive, legislative, and judicial, firmly but admirably constructed to serve as checks against usurpation, without controlling each other, in any constitutional right or power. Yet if you shall forget your most important duty and suffer party rage, angry passion, individual animosities, or interested motives to influence you in this high office of an Elector, you will but have changed the name. Really tyranny and oppression will as assuredly be entailed in your prosperity, as if you were governed by Despot, usurping absolute power over you, and will in the end lead to this awful issue.

If your representatives are ignorant, venal, immoral or self conceded merely seeking personal emoluments and honor or possessed with pride of office and love of power, the restrictions provided by the wisdom of the convention will be found but a feeble defense; and the bonds of union contained in your excellent Constitution, a mere rope of sand.

Have I said too much in favor of this invaluable instrument? Let me appeal to the experience of past years. It will justify all that has been suggested in favor of this central pivot of your political happiness.

Look back to the time of its date. Many of you must remember the deplorable state of our publick affairs. A treasury without money or credit. Trade and commerce clad in mourning and covered with tears. Your farms in a state of dilapidation. Your tradesmen and manufacturers almost without employ. Your numerous public predators wandering about your streets, accusing themselves for their blind incredulity in entrusting to the public faith. In short, fear and trembling had reigned in every breast.

But no sooner was the confirmation of this welcome Constitution announced as adopted by the several States and our highly respected *Commander in Chief,* seated in the executive chair, by the universal suffrage of his fellow citizens, then every countenance glowed with life and vigor. Every breast beat with grateful devotion and thankfulness to that almighty Being, who had never forsaken us in the greatest distress. Prosperity and industry took place of misfortune and indolence.

So many years of happy experience, while virtue and integrity influenced our elections and governed our publick affairs, has raised our county to an eminence among Nations, truly enviable.

The salutary influence of this new government, became every day more clearly evinced by the universal satisfaction given to almost every class of honest citizens. Publick confidence speedily took place of doubt and fear. The arts and manufacturing, with trade and commerce, soon revived. Our treasury became full and overflowing. The publick debt was organized, provided for, and greatly reduced. The nations of Europe courted our alliance and favored our intercommunion. Every part of the globe open to trade and commerce has been visited by our hearty seaman. Our numerous harbors had been crowded with ships from all the nations of the European world. Our farms have laughed for their plentiful harvest and every neighborhood has resounded with the noise of labor, joy and industry.

Let this view, arising from certain experience, of what might be constantly realized from our new form of government, if it were wisely and judiciously carried into execution, animate you my fellow citizens of every denomination to make the proper reflections and to draw the necessary conclusions. But is there no dark side to this pleasing picture? Has not our welfare been endangered, our happiness threatened, our fair prospects become clouded, by *party distinctions, names and measures?* I mean not to descend to particulars, the fact, I fear is indisputable.

And are we fellow citizens, ever to be a divided people? If you answer in the affirmative (which may God forbid) who among you, is bold enough to look at the consequence and not tremble? Are these political or rather personal and selfish finds to grow with our population, expand over our territory and fasten their poisonous fangs on the vitals of the Republic? Have we fairly and coolly considered the *end of these things?* And what can there be but individual suffer ing, national weakness, disgrace, and final disunion? If our treason did not tell us, do not the numerous examples of lost liberty and all history pervade us to banish the fiend of *party spirit?* Is it not to be feared, that by discords and animosities we are treading in the errors and hastening to the fate of so many ruined Republics? Those in Greece and Rome, and the more recent pretender The Republic of France, ought to be flaming beacons to warn us of the natural and inevitable consequences of such unjustifiable misconduct.

How fatal the mistake, which makes the hostility of factions and citizens with each other, and against the measures of government, synonymous with a cautious but candid watchfulness of constituents over the conduct of their publick agents! Is it indeed pretended that our divisions have no other consequence, but to repress and correct the usurpations and the errors of government? The truth is that they assume no such character, nor do they perform these salutary offices. They are conflicts over the wide face of our country and in all its departments, for office and emolument or deadly animosities engendered by mutual distrust and alternate proscriptions.

Need we to point to the final consequences of these deep-rooted prejudices and political enormities? They are baneful and ruinous beyond description in *party spirit*! How does it interrupt the charities of life; destroying the sweetest and most rational enjoyments, those which spring from social intercourse and feelings of love and respect for each other? The result of this mistaken and unhappy conduct, as affecting the Nation and all its great interest is manifest beyond contradiction, and alarming enough to make even the resolute almost despair of a remedy. If one is to be speedily and effectively had, under God, it must arise from the wisdom and magnanimity of the first great executive officer of the United States. The time is ardently to be wished for when the President of these States, possessing the wisdom to perceive this wide spreading evil shall stake his fame upon a sincere and resolute attempt to provide the remedy, by destroying every faction by whatever name it may be called, and uniting all the talents and wealth and influence of our citizens, by comprehending all in his confidence and favour.

No administration of the federal government, whatever be its name or pretensions, supposing it both virtuous and able, can long proceed with honor or success, opposed in the Cabinet and Congress and in the States by a persevering and powerful opposition of any party, aided by the press, availing themselves of talent and riches, watching and exposing the errors, difficulties, and even misfortunes of the ruling party. They will in time break its system, if not per chance destroy its popularity.

There my fellow citizens you have heard the great, the all-important part, you are to act in this interesting drama. If you are venal, faithless, or even inattentive to this sacred trust, all will still be lost.

But amidst every pursuit, never forget to let your gratitude arise in devout strains of praise and thanksgiving to the Divine Author of all our blessings, whether political, civil, or religious for the special and distinguishing privileges and publick favors, we this day enjoy.

But the passing time warns me of the necessity of turning in a more special manner to my brethren and compatriots, members of the American Cincinnati. If I have addressed this audience in general, on the important subject of their duties as citizens, with any degree of comparative propriety, with how much greater emphasis may I press these essential obligations on you.

The design of our meeting together on this anniversary professedly is to perpetuate as well the remembrance of the freedom, independence and sovereignty of the United States, as the mutual friendship which have been formed under the pressure of common danger, and in many instances cemented by the blood of the parties. To give an incessant attention to preserve inviolate those exulted rights of liberties of human nature, for which the army have fought and bled, and without which the high rank of a national Being is a curse instead of a blessing. To promote and cherish between the respected States, that union and national honor (which we have just seen) is so essentially necessary to their happiness and the future dignity of the American Empire. To render permanent the cordial affection subsisting among the officers. To promote the spirit of brotherly kindness in all things, and particularly to extend the most substantial acts of beneficence, according to the ability of the Society, towards those officers and their families who unfortunately may be under the necessity of receiving them.

I know of no period since our first organization as a society, that could more fully justify an enquiry into the origin of our institution, than the present; that by contemplating former circumstances and distresses we may be better enabled to field the obligations of our present political privilege and thence to fulfill our duties as a Society and good citizens of the State, and thereby answer the great design of our union as brethren.

Our fellow citizens, having now had experience of our principles and conduct for upwards of twenty-seven years, they can no longer be affected by the groundless fears and political jealousies that at first were fostered in the breasts of some against us.

Instead, then, of expatiating on subjects of comparatively small importance, by way of our justification, let the glorious subject of our union, the independence of our nation, and the perfection of our happy Constitution fill our mind with joy and chase away every meaner object. Forgetting or suspending every party feud or inflamed passion, let us consecrate this festive day to the Constitution under which we enjoy so many political benefits sacred to the fathers of our country and to the defenders of our liberties, many of whom are now sleeping in the dust. Let it be devoted to reconciliation and unity. To the contemplation and praise of every moral and social virtue; and whatever can promote the true glory, the strength, and character of the United States of America. If such should universally become the uses and improvement of this day, it would indeed be annually welcomed as a jubilee of national sympathy and sentiment, no less than the era of national independence.

Time the great impairer of the memory of past events has, no doubt, weakened the remembrance of those very peculiar circumstances, that induced the establishment of our Society, and which many of our fellow citizens may be totally inattentive to. It shall then be my present business to retrace them in as concise a manner as possible.

At the conclusion of the late revolutionary war, the Army of the United States (formed of citizens, called to the defense of their country from their various avocations and beloved families) having this peril and dangers before unknown to Americans, more than accomplished the expectations of their country, was about to be disbanded, and to return to the masses of their fellow citizens. They had deserved well of their country. Were I to give an account of the uncommon sacrifice of this patriotic band in the cause of that liberty they had been seeking with so much ardor, tho' I should confine the facts to my personal knowledge, I might be suspected of flattery or even paying undeserved compliments to those with whom I am associated.

I will therefore confine myself to testimony arising from sources that will not be doubted by any genuine American.

It is well known to all, that the subjugation of the thirteen British colonies, arising from very mistaken ideas, to the unlimited power of parliament was intended. Many injudicious and oppressive measures were resorted to, and severe threatenings announced, to intimidate a plain and unoffending people, to unconditional submission. Acts of Parliament were passed one after another of the most violent and irritating complexion.

One arbitrary step after another was repeated till the climax was finished by the act putting all of the colonies, without discrimination or reason, out of the king's protection, by which the Gordian knot was cut and the tender consciences of good men and obedient subjects were legally discharged from the obligations of their allegiance. The American citizen, being thus reduced to a state of nature, having no sovereign to look to for protection, had only to become his own protector.

The dye was cast. Terror and dismay stalked this our late peaceful colonies, by reason of the most formidable invasion, both by land and sea, from one of the chief powers on Earth, against a people unsuspecting, unprovided, unarmed, and ignorant of the usual needs of defense.

Aided by the wonderful providence of God, we struggled through a contest, unknown before to a great part of Mankind. After suffering eight years of peril and hardship of every kind, hoping against a hope, a glorious end was put to a bloody war; in all its circumstances, one of the most arduous and doubtful that ever was raged against an unoffending People. It was indeed, that of David with a sling and the stones of the brook against Goliath of Gath, clad in all his impenetrable armor.

Congress in their address to the States in April 1783, bears this unequivocal testimony to the merits of the Army. Speaking of the publick creditors, they say

> *Another class of creditors, is that* illustrious and patriotic band of fellow citizens, whose blood and whose bravery have defended the liberties of their country; *who have patiently born among other distresses, the privation of their stipends, while the distress of their country disabled it from bestowing them. And who* even now *asks for no more than such a portion of their dues as will enable them to retire from the field of victory and of glory, into the bosom of peace and private citizenship; and for such effectual security for the residue of their claims, as their country is now unquestionably able to provide.*

General Washington whose praise is in all the Earth, in his letters to Congress of March 18, 1783 says,

> *And here I humbly conceive it is altogether unnecessary, while I am pleading the cause of an army, which have done and suffered more than any other army ever did, in the defense of the rights and liberties of human nature, to expatiate on their claims, to the most ample compensation for their meritorious services, because they are perfectly known to the whole world. . . . But of besides the simple payment of their wages, a further compensation is not due to the sufferings and sacrifices of the officers, then have I been mistaken indeed. If the whole Army have not merited whatever a grateful people can bestow, than have I been beguiled by prejudice and built opinion on the basis of error.*

These voluntary proofs were not the effect of blind attachments or unreasonable prejudice, but the spontaneous effects of experience and an intimate knowledge of facts. In proof of this recollect the state of the Army at this period. They had arms in their hands and ammunition in their arsenals; but this was all. Though in a plentiful country, "Their distresses were brought to a point—they had borne all that men could bear—their property was expended—their private resources were at an end and their friends were wearied out and disgusted with their incessant applications."

This was their own confession in their address to Congress. In this situation, then, and under these untoward circumstances were they assailed by some incendiary, claiming to belong to the Army, in an address to the officers, the most artful, insidious, eloquent, and pervasive, that the most determined foe to the real welfare of peace of the United States could have devised. He advised them to meet together without delay and while they had arms in their hands to consult their present welfare. The writer thought, from the experience of the state of other armies, that it was only necessary to apply the match, and an explosion must take place, producing noise, rebellion, enmity, and confusion.

The general, with every patriotic friend and his country was alarmed and terrified at the awful crisis. The hard earned laurels of eight years of arduous service were likely to be sacrificed to the impudent zeal or traitorous views of unknown individuals.

The wisdom and firmness of the Commander in Chief, at this critical and important moment, shown forth most conspicuously.

Instead of a consuming jealousy of all around him, he without hesitation, summoned the whole body of officers to meet him, thereby manifesting the utmost confidence in their patriotism and honor. He personally addressed them on the occasion, and then left them to their own deliberations.

Instead of mutiny and unbridled complaint, with threatenings and fury, they calmly and unanimously resolved

> *That the officers of the American army, view with abhorrence and reject with disdain, the infamous propositions contained in a late anonymous address to the officers of the Army; and resent with indignation the secret attempts of some unknown persons, to collect the officers together in a manner totally subversive of all discipline and good order.*

Many of the officers though "relieved from the distress of beholding a brother shedding a brother's blood, from hearing the shout of the victor and the groans of the dying," and hoping to enjoy the blessings of peace purchased at so dear a rate, in the bosom of their country; now beheld,

> *their families fallen from a state of affluence to the most trying circumstances. The States, not having in their power to comply with their engagements to them, they had no means of relief. The officers would only present their families with scars, instead of cash; and ruined constitutions in lieu of the spoils of war. Yet filled with compassion for the still more wretched situation of the bereaved relatives of those who had bravely fallen in the contest, from their small pittance, they raised funds for the relief of their widows and orphans.*

Under these afflicting and indeed, all things considered, humiliating circumstances, the Army was disbanded and dismissed to their several States.

Before they separated, they proceeded one step further, to show the firmness of their mind, their unsubdued spirit of patriotism, and their wishes to prevent any turbulence of spirit that might arise among individuals from such a trying state of things, for truly this was a time that tried men's souls. They determined to form some basis of union, that might concentrate their influence with their fellow soldiers, preserve their friendships and aid their distress.

The Society of the Cincinnati was thus established and became the effect of the joint wisdom of the Army and the first fruit of the Revolution. We had already heard the Principles impressed in the instrument of your Constitution.

It becomes us then, beloved brethren in a very special manner, to watch over our conduct—to be circumspect in all things, how we fulfill the expectations of our country and perform every duty of good citizens, which we have so solemnly promised. Let us then religiously maintain our principles and professions with uniform integrity. Let no selfish or other unworthy considerations lead us to act contrary to our civil, political, or religious characters. May we never lose sight of the particular duties we have been contemplating, by doing all in our power to promote the union of the states. This is our sheet anchor, without which the ship must be lost. Rally round the Constitution as the standard under which you expect death or victory. Preserve it inviolate in all its fundamental principles as a great palladium of your liberty and safety.

Let it never be said, that we who have experienced an almost miraculous interposition of heaven in our favor during so trying and dangerous a struggle, have now in the days of prosperity forgotten our obligation to His overruling Providence or neglect to pay the constant tribute of gratitude and praise for so much love and beneficence, by surrendering up the blessings bestowed without a struggle.

I might now go into a strict examination of your conduct, as good citizens, since your institution, contrast it with the constitutional professions of our society, and compare it with that of the rest of our fellow citizens at large to show how far the Nation has been benefited by the event.

But here I rejoice that I am saved a duty, which however delicately executed, might by some, be considered as an invidious attempt, inconsistent with the business of so festive a day. Your fellow citizens, who best know your public and private characters, have fixed a deeper stamp on your virtues, than anything my feeble powers could accomplish.

When I review the long list of officers, as well of the united, as the individual States, I find the names of some of my brethren of this and the other States, among the members of both state and general conventions, Presidents of Congress and the United States, members of both Houses of Congress, Presidents of the Senate and Speakers of Congress, Electors of President and Vice President, Governors of the State, judges and justices of your Supreme and other courts, members of both Houses of your State Legislature, Commanding and other officers of the Militia, State Magistrates, Ministers of Religion and inferior officers civil and religious with private offices in high places of trust and confidence. I repeat it with pleasure, that in this long list, I find a great proportion of the names of my brethren of this and other state societies, and all first or last, the choice of the people. This has closed my lips on this subject being convinced that no language could give additional weight to testimony so conclusive, to witness so dignified and unexceptional, to proof so satisfactory and honorable.

I confess that I feel a becoming pride in your having so effectually proved the sincerity of your views and the successful efficacy of your engagements.

Again, I have examined the records of your finances and there I find full proof that your "substantial acts of beneficence," have agreeably to your promises, been only limited by the ability of the society to afford them. That the tears have been annually wiped from the swollen cheeks of the distressed widow, and the helpless orphan's breast has been made to sing with joy.

Go on then respected friends and brethren. Continue to manifest to the world, the purity of your principles and the correctness of your conduct in supporting those principles. May our common country always find that support and confidence in you. That your active zeal and animated exertion, during the severe conflict for our freedom and independence, and your exemplary behavior since your return to private life, have given her so great a right to expect.

Confirm to your fellow citizen and to posterity that you persist in "recognizing that most important principle, of inculcating to the latest ages, the duty of laying down in peace arms assumed for publick defense in war." Thus will you leave an example to future ages, which may benefit the world, when you are no more.

And now my highly respected and worthy brethren, I most sincerely congratulate you on the views here taken in this short and imperfect statement of the commencement of our institution and its essential principles, with our progress to this twenty-seventh anniversary of our freedom and independence, most devoutly wishing you every blessing here and that you may be crowned with glory and immortality hereafter.

I should be greatly wanting in the high respect and veneration I certainly have for the most brilliant part of my audience, were I to conclude this address, without particular attention to the ladies of New Jersey, who have so politely honored us by their presence.

Altho' I have endeavored to delineate and stir attention to duties, that particularly belong to our sex, think not my fair friends, that you are excluded from having a very material part to act in this business.

It is just observed by an eminent writer

> *that the meek—the modest—the noiseless exhibition and exercise of female excellence, occupy a smaller space in the annuals of human nature, than the noisy, bustling, forensic pursuits and employments of our sex. But when feminine worth is gently drawn out of the obscurity which it loves, and advantageously placed in the light, which it naturally shuns—how amiable—how irresistible—how attractive is it! A wise and good woman, shines by not seeking to shine—is most eloquent when she is silent and obtains all her will, by submission, by patience and self denial.*

In short, it is to you ladies we must look for the foundation and first improvement of every principle and sentiment that is to preserve and benefit our country.

To your impressive example and early instruction on the young and tender mind of our rising generation, are we to owe the fruits that in future life, are to adorn and benefit the Citizens, the Legislator, the Magistrate and the Hero.

To first impressions and early habits are we frequently indebted for the prospects of future glory. Domestic discipline and an early virtuous education. Habits of subduing the temper and curving the passions in the youthful part of life, must come from you: and if you are negligent or inattentive to this all-important duty, the consequences may be dreadful to society. It is an old observation, that a child gains more ideas in its first five or six years, than during his whole afterlife.

The importance, then, is manifest, of your most powerful exertion—of your incessant care and unswerving attention to train up your children with such principles, habits and command of temper, and appetites, with an ardent love of country, as may fit and prepare them for the most useful and important publick services in their advancing age.

I repeat it, this important branch of female duty, must be manifest, and become the most binding obligation on you, to discharge it with faithfulness, conscientiously, and laboriously.

> Delightful task! To rear the tender thought,
> To teach the young idea how to shoot,
> To pour fresh instruction o'er the mind,
> To breathe the enlivening spirit, and to fix
> The generous purpose, in the glowing breed.
>
> —*Thomson*

"The mother's influence over a child," says the eloquent Hunter,

> *as it begins earlier, so it is of much longer duration than the father. The first object he distinguishes, is the smiling face of his guardian angel. The first sound that strikes his opening ear, is the murmur of maternal affection. The first idea he forms, is that of seeking refuge from want, pain, and danger, in the fond bosom of a mother. . . .*
>
> *And if we follow the child to a more mature age, when the fire of youth makes the restraint of a prudent father uneasy, do we ever find an ingenious young man, who feels a mother's yoke galling, or who longs for emancipation from the silken fetters in which her gentle fingers has entangled his soul?*
>
> *In the perfection of understanding—in the plentitude of power—in the self gratulations of independence—to her milder reason he still submits. Her unassuming sway he readily acknowledges, and independent of all things else, he feels he cannot do without the smiles of material approbation—the admonitions of material solicitude, the reproof of maternal tenderness and integrity.*

Thus ladies do you become not only essential to individual happiness, but you are equally so to the happiness and well-being of your generation. And while if you act your part well, your children shall "rise up and call you blessed," your country also will hail you among the best friends and promoters of her glory and independence.

Once more to my fellow citizens of every description would I now present our warmest congratulations on this happy day. We have great cause of comparative joy—look around the nations of the old world. What do you hear, but the sounding din of war? What do you behold, but garments rolling in blood? Governments established for centuries, passing away as a shadow and political institutions matured by ages, becoming "like the baseless fabrick of a vision, leaving scarcely a wreck behind." Emperors and kings dethroned by a word, as in a moment—and potentates and princes rising, like mushrooms from the very dregs of the people, in a night. Liberty wholly lost. Property rendered useless, by its uncertainty and personal safety and even life itself dependent on the will of a single man. Contrast this with the state of your own county—what must be the issue—will it not force upon the grateful heart, the highest degree of profound veneration and praise to the divine author of these inestimable favors? Will not the safety and protection afforded by your excellent Constitution and form of government, decidedly determine you to fulfill every duty of a good citizen, and to hand down to prosperity, their principles inviolate? To use every means in your power, to keep the great machine with all its detailed dependencies, in perfect harmony and order.

This, as you have seen, can only be done by your representatives being always men fearing God and hating covetousness. Men of knowledge and understanding—possessing a sound mind and known for their prudence, integrity and freedom from mean selfishness or interested views. Keep in mind, the high character who formed your Constitution, with the peculiar advantages they enjoyed for so important a trust. That they saw and fully considered every principle in all its bearings on the different interests and necessities of every part of the union. That it was founded in mutual sacrifices and in mutual conciliation.

Be not then easily or hastily persuaded to alter a little of it, for as in an even scale, a grain taken from one, will immediately depress the other. Bear with patience, temporary or supposed inconveniences for a time, till long experience has ripened into conviction, lest that hallowed instrument should be touched with unhallowed hands. Rejoice then in your privileges and be appraised that if these citizens of this union will be only united—if they will only banish all improper party spirit from their councils. If they will act their part with fidelity. If by their example and watchful conduct, they will promote in their families and neighborhoods and impress on the rising generation, the love of God and the love of one another. If they will always bear in mind and if practicable, as the Jews of old did, in another instance, write on the border of their garments, and in the palms of their hands, that "united they stand, divided they fall," then the powers of Europe could not shake our safety, nor the world in arms ultimately force from us, the smallest right of an independent Nation.

That you, my [?] respectable audience, suppose that I stand alone in these opinions, suffer me as a conclusion to this address to quote a few sentences from our beloved Washington's eloquent and invaluable address to the United States, on his retiring to private life:

> *The citizens of America are placed in the most enviable condition, as the sole lords and proprietors of a vast tract of continent, comprehending all the various soils and climates of the world, and abounding with all the necessaries and conveniences of life—they are surrounded, not only with everything that can contribute to the completion of private and domestic enjoyments, but Heaven has crowned all its other blessings, by giving a surer opportunity for political happiness, than any other Nation has ever been favored with.*

Such is our situation and such are our prospects, but not withstanding the cup of blessing is thus reached out to us, not withstanding happiness is ours, if we have a disposition to seize the occasion and make it our own; yet it appears to me, that there is an option state left to the United States, whether they will be respectable and prosperous, or contemptible and miserable. This is the time of their political probation—or this may be the ill fated moment for relaxing the powers of the union, and exposing us to become the sport of European politics, *which play one state against another, to prevent their growing importance and to serve their own interested purposes*. For according to the system of policy the States shall adopt, they will stand or fall—and by their confirmation or lapse, it is yet to be decided, whether the revolution must ultimately be considered as a blessing or a curse—a blessing or a curse, not to the present age alone, for with our fate, will the destiny of unborn millions be involved.

And now nothing remains but my ardent supplication and prayer to Almighty God, that my country may continue in peace and happiness to remotest ages and become an asylum and a refuge for the distressed of all the Nations of the Earth, and finally to conclude, with that pious wish in her favor. *Esto Perpetua.*

FIVE

AN ORATION

Ebenezer Elmer, 1812

Surgeon Ebenezer Elmer, 1752–1843 (Original Member), was an Ensign of Captain Bloomfield's Company, Third Battalion First Establishment, New Jersey Continental Line, February 9, 1776. He was promoted to Lieutenant two months later, and in six months became a Surgeon's mate. In 1778, he was promoted to Surgeon and served in the capacity until 1783. During the War of 1812, he served as Brigadier-General of the Militia of New Jersey and commanded the brigade of the New Jersey Militia. His political career was also outstanding. He was a Member and Speaker of the New Jersey House of Assembly, 1791–1795; Vice President of the Council of New Jersey; Member of Congress from New Jersey, 1801–1807 and Adjutant-General of New Jersey, July 5, 1804. He was also Vice President of Burlington College, 1808–1817. In the Society of the Cincinnati in New Jersey, he served as Assistant Treasurer, 1783; Treasurer, 1826–1829; Vice President, 1824–1838 and President, 1839, and 1842–1848 (see illustration 8). Ebenezer Elmer is represented in the society by Elmer Mompere of Williamston, Vermont.

Delivered at Trenton,
before the Cincinnati Society
and a numerous audience,
July 4, 1812

My very respectable Audience,

On me has devolved, by the appointment of my revered friends, the task of directing your thoughts for a few minutes on this eventful anniversary. Happy should I be were it in my power to realize the expectations of my friends, and afford you, on this occasion, some instruction or amusement. But incapacitated at all times for the higher species of Oratory, and that picturesque description that is calculated to interest the imagination; added to a faltering voice, I feel at this time almost insuperable embarrassment at the very threshold. Nothing but an earnest desire to perform every duty assigned me, however feebly, and that kind indulgence which you have heretofore showed, could embolden me to appear before you.

On the ever restless pinions of time, the 36th year of our political existence has passed away. Penetrated with lively gratitude to that Divine Being, from whom descendeth every good and perfect gift, should we celebrate every return of this national festival. Another year is erased from the records of time; but the events of the past call for a durable recollection. A transient retrospect of the past may be productive of amelioration and improvement. Contemplation on the future may be attended with an alternation of gloomy and cheerful views. And by surveying the inconstancy, the fleeting nature and unsubstantial good of all earthly enjoyments, our desires may be drawn forth towards that new Heaven and new Earth wherein harmony and righteousness forever dwell.

Uncertain and fluctuating at every period are the events which mark the progress of all subliminary things, and the destinies of Nations. No objects that present themselves for contemplation, but the ever-adorable Jehovah, and virtue, remain invariable. When we descend from these sublime meditations to take a view of the vicissitudes which take place in this world, we behold, indeed, the footsteps of a wise and gracious Governor, but they are in the great sleep, and he hideth his face in the recesses of his own immensity. Sometimes displaying in astonishing and palpable manner the operations of his Providence in the rise and fall, the prosperity and adversity of nations. Sometimes causing the wrath of man to praise him, and restraining the residue thereof; but often apparently suffering Generals to conquer or yield, and nations to flourish or decay, according to the vicissitudes of human affairs, or the wisdom or folly of the actors. It is however a consoling reflection that the throne of the unchangeable Deity is at all times accessible by every individual and nation who by Piety and virtue are made fit objects of his benedictions.

We, my friends, have been highly favored of the Lord. Through a long and arduous struggle for Independence he has helped us, and has crowned our past days with every blessing, both spiritual and temporal, which a sober and contented mind could desire. The means that led to the establishment of our Independence, the pleasing prospects which that event opened before us, and the combination of favorable circumstances which caused the adoption of that excellent form of Government under which we live, have so often been delineated by masterly pens, that I shall not at present dilate on those subjects.

As we are now under the frowns of Providence, as the times are perilous and difficult, the sword of man being unsheathed, it will be more propitable to pause—to consider—to enquire of our own Hearts, have we individually, and as joint citizens of this great republic, wisely and religiously improved the privileges and advantages which we have enjoyed? The blessings of peace, prosperity and happiness have been strewn before us in an unusual profusion. Corresponding obligations were clearly laid on us to improve them to the glory of the giver, and to promote and increase the sum of human happiness on Earth. As Children of the same family, heirs of the same inheritance on Earth, and expectants of the same immortality, we are bound by the plainest sense of propriety which can influence an ingenious mind to love as brethren, to cherish the kind and tender affections of our nature, and to promote the peace and happiness of our beloved Country. Living under a free Government formed by the wisest and most patriotic of our citizens, in the hours of cool deliberation and calm reflection, and freely adopted by the voice of the whole, the most solid basis was laid for general content and universal satisfaction. Such a form of Government, established under circumstances so favorable, and administered by citizens of our own choice, acting under the strongest possible restraints of responsibility, opened the purest sources of consolation to the political philosopher and the genuine philanthropist. That being beyond example was the prospect and precious have been the benefits which have resulted therefrom. But have these benefits met with a suitable return of gratitude from us? Have we rendered to God, who Providence ruleth over all, that homage, reverence and service which are his due? Have we devoutly regarded all the operations of his hand and thoughtfully acknowledged him in all our ways? Have we yielded that quiet and faithful obedience to the laws of the land, and that respect and submission to the constituted authorities of our Country, which the nature of the Government and the authority of the most high required? Have we in love professed one another? Has neither ambition, self interest, nor the formation of a party, entered into any of our views in any of those political discussions and transactions in which we have been and are still engaged? In a word has pure patriotism and disinterested love of our Country dictated every word we have uttered or written in cool deliberation and entreated every movement we have made in our political career? That we ought to have been so actuated and influenced, under the smiles of Providence which we have enjoyed, appears to be one of the plainest dictates of common sense. But who can say I have hitherto washed my hands in innocence, and cleansed myself from all political inequity? The Speaker is ready to acknowledge he is not altogether pure, and let him who is without sin cast the first stone.

Will my kind and endeared audience now indulge me a few moments while I cursorily account some of the most remarkable phenomena and transactions of the past year? In the Heavens we have beheld a "burning sphere," a "fierce fiery form," "an illimitable torch," stupendous in its dimensions, threatening in its aspect, and of inconceivable rapidity of motion. This Comet, the greatest perhaps of those erratick bodies which at time light up the Heavens over our heads, made its appearance in the North and having swept the immense arch disappeared in the South. No longer influenced by those superstitious forebodings which ignorance and fanaticism formerly produced, we should prove ourselves perversely stupid not to contemplate with awe the immensity of space in which such huge bodies wing their way, and to adore and reverence that august being, with whom we have to do, whose finger points out their trackless path and whose presence filleth that immensity.

On Earth, the fabrick of nature has been shaken to its foundations. Tempests, Hurricanes and tornadoes have locally prevailed, and spread desolation in the train. Earthquakes beyond example extensive, have caused our Hemisphere to stagger to and fro like a drunken man. Set in motion probably by some volcanic eruption, like the blood in the human body by the systole of the heart, the electric fluid circulating in the circumambient Atmosphere of our Earth, like the pulsation of the arteries, has extended the affects thereof to remote parts.

On these terrific scenes of nature we might at another time profitably expatiate. But we will proceed passingly to notice a casual event, the most melancholy that has ever been recorded. An event at which imagination starts appalled from its horrors, and fancy sickens at the Panorama of woes which it exhibited. In the conflagration of the theatre at Richmond perished, in fierce devouring flames, the wise sage, the hoary headed father, the tender and palpitating mother, the spritely and heroic youth and the gay, charming, captivating virgin. An incident attended with such unutterable anguish meagers all description. It is noticed as yielding some insight into the nature of surrounding casualties and the fragile tenure of human life.

My Brethren of the Society, in the events of the past year, we have the melancholy task of recording the removal of some of the members of the Cincinnati to the mansions of the Grave, the house appointed for all living. Among others the illustrious Clinton, the Hero, the Statesman and the Christian is sleeping in the dust. He lives now only in the hearts of his countrymen [and in] "The bosom of his Father and his God." Most of us who survive are tottering under the weight of years, and must shortly, very shortly, follow him to the shores of immortality. Wash, O blessed Immanuel! Wash our sin stained souls with thy purifying blood, invest us with the long white robe of thy spotless righteousness and impress on our hands the palms of the just, before we shoot the awful Gulf that we may appear in thy presence without dismay.

The political transactions of the past era have not been barren or uninteresting. In the Spanish American provinces, civil war has lighted up her tremendous torch, and raised her crimson banner. The Father's arm has been lifted against the son, the son's against his sire, and a brother's hand has been deeply tinctured with a brother's blood. In short, on the plains of Mexico and Paraguay, Peru and Caracas have been renewed those direful scenes which formerly were exhibited at Philippi and Pharsalia.

In Europe the two great belligerents continue to cast about firebrands, arrows and death. Without leading to conquest, or the security of either, they are slaughtering thousands and spreading death and desolation through different lands. Nothing better has been produced by their mighty efforts, than human carnage and the extension of human misery. Not content with doing each other all the harm in their power, in the madness of their career they have extended their acts of injustice and oppression to neutral and unoffending nations. We have long suffered, amidst all our efforts for amity and peace, by their cruelty and injustice, until the extent of the injury and the persevering obstinacy of one of them, have filled up the measure of our forbearance and driven us to the last resort—the resort to arms; we are now called upon by the constituted authority of our country to defend that independence and those privileges with our arms which we obtained by them. The die is cast. He that is not for us is now against us. If incapable and unworthy men have seats in our Councils, chasten them with the Election rod, and place in their stead wiser and sounder statesmen. But let not discontent, envy, jealousy and a party spirit mar our efforts for a redress of grievances, and embolden the foe to heap upon us accumulated woes.

From the dawn of our Independence it has been the fear of our friends, and the hope of our enemies, that our Citizens would not coalesce under a Government sufficiently energetic as to secure the prosperity and preserve the internal peace of Society. Should their feats and hopes ever be realized, it will afford one of the most decisive evidences of the fatal depravity of the human heart. The advantages which we have enjoyed under our free form of Government are vastly superior to any of our brethren of mankind; and it is believed that the public good has been the pole star by which the operations of government have generally been directed, whatever aberrations the fallibility of the human understanding may at times have produced. And as we have a constitutional remedy for the correction of error, both interest and duty press upon us to unite in support of the laws and legitimate authorities.

On this subject the observation of the enlightened Hamilton meets our understandings, and comes home to our bosoms: "A new government constructed on free principles is always weak, and must stand in need of the props of all the wise and good men of the community." And also of the virtuous Washington, the political Father of our county, who speaking of our Government says "Respect for its authority, compliance with its laws, acquaintance with its measures, are duties enjoined by the fundamental maxims of true Liberty."

We should, my Countrymen, at this time bear on our minds that the Sovereignties of Europe are adverse to the prosperity of these States. Our difference of Government, participation in commerce, improvement in policy and magnitude of power, are objects of envy and jealousy to them. They estimate our loss as their gain—our fall their rise—our shame their triumph. Hence they strive to divide that they may distract, dictate and destroy. But by uniting we shall cause all their efforts to evaporate like waves dashing themselves into foam against a Rock.

All our conciliatory measures with England have proved abortive and we are now called upon to rally round the standard of our country, and harness for the battle. But it may be said, Peace might have been preserved by different and better councils. Be it so; but who among us can pretend to so high a degree of insight into the decrees of Heaven as to pronounce that a continuation of peace at this time, might not eventually prove a curse instead of a blessing? These same observations were frequently made in the years 1775 and 1776, yet, none at this day will say it would have been well for us if peace had then been preserved upon any practicable terms. And future events, perhaps, may hereafter develop the wisdom of the present measures.

We have, my friends, all of us, offended the Majesty of Heaven and the sword of our foe it seems is to be lifted up for our Chastisement. Repentance of our personal and national crimes is a duty peculiarly incumbent upon us at this time; that repentance which eventuates into reformation. Let not passion or prejudice hence forward pervert our judgments, nor influence our conduct. To be persuaded in our own minds is a prerogative of human nature; but there is a strange and malevolent propensity in us, not to rest content with being in the right ourselves, we too often do perversely condemn all who differ from us as being in the wrong. Whereas science and common sense wholly repudiate such a conclusion. We know that in many cases very different means will answer the same ends. In demonstrative science different modes of operation will lead to the same infallible result. And are the avenues to contingent and casual truths more circumscribed? Certainly not.

We have divine authority and universal experience to prove to us that the indulgence of discontent, envy, jealousy or any of the irascible passions bring misery on the individual and ruin on society. The fatal effects of a jealous, fretful and discontented temper on a nation is fully exemplified in the history of the Jews. The Israelites were proud and jealous of their new acquired rights and liberty upon being freed from the Egyptian bondage, yet, not withstanding many miracles were wrought for their deliverance, they were seldom easy satisfied. Being instigated by Corah and other artful men who wished to supplant Moses and Aaron in authority, they presently rebelled against the Institutions of their lawgiver; and unjustly charged him with having the ambitious views of making himself an absolute Prince, and of peculation and knavery. And when Moses with great dignity repelled the charges, 250 of their principal men excited the populace to cry out "Stone him!" Several ages afterwards, when they had by the traditions of their reputed wise men sadly defaced and corrupted the Institutions of Moses, and the divine and all adorable Messiah appeared among them, for the express purpose of restoring the desolations of many generations, and introducing a new and better code, having not only the promise of the life that now is, but also of that which is to come; through the artifice and influence of the Scribes and Pharisees, who boasted much of their intelligence and purity and whose selfish view the doctrines of the Messiah condemned, they with the same temper and increased malignity cried out "Crucify him, crucify him." From this awful example we ought to take warning, lest we incur the same Judgments which lighted on them. This sacred history proves incontestably that opposition be excited and maintained by men of reputed wisdom and great distinction.

Reason and the cool suggestions of deliberative wisdom can have but little connection with a party spirit, for that is almost universally a spirit of intolerance and violence. "A principal cause" says Senator William Temple,

> *of those discontents which arise among mankind is a certain restlessness of thought which seems universally and inseparably annexed to our very natures and constitutions; unsatisfied with what we are, or of what we at present enjoy, still craving after something passed or to come, and by griefs, regrets, desires or fears ever troubling and corrupting the pleasures of our senses and of our imaginations, the enjoyments of our fortunes or best productions of our reason, and thereby the content and happiness of ourselves and the peace of society.*

This weed so pernicious to our peace and welfare, like other noxious ones, grows on all soils, but most luxuriantly in the heart. Under the most favorable circumstances, discontent often rears its head the highest and shoots forth the greatest number of branches. From the influence of such a direful temper may the people of these States ever be preserved; that in these trying times of trouble and difficulty we may all of us possess our souls with becoming serenity and propriety. On this memorable day in this Temple dedicated to the service of the august Jehovah, and bowing ourselves before the altar of the most High, let us resolve to rectify whatever has been amiss in our private or political conduct. Let love to God and true Patriotism hush every conflicting passion, and warm every bosom. Let the genuine spirit of an American Hero, and a Christian Philosopher animate every soul; then shall we have reason to hope that the contest, in which we are engaged will be short and attended with little misery. Then may we confidently trust that the Lord of Hosts will be on our side, the munition of riches our defense and the divine Pavilion our secure dwelling. Then may the pensioned Campbell sing and the renowned

Statesman of Roanoke echo the stanza:

> Britiannia needs no bulwarks,
> No Towers along the steep;
> Her Mark is on the mountain waves
> Her home is on the deep.

The sling and the stone of the American people, directed by the unerring hand of Jehovah, shall prostrate their formidable Armada. Nor leave the Poet room to add,

> The Meteor flag of England,
> Shall yet terrific burn.

SIX

AN ORATION

Peter Phillip James Kean, 1823

Colonel Peter Phillip James Kean, 1788–1828, was graduated from Princeton in 1807. He became prominent in military affairs in New Jersey and was Colonel of the Fourth Regiment of New Jersey at the time of his death. He was fluent in French and was appointed to escort Lafayette on the latter's tour of New Jersey in 1824. The inscription on his tombstone in the graveyard of the First Presbyterian Church, Elizabeth, New Jersey, reads,

Peter Kean, Public spirited as a Citizen; Faithful, affectionate and devoted as a Son, a Husband, a Father. Sincere and firm in his Faith as a Christian; Sound and enlightened in his principals as a Churchman, an exemplary and valuable member of this congregation. With talents and zeal that fitted him for extensive usefulness, he died deeply and universally lamented October 2nd, 1828, aged 40 years.

Oration Delivered in the First Presbyterian Church in Elizabeth Town, N.J. by the Request of a Committee of the Honorable Cincinnati Society of New-Jersey, Before His Excellency the Governor, the Hon. Cincinnati Society the Inhabitants of the Borough of Elizabeth, and the Township of Union, July 4, 1823

At a meeting of the Society of the Cincinnati of the State of New-Jersey, held at Elizabeth-Town, July 4, 1823—Present, Gen. Joseph Bloomfield, President, and twenty-five Members.

RESOLVED, UNANIMOUSLY, That the thanks of this Society be given to Major PETER KEAN, for the very eloquent and truly patriotic Oration publicly delivered by him this day, in presence of a very large and respectable assembly of the public authorities, citizens and military of this borough and its vicinity, convened on an occasion so deeply interesting to the whole American people.

RESOLVED, That the very pathetic and affecting eulogium bestowed by him in his address upon the surviving members, and in an especial manner upon our departed brethren of the Cincinnati, be held in most grateful remembrance by the Society, and that our just sense thereof be manifested by the entry of these resolutions upon our journals, and by requesting the President to cause a copy thereof, under his signature, to be addressed or delivered to Maj. KEAN by the Secretary, accompanied with a request that he would furnish a copy of the same to be deposited in the archives of the Society.

A true copy from the minutes,

—*JOSEPH BLOOMFIELD, President.*

JULY 4, 1823.

SIR,

BE pleased in my behalf to express to the Honourable Society of Cincinnati, the high sense I entertain of the honour they have done me in their resolutions of this day.

HOWEVER unworthy the Speech I had the honour of pronouncing before them, of the encomiums the Society's indulgence has been pleased to bestow upon it, and of the distinguished place they have assigned it, I cannot refuse any request made by a body whose claims to respect, confidence and obedience are so transcendent.

With sentiments of the greatest respect and veneration,
I have the honour to be, Sir,
Your and the Society's
Very humble servant,
PETER KEAN.

To Major General
The Hon. J. BLOOMFIELD
Pres't of the Hon. Society of Cincinnati.

Gentlemen of The Cincinnati, And Fellow Citizens!

If it be wise in other nations to commemorate great events by public rejoicings, we need no apology for this meeting. They celebrate victories and the birth of princes; we, the triumphs of a people and the birth of a nation.

Millions, who this day forty-seven years [ago] were not in being, are now assembled to offer up fervent thanksgivings for unprecedented blessings. Our best feelings prompt us to unite in this tribute of gratitude and praise to that Omnipotent Being who has "vouchsafed to guide, govern, and direct us, and to cause all things to work together for our good."

To you, Gentlemen of the Cincinnati, to your brothers in arms, and to your and our common political father, next to God, is our gratitude most justly due. In behalf of my fellow citizens I tender you their thanks, for the zeal, patience, perseverance, gallantry and heroic resolution with which you commenced, prosecuted, and terminated the contest.

Nor are we unmindful of the trials to which you were subjected at the close of the war. Wasted fortunes; ruined hopes; impaired constitutions; "ingratitude, marble-hearted fiend." "You asked for bread and they gave you a stone"—yet you were true to your country. Treason, assuming the garb of friendship and the language of sympathy, assailed your passions with an ability second only to that of an "archangel fallen": there was a voice which said to the troubled waves, "peace, be still," and they were calm. The spot the tempter intended to render memorable by your disgrace, was hallowed by the formation of an institution "calculated to inculcate to the latest ages, the duty of laying down in peace, arms assumed for public defence." "Had the trials of March, '83, been wanting, (I use the words of Washington,) the world had never seen the last stage of perfection to which human nature is capable of attaining."

Gentlemen, on an occasion like this, yours must be no common emotions. With passions and feelings mellowed by age, with minds fraught with the lessons of experience, you stand on the verge of time, a connecting link between your departed brothers and the rising generation. While on each anniversary, you look with satisfaction to the past, and with pleasing anticipation to the future, you are equally called to drop a tear to the memory of companions who yearly precede you to the tomb. "The good that men do lives after them": the tribute paid to departed worth, is an assurance, that yours will be remembered.

Gentlemen! your country greets you with a fervent prayer, that, the splendour of your setting sun may be as refulgent, as its rise was glorious; that, the gratitude of America, and the consolations of religion, may cheer your latest hours, and that, your sons may be worthy of you.

Fellow Citizens! The causes that led to the revolution, the victories that crowned our arms, all crowd on the memory. Can words add force to the statement of the first made in the declaration of '76? What but an inspired tongue can increase the vivid recollections of the last that glow in every bosom? Need we apologize, then, for not dwelling on subjects so deeply engraven on our hearts, that an attempt to illustrate would, like an effort to explain the axioms of science, only render the intuitive perceptions of the mind less distinct? Let us rather attend to their consequences, and endeavour to lay "deep and broad" the foundations of republican principles.

At the end of the war, these United States entered upon "a new and untried state of being." The confederation was soon found inadequate; state interest and state pride militated with the general good; visionaries were not wanting, who believed, or, who affected to believe, that freedom might be maintained without a government; private and public bankruptcy palsied every effort for the attainment of competency; insurrection and sedition were busy; the enemies of freedom smiled, and presaged her ruin; her most sanguine friends were oppressed; the boldest doubted; a gloom diffused itself over the well affected. A paternal voice called on them to rouse from their despondency and save their country—it was the voice of Washington! who could refuse obedience?—The Constitution was adopted.

That it was admirably calculated to effect the ends intended, is proved by the increased and increasing intelligence, wealth, power and happiness of the republic.

Our institutions are founded on the virtue and good sense of the people—the only legitimate source of power. How is the source to be kept pure? It would be worse than utopian for a Christian people, accustomed to consult that Book in which the springs of human action are laid open by "Him who knoweth what is in the heart of man," not to feel a firm conviction, that they must keep a vigilant guard over their own passions, and use every means to repress and control inclinations that might lead to ruin. A sincere lover of freedom will never forget, that there is but one step from the excess of liberty to the gloom of despotism, and that that step must be through anarchy and crime. How, then, is the source to be kept pure? Happily, our own history answers the question. It teaches us that the source is to be kept pure, that Government is to be kept in perennial vigour, by the diffusion of moral and religious instruction; by encouraging industry, in all its various branches; by giving a firm support to the authority of magistrates, and yielding a willing obedience to law; by a temperate discussion of public measures; by a frequent recurrence to first principles, and their judicious adaptation to the exigencies of the moment; thus gradually moulding our institutions to conform to that perfection in the moral and physical condition of man, to which the march of mind is in a state of slow but sure approximation.

As citizens of New-Jersey, peculiar duties devolve upon us. All history proves, that, in federate governments, the smaller members are constantly in danger, from the power and ambition of the larger states. It would be sinning against experience to believe that we are to be exempted from dangers that have proved destructive to others. The union then is the only palladium of our state rights, and it is both our duty and our interest to strengthen the hands of the general government in the exercise of its constitutional powers. To this end, our representatives in congress should be men capable of making up by their abilities and statesmanlike views, what they want in numbers; men fitted to command the respect and confidence of the union, in order to give a due preponderance to a state, which, although small, deservedly claims, from its internal resources, its revolutionary services, the virtue of its people and its tried patriotism, great weight in our national councils.

Nor should we be unmindful of our state affairs. Situated between the two great marts of commerce and manufactures, possessing a territory rich in mineral treasures, and not unfitted for great agricultural improvements, watered by rivers and streams that afford abundant facilities to commercial intercourse and the increase of manufactures, we should be wanting to ourselves were we to disregard these bounties of providence.

Above all, let us not neglect the rising generation. To your maternal care, my countrywomen, New-Jersey entrusts her future hopes. If you love virtue, if you desire praise, if you would deserve the gratitude of your children, cultivate their minds. Teach them, early to tread in the paths of virtue. Let the volume of inspiration be the guide of their youthful ways, and it will be the light of their manhood. Point them to the life of Washington, and teach them to love and venerate his virtues. Bid them practice "whatsoever things are true, whatsoever things are honest, whatsoever things are just, whatsoever things are pure, whatsoever things are lovely, whatsoever things are of good report; if there be any virtue, and if there be any praise, teach them to think on these things,"[1] and their after lives will be your reward.

Fellow citizens! Opportunities of performing distinguished services are of rare occurrence; they are afforded by periods of difficulty and danger, that call for the exertion of great powers; but we all have the ability to render essential benefits, and our conduct will be the more meritorious, as it will meet no reward but that which proceeds from a consciousness of duty performed. Your sons are daily migrating; their usefulness and respectability in the new states depend upon their education and on the examples of virtue your lives afford them. Surely you will not count it an unacceptable service, to have aided in the advancement of civilisation and the spread of Christianity; or reflect with other than pleasurable emotions, on having contributed to the diffusion of happiness.

The reputation of a state and consequently its weight in the union, depends upon its civilisation; that is, upon the progress it has made and is making, in wealth, refinement and moral worth. By a fixed law of our nature, these are inseparable from and have a direct effect on political institutions. In Europe, the accumulation of commercial capital and the improvements of science are opening the way for civil liberty. In America, free institutions

[1] *Philippians iv. 8.*

and the extension of education have given an impetus to industry and laid the foundation of national greatness. The source of our prosperity is the more pure, its effects have consequently been more immediate. No country can remain stationary; its condition must improve, or, it will go back. By what powerful motives then, are we impelled to exertion! To what scorn would we not be justly liable, were we to relax! With what ingratitude would we not be chargeable, were we to refuse to our children, advantages conferred on us by our fathers!

May it please your Excellency! Called to preside over a state, capable of high destinies, we look with confidence to the exertion of your best talents. This confidence is strengthened by a recollection of your past administration. Persevere sir, in the liberal policy that has marked your course; give force and consistency by your legal learning, to our highest court of judicature; husband the means set apart for common schools; encourage well organized schemes for the advancement of the arts; unite your name with plans of internal improvement, calculated to develop the resources, stimulate the industry and augment the wealth of your native state, and the gratitude of her sons, while it assigns you no undistinguished place among your worthy predecessors, will reward your labours.

The effects of the revolution are not confined to this country. The spectacle of a youthful people successfully grasping with a great nation attracted attention and gave a powerful impulse to the friends of liberal principles in Europe. Unfortunately for humanity, the cause was disgraced by the excesses of its first advocates and a re-action was produced. A bold effort was made to wed the Genius of Freedom with Infidelity and Crime; she shrank from the contaminating impurity of the base alliance and fled. America was her place of refuge; the good sense of the American people has preserved her unsullied. Here she found a resting place, where to renew her strength for another and a more vigorous flight. She has ascended, and while with untired wing and undazzled gaze she hovers in mid air, ready to dispense her blessings on Greece, once her favourite abode, and o'er the civilized nations of Europe, no less fitted for her dwelling place, who can be an uninterested spectator of her towering soar?

Connected with Europe by commercial relations, a common ancestry and a common literature; anxious, from the convictions of reason and experience, for the extension of constitutional freedom, we deeply sympathize with the liberal party.

At the restoration of the Bourbons it was hoped, that, the governments of Europe would learn wisdom from experience, yield to the spirit of the age and lead the way in reform; that they would adapt the administration of affairs to the altered condition of the people, and hasten to remove the vestiges of feudal institutions that time and civilization had gradually undermined. It was emphatically called, "the era of good feeling," and the friends of humanity longed for its perpetuation. Alas! the feelings have subsided and nothing but professions remain.

The Holy Alliance! I shudder while I pronounce the name. What a combination to retard the progress of civilization; to benumb and freeze the energies of the human intellect; to revive antiquated and exploded superstitions; to replunge mankind into the more than midnight darkness of the barbarous ages; to arrest the wonder-working hand of the Almighty, in its adaptation of human means to the fulfilment of prophecy; undertaken and sworn to in the name in which a Triune God has vouchsafed to reveal his mercies to man, and the earth born worms who have thus dared to profane that name, are spared! Yes they are spared! But only spared to be rendered memorable examples to future generations, and by their signal defeat more assuredly to accelerate the advent of that period, when the human race shall be fitted for the happiness of the latter times.

The indignation due to their enormity is equaled only, by the contempt their imbecility merits. The page of history was open to them, the follies of the house of Stuart were there traced in indelible characters; the glorious revolution of 1688 was blazoned, with no common splendour; yet, they would not read. The hundred days compelled Louis 18th to confess his errours and to grant the charter to France. Temporary tranquility has re-produced a blind security; men incapable of learning the lessons of wisdom, although taught in the school of adversity, again surround his throne and direct his councils. The property, the talent, the people of France have again and again evinced their attachment to civil freedom, yet, her emigrant nobles and her king wage war on Spanish independence.

Not a rivulet, not a fastness in Spain, but tells of triumphs over invading Frenchmen; not a true hearted Spaniard but is ready to shed his blood for his country's honour; and yet, a "Son of France" (degenerate scion of a noble stem) leads an army beyond its resources, into the heart of Spain, unappalled by the difficulties of the route, by the retreat of the king to Seville, by the preconcerted abandonment of the country, by the solemn and death-like stillness that surrounds his march, giving "dreadful note" of the coming storm. Yes, the storm will burst, the dark and midnight cloud that o'ershadows him will be livid with lightnings and pour out its torrents of desolation. Spain will arise in her might, and hurl the invaders back. From the days of Charlemagne to the days of Napoleon, when was Spain ever invaded with Impunity? The contest will not be confined to her limits; it will be as dreadful, as its consequences will be important. All former efforts will sink into insignificancy, when compared with this shock of embattled millions—all future wars lose their interest in the recollections of this mighty conflict; but the result will be glorious. Success is insured by the development of moral causes that no physical force can elude or counteract.

What though the moral elements of Europe be in a state of tempestuous commotion! what though the fountains of the great deep be broken up! the hand that can stay them is raised; the spirit that will breathe on the face of the waters is ready; the ark of safety is moored, and the dove will return with an offering of peace. France must and will be ruled by a constitutional king; Europe must and will be free.

Americans! Citizens of a free and independent republic! Descendants of the soldiers of the revolution! You are this day called, by the wisdom of your institutions; by the rising greatness of your country; by the blood of your fathers; by the silvered locks and honourable scars of the venerable men who grace this assembly; by recollections of recent victories both by land and sea; by the loveliness and purity of your wives and daughters; by the interests of your sons; by the interests of the whole human family; by every religious and every moral tie, to fan the sacred flame that is kindled, and by the purity of your lives and devotion to your country, to add new brilliancy to the light that cheers the friends of civil liberty. Will you listen to the call? or, will you by supineness and indifference hazard its extinction, jeopardise your own liberties and the world's, and give cause of triumph to the Genius of despotism, to whose malignant hate your follies would afford an eternal theme for bitter scorn and derision? I pause not for a reply. The spirit of your fathers burns within you, and Freedom has marked you for her own.

SEVEN

EULOGY ON LA FAYETTE

Aaron Ogden Dayton, 1835

Aaron Ogden Dayton, 1796–1858 (admitted 1832), was the nephew of Captain Jonathan Dayton (Original Member), Third Regiment, New Jersey Continental Line.

He was graduated from Princeton College in 1813 and obtained a degree of Master of Arts in 1816. Ogden was a member of the House of Assembly of New Jersey, 1823, and a member of the Legislature of New York, 1828. He served as Chief Clerk of the State Department in 1836 and as Fourth Auditor of the United States Treasury from 1838 to 1858. Aaron Ogden Dayton is not currently represented in the society (see illustrations 9 and 10).

Eulogy on La Fayette,
Pronounced Before
the Society of Cincinnati
of the
State of New Jersey
on the 4th of July, 1835

On the 4th of July, 1834, the Society of Cincinnati of the State of New-Jersey passed the following resolution:

Resolved, That the Orator of this Society for the next Anniversary pronounce a eulogium on the character and services of General La Fayette, to be preserved among their archives for ever.

In compliance with this resolution, the Oration now published was prepared, and such portions of it were delivered as the time would allow. It is printed by permission of the Society, granted at the request of the citizens of Elizabeth. The writer is well aware that whatever interest it may possess, is owing more to the subject than to the manner in which it is treated. He may be allowed to observe, however, that the facts have been carefully compiled from the most authentic sources, and to express the confidence which he feels, that they may be relied on as accurate.

Brethren of the Cincinnati, and Fellow-Citizens—

The day and the place in which we are assembled, are full of interesting associations. The Declaration of Independence, with all its moral grandeur; the toils and sufferings, the doubts and fears, the glories and triumphs, of the seven years' war by which that independence was achieved; the never-dying memory of the patriots and heroes, in the cabinet and the field, who staked their fortunes and their lives upon the issue; our constitutional union; the influence of our example throughout the civilized world, manifesting itself in the gradual but irresistible progress of liberal opinions and free institutions; grateful recollections of the past, the multiplied enjoyments of the present, and cheering anticipations of the future, rush upon the mind, on this the anniversary of that great day to which we owe them all. To those of us who have been reared from infancy in the lap of liberty, whose bosoms have never been stirred up by oppression, the imagination essays in vain to paint, with the force and vividness of reality, the feelings that pervaded the Continental Congress and the people of the Colonies, at that important epoch which we are assembled to commemorate. The Fourth of July, 1776, was not, like this, a season of rejoicing. The tremendous consequences which hung upon its decision gave to it a character of profound solemnity. The council of patriots that assembled on that eventful morning were strongly impressed with the responsibility they were about to assume:

> "Deep on" their "front engraven,
> Deliberation sat, and public care."

They knew the power against which they were to contend, they knew the poverty of their own resources, they knew the consequences if they failed. Success alone could save them from the infamy and punishment of rebels and traitors, and to the eye of reason success was almost hopeless. This was not all. Even if the object of the hopes and exertions should be attained, it could only be at a fearful cost. The young fields of their country were to be crimsoned with the best blood of its sons; its fruitful plains were to be ravaged; its towns and villages plundered and burnt; the frame of society was to be shattered and unhinged; the sources of individual wealth and happiness were to be dried up; brother was to come into conflict with brother, and parent with child; the air was to be rent with the cries of widows and orphans; and all the horrors of protracted civil war were to spread desolation, and ruin, and death, over a hitherto peaceful, and in most respects a happy people. But the statesmen to whom the interests of America were intrusted were equal to the emergency. Independence was declared. It was proclaimed through the towns and villages of the country, and every where ratified by the approving voice of the people. To the mass of citizens, even more than to their delegates in Congress, the prospect was dark and cheerless; but they had a spirit within them that would not brook oppression; they had confidence in their leaders, and a firm conviction of the justice of their cause, and they trusted in God to deliver them. The loud acclamations with which the tidings from Congress were received, were not the sounds of joy and merriment that now rise from every part of our country on the annual return of the day of Independence: they were the outbreakings of a spirit determined to be free; they were the animating shouts that precede the desperate encounter; such as may have risen from the Spartan band of Leonidas, when they rushed upon the countless hosts of Xerxes at the pass of Thermopylæ. Over many of these brave men, too, with a slight variation, the touching inscription might afterwards have been graven, which was sculptured upon the monument that marked the spot where the Spartans fell: "O stranger! tell it in Lacedæmon, that we died here in obedience to her laws." The valor and virtue of our fathers met their reward. Heaven smiled upon their exertions, and the day on which they staked all for liberty against such fearful odds, has become the brightest in the annals of our country. Hail then to the anniversary of that day! All that meets the eye and the ear proclaims the general joy at its return. The thunder of artillery that salutes the dawn, rolling along every river and valley, and reverberated from every hill throughout the wide extent of our country; the incense of gratitude and praise ascending to heaven from a thousand altars; the vast landscape radiant with the stars and stripes of our national banner, floating over every town, and village, and hamlet, from the Northern Lakes to the Gulf of Mexico, and from the Atlantic to the Pacific, all proclaim the arrival of the great jubilee of American freedom. Well may we rejoice! for never since the sun was fixed in the firmament, has he shone upon a country so widely extended, so prosperous, and so free as ours.

The place in which we are assembled was conspicuous in the revolutionary contest, not indeed as the theatre of any important engagement, but as for a long time included in the seat of war, and the scene of varied and protracted suffering, as some who now hear me can probably bear witness. The very walls of this sacred edifice which surround us, were erected on the ruins of a conflagration, kindled by the sacrilegious hand of an enemy. Along the street from which we have just entered, passed the half-clothed, dispirited remains of the American army, with their unconquerable leader at their head, on their memorable retreat before the numerous and well-furnished hosts of Britain. The proximity of the town to Staten-Island and New-York, so long in possession of the enemy, exposed it for years to frequent alarms and incursions, from detachments of the British army and from bands of refugees. During the whole winter of 1776 and 77, it was occupied by a hostile force. In February, 1779, an unsuccessful attempt was made by General Gray, with a considerable corps, to surprise the Jersey Brigade which was quartered here, and to carry off the Governor of the State. On the 6th of June, 1780, General Knyphausen landed at the Point with a force of about six thousand men, and advancing as far as Connecticut Farms, he there received so severe a check from the Jersey Brigade and the neighboring militia, that after setting fire to several houses in that village, he retired to Elizabeth-Town Point, where he remained until the 23d of that month, when he again advanced as far as Springfield, which he burnt, and then retreated to Staten-Island. In the City of New-York, a company was organized for purposes of depredation, under the name of "The Honorable Board of Associated Loyalists," which spread terror and distress through the whole surrounding country. In a place situated like this, the sufferings of the inhabitants must necessarily have been peculiarly severe. Families were driven from their homes and from their means of living; time after time their houses were robbed, and their fields laid waste; females were left defenceless and unprotected against the outrages of lawless ruffians, while their fathers and brothers were fighting in the cause of their country; and the fate of two neighboring villages, as well as their own experience, admonished them that they were at no hour secure from the torch of the incendiary, or the incursions of armed robbers; while the melancholy death of Mrs. Caldwell proclaimed to them that their sex was not always a protection against inhuman butchery. But if the town in which we are assembled had its full share of suffering, I am proud to say it contributed its full share also to the success which finally crowned the American arms. It was the testimony of the Commander-in-chief himself, that the Jersey officers had not been outdone by any others in the qualities either of citizens or soldiers. Of these officers commissioned in the regular line of the army, Elizabeth-Town alone, then possessing less than one-third of its present population, furnished the number of twenty-eight. It may not be uninteresting to some of those whom I address, to recount the names of these brave men, which, especially in this the place that sent them forth, should never be forgotten. They are the following:

> *Elias Dayton, Matthias Ogden, Oliver Spencer, Francis Barber, William Barber, Elias Boudinot, Thomas Morrell, James Caldwell, William Barnet, Aaron Ogden, Jonathan Dayton, Andrew McMyers, Aaron Clark, Cyrus Dehart, Seth Johnson, Jonathan Pierson, David Lyon, Joseph Periam, Absalom Martin, Ephraim L. Whitlock, William Shute, Edmund Thomas, Luther Halsey, William Crane, Moses Ogden, Morris Dehart, Thomas Clark, Robert Spencer.*[1]

Scanty remnant of this gallant band that I see before me! where are your comrades? Those who fought with you side by side, who bore with you the heat and burden of many a weary day—where are they? We are met to perpetuate

[1] *Since the delivery of this oration, the writer has been informed that the name of Captain William Brittin should be added to the list of officers who entered the army from Elizabeth-Town.*

the remembrances of the great event for which they toiled and bled; to keep alive those friendships which were formed under the pressure of common danger, and in many instances cemented by blood;—and they are absent. Absent! Ah! those hoary heads remind me that threescore years have run their round, since the day that first called those gallant spirits forth in their country's cause. I seem to hear, in the remote distance, the hoarse beat of the muffled drum, and the wailing of the shrill fife; and my memory recalls the solemn hour, when my youthful footsteps joined in the procession, which, with arms reversed and shrouded ensigns, conveyed the remains of him who was the eldest of your number, to their final repose in yonder cemetery.[2] Most of those patriotic men, though now departed, had the happiness to live until the object of their warfare was accomplished; and passed from a quiet death-bed to the grave. A few there were whose glory it was to die for their country; for whose last moments no couch was spread, under the domestic roof, by the sympathy of sorrowing friends—whose destiny it was

> ________________ to lie,
> Stretch'd out on honor's nobler bed,
> Beneath a nobler roof–the sky.

Three of the number still survive; and two of them have come up on this joyful occasion, with their few remaining brethren in arms, still to cherish those ancient friendships, which were formed more than half a century ago, and to unite with another generation in the celebration of those great events, of which they themselves were eye-witnesses, and in which they bore a part. Venerable fathers! relics of the days that tried men's souls! happy are we that you are yet amongst us. May many returning anniversaries of this glorious day find you still, as now, rejoicing in the "fruits your valor won"; and when, in the course of Providence, you shall have passed from human sight, each succeeding anniversary shall revive the memory of your services and your virtues.

Brethren of the Cincinnati—Shortly before our last annual meeting the whole country was covered with gloom, by the intelligence received from France of the death of one whom we all venerated and loved—the generous, the brave, the virtuous La Fayette. The Society hastened to express its sorrow at the decease of the last surviving general officer of the Revolution, by assuming

---

[2] *General Elias Dayton*

the external badges of mourning, and by offering to the family of the deceased its deep condolence in their afflicting bereavement. The duty was at the same time imposed upon me of pronouncing before the Society, on the present occasion, a eulogy on the life and character of this extraordinary man, to be preserved in the archives of the Society. I did not consider myself at liberty to decline the task, although I felt, as I now most painfully feel, my inadequacy to its fulfillment. My diffidence is much increased by the reflection, that the subject has already been treated at the hands of others, whom I can aspire to follow only at a very humble distance. The best eulogy upon La Fayette would be a simple unadorned narrative of the events of his life. With these events you are all more or less familiar; I have not even the aid of novelty, therefore, by which I can hope to attract your attention—I must rely for a hearing upon your indulgence—upon that indulgence which affection is wont to show to the repetition of the virtuous deeds of a departed friend.

The darkest period of the American revolutionary contest was unquestionably that of the retreat through the Jerseys, in the fall and winter of 1776. The great accession to the British army, the disastrous issue of the battle of Long-Island, the evacuation of New-York, the loss of Fort Washington, with its garrison of 2,000 men, the abandonment of Fort Lee, had followed each other in rapid succession; and the American army, reduced to three or four thousand men, was flying, ragged and barefooted, at an inclement season, closely pursued by a well-disciplined, well-furnished force of three times its number. A few weeks before, General Washington was at the head of 27,000 men, full of confidence and high in spirits. During the late reverses, thousands of these had been killed or captured; multitudes had become panic-stricken, and fled; the remnant, composed in part of regulars, whose terms of enlistment had nearly expired, and part of raw militia, was dispirited and discontented. The currency had become depreciated to a fearful degree, and disaffection was spreading among the people. The stoutest hearts palpitated with anxiety and apprehension. Even the fortitude of the Commander-in-chief, which seemed "fixed as the everlasting hills," trembled in the general convulsion; and he expressed, in his letters to Congress, the most serious alarm lest the hopes of the country should be utterly blasted. The struggle, which at this agonizing crisis was a subject of such intense solicitude in America, had yet excited but little sympathy or interest in Europe; if we except the mother country itself. By most it was regarded as a family quarrel, which would soon be healed; as the rising of refractory children against parental authority, who, by proper correction, would soon be reduced to their former subjection. Little did the princes and potentates of the old world, reposing upon their honors in the fancied security of divine right—little did they anticipate the mighty consequences with which the rising contest was fraught. Little did they imagine that the cloud which they saw as a speck in the western horizon, was gathering the electric fire which was to burst in thunder over their heads, shaking down thrones, and riving institutions compacted by the duration of centuries; but dissipating, at the same time, the noxious vapors by which the political atmosphere had been so long corrupted. While this general indifference prevailed—while monarchs and statesmen the most sagacious and experienced, exhibited a total blindness to the importance of the events that were transpiring on this side of the Atlantic, there was one individual whose eye was keenly fixed on every movement of the American colonists, whose heart glowed with the warmest sympathy in their cause. This was a youth of one of the noblest families of France. At the early age of nineteen, an age devoted by most of the young men of his country to pleasure and dissipation; possessed of an ample fortune; cherished by affectionate and influential friends; wedded to a young and interesting wife; surrounded by the splendor and fascination of a luxurious court; a favorite of the young king, for whose immediate predecessor on the throne a father and an uncle had shed their blood; bearing a commission in the army of France, with a certain prospect of rapid promotion; with every thing, in short, to rivet him to his own country; the first tidings that reached his ear of a people beyond the Atlantic struggling against oppression, and fighting for *freedom*, stirred up the noble spirit within him, and he panted for an active participation in the conflict. His ardent and disinterested sympathy in the cause is best expressed in his own impassioned language, employed in a letter addressed to Congress two years afterwards: "The moment I heard of America I loved her; the moment I knew she was fighting for freedom I burnt with the desire of bleeding for her; and the moment I shall be able to serve her, at any time, or in any part of the world, will be among the happiest of my life." A spirit like this [creates] difficulties but inspires with increased energy. Happy for us, in this instance, that it was so! Else La Fayette had declined our cause as hopeless; and what, in that case, would have been the issue of the struggle, is known only to the Omniscient. The same Providence that raised up, and conducted to our aid, in the time of our greatest need, this zealous and powerful friend, might of his unsearchable pleasure have used some other instrument in the accomplishment of our deliverance. But in all human probability, if La Fayette had yielded to the obstacles which rose up before him at every step, the independence of America, if achieved at all, would have been obtained only after a much more protracted, expensive and bloody contest. I believe I may say, without injustice to the memory of any among that host of noble spirits, who, for wisdom and courage in council, bravery and energy in the field, and zeal and self-devotion in the cause of freedom, was never surpassed, that there was but one man who contributed more to the happy result of the revolutionary war than La Fayette. This gallant and noble-minded youth, spurning the seductions of a life of ease, bursting the ties which bound him to his family and his native land, against the advice and the urgent entreaties of his friends, with perils and difficulties innumerable staring him in the face, in opposition to the known wish of his sovereign, at the risk of the confiscation of his large estate, and of personal degradation and punishment, had already offered his services to the American commissioner in France, as a volunteer in the cause of the revolted colonies. The offer had been accepted, and a passage was promised him in a vessel which was expected soon to sail for America, with stores and equipments. At this juncture arrived the dismal tidings of the evacuation of New-York, and the retreat of the American army through New-Jersey, almost annihilated before its pursuers. The hearts of the commissioners sunk within them; the shrieks of American freedom, expiring in its infancy, seemed wafted to their ear across the Atlantic; the credit of the country was gone; hope itself was almost extinct. This melancholy reverse was announced to La Fayette: his projected enterprise was discouraged; and he was informed that the idea of sending out a vessel to America was necessarily abandoned. Mark his noble reply—Americans! Freemen! whose destiny it may be turned on that resolve! Mark his magnanimous reply: "Hitherto I have only cherished your cause, now I am going to serve it. The lower it is in the opinion of the people, the greater will be the effect of my departure; and since you cannot get a vessel, I will purchase one, which shall convey your dispatches to Congress, and myself and my companions to America." A ship was purchased, and for greater safety was conveyed to a port in Spain. An order was issued by the King prohibiting his departure, and he was compelled to return to France. He afterwards fled to his vessel in the disguise of a courier, pursued by officers with a warrant for his arrest. He put to sea immediately with a clearance for the West Indies; but altering the course of the vessel, at the imminent risk of capture and imprisonment by the enemy, under such circumstances as would preclude the hope of an exchange, he steered for the American continent, and escaping the cruisers, which had been fortunately blown off by a gale, he landed near Charleston, in South-Carolina.

Here let us pause, and inquire what powerful motives induced this young member of a proud aristocracy, reared and educated under the dominion of a despotic king, to sympathize with the rebel subjects of a neighboring prince; what considerations impelled him, when the millions around him were standing aloof, at the risk of all his possessions and prospects, to rush with the burning zeal of chivalry to the support of a sinking and almost desperate cause in a strange and distant land. Open the history of his life, and at the head of every page, from the commencement to the close, you see inscribed, in conspicuous characters, LOVE OF LIBERTY—LOVE OF GLORY. These are the principles by which he has been swayed through the whole of his eventful career. Love of liberty, and ever in subordination to that, the love of glory. Not that liberty which consists in the absence of all government, in the destruction of all orders in society, and the overthrow of the most sacred and valuable institutions, and whose licentiousness terminates inevitably in despotism; but that rational genuine liberty, which admits of no restraint upon individual action, or the expression of individual opinion, beyond that which is necessary to the well-being of the society in which it exists, but which at the same time allows no license inconsistent with the morals and good order of the community. No that glory which seeks a selfish gratification in wantonly shedding human blood, and spreading misery and ruin and desolation over the face of unoffending nations, and with the blood-stained laurel on its brow, weeps for more worlds to conquer: but that glory which springs from noble actions achieved for noble purposes, from the gallant defence of a nation's liberties, from a manly resistance against oppression, from the promotion of the general happiness.

On the 31st of July, 1777, La Fayette, then not twenty years of age, received from Congress the commission of Major General in the army of the United States. By his own desire, he was to serve as a volunteer, and without pay. The interest which had been excited among the friends of the Revolution by the expected arrival of a personage so eminent by his rank and his illustrious connexions, who had exhibited so extraordinary a zeal in favor of the American cause, was not disappointed by his presence. Tall and slender in his person—his youthful countenance beaming with intelligence and vivacity—frank, and courteous, and affable in his manners—the warmth of his affection and the ardor of his feelings shining through his whole deportment—he inspired at once that attachment and confidence which, when yielded, were never withdrawn. He was adopted as an American citizen, a privilege which from that time was his pride and boast; a distinction to which he clung with fondness and exultation long after he had cast away the title derived from his noble birth, and had rejected as lighter than vanity the honorary insignia which princes can confer. It was his first request upon accepting his commission, that he might be near the person of Washington; and so favorable was the impression which he made upon the Commander-in-chief at the first interview, that he, whose confidence was hardly ever rashly given, invited the young volunteer to become one of his family. The invitation was accepted with avidity, and a connexion of the tenderest friendship was formed, which terminated only with life: a connexion, indeed, more intimate and endearing than the closest friendship; a filial veneration and affection on the one part, and a paternal fondness on the other. The sword of La Fayette was now to be unsheathed, and he was to encounter, under the eye of his paternal chief, the terrors of the first battlefield. It was at Brandywine that the young hero first found himself face to face with the enemy. His gallant spirit mocked at fear; and novel as the scene was, his displayed the courage of a veteran. When the fortune of the day was inclining against the American arms, he was to be seen on foot in the thickest of the danger, endeavoring to rally the retreating troops; and while thus engaged, he received a severe wound, which compelled him to retire for some weeks from active duty. During his confinement, his mind was not unemployed, nor was his zeal in the cause of American liberty in the least degree abated. While thus withdrawn from the field, he prepared and sent to Versailles a written project, which he hoped might bring about a declaration of war against England: and with the same view of producing a disagreement between the two countries, which might lead to active hostilities, he proposed to the Governor of Mississippi a joint expedition under American colors, against the English West India Islands; toward the expense of which he intended to contribute out of his own fortune: a measure which met with the approbation of the governor, and in favor of which that functionary addressed the French Court. In November we find him again in the field, acting as a volunteer in a detachment under General Greene, which was sent to succor Fort Mercer. In the course of this expedition, he distinguished himself by a spirited and successful attack with one hundred and fifty riflemen and as many militia, upon a picket of three hundred men, belonging to the army of Lord Cornwallis. Congress and the Commander-in-chief were satisfied, from the short experiment which had now been made, that property and influence were not all that the newly constituted General had brought into the service of America. They perceived that he had military talent, which ought not to remain inactive for want of proper opportunity of exertion; and soon after he had recovered from his wound, the Commander-in-chief was informed that it would be agreeable to Congress, that General La Fayette should have command of a division. In the next month an appointment was conferred upon this young soldier, which, while it was a flattering mark of the confidence reposed in him; brought into prominent relief another of that rare assemblage of qualities, which his life exhibited in such beautiful equilibrium. It was resolved to invade Canada with an army of 2,500 men. This expedition was to have a double aspect, and was considered one of great importance. To capture St. John's, Chambly and Montreal; to seize the public stores at those places; and to obtain supplies for the American army in the States; constituted one class of objects in view: the other was to conciliate the inhabitants; to take advantage of their supposed disaffection to the British Government, and to induce them to join the Confederacy of States, submitting to the resolves of Congress, adopting the American currency, and sending delegates to represent their interests in the general body of representatives at Philadelphia. La Fayette, at that time but little more than twenty years of age, was unanimously elected by ballot to command this expedition. What an enviable opportunity for distinction was here presented to the young and chivalrous officer! With what elation of spirits, with what tumultuous joy, must he have received the unexpected tidings! He, a youth of twenty, intrusted with the separate and independent command of an army of 2,500 men, the superior of officers grey with years and service, the head and conductor of an invasion of great difficulty and moment, requiring the exercise of the utmost skill, courage and address; with what eagerness must he have rushed to slake his burning thirst of glory at the fountain thus opened before him! With what alacrity and precipitation must he have hastened to the field, to reap the bright harvest of fame that waved before him! But no! Covetous as he was of glory, and full as he was of zeal, neither his ambition nor his ardor ever outran his prudence. When his appointment as the leader of the projected expedition was announced to him, he exhibited all the coolness, and wariness, and circumspection of a veteran. In his letter to the President of Congress, he said: "You will find me, Sir, very difficult, and rather too cautious; but it comes chiefly from my being strongly convinced how far indebted I am to the Congress of the United States for the confidence they honor me with." He expressed his willingness to accept the command, only on condition of the most thorough preparation being made. He requested that the force to be employed might be considered as a detachment of the main army, and subject to the command in chief of General Washington; and that an additional number of general officers might be attached to the expedition, with whom he could consult. He had an eye to the most minute arrangements, urging the adoption of every precaution to prevent a failure; and after a considerable expenditure incurred by himself, in making the necessary preparations, the expedition was finally abandoned at his recommendation, from a supposed deficiency in the means for securing its success.

I should exceed the time allowed me on this occasion, were I to enter into a detailed account of all the scenes of the Revolutionary War in which the subject of this eulogy bore a conspicuous part. He always courted active service, and he never entered a field of battle without gathering fresh honors, and acquiring increased claims upon the admiration and gratitude of the American people. His masterly retreat with an advanced guard of 2,000 men from Barren Hill, in the spring of 1778, for which he was complimented by General Washington; the gallantry and judgment displayed by him, in the battle of Monmouth, in which he had a principal command; his unremitted and successful exertions in healing the alarming feud between the American and French officers, arising out of the unhappy jealousy evinced by Admiral d'Estaing at the attack on Newport; his courage and good conduct in aiding the retreat of General Sullivan, after the departure of the French fleet, for which he received the particular thanks of Congress; each presenting a fruitful theme for the biographer or historian, can now receive but a passing notice.

With all the enthusiasm and devotion which La Fayette had manifested in the cause of America, he had lost none of his attachment to his native country, or of his loyalty to its king. With that high and delicate sense of duty, for which he was distinguished, now that war had been declared by Great Britain against France, he resolved to present himself before his sovereign, and place his services at his disposal. It was a time, too, when his influence and exertions at the Court of Versailles might be of immense importance, in procuring the active and energetic co-operation of France, in the efforts which [they] were making to drive the common enemy from their former possessions on this continent. Under these circumstances, much as his loss might be felt in America, his departure could not be opposed; and Congress, while granting him an unlimited furlough, returned him their thanks for the zeal and ability he had displayed in their cause, directed an elegant sword to be presented to him, as a testimonial of their gratitude and esteem, and gave him a letter to the King of France, in which they say:—"We recommend this young nobleman to your Majesty's notice, as one whom we know to be wise in council, gallant in the field, and patient under the hardships of war." He, on his part, assured them that the affairs of America should be his first business while in Europe; that any confidence he might have with the king and ministry, any popularity with his countrymen, and every means in his power, should be exerted in behalf of an interest he had so much at heart. And faithfully was his promise kept. During his absence, he was almost constantly in correspondence with the representation of the United States at Versailles, and with the French ministry, and exerting his influence at court, to procure contributions in men, ships and money, for carrying on the war. His mind was replete with resources, and his efforts were unceasing to render them available. At one time, we find him proposing that vessels of war should be hired from Sweden, upon the responsibility of France; at another, that a loan should be procured from Holland, with a French guaranty; and again, pressing upon the French government itself to send out a large military and naval force to the assistance of its allies. He urged their co-operation in a joint expedition against Canada and Nova Scotia, which had been specially recommended to his attention by Congress, previous to his departure from America; and he only ceased his exertions to this respect, when he was informed by its authors that the scheme was abandoned. In his solicitude to recruit the American finances, he projected with the celebrated Paul Jones, a descent under American colors upon the western coast of England, for the purpose of levying contributions from Liverpool, and other towns upon the seaboard, for the American treasury. This project was superseded by a contemplated invasion of England, upon a much larger scale, by the united forces of France and Spain; which, however, was never undertaken. The reception of La Fayette in his native country was gratifying even beyond his expectation. His kindred and friends beheld him with increased interest and pride, as he came invested with the honors he had won in a foreign service; and after atoning, by a formal exile of a few days, for the disregard he had shown to the king's wishes, when he embarked for America, he was received with the fullness of royal favor, and was soon after appointed to the command of the king's own regiment of dragoons, and subsequently served with an honorable command under the Count de Vaux in Normandy. But beloved and cherished as he was in France, his heart was in America, and he yearned to be at the side of his former comrades, fighting in the cause of freedom. He writes in a letter of June, 1779:—"Never any thing was so warmly and passionately wished for, as I desire to return again to that country, of which I shall ever consider myself as a citizen." At length the wish of his heart was gratified. In April, 1780, he arrived at Boston, with the joyful intelligence that France had agreed to send out large succors to America, and that a formidable military and naval force might soon be expected to cooperate against the enemy. Cordial was the welcome, and great the rejoicing, with which this generous and tried friend of the American cause was greeted on his return. It seemed as if a new star of propitious aspect had risen upon America, toward which every face was turned, beaming with joy and hope. The news of the coming reinforcement flew with electrical rapidity to every quarter of the continent. The spirits of the whole country were revived, and renewed exertions were made, in the confidence that a speedy termination would be put to the war.

We are now approaching the most interesting and eventful period of La Fayette's service in America; a period which called forth all his talents and energies, and shed a luster upon his military reputation, which, at his age, a Turenne or a Malborough might have envied. In the summer of 1780 he was placed at the head of a separate corps, formed of the flower of the army, and ever after designated by him, with feelings of affection and pride, as his "beloved light infantry." When he obtained the command of this fine body of men, his fondest wish was gratified; and with them all his anticipations of future glory seemed to be identified. His private fortune was liberally expended in giving them a soldierlike appearance, and every effort was made to infuse into their breasts that lofty martial spirit which glowed in the bosom of their leader. In toil, in suffering, and in triumph, they were still his "beloved light infantry." From the time of his taking the command, through all the vicissitudes of the war in Virginia, until he bid them an affecting farewell, on his departure for Europe, after the surrender of Yorktown, he exhibited toward them the same parental fondness and sympathy. When they were destitute of clothing on their march to the South, he relieved them with means obtained upon his own private responsibility; and when, pressed with accumulated suffering, they threatened to desert, he secured their adherence by giving them leave to retire. The sight of their uniform, worn by a company in Boston, upon his last visit to the United States, filled him with the deepest emotion. The tear glistened in his eye, as he turned again and again to view this affecting memento of former days, and he repeatedly exclaimed, "My brave light infantry! such was their uniform! What courage! What resignation! How much I loved them!" It was with this corps that he achieved the memorable campaign of 1781, which, doubtless, paved the way to his subsequent elevation, in his own country, to the command of the National Guard of Paris, and to his selection as the leader of one of the three great armies employed against Austria. It was in the spring of 1781 that he entered upon this celebrated campaign. For some time previous, the enemy had been directing their principal operations against the Southern States. The fall of Charleston, the calamitous result of the battle of Camden, and the surprise of Sumpter at Catawba, had almost annihilated the American army at the South, and with it, the hopes of the friends of the cause in that quarter. The whole southern section of the Union was in imminent danger of falling to the undisputed control of the invaders; and although the reverses alluded to had been a measure retrieved by subsequent successes under General Greene, in South-Carolina, the aspect of affairs in that quarter was still discouraging. The occupation of Virginia at this crisis was of the utmost importance; and so utterly defenceless was it that the traitor Arnold, who had recently been invested by Sir Henry Clinton with the command of an expedition to that State, left his vessels, advanced with 900 men to Richmond, and returned almost without opposition, laying waste the country along his whole route. It was to capture this traitor, that a joint expedition was planned by the Commander-in-chief, in execution of which, on his part, General La Fayette was dispatched by land with 1,200 men, while the French were to transport about the same number to the Chesapeake by water. The French having failed to execute that part of the project which was assigned to them, and General Philips having been sent to the relief of Arnold, with 2,000 additional troops, La Fayette was then ordered to take upon himself the defence of Virginia. The situation of La Fayette at this point of his history was deeply interesting. A youth of twenty-three, with little experience in war, he was directed to advance with less than a thousand regular troops, literally almost naked, and without tents to cover them from the weather in an uncongenial climate,—many of them sick, and all dispirited and dissatisfied,—for the purpose of defending the most important State of the Confederacy, the key to the whole southern country, against a disciplined and well-appointed army of 3,500 men, including a numerous corps of cavalry, and having command of the water. He who had been accustomed, on all former occasions of difficulty, to look up with filial confidence to his paternal chief for guidance and direction, was now to assume what was, in effect, a separate command, where every movement must be made upon his own judgment and responsibility, against officers of high and established military character. General Philips, with whom he was first to cope, had served with great credit while young under Prince Ferdinand of Brunswick, and had acquired additional reputation as a commander of a division of the army under General Burgoyne. It was now to be determined by a severe test, whether the extra-ordinary confidence which Congress, and the Commander-in-chief, and the country, had reposed in La Fayette was to be justified; whether the high hopes and expectations which had been excited in America and Europe by the incipient career of this noble adventurer in the cause of freedom, were to be realized, and the luster of a new renown, such as he had never before acquired, should shed its light along the path of his future life, or whether his own eager aspirations after fame, and the fond anticipations of his friends, were to be blasted by a want of success, which, in the candidate for military fame, is so apt to be construed, however unjustly, into a want of merit. The prospect was appalling, and a bold heart might have trembled at the danger. Did La Fayette falter? No—not for a moment. With his other qualities, he possessed, in a high degree, that *self-confidence* which is so essential to the accomplishment of great enterprises, without which, in situations of command and in critical emergencies, great talents, if not wholly useless, are comparatively ineffective. He never lost a cause from fear of losing it. He received the order, and it was his duty as an officer, disregarding personal considerations, to do his utmost to execute it. He was to fight against a traitor, whom from the depths of his noble soul he execrated and despised; and against a commander before whose battery his gallant father had fallen on the field of Minden. It is not for me to narrate the details of this campaign, in the progress of which the young General was called to encounter, in the person of Lord Cornwallis, an officer who, in all the qualities required for such a contest, in courage, activity, circumspection, and skill in manœuvre, had no superior in the British army; and in Simcoe and Tarleton, men whose enterprise and agility had struck terror into the country, and rendered them most dangerous adversaries. There is one at least among us[3] who shared with him the trials and the triumphs of that memorable summer. He can tell you of the forced marches, the rapid advances, the hurried retreats, the frequent alarms, the narrow escapes, which rendered their days wearisome and their nights sleepless: he can tell you how often his heart has ached to behold those brave and devoted men hurried long from post to post, in miserable destitution of all conveniences and comforts on the road and in the camp, sinking under the oppressive heats of the day and the chilling damps of the night, yet striving to present a bold and warlike front to a formidable enemy. History will tell you, for she has inscribed it upon one of her fairest pages, how the young commander met and surmounted every difficulty, as the gallant ship rides the crested waves. She will tell you of the *cautious prudence,* which held in restraint the ardor of his youth, and the enthusiasm of his temperament, and led him, with Fabian policy, to act on the defensive, in spite of every artifice of the enemy and every temptation to act otherwise, and thus to harass and wear out the superior force of his adversary; of his *courage and enterprise,* which kept him with his comparatively small band upon the very skirts of an army of three times his effective numbers, and enabled him ever and anon to strike at some detached portion of the opposing forces: of his *untiring vigilance,* which, notwithstanding that he was incessantly hovering about the enemy, never suffered a surprise: of his *military sagacity,* which saw with eagle eye an advantage was to be gained, or a danger escaped; and his *skill and agility in manœuvres,* which enabled him repeatedly to thrust himself between the enemy and his object, to check and foil him in his movements, and to extricate himself from all the snares laid for him by his dexterous opponent, even when he fondly hoped and boasted, that "the boy" could not escape him. History will tell, too, of the glorious consummation of his anxieties and toils, in the surrender of his lionlike adversary in

[3] *Colonel Aaron Ogden—Capt. Wm. Tuttle, a member of the Society also served in that Campaign.*

the lair to which he had tracked him; she will tell of the luster which surrounded the young hero on the battlefield, when, detached upon the most perilous service of the siege, his gallant spirit, freed from all restraint, rushed to victory in the face of danger and of death itself. The fall of Yorktown was decisive of the war; but the exertions of the Commander-in-chief were not for a moment relaxed. At his suggestion, La Fayette resolved again to visit France, and exert his powerful influence in procuring further aid for the next campaign. Previous to his departure, Congress expressed in the strongest terms their sense of the services rendered by him and his brave troops in Virginia. He was again recommended to the King, and the ministers plenipotentiary of the United States abroad were directed to confer with him respecting the affairs of the country. From the period of his arrival in France, his efforts were unremitted to promote the views of Congress, and the interests of his adopted country, by every means within his power; and, to use his own language, he became the political aid-de-camp of Dr. Franklin, then the minister of the United States at Versailles. The public documents of that day contain abundant evidence of his zealous and active interposition, both in providing for a vigorous prosecution of the war, and in promoting the negotiations for peace. He who, a few months before, first bore to our shores the welcome tidings of those succors from France which he had been so instrumental in procuring, and which hastened the close of the war by their co-operation at Yorktown, was now the first to announce by letter the joyful news that peace was concluded, and the Independence of the United States secured. At the time of the occurrence of this happy event, a French and Spanish force of forty-nine ships of the line and 20,000 troops was lying at Cadiz, in readiness for the next campaign in America; and he himself, who had marched 8,000 of these men from Brest, and who had been appointed chief of the staff to this expedition, was to enter the St. Lawrence at the head of a French detachment, and prosecute his favorite scheme of annexing Canada to the United States. Having remained in France at the earnest solicitation of the commissioners who were conducting the negotiations for peace, until his services were no longer required in the field, anxious as he was to take his old comrades by the hand, and exchange congratulations upon the accomplishment of the object of their labors and anxieties, he sacrificed his personal feelings to the public interest, and hastened to Madrid at the call of the American representative there, and with the skill and address of an experienced diplomatist, exerted himself successfully to remove the difficulties that obstructed the establishment of friendly relations with that government.

On his return to France, he was still occupied in seeking advantages for American commerce, and facilities in the payment of the public debts of the United States, which had been contracted in Europe; and it was not until the spring of 1784, that he was enabled to make his long desired visit to this country. He was received with enthusiasm, and his stay was accompanied by all those marks of admiration and attachment which his character and his services had justly inspired. At the close of that year he took an affectionate leave of Congress, and his old companions in America, and left these shores, never again to return, until after the lapse of forty years, (Oh! what eventful years!) and then to re-appear before another generation, with circumstances of indescribable interest and grandeur.

The scene of the exploits of La Fayette is now to be changed from the new world to the old. The Revolution in America had been brought to a happy conclusion, and the patriots of France, roused by the example, were about to erect the standard of popular rights in that country. This Revolution, which was commenced upon just grounds, for the redress of actual grievances, and which excited the sympathy of the friends of freedom every where, was soon perverted by unprincipled demagogues, to the overthrow of all social order, and the commission of excesses which outraged humanity. It were vain to attempt to picture to the eye or to the imagination the horrors by which France was devastated under the abused and prostituted name of liberty. The most awful exhibition of destructive power that nature presents—the volcano, rolling forth its burning floods, amid thunderings, and earthquakes, and flames, desolating fields that but yesterday rejoiced in verdure and bloom, and burying villages that a few hours before were instinct with life and gayety—affords but a faint image of the moral blight and ruin spread over the face of society by the atrocities of this dreadful period. A monarchy, hoary with the antiquity of fourteen hundred years, shivered to atoms by the fury of a mob; the crown which had sparkled upon the brows of sixty-six successive kings, trampled in the dust; the last of that royal line deposed, insulted and murdered; princes and nobles sent forth to exile and beggary; society upheaved from its very foundations, and the most ancient and valuable institutions overturned; the leaders of opposing factions butchering each other in their struggles for power; the prisons choked up with the victims of jealousy and revenge; the guillotine streaming incessantly with fresh blood; the temples and altars of religion desecrated and overthrown,—such were the scenes enacted by men with the cry of freedom on their lips. But what connexion have these horrible details with the character or conduct of La Fayette? It was declared by Burke, upon the floor of the House of Commons, and the accusation has been often repeated, that La Fayette was the origin and author of all the calamities of that frightful period. Never was a fouler calumny uttered by the lips of party virulence. As the candid eulogist of La Fayette, I would exhibit him to view upon this awful theatre, as an example of the purest consistency of character ever displayed by man, under circumstances of equal difficulty. Could I follow him, step by step, from the commencement of the Revolution, to the moment when he abandoned his country in despair, you would see at every stage an exhibition of heroic virtue which has never been sufficiently applauded, even by his warmest admirers. The same qualities by which he was distinguished during his youthful career in America, still constituted the beautiful symmetry of his character; but the trying circumstances under which he was now called upon to act, brought out those qualities with a strength and boldness of relief which they had never before presented. All the powers and energies of his mind were called into action, and gave to his character a sublimity which can only be displayed in times of great difficulty and peril. Surrounded by the most unprincipled licentiousness, he was the consistent advocate of liberty regulated by law; in the midst of temptation and corruption, he preserved the most unblemished integrity; familiarized to scenes of cruelty, and subjected to the strongest provocation, he was always humane; thrown, time after time, into situations of the utmost perplexity and danger, his prudence and firmness never forsook him: while his rivals and his enemies were seeking the means of his destruction, by degrading themselves to a level with the lowest dregs of a Parisian populace, and while he himself was dependent for all his power and influence, and for life itself, upon popular favor, he never stooped to conciliate the multitude by the smallest sacrifice of principle, or the slightest departure from personal dignity. That he was a friend and chief promoter of the Revolution, is most true. In the first assembly of the Notables, it was he that moved the convocation of the States General. In the second assembly, it was he that insisted upon that most important measure, which secured the popular ascendancy, and lay at the foundation of all popular reform—the double representation of the Commons. He was a leading member and one of the vice-presidents of the National Convention. He was the first to present to that body for its adoption a declaration of popular rights, and was one of the principal framers of the Constitution of 1791; and he was, moreover, the commander of the National Guard of Paris. And was he to be blamed for all this? In the part which he acted, he but followed the examples of a Hampden, a Sydney and a Washington. He was a lover of liberty from his cradle. He fought for freedom in America, he yearned to give freedom to oppressed Ireland, and was he to look with submissive indifference upon the servitude to which his own country was subjected? The government of France was not always an absolute monarchy. For centuries the royal prerogative was strictly limited; and in the early ages of the monarchy, the people even exercised the right of electing and deposing the king. Nor was nobility hereditary until the tenth century. To the question of Hugh Capet, "Who made you a noble?" the Viscount of Perigneaux replied, "Not you, but those who made you king." The people had a share in legislation, and no taxes could be imposed upon them but with their consent. From the time of Charles VII, the kings of France had exercised despotic power; and although in succeeding reigns, the States General were occasionally convened, the people were virtually excluded from all participation in the government. For nearly two hundred years before the accession of Louis XVI, they had ceased to be represented or consulted even in name. It is unnecessary to enter upon a particular detail of the numerous causes which conspired to bring about the Revolution. Although the nation had reached its highest splendor under the absolute government to which it had been subjected, and although the condition of the people under Louis XVI was happiness itself, in comparison with the anarchy and wild misrule of the Jacobins, yet no friend of freedom can deny that the situation of public affairs in 1789, was such as to justify an attempt at reform. The people were subjected to oppressive taxation at the will of the monarch, and were excluded from the highest offices; the public finances were in a state of almost hopeless embarrassment; the numerous body of nobles was exempt from contributing to the expenses of the government; titles conferring this exemption were bought and sold; the administration of justice was corrupted, and the personal liberty of the subject was constantly in jeopardy from the *lettres de cachet* of the king. Our fathers were far from having suffered, or even apprehended, evils like these, when they rose against their oppressors, and threw off the yoke. How, then, can any American condemn the authors of the French Revolution? The friends and advocates of salutary reform and rational liberty cannot justly be held responsible for the excesses which were afterwards committed by those who proved themselves to be the most rancorous enemies of genuine freedom. They who held up the torch to show to an oppressed people their rights, and the way to obtain them, are not to be condemned for the acts of vile incendiaries, who plucked it from their hands, and fired the whole social edifice, involving life, liberty and property in one common ruin. The Constitution of 1791, defective as it was, if it had been suffered to remain, would undoubtedly have improved the condition of the French people, and to the principles asserted by the framers of that Constitution is France indebted for all the protection, imperfect though it be, which is afforded to popular rights by her present system.

It must be acknowledged that the original movers in the French Revolution, with honest intentions, committed great errors of judgment. They aimed to accomplish too much at once, and paid too little regard to the character of the people, and to their former habits. Let it be remembered, however, to the credit of La Fayette, that he never was favorable to the establishment of a republican government in France. During the Revolution of 1789, he never even suggested such a change; on the contrary, he more than once avowed his opinion to be in favor of a hereditary executive; and in the Revolution of 1830, he expressly declared himself opposed to the foundation of a republic, and in favor of "a popular throne surrounded by republican institutions." He was never so unreasonable as to believe that the same form of government was adapted to every people, whatever might be their dispositions, their habits, or their circumstances. Looking upon the American government as the best that had ever been framed, he knew the French people too well to attempt to introduce it among them. The declaration of rights which he proposed to the National Assembly, contained the same leading principles as the Declaration of Independence of the United States, placing all power where it rightfully belongs, in the body of the people; but the government which he proposed to base upon those principles was not a republic. He foresaw that the first popular election of the chief executive officer would shake the constitutional fabric to pieces. The form of government established by the Constitution of 1791, which was the foundation of all his hopes, and to which he adhered to the last, was a limited monarchy. The kingly office was to remain hereditary, and the royal person to be sacred and inviolate. It was a radical and a fatal error, however, that in abolishing the hereditary peerage, no substitute was interposed as a barrier between the king and the popular assembly. There were other conspiring causes, undoubtedly, which tended to produce the disorganization of the newly established government, and not the least were the irresolution, the vacillation, the insincerity, and the weakness of the King himself, and the ignorance, degradation, and excitability of the Parisian populace: but, after all, the defect of which I have spoken was the rock upon which the Constitution split. The too popular cast given to the new system, including this want of protection to the King against the waves of popular excitement, appears to have been foreseen by La Fayette; for in a letter addressed to his constituents, in the year 1831, he expressly states that the experience of the world upon this subject, anterior to the year '89, led him to regret that the Constituent Assembly preferred the unity of the legislative body to its division into two elective chambers. Afterwards, too, in a speech delivered by him in the Chamber of Deputies, against a hereditary peerage, he declared that he had always been in favor of the system of two chambers; and during the same session he voted for a Chamber of Peers, the members of which should be constituted for the term of fifteen years. As it does not appear, however, that he exerted his influence, which at that period was very great, to procure the adoption of this feature in the Constitution of 1791, it may fairly be inferred that he was not aware of its vital importance; and herein, it must be confessed, that he showed a want of due sagacity as a statesman, the less excusable, as the omission was a departure from the only free constitutions then existing, those of America and England. But if he committed an error in judgment, the honesty of his intention was proved beyond controversy, by his unwavering support of the new Constitution, through evil as well as through good report; and by his sufferings and sacrifices in the cause. He supported the constitutional king from the first to the last moment, with as much zeal and devotion as he manifested in favor of the constitutional parliament. His language to the Duke of Orleans, when he advised that prince, for the sake of the public peace, to quit the country, was: "The throne itself still exists, and will always exist, for it is the rampart of the Constitution, and of the liberty of the people." Again and again he periled his influence and his life for the personal safety of the monarch. On the memorable 5th and 6th of October, when the palace of Versailles was attacked by an infuriated rabble, crying out for bread, and thirsting for revenge against the King and Queen, who were suspected of a design to reduce the city of Paris to submission by famine, La Fayette rushed into the midst of the exasperated crowd, from which cries for his head were heard to issue, and after rescuing several of the King's body guards from assassination, passed into the palace, and took the royal family under his personal protection. It was by his courage and devotion alone, as they ever afterwards acknowledged, that their lives were preserved on this occasion. When the departure of the King to St. Cloud was successfully resisted by the populace and a part of the National Guards, La Fayette, in disgust, resigned his commission as commandant of the Parisian guard; and it was only upon the most urgent entreaties of the municipality of Paris, of the troops themselves, and of the royal family, and after the most solemn assurances that he should be sustained in repressing future disorders, that he consented to resume the command. The flight of the royal family to

Varennes, with an intention of leaving the kingdom, was undertaken without the knowledge of La Fayette, and after he had been induced, by the promises of the King, to declare publicly that such an attempt would not be made. It was a step which threatened to overturn the Constitution, and to involve France in internecine and foreign war; and in such imminent jeopardy did it place La Fayette himself, that Louis upon his arrest expressed his surprise that the General yet lived and commanded the National Guard. Still the solicitude which he had always manifested for the personal security of the monarch was not relaxed. At the risk of his popularity, he dispersed by force of arms the crowd assembled in the Champ de Mars, for the purpose of signing a petition for the dethronement of the King. A few days before the memorable 10th of August, he offered to conduct the unfortunate monarch in safety to Compeigne, where he would be out of the reach of his enemies; but the offer was only accepted when it was too late to accomplish the object. He denounced the Jacobins at the peril of his life, when they threatened to overturn the throne; and, finally, when the royal authority was suspended, he abandoned the army and the country.

We are thus brought to the consideration of an event which was probably the most painful of all the varied occurrences that chequered the life of La Fayette—his flight from France. What tongue can tell the anguish that must have wrung the bosom of this faithful solider and patriot at the necessity of taking such a step! His country, dearer to him than his life, seemed to stretch out her bleeding hands and implore him not to leave her in the hour of her greatest need. Liberty, the object of his earliest affection, for whom his youthful blood had been shed, and to whom he had consecrated the labors and sufferings of after years, pierced his ear with her plaintive cries, and conjured him to rescue her from the grasp of enemies in the guise of friends. Those visions of happiness for his beloved France, which had hitherto sustained him through every vicissitude, and cheered him onward in his course, were now dissipated like morning dreams. The sun of freedom, whose rising beams he had hailed with so much rapture, and whose struggling rays gilded to his eye every cloud that intervened to obscure their radiance, was "going down while it was yet day"; and the lurid clouds, that now swept with fearful rapidity across the horizon, portended a night of darkness and blood. The allurements of military glory, which to him were so inviting, and which glittered almost within his reach, were to be foregone. He was about to take a step, the motives of which were likely to be misunderstood, and certain to be misrepresented; he was to incur the charge of flying from danger, of deserting his standard, of forsaking in an hour of peril, the brave troops that looked up to him as their leader, and above all, of abandoning, from cowardly despondence, the glorious cause of liberty, of which he had professed to be the fearless and zealous champion, which it would be said might still, peradventure, have been redeemed by his exertions, in the defence of which, at all events, he should have conquered or died: a family, too, to which he was tenderly attached, and whose natural protector he was, must be left to rely upon the mercy and forbearance of blood-thirsty ruffians, to whom his very name was hateful, and whose rage would be excited to desperation by the news of his escape from their fangs. He paused to consider. On whichever side he looked he saw his enemies triumphant: the constitution and laws were prostrate, and the "reign of terror" had commenced. He had contended for his principles until he stood almost alone; corruption and intrigue had shorn him of his power and influence, seduction had even been busy in the ranks of his army; he had been denounced by the National Assembly as a traitor and a monster, and a price had been set upon his head. If he remained in France there was naught before him but an ignominious death, at which his adversaries would exult, and the friends of freedom would despond. He determined to withdraw, and await a more auspicious day, when the advocates of liberty might again be rallied, and led on to victory. Having provided for the safety of the army under his command, he passed the frontier, with some members of his staff, with a view of proceeding to Holland and England; but was arrested by an Austrian corps in the neutral territory of Liege, and having refused to take part against his country in the war that was waging, he was subjected to incarceration as a prisoner of state. I must pass over his long and cruel captivity in the dungeons of Prussia and Austria, from which he was at length released upon the intercession of the French Directory, and through the influence of Bonaparte. Those principles which neither time nor suffering had changed, forbade his return to France until after the revolution of the 18th Brumaire, which established the consular government. He then repaired to his native country to live as a private citizen, and it was in vain that Bonaparte, who was anxious to attach him to his government, sought, by personal solicitation, to draw him from his retreat at La Grange. Full of gratitude as he was to the First Consul, for the interest he had taken in procuring his discharge from imprisonment, and for his uniform kindness, that consideration was not permitted to prevail over his love of country; and he firmly refused his consent to the establishment of the Consulate for life, unless some guaranty should be previously given for the liberties of France. Thus separated Bonaparte and La Fayette, never again to meet; like two majestic rivers, whose near approach had almost mingled their waters, now parting to roil their floods by different courses, and at a wider and wider distance asunder, toward the same ocean; the one pursuing its way over rocks and precipices, displaying at every obstruction new beauty or grandeur, in the glittering waterfall or the thundering cataract, widening and deepening as it proceeds, and acquiring increased rapidity, until all its original transparency lost, it presents to the view the sublime but fearful spectacle of a capacious sea lashed into fury by storms and tempests, and bearing upon its agitated surface the weight of contending fleets—the other pouring its smooth and fertilizing current through valleys and plains, every where ministering to health and convenience, till its accumulated waters, flowing from nation to nation, wash the feet of mighty cities, bearing upon their brimming surface the freights of distant climes and throngs of joyful people, and through all their course reflecting from their crystal bosom, as from a mirror, the purity of the o'er-arching heaven. The great object of Bonaparte's life was personal glory; the great object of the life of La Fayette was the happiness of mankind; and, wide as the objects were from each other, so widely different were the means by which they were sought to be attained.

From this period until the restoration of the Bourbons, in 1815, La Fayette remained in retirement at La Grange. After the return of Bonaparte from Elba, when hosts of foreign enemies were marshaled again him, and the fearful struggle was about to commence upon the issue of which his destiny was suspended, the confidence of the people was sought to be regained, and the nation roused to vigorous exertion by promises of liberty, on the part of him by whom nearly every vestige of freedom had been long since destroyed. La Fayette, diffident as he was of the fulfillment of these engagements, felt it to be his duty, upon the urgent solicitation of the brother of Napoleon, to come forth from his retreat at such a crisis; and having been elected a member of Chamber of Representatives, he became one of the vice-presidents of that body. He urged the adoption of active measures for the national defence, but at the same time boldly asserted the rights of the people, and refused to hold personal intercourse with the Emperor. When Napoleon, driven to desperation, meditated the dissolution of the Chambers, and the assumption of the Dictatorship, La Fayette proposed that the Assembly should declare its sitting permanent, and that it would consider as a traitor any one who should attempt to dissolve it. The proposition was adopted, but the face of affairs was soon changed by the battle of Waterloo and the abdication of the Emperor. A provisional government was formed, and La Fayette, being excluded by the intrigues of Fouché, was sent to treat with the enemy for an armistice. In the course of this negotiation, still mindful of the generous part which Bonaparte had taken in procuring his release from the prison of Olmutz, he indulged his grateful feelings by endeavoring to secure to the fallen Emperor a safe passage to the United States. In the meantime, a capitulation was signed at Paris, and Louis XVIII was soon after placed by the allied powers again upon the throne. La Fayette retired once more to La Grange, and was elected to the Chamber of Deputies. In this body he continued until the year 1824, contending on all occasions for the principles of 1789. At length the loss of his election afforded him an opportunity, without deserting his duty at home, of gratifying an inclination which he had long felt, to visit in his old age the country to which the flower of his youth had been devoted, and which, in its rapid career of prosperity and happiness, had transcended the most enthusiastic anticipations of his early years. You remember, my hearers—and were ages to pass over your heads, they could not efface the remembrance—you remember that joyful day, when it was announced that this patriarch of liberty had landed upon our shores. You remember the pause of incredulity with which the tidings of this expected event were received, as though it were proclaimed that one had risen from the dead. You remember how millions of grateful people, with one heart and one voice, sent forth the shout of "Welcome La Fayette!" until inanimate nature seemed to catch the strain, and every mountain, and rock, and grove, echoed back the sound "Welcome La Fayette!" You remember the magnificent spectacle exhibited in his progress through the Union; the living floods that poured forth to meet him on his way; the military pageantry; the acclamations of the multitude; the thunder of cannon, and the pealing of bells; the crowns and garlands of laurel that were showered upon his head, and the flowers that were every where strewed in his path; the splendid banquets; the blazing illuminations by which the nation manifested its joy at the arrival of its guest, and afforded him a prouder triumph than Rome in her loftiest day awarded to her returning conquerors. You witnessed the emotion with which the aged fathers of our country grasped once more the hand of their early, and long-absent friend; the eagerness with which another generation, in the vigor of life, who had been taught by their sires to venerate his character, gathered around him to express their gratitude, and to bid him welcome to the country for which he had shed his youthful blood; the ardor with which even infants, uniting in the feeling that filled every heart, pressed forward to share his smile or receive his blessing.

The eventful life of this extraordinary man was not yet full. The Bourbons, since their restoration to the throne, had broken down, one after another, the guards which had been established for the preservation of popular rights, and the country was fast sinking back into the despotism, which she had made such fearful sacrifices to overthrow. These oppressions at length became intolerable; the patience of the community was exhausted; and the cry of Revolution again issued from the capital. La Fayette, whose aged frame had now encountered the storms of threescore and twelve years, was reposing at La Grange. The voice of liberty crying out against oppression fell upon his ear, and he started like an old war-horse at the sound of the trumpet. He hastened to Paris, and offered his services to the insurgent patriots. He was received with enthusiasm. The friends of freedom rallied around the veteran chief. His well-known voice was heard in all their councils, and the whole military force was subjected to his command. He thus became the head of another revolution. The last words of Charles X to the officer who conducted him to England, were; "It is that old Republican, La Fayette, who has done all this." A new government was formed under Louis Philippe as the head, and La Fayette now hoped to see the wish of his heart accomplished, in the firm establishment of "a popular throne surrounded by republican institutions." But this hope was not destined to be realized. The gradual departure of Louis Philippe from those principles of constitutional freedom, to the profession of which he owed his elevation, at length induced La Fayette to withdraw his confidence from the new administration, and to resign his office as commander of the National Guards. He continued, however, to represent the district of Meaux in the Chamber of Deputies, and to raise his voice on all occasions in favor of liberty, and the principles of the Revolution of July. On the 27th day of May, 1834, the toils and cares of this friend of mankind were brought to a close. Agreeably to his own request, his remains were deposited in the family vault at the private cemetery of Picpus. Simple and unostentatious in death, as in life, a plain stone points the stranger to the humble spot, where, by the side of his beloved partner, the ashes of this great man repose. There he sleeps—he the champion of liberty, before whose moral power monarchs trembled on their thrones—he the patriot and the statesman, whose honest and manly eloquence so often swayed a tumultuous senate, and calmed the waves of popular fury whose voice animated and cheered the friends of freedom wherever it was heard—he the warrior and the hero, to whose youthful prowess the fields of our own country, and the records of our own history bear witness, and by whose word of command, in later life, a million and a half of men were marshaled and controlled. The storms of party violence may sweep over his lowly dwelling; the cries of the oppressed may pierce the surrounding air; the tread of armies, or the clash of conflicting hosts, may shake the earth in which he rests; they shall be alike unheard and unheeded. But the place in which he lies shall not be neglected nor forgotten. Liberty shall hold there, through every age, her unseen vigils, and the friends of freedom of each successive generation shall resort as pilgrims to his tomb.

Thus lived and died the man, who, if we consider the opportunities of influence which he possessed, the great and varied powers of his mind, the honesty and perseverance with which he devoted them all to the improvement of the civil condition of mankind, may be pronounced the most remarkable of his times. In an age emblazoned as this has been with great events, and thick-studded as it has been with great men, it is venturing little to say, that there is no one whose moral power has been more felt, or has left a deeper impression upon the civilized world, than that of La Fayette. By the impulse which he has given to the spirit of popular freedom, he has founded a monument to his fame, which each emancipated nation in its turn shall contribute to raise, until the top-stone shall be laid by a liberated world.

From the conspicuous part which La Fayette acted on the theatre of human affairs, and the frankness and openness which marked every step of his career, the lines of his character are so distinctly visible upon his history, that it seems almost superfluous to point them out to view. The brief allusion to them which will now be made, is designed chiefly to afford an opportunity of directing your attention to a few prominent incidents of his life by way of illustration.

That feature of his character which was most strongly marked, and to which observers of every description would first point, is undoubtedly, his LOVE OF REGULATED LIBERTY. For such an instance of early, persevering, extended, and self-sacrificing devotion to this noble cause, the records of the world, ancient and modern, will be searched in vain. Thousands have suffered and died rather than be slaves themselves, and other thousands have suffered and died that their country might be free. But the liberty for which La Fayette underwent labor and pain, and for which he staked his fortune, his friends, his health, his life, and even his temporary reputation, was not confined to himself or to his country. It was the liberty of mankind. At one time we find him contending for the independence of America; at another time, seeking means to effect the enfranchisement of Ireland; his exertions in the cause of his own country are known to all; he made repeated efforts to procure the abolition of negro slavery; his sympathies and his counsels were given to the patriots of South America, of Belgium, of Poland, of Italy, of Spain, of Greece; in short, wherever in the wide world a friend of liberty existed, he was sure of a counsellor and a friend in La Fayette.

But this zeal in the cause of freedom, however noble and amiable in itself, would have been of little utility, and might, indeed, have been productive of more injury than benefit, had it not been regulated and controlled by other qualities. Among these was a remarkable DISCRETION. Even during the ardor of youth, and with a most excitable temperament, he had the circumspection and prudence of sober age. It was the testimony of General Washington, communicated to Congress in 1778, that he united to all the military fire of youth an uncommon maturity of judgment; and the truth of this observation was evinced by his whole career in this country, and more especially by the campaign of 1781 in Virginia. He was no fanatic in the cause to which his life was devoted. He was not for giving to every people the utmost degree of liberty of which organized society is susceptible; but so much as was adapted to their particular circumstances, as would conduce to their greatest happiness, and be most enduring. His proposed "Declaration of Rights" contained the broadest principles of freedom and equality, and it was his frequent declaration that he regarded the Constitution of these United States as the best ever invented, and yet upon two occasions, when his opinion would probably have been decisive, he favored the establishment of a different system of government in his own country.

Another striking trait in the charter of La Fayette, is his COURAGE, moral and physical. The same leading principles which he adopted in early youth, in opposition to the seductive allurements of a luxurious and despotic court, he preserved unimpaired to his latest breath, through all the vicissitudes of half a century, and of three revolutions, under circumstances, at one time, of prosperity and temptation that would have turned any but the strongest head, and at another, of danger and adversity which would have subdued any but the stoutest heart. No considerations of personal security, no fear of losing the popularity which he at times possessed, and with which most men would have been intoxicated, ever induced him to abandon, for one moment, or in the slightest degree, a single important principle. When the public good required it he was ready to throw himself into any situation of peril or responsibility; and, when surrounded by danger, he never lost his presence of mind. Over and over again he rushed unprotected into the midst of the infuriated multitudes of Paris, when thousands upon thousands in dense mass extended as far as the eye could see, raging and roaring like an angry ocean, and interposed himself between the excited populace and the objects of their fury. At the risk of his popularity, and of the vengeance of the mob, he commanded the National Guards to fire upon the throngs of people assembled in the Champ de Mars, to plot the dethronement of the King; and when the Jacobins, with their forty thousand affiliated clubs, were obtaining the ascendancy in the Legislative Assembly, and threatening to overturn the government and deluge the nation in blood, he left a powerful army, strongly attached to his person, and presented himself alone at the bar of the Assembly, in the very jaws of these bloodhounds, and fearlessly denounced them to their colleagues and the country, as the instigators of all the calamities that were impending over France.

His courage was not more remarkable than his HUMANITY. While all around him was calculated to harden the heart against human suffering, and to provoke to acts of unjustifiable severity; while scenes of atrocious cruelty were daily presenting themselves to his view, and the very air was scented with human blood; when compassion seemed to have "fled to brutish beasts, and men" to "have lost their reason," he once and again jeopardized his own life to save the lives of others, but never, throughout his whole career, committed, or designedly caused, a single act of wanton or unnecessary bloodshed.

Finally, to give the highest of values to all of his other qualities, he was DISINTERESTED. He never suffered consideration of personal advantage to interfere with his duty to the public. Wealth and distinction, and popularity, were alike disregarded, when they came in competition with the advancement of those great principles which it was the business of his life to promote. Born to fortune and rank, he sacrificed both in the cause of freedom. He steadily refused all compensation for his services both in America and France. The highest honors were repeatedly laid at his feet, but he refused to accept them. During the first Revolution in France, fond as he was of military distinction, he declined a marshal's baton, a constable's sword, and the lieutenant-generalcy of the kingdom. When at the summit of his popularity, he refused the command of a greater military force than was ever subjected to the orders of one individual. The fourteen thousand deputies who represented the National Guards of the kingdom at the Grand Federation in 1790, came prepared to confer upon him the command in chief of the whole body, consisting of between four and five millions of men; but, anticipating their design, he procured the passage of a law by the National Assembly, that no individual should command the guards of more than one Department. He had previously resisted and defeated a proposition for the accomplishment of the same object, introduced at a meeting of the municipality of Paris, and unanimously supported by the members of that body. Although it has often been stated, it is nevertheless untrue that he ever commanded the whole body of National Guards of France during the Revolution of 1789. After the proceedings of the famous 10th of August, the new ministry wrote him the most flattering letters; and the deputies who were commissioned by the National Assembly to proceed to his army, proposed to him the establishment of a republic, and offered him a place at its head; but he had sworn to be faithful to the Constitution of 1791, and he refused to listen to the proposal. In the interval between the dethronement of Charles X and the accession of Louis Philippe, the patriots who had accomplished the Revolution insisted upon the establishment of a republic, with La Fayette as the President; but he resisted all the solicitations that were addressed to him on the subject. There were even those who demanded, that if they must have a monarchy, he should be the king. After the insurrection at Brussels, the Belgians sent deputies to propose to him the acceptance of the presidency or the crown. He declined both, upon the ground that his presence in France would be more useful to the cause of liberty.

Such was La Fayette—the prudent, courageous, humane, disinterested friend of regulated freedom throughout the world: so judicious, so honest, and so consistent, that, in reference to all important subjects of public concern, it may be truly said of him, in the language which he himself used in his letter of June 30, 1792, to the National Assembly, that he never changed his principles, nor his opinions, nor his language. Had all the leaders in the Revolution of 1789 been like him, how different would have been the fate of France! The great Charles James Fox thus spoke of him in the British Parliament:

> *If ever there existed a man, who, in a great and hazardous situation, amidst the conflict of opinions carried on either side to extremes, could claim the merit of having steered a temperate and middle course, uninfluenced by the violence of the moment, and directed by preconceived opinions, that man was La Fayette.*

In private life he was a pattern of moral excellence. He was eminent for that simplicity of character, which is so frequent and so delightful an accompaniment of true greatness. He was a warm friend, a kind father, an affectionate husband. His greatest happiness appeared to consist in the cultivation of the domestic virtues, and in the exercise of an unbounded hospitality, of which his residence was at all times the seat, and of which so many of our own countrymen enjoy the grateful recollection. But the main spring of his prodigious moral power was his rare and incorruptible integrity. To him may be applied, with great truth and justness, the sentiment inscribed upon the monument erected to the memory of the famous Duke of Marlborough: "He acquired an influence which no rank, no authority can give, nor any force but that of superior virtue." It might be exaggeration to say that his mind was of the very highest order, but he possessed a singular assemblage of great and good qualities, admirably balanced, and exercised on all occasions with a peculiar nicety of perception. The Revolution of 1789, in France, brought out a host of men, eminent alike for the brilliancy of their talents and for their zeal in the cause of liberty. These have nearly all passed off the stage; but which of them has left a reputation like that of La Fayette?

> He was the noblest Roman of them all:
> . . .
> He–in a general honest thought,
> And common good to all, made one of
> them,–
> His life was gentle; and the elements
> So mix'd in him, that Nature might stand up,
> And say to all the world–"This was a man."[4]

[4] *These lines are adapted from the speech by Marcus Antonius (reporting to Julius Caesar) at the end of Act* IV*, Scene* V*, of* Julius Caesar *by William Shakespeare.*

EIGHT

AN ORATION

Joseph Warren Scott, 1846

Joseph Warren Scott, 1778–1871 (admitted 1825), was graduated from Princeton College in 1795 and received his Master of Arts from Princeton College in 1798 and his Doctor of Laws in 1869. He served as a Lieutenant in the Third Regiment, Middlesex County, New Jersey Militia, May 24, 1808; Captain, June 24, 1811; Lt. Colonel and Deputy Adjutant-General of the Third Division, May 21, 1818; and Colonel, Independent Battalion, Middlesex Brigade, February 20, 1829. He was Vice President of the New Jersey Society from 1840 to 1842; President, from 1844 to 1871; Assistant Treasurer-General from 1832 to 1838; and Treasurer-General from 1838 to 1871 (see illustration 11).

Oration delivered at Newark before the Cincinnati of New Jersey, Fourth of July, 1846

On a day auspicious as the birth of our country our hearts dilate with joyful enthusiasm and with mingled emotions of honest pride and grateful sensibility do we hail this interesting anniversary.

This was our nation's birthday. This day was empire born into existence. This day our fathers having drained up the cup of reconciliation to the very dregs, having appealed in vain to the Justice, the magnanimity and even the interest of the proud government, Great Britain, and her vicious and infatuated counselors and firmly relying on the protection and justice of Him who "ridith on the whirlwind and directeth the storm" recorded that Declaration of Independence which you have just now heard.

From this dread stand there was now no retreat. Liberty or death was the alternative. The spirit of liberty animated the fathers and it glowed in their sons. The electric fire spread from heart to heart. Every boson beat with ardour. The mountains, the plains, and the vales reechoed with the shout "Let us march against our oppressors, let us fight for our liberties, let us conquer or die" and the college, the counting house, and the plow teemed with thunderbolts of war. The hardy veteran whose nervous arm had dealt death and destruction in the well-fought field and the generous gallant youth of life's earliest summer marched together in the same battle ranks well lead on by that noble impulse.

Oh day of vast anticipation. Oh time pregnant with an empire's fate.

The mighty event of which this day is the anniversary forms one of those decisive and brilliant eras in the history of man followed by consequences and blessings not dreamed of in the imagination of conscience and which mock all the calculations of Political Science.

The American citizen delights in the certain creation of it. He sees the source of his enjoyment and the pledge of his security.

It is interesting to the moralist because he sees religion and virtue and truth flourish under the benign influences of our republican institutions.

To the statesmen I present the development of new salutory and conservative principles which already have baffled the calculations of the wise men of the Old World. They could see nothing but anarchy and confusion in our councils when we should be freed from the authorities and separated from the fortunes of the mother country.

But to the Patriot it is a theme of peculiar interest. What thrilling emotions agitate his name. How does his bosom swell when he looks around and beholds the rising glory of his country.

Twenty millions of his fellow citizens, industrious, frugal, prosperous and happy. Agriculture, commerce, and the arts flourishing stretching far and wide over the vast continent and his country advancing in wealth and power with more gigantic strides.

The colonies out of which these United States were formed were planted after the midnight of despotism had passed away and the light of civil and religious freedom had dawned upon the world. The nation of England was early distinguished for [its] enlarged view of policy and for no inconsiderable measure of liberal principle. In these respects they have gone in the way of the other nations of Europe. She has been marked, as has been observed by an eloquent orator, "by a natural avarice for freedom which she is studious to engross but most unwilling to impart."

While the inhabitants of the European continent were wrapt in the slumbers of feudal despotism the people of England were shaking off their lethargy and opening their eyes to the morning star of light. So early as the commencement of the 13th century, recalling some of the vestiges of Saxon liberty, they asserted their inalienable rights with arms and with blood and in the plains of Runnymede extorted from the dastard tyrant John the Magna Carta of British liberty. That sacred charter to which they still look as the great palladium of their security while battling with the agitated waves of arbitrary encroachment has served as the beacon to guide them to safety.

There also religious freedom was first promulgated. So far back as the 14th century their Wickliffe proclaimed the true spirit of the gospel and warned his countrymen against the alarming encroachment and gross superstition of the papal hierarchy.

These however were but occasional flashes. They appeared like meteoric lights in the heavens and were soon obscured by the lowering tempest and the darkened sky. It was not until the reign of Elizabeth, haughty and tyrannical as she was, that the grand discussion was opened which ages shall not close. The great truth was unfolded and the lesson was taught that never shall be unlearned.

Freedom is that hardy plant which strikes deep roots and becomes indigenous to any soil.

In this reign it was that the first colony was founded on these Western shores, deriving its name from the Virgin Queen.

James her successor was the first of the infatuated and doomed House of Stuart. He greatly excelled at literature but was as deficient in rectitude of understanding as he was infirm in integrity of purpose. He was noted for the boldness and audacity of his pretensions and the contemptible feebleness and debility of his exertions. His mind was active but not vigorous; contemplative but neither enlarged nor practical. His intellect was not of that plastick character which moulds its plans according to the exigency of circumstances. Instead of making himself acquainted with political knowledge and studying the interests, the habits and the wants of his people, he was pursuing the ugly values of a wild absurd theological philosophy.

While the spirit of civil and religious liberty, like the electric fluid, was spreading through the land and thrilling and agitating every bosom, he was brooding in his closet over the divine right of kings. He was, says a shrewd and sagacious contemporary, "the wisest and the most learned fool in Christendom."

His successors of the Stuart name followed in his path with equal pace and folly and perverseness but without half his learning.

The genius of inquiry found no obstacle. Its pulse became morbid, almost rabid.

The people of that country looked back with fond regret to their ancient charters. These had been trampled underfoot by Henry the seventh and his tyrannical son.

But again they were to be reclaimed with eager avidity. Every branch of the Royal prerogative was scrutinized with a keen and jealous eye. The Stuarts on the other hand were madly endeavoring to stretch that prerogative beyond even the exactions of their most arbitrary predecessors.

Such a contest between such parties could have but one termination. England was deluged with the blood of her sons—but I forbear.

During these throes and convulsions the American Colonies were successfully planted.

The Stuarts were as remarkable for their selfishness and love of ease as for their spirit of domination. Their hearts' desire was to reign with a rod of iron, but they were willing to get rid of their discontented subjects without the trouble of subduing them. While these misguided and obstinate sovereigns were endeavoring to quash all power and to reign independently of their Parliament and the opinions of their subjects, they permitted these colonies to be peopled by a brave hardy independent race of men who differed from them radically in their principles of civil and religious government. They were the brave descendants of those hardy Barons, the heroes of Runnymede. They could not brook a state of servitude.

They embarked on the "roaring ocean rolling wide" to seek in a foreign land that virtue, liberty, and independence which then were well nigh smothered in their native home.

Mark the indomitable and the unyielding spirit of freedom which animated our forefathers at that early period. They were not insensible to the ties which bound them to the land of their birth—the land associated with their earliest fondest recollections. Like the children of Israel they could weep when they thought of their beloved Zion.

There were the fields in which they had often gamboled in all the sportiveness of youth. There were the vales which had oft times been made vocal with their song. There were the tombs of their ancestors. Powerful appeals to the love and sympathy of man. But there were high and important and paramount rights to which they were entitled as moral, rational and intelligent beings which *there* they could not enjoy. Home was dear; but conscience and liberty were of higher estimate.

They resolved to leave all that soil, which seemed to them destined for servitude. Their search, the privileges of free men in an unknown land. They left the shores of Britain and threw themselves upon the mercy of the waves. Liberty was their polar star pointing their course over the trackless ocean. A wilderness their place of destination.

Our ancestors were jealous of their liberty. When they left the British Isle they did not abandon their freedom. They came here to enjoy it. They brought charters securing their franchises and guaranteeing in all respects their great and substantial rights as Englishmen. The great charter was their birthright and fast inheritance.

They made assurance doubly sure. They adopted in their local governments fundamental constitutions containing all the essential principles of Magna Carta's Petition and bill of rights, Habeas Corpus, and other charters of English liberty.

They were colonists it is true; but they were not in a state of colonial servitude. They brought with them all the rights and privileges of Englishmen and among the rest that vital and cardinal principle of freedom that no tax shall be imposed upon them but by their consent.

Read these charters. Examine attentively these fundamental constitutions. Freedom is in every line. Liberty and non-vassalage was their determined choice.

Can we then be in any doubt as to the source of those genuine Whig principles held forth in high belief in that Declaration of Independence which has just been read in our hearing?

When our ancestors settled upon the shores they were left in a great measure undefended and unprotected by the mother country. Unaided they cleared the forest. Undefended from without, they defended themselves. The savage and the barbarian felt their prowess and acknowledged their fidelity.

In their respective colonial legislatures they enacted wise, just and wholesome laws for the protection of life, liberty and property.

Heaven smiled its rich approbation on their enterprise and their industry.

I said that from the mother country they received but little aid or benefit. They did not require, they did not desire it. But the converse of the proposition is far from being true.

Before their establishment the manufacturers and the commerce of England were at a low ebb. The woollen alone flourished. She derived the greater part of her utensils in iron and other metals from Germany. Her silks, linen and wines were received from France. Portugal supplied her with sugar. All the products of America were poured into her by Spain. Venice and Genoa retailed the commodities of the East at their own enhanced prices and other articles were brought from other parts of Europe.

But when the colonial system was adopted, how fast the change. England then could and did turn her attention to manufactures; and the heretofore neglected colonies became her great vending marts.

Hence she was jealous of all competition. The colonies without a murmur yielded that their trade should be chiefly confined to her; so long as this demand was asserted with any show of justice or restrained within any reasonable bounds of moderation or propriety. The regulations of the colonial trade became the fruitful source of profit advantage and wealth to the mother country and England soon became a great maritime and commercial power. The trident of the ocean for a long time wielded by Holland passed over to Albion's isle.

In 1651 the first great navigation act was passed. This was during the protectorate of Cromwell. I mention this name without intending either censure or applause. This is not the time nor the place for either. But I cannot help adding that he was a man as great and enlightened in his public conduct as he was strange and mysterious in his private character.

The grand object of this regulation was to secure the carrying trade between the colonies and the mother country to the exclusion of the Dutch by whom it had been principally conducted.

This system was wise and it was equitable too in regard to the colonies; and it was vastly more liberal than that which succeeded it. On the restoration of the monarchy in the person and reign of the profligate, selfish, and sensual Charles II, a new plan was adopted—fetters were invented—the colonies were prohibited from trading with any other nation—their exports and their imports had to pass through England; and before they could enjoy the production of foreign climes heavy duties were required to be paid to the British exchequer.

And why should we be surprised that oppressions began in those days? They were days, says McAuley, never to be remembered without a blush; days of servitude without loyalty and sensuality without love, of dwarfish talents and gigantic vices. The paradise of cold hearts and narrow minds, the golden age of the coward, the bigot and the slave. Charles cringed to his rival that he might trample on his people—sunk into a viceroy of France he pocketed with complacent infamy her degrading insults and her more degrading gold.

The caresses of harlots and the jests of buffoons regulated the measures of a government which had just ability enough to deceive and just religion enough to persecute. The principles of liberty were the scoff of every grinning courtier and the anathema [?] of every fawning dean. In every high place worship was paid to Charles and James: Belial and Moloch. And England propitiated those obscene and cruel idols with the blood of her best and bravest children. Crime succeeded to crime and disgrace to disgrace till the race accursed of God and man was a second time driven forth to wander on the face of the earth and to be a by-word and a shaking of the head to the nations.

Notwithstanding all the impediments which have been mentioned and many more, the American colonies grew and flourished. Their increase in wealth and population and internal resource amazed and confounded the calculations of British statesmen and awakened a cupidity and lust of power, and produced a series of oppressions and injustices, that terminated in the disruption of every tie that bound the infant settlements to their mother country.

Nations become objects of interest and attention to each other only as they become considerable and important. It is no less true in political than in moral life that inordinate cupidity is the prolifick source of a thousand ills.

Virtue is the principal and life of a republick. Indignant and chivalrous honour impels to action in a monarchy of law—while servile fear and pale-faced apprehension minister to the caprice, the wantonness and the cruelty of the despot.

Transported to the times when America rose to repel her wrongs and to claim her destinies, a scene of boundless grandeur bursts upon our view. Long had her filial duty remonstrated with parental injustice. Long did she deprecate the rupture of those ties which she had been proud to cherish, preserve and display.

But her humble entreaty spurned—aggression followed by the rod and the rod by scorpions—having changed remonstrance into murmur, and murmur into resistance, she transfers her grievances from a throne of earth to the throne of heaven and proceeds by an appeal to the God of battles, her appeal to the sword of war.

Let us contemplate for a moment that august Congress to whom under him whose kingdom ruleth over all seemed to be committed the destinies of America.

The Declaration of Independence was not the work of a day.—It was no violent effusion of passion and fury. It was tempered and calm.—It was conned with anxious care.—It was made subject to the most rigid criticism.—It was that dignified and firm, that deliberate and awful ordinance which severed the bonds of an empire and gave the nation birth. No vulgar penalty cemented it. The pledge was, and it is and shall be, our lives, our fortunes and our sacred honour.

Nor were there wanting those in that illustrious assembly who thought the deed too daring and that it was premature. It was censured as precipitate and rash, and the eloquent voice of warning and of threat was heard with attention, but not with heed.

I will not be so unjust as to withhold from you an anecdote of that day which in early life I received from one of the actors in that drama of astonishment and wonder.

The celebrated John Dickinson was a member of that Congress. Tradition and many evidences confirm that he was eloquent, impassioned, faithful and true.

He opposed of the Declaration of Independence. In a powerful speech near the close of the debates, he argued vehemently against the decisive step. He augured the capture of our towns, the desolation of our villages, the waste of our fields, our cities wrapt in flames and the imprisonment, chains, torture, carnage, and death of our brothers and friends.—He expiated at length on our want of means.—That they were totally incommensurate with the mighty end. He prophesied of the raw recruits and irregular supply lines across distant colonies.

He invoked the aid of the God of Eloquence to assist him in impressing these alarming views upon his infatuated auditors. And when in our fancy's eye he portrayed the prospective distresses and sufferings of his country, unbidden tears came to his eyes. He wept from the fullness of his feelings and overpowered by his emotions he ceased to address the assembly.

None were inattentive to this impressive address. After the unbroken and solemn silence of some minutes, old John Adams rose. A bolder or more heroic spirit than his never animated the heart of man.

He seemed deeply oppressed and scarce could he give utterance to the mighty thoughts that engrossed and overwhelmed his soul. Slowly recovering he said,

> *Mr. President, the orator from the counties has warned, entreated and threatened. His pencil did not languish when he painted the horror and the carnage and desolation and death which must ravage our beloved country. 'Tis true the work of murder and butchery is begun. Lexington and Concord and Bunker Hill and Charlestown have marked the tender mercies of our oppressors. Already have corruption and venality proclaimed their infernal offices. Already has the royal herald commissioned the incendiary and the robber and promised to traitors the degrading emolument of statutable plunder. The blood of Massachusetts has been shed. The martyr's blood has sealed the patriot's truth. Its cry from the ground is vengeance and freedom. It is a voice which ages cannot stifle. The soil that drank that stream of life shall grow more holy with every passing age. It was precious blood that shall give life to the tree of liberty. The orator who addressed us appealed to the God of Eloquence and invoked his aid. He appealed to a heathen god, a god who not I nor my fathers ever knew. But I appeal to the God of Battles and the Lord of Hosts and invoke His aid. I implore His keeping and protection, and in His awful and tremendous Name swear that our nation shall be free.*

The silence as of death followed this reply. At length it was broken by the venerable Witherspoon, our own Witherspoon.

"The duty before us," he said, "is grave, dignified and portentous. We are called upon to subscribe our names to that sublime charter of American independence. Let it not be in the burst of feeling. Let it not be in the pulse of passion. Let us adjourn to the morrow: And then assembling in this Hall under the protection and blessing of Him whose blessing maketh rich let us affix our signatures in the fear of God and as we love our country and her rights."

Twas done. The resolve was firm. The probation was terrible. The theater of action was to be a world. The charge of interest, a family of nations, and the internal stake, the prosperity of millions unborn in ages to come. A tremendous issue now with the mistress of the seas—unfurnished with equal means of defense—the convulsive shock approaching in every evil omen passing before her, one step of rashness or of folly might seal the doom of our country.

In this accumulation of trouble who shall command her confidence and face her dangers and conduct her cause?

God rules from afar and prepares the instruments best adapted to His purpose. By an influence which it would be as irrational to dispute as it is vain to scrutinize, he stirs up the spirit of the statesman and the soldier. Minds on which he has bestowed an element of greatness are brought by His providence into contact with exigencies which rouse them into action.

It is in the season of effort and peril that impotence disappears and energy arises. The whirlwind which sweeps away the glowworm uncovers the fire of genius and kindles it into a blaze that radiates at once both the zenith and the poles. America required in her leader a man reared under her own eye—who combined with distinguished talent a character above suspicion—who had added to his physical and moral qualities the experience of difficult service. A man who should concentrate in himself the publick affections and the publick confidences. Who should know how to multiply the energies of every other man under his direction and to make disaster itself the means of success. His name a fortress and his arm a host.

Such a man it were almost presumption to expect, but such a man all ruling heaven had provided, and that man was Washington.

My brothers and friends I anticipate the response of your heart. Yes, the name of Washington is associated with all that is most brilliant in the history of our country and in human character. That it awakens sensations which agitate the fevers of youth and warm the chill bosom of age. How he redeemed the holy pledge—how he inspired confidence—how he dissipated irresolution and despondence—how he gave temperance to victory and cheerfulness to disaster—all this and more is familiar to your memories—your fathers have taught it to you and faithful history has recorded it in undying remembrance.

It was the purpose of high heaven to conduct us through toils, and through dangers to give victory to our arms—to deliver this people from the yoke of oppression, and to bring them finally to the full enjoyment of the greatest of all earthly blessings.

America shall be free was the decree of the infinite benevolence; but she must know to value the blessing by the enormous price of the acquisition. Many a generous youth must bleed and many a gallant youth must sink into the surprised grave. The field must be heaped with the slain. The humble torrent must roll and vengeance must be bloodied with her unnumbered victims ere the angel of peace shall descend with her olive. It is here amid carnage and horror and desolation and death that the much loved leader of the army of freedom and his sublime compatriots must reap their laurels and engrave their trophies on the shields of immortality.

A celebrated general of olden time marching to battle in defense of his beloved country addressed his troops:

> *Fellow soldiers, behold the roof under which you drew your first breath. Lo, the fields that give you nurture, the cradle in which is hushed to sleep your infant offspring, the bed of your wives, the tombs of your ancestors and the alters of the gods.*

It was with emotions and reflections akin to these that our fathers met and repulsed the rude invader. Yes, the best troops of Britain led on by her most consummate generals fled and were conquered.—They were conquered by men who had consecrated their lives to the publick defense, by men who well remembered the roof under which they drew their first breath, the fields that gave them nurture, the cradle of their infants, the bed of their wives, the tombs of their ancestors, and the alters of the living God.

The war of the revolution was not, nor could it be, one continued scene of triumph and success. In the dark and lowering period of the first march through this state, gloomy was indeed the prospect. With raw recruits and undisciplined levies, almost naked and worn out with fatigue and cold and hunger, it was necessary to avoid a pitched battle with a foe at once haughty and excelling, disciplined and well provided.

The autumn of 1776 and the winter following were a trying period. How many hearts were then chilled with despair? Where then was the summer soldier and the sunshine patriot?

The undaunted mind of the commander in chief remained erect, unmoved, invincible. He looked forward to deeds of high daring, and to results the most glorious.

He leads his little, half famished army beyond the Delaware; but his eagle eye did not forget its steady gaze. Failing in their plan of overtaking and forcing him to a battle which then in all human probability would have been as fatal as decisive, the enemy were scattered in different directions and resting in fancied security.

O! Fatal false lethargic security.

The little remnant of our patriotic troops who had endured hunger and cold and nakedness and privations almost intolerable, had once again been saved by more than Fabian caution; but the period was now arrived when they were to be avenged deeply by Carthaginian boldness and rapacity.

The swelling and tempestuous Delaware offered such impediment only as become the incentive to more vigorous exertions and the prelude to more signal success: and the plains of Trenton and Princeton reeking with the blood of the foe—his captured legions and his broken plans bear testimony to the wisdom and fidelity of our unmatched General and his bold and masterful execution.

There is anecdote in relation to the capture of the Hessians at Trenton and the measures immediately subsequent to it which ought to be rescued from oblivion.

Instantly after the Hessians had surrendered, measures were taken to assemble a large force of the British army quartered in that vicinity. They arrived in the evening and a Council of War was immediately summoned. Sir William Erskine, who was confessedly second in point of talents and military skill to no officers in that army, proposed an immediate and night attack on the American lines. He was overruled by a large majority who decided for battle on the morning following. It was in vain that Sir William Erskine remonstrated with them. "If I judge him right," said he, "in the morning you will have no Washington to contend with. I strongly suspect that he is a general, and if so, he will not be here. Princeton will be the place of his attack and he will have eluded our vigilance." The Council of War thought otherwise and postponed the battle.

It is well known the American fires were kept up during the night and that the appearance of a camp remained. But it was appearance only. Early in the morning some of the officers of the Council of War called to Sir William Erskine to rise for the conflict. "Here," they said, and they thought it to be true, "here is Washington completely in our power. He cannot escape us now. His destruction is inevitable. What think you now?" Sir William instantly arose and prepared to obey the orders. "I may," said he, "have been greatly deceived. I did not believe that he would have remained." While they were yet speaking the sound of distant cannon was heard. "O!" said he, "did you hear that? Last night I thought that Washington was a general and a soldier. Now I know he is." Frequent reports of distant cannons were heard in rapid succession. "That attack is at Princeton," said Sir William, "and it is and must be successful too. In less than a week he will be in the hills of Morris and bid you defiance. We have lost the fruit of the whole campaign."

The prediction was verified. In a week he was with a victorious army in the hills of Morris proudly bidding defiance to the enemy and menacing his security in the stronghold of his power.

I may not particularize the brilliant events in this war of virtue, liberty and independence. It is a theme which babes recite, and poets sing and fame has published to a listening world.

These were the times, I quote a distinguished speaker of our own country, these were the times that tried the souls of men; but never did any country or any age produce a race of men whose souls were better fitted to endure that trial.

Patient in suffering, firm in adversity, calm and collected amid surrounding dangers, cool in council and brave in battle, they were worthy of the cause and the cause was worthy of such noble defenders.

The peace of 1783 acknowledged the independence of the United States of America: and the adoption of the Constitution of 1787 ratified, established and confirmed our liberties and our interests on a basis broad as virtue; and erected a column high as glory's head.

In the full enjoyment of every civil and religious privilege—with laws mild, temperate and wholesome—with a soil and climate fitted to all the desires of man: the march to prosperity and greatness is no longer the problem for solution.

In the infancy of society men were usually occupied with the business of the present hour, forgetful of the past, and careless of the future, or at most, careful for that which is near at hand and close before them. Ages carry them through youth into maturity and strength. But these states like the infant Hercules seem to spring from the cradle in all of the maturity of vigour and of power.

Commerce now ploughs the wave—our canvas whitens every sea—agriculture smiles upon the land and the labor of the husbandman is rewarded with a rich and plentiful return.

The dark forests recede—scarcely do they have a trace of their antecedent existence. Cities, towns, and villages spring up as if by magick—science and the arts are cherished and prevail—railroads and canals annihilate distances. The immense inland seas of the West have kissed the Atlantick; and the majestic Hudson, the Delaware, and the Susquehanna bear on their broad bosoms the wealth and the produce of a world. In the far West the wondrous Mississippi, the parent of rivers, receives the tribute of her hundred children, at once imparting and receiving the product of far and distant climes.

Here upon this vast and wide expanse appears the truth impressed in characters indelible and broad, that the rights of man are not the gift of princes—they are his birthright and inheritance—and richer and more auspicious than any other inheritance, the son and heir is joint tenant with his sire—no invidious primogeniture excludes. All receive and all enjoy the whole. So rich and ample is the source, and so bountiful is the supply that division cannot diminish.

Here is an axiom admitting neither contradiction nor controversy: that government is formed for man's protection and security; and not for its indolence, luxury, or injustice.—The slanders and apologies of tyranny and vice are confounded by the practical demonstration that man is equal to his own government.

May we not then exult that we are Americans? May we not augur to our country all that is great and good and happy? And is it not just and reasonable to ascribe these wonderful changes under the good providence of High Heaven to the great event we this day commemorate?

To the Society of the Cincinnati in a peculiar manner does this day recall recollections the most tender and heroic remembrances, the most affecting and elevated. Emotions and feelings overwhelming and unutterable rush tumultuously upon the mind.

My brothers and friends I well remember the first time it became my duty to address you. It was a day of heart-felt recollections and commingled feelings.

On that day we counted six survivors of the original members of this society.

It was a melancholy reflection that there were no more. It was consoling that these still remained; and that they were all present at our meeting.

This was shortly after the magnificent reception of La Fayette throughout our land.

O! that was a nation's pulse. That was an empire's grateful remembrance.

Kings, princes, mighty men of the East, stand forth and behold the august, the astounding triumph. 'Twas such as Roman emperor never knew.

Alas at this day we have not even one surviving of that noble band. Of two hundred and forty-seven officers commissioned by New Jersey during that sanguinary conflict, not one remains.

In the states south of the Hudson, all are gone.

In the state of New York the venerable Popham [seventh President General; lived to 1848—Ed.] remains solitary and alone. He still survives and still we record his honourable name as the President General of the Cincinnati of the United States.

My brothers and friends I had reason to believe until very recently that he would have been here this day. Closely connected as he was with the gallant army of New Jersey, he desired to come, and mingle his sympathies with ours. Loving and honouring our fathers in those days of convulsion when our fields were the battleground of freedom, he desired once more to see their sons. I did expect to introduce you this day to the last surviving officer from many, perhaps from all the states. A noble specimen of ancient days, a venerable and stately relic of that courtesy, urbanity and chivalrous feeling which particularly marked and distinguished the officers of the American Revolution. Had he come, were he now here, with what melting sympathy, with what tender yet contending [feelings] should we look upon him, the last survivor standing as it were alone, and leaning on the top of his staff asking for the friends of his youth, those who with him had fired the soul and nerved the arm of our injured and oppressed country.

The heart has memories which cannot die. The rude and rough occurrences of a jarring and conflicting world cannot obliterate these.

> Where is Dayton, that thunderbolt of war?
> Where the youthful and gallant Ogden!
> In war no lion ever rag'd more fierce.
> In peace was never gentle lamb more mild.
> Where Voorhees, that young Mars of men
> Mature in glory, ere the Spring of life was o'er.
> Where McMyer, covered o'er with wounds
> Borne on the shields of his surviving warriors
>   from the fields of his fame fresh and gory.
> Where the thrice lamented and beloved
>   Barber?
> The mark and glass, copy and book that
>   fashioned heroes.

Where is Cumming, Spencer, Howell, Bloomfield, Beatty, Ross, Dehart, Conway, Pratt, Maxwell?

Where is Shreve, Rhea, Hugg, Tuttle, Kinney, Neil and Clark?

Where is Shute and Bennington and Halsey?

Where is Bowen and where is Buck and Cox and Gifford and Lane?

But why do I mention some. It is injustice to the residue. Where are our fathers? Alas, all are gone, not one is left.

Shall I for a moment imagine this venerable and war-worn veteran here in the midst of us giving his last council, and pronouncing his parting benediction. What think you would be his language and with what devoted and deep attention should we hang on every accent, and listen to his injunctions?

That he would deplore the injustice to his companions in war is most obvious. Deeply indeed would he lament and mourn that they had gone to their silent and narrow house, the recompense of their reward unjustly withheld, or at best doled out in scanty allowance.

True, he would say, all of this and more. But he would speak to us of other things. He would call our attention to the original formation of this society. He would dwell with force and energy upon the time, the object and the principles; and he would command that these shall never be forgotten.

He would point to an army suffering under multiplied privations. He would show that army flushed with conquest and victorious for the publick weal. Such an army indignant against injustice is rarely a humble supplicant for its rights.

He would tell us of the eloquent but insidious appeal and counsel to redress their own wrongs. He would remind us that they were advised to retain their arms, and compel that compliance which justice demanded and the opportunity made easy.

He would exhibit the officers of that army: its bond of union, its very life blood, soul and spring. He would talk to us of our fathers, those who had labored, toiled, and bled for their country, who had sacrificed for it everything but their honour.

Now they were to return to their houses and families victorious for America, victorious for freedom, triumphant in the great cause of justice and truth and honour and liberty and independence but with health impaired and constitutions broken.

The states were unable to comply with their engagements, and the defenders of their country were compelled for present necessities and immediate life to sell for a price almost nominal the unavailing paper promises of the government. He would show forth in broad relief the noble example set by them. He would tell you of their efforts, almost incredible and nearly beyond the power of man, to counteract the influence of that insidious address. And he would exult in the final and glorious triumph of virtue, patriotism and truth.

The army obeyed their officers and yielded to the command of law.

The solemn and affecting moment was near at hand. A grand moral spectacle was to be exhibited to an amazed world. They were to lay down those arms which had been assumed for the publick protection and the publick defense.

They were to separate from the companions of their youth, their toils, their sufferings and their dangers.

This was a difficult and a painful task. He who has no tenderness, has no magnanimity.

Go search the foremost ranks of dangers high career, be sure the hand, most daring there has wiped away the tear.

To separate at once, under the strong sense of injustice to all. Never again to meet, until assembled with an assembled universe. I dare not attempt the description.

The clasped hand, the strained embrace, the silent wishful look, the tear trickling down the scarred sunburned cheek, the expression of that scar, the overwhelming remembrance of mutual defenses, the throbbing bosom and the bursting heart as brother parted from his brother and friend from friend. O! This is a scene for nature's painter and for nature's bard.

They retired like Cincinnatus of old to cultivate the earth. They relied upon the slumbering justice of their country: but the sleep seems like the sleep of death. O! When shall it awake?

It was on the very eve of this heart-rendering disruption, when the last link was on the point of severance, that the officers of the American army formed and established the society of the Cincinnati. Their principles and objects are set forth in terms so decisive and so plain, that he who runs may read. Let them not be mistaken, let them not be forgotten.

I turn to the record of their proceeding, and I behold their first act. It is an act of adoration, thanksgiving and praise to Him that sitteth upon the throne and reigneth forever and ever.

To commemorate the great event, to inculcate the duty of laying down in peace arms assumed for the publick defense, to unite in acts of brotherly affection and bonds of perpetual friendship, are a few of the immutable principles of the Cincinnati. And who can doubt their purity or their propriety? In the exercise of a rational understanding, none. Who shall deny their benevolence, their honour, or their truth? None but an idiot will now question the right, the tenderness or the benevolence of such objects and principles.

Who was there to deny to our fathers the luxury, the honourable privilege of providing out of their own scanty pittance, poor as it was, a fund for the relief of the widows and orphans of their brethren in arms? And what madman or tyrant is it that shall dare to say that our honourable and patriotic fathers shall not leave it an injunction on us their sons to cherish, defend and protect these interesting objects of their tenderness and care.

The statement of the question brings forth its own unanswerable reply.

And yet we know, for our fathers have told us, that ignorance and vanity and the love of mischief and the love of paradox did sound a false and hypocritical alarm. That the same envenomed pen which ever on evil purposes intent had traitorously addressed the American army and has dissuaded them from obeying the mandate of their country and the orders of her beloved Commander in chief; foiled in the work of ruin which it had designed, by the vigorous and virtuous exertions of the officers of that army, now perfidiously attacked these officers and the society which they had formed.

The envenomed author could not forgive his signal defeat. He could not forgive nor forget that it was the Cincinnati who had repulsed and crushed his daring treason. There could be no oblivion for such offense. They were marked for ruin.

To that end publick jealousy must be excited.

The most fiendish arts of sophistry and malevolence were called into requisition. Hatred, malice and revenge did perform their demoniack offices, and to the utmost of their fervor.

The simple tale of truth told with the energy of manly sincerity once more repelled calumny and dissipated the unfounded alarm.

We claim a right, they responded, to love our brothers in arms. We claim a right to hold in affectionate remembrance friends of approved virtue. That friendship commenced with the contest; it increased through every danger; it was tried through calamities. It was cemented with blood. We claim a right to relieve the widows and the orphans of our martyred brothers and friends. We claim a right to command our sons as they value our benediction, as they value their own honour, to hold in fast remembrance and forever to obey that sublime and elevated injunction.

Remember thou thy friend, and the friend of thy father forget thou not.

To such a Bill of Rights no negative voice was heard.

Maddening into desperation by this second abortive effort of malevolence and fraud, the snakes of envy recoiled upon the head of their mistress, and burrowed into the brain that supplied their venom.

And now does any one ask how the funds thus provided by sympathy, by affection, and by the most honourable remembrances had been distributed?

Ancient widows of the brave who periled the storm when the tempest raged, come forth and answer ye, and put to shame the despicable suspicion.

Daughters of the brothers of our fathers in arms, answer ye and silence the dastardly insinuation.

The relief is of that peculiarly delicate character, which does not depress the recipient. In it is no painful humiliation. It is claimed as a right. It is as proudly received, as it is liberally given.

Oft times has it soothed the widow's sigh, oft times has it wiped away the orphan's tear.

ILLUSTRATIONS

1. New Jersey Society Stationery Die

Reproduced from book printed in 1908 by W.T.B.S. Imlay for this Society.

2. New Jersey Society 1838 Flag

It dates from about 1838, is made of silk, and is painted on both sides by John Archibald Woodside (1781–1852).

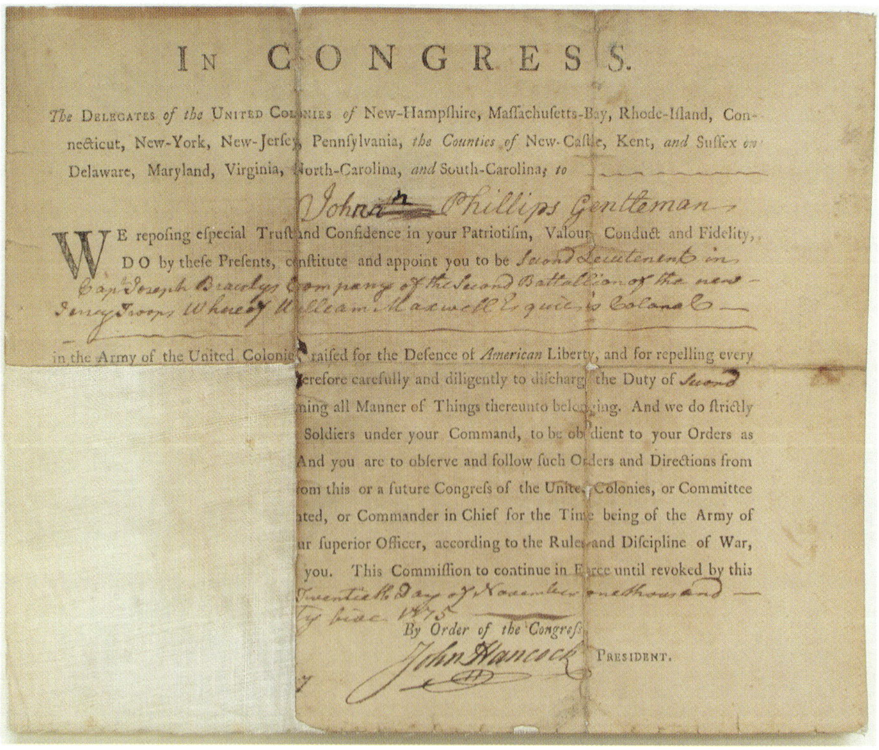

IN CONGRESS.

The DELEGATES of the UNITED COLONIES of New-Hampſhire, Maſſachuſetts-Bay, Rhode-Iſland, Connecticut, New-York, New-Jerſey, Pennſylvania, the Counties of New-Caſtle, Kent, and Suſſex on Delaware, Maryland, Virginia, North-Carolina, and South-Carolina, to

John Phillips Gentleman

WE repoſing eſpecial Truſt and Confidence in your Patriotiſm, Valour, Conduct and Fidelity, DO by theſe Preſents, conſtitute and appoint you to be Second Lieutenant in Capt Joseph Bracly's Company of the Second Battalion of the new-Jersey Troops whereof William Maxwell Esquire is Colonel

in the Army of the United Colonies, raiſed for the Defence of American Liberty, and for repelling every … erefore carefully and diligently to diſcharge the Duty of Second … ming all Manner of Things thereunto belonging. And we do ſtrictly … Soldiers under your Command, to be obedient to your Orders as … And you are to obſerve and follow ſuch Orders and Directions from … om this or a future Congreſs of the United Colonies, or Committee … ated, or Commander in Chief for the Time being of the Army of … ur ſuperior Officer, according to the Rules and Diſcipline of War, … you. This Commiſſion to continue in Force until revoked by this … Twentieth Day of November one thousand … ty five 1775

By Order of the Congreſs,

John Hancock PRESIDENT.

3. Phillips original commission

4. Phillips membership certificate

Original certificate of membership in the New Jersey Society of the Cincinnati of Horatio Gates Phillips dated January 7th, 1809 and signed by Joseph Bloomfield, President.

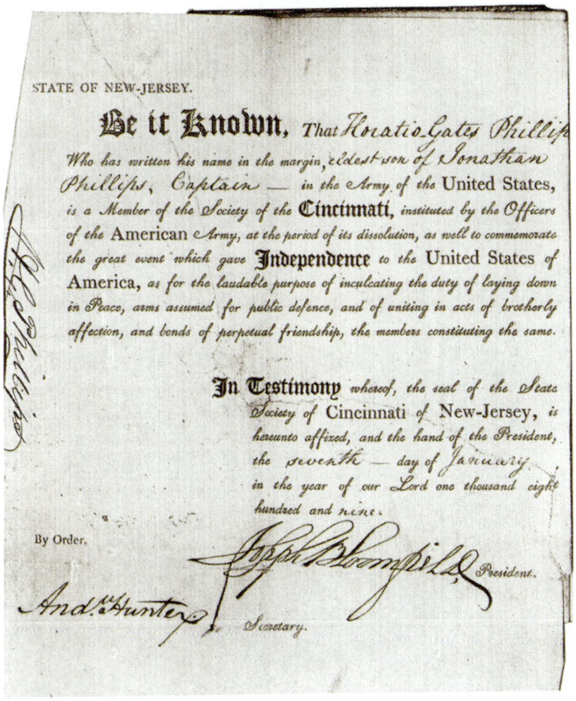

STATE OF NEW-JERSEY.

Be it Known, That Horatio Gates Phillips Who has written his name in the margin, eldest son of Jonathan Phillips, Captain — in the Army of the United States, is a Member of the Society of the **Cincinnati**, instituted by the Officers of the American Army, at the period of its dissolution, as well to commemorate the great event which gave **Independence** to the United States of America, as for the laudable purpose of inculcating the duty of laying down in Peace, arms assumed for public defence, and of uniting in acts of brotherly affection, and bonds of perpetual friendship, the members constituting the same.

In Testimony whereof, the seal of the State Society of Cincinnati of New-Jersey, is hereunto affixed, and the hand of the President, the seventh — day of January in the year of our Lord one thousand eight hundred and nine.

By Order.

Joseph Bloomfield President.

Andw. Hunter Secretary.

H. G. Phillips

5. Frederick Frelinghuysen

Pastel on Paper attributed to James or Ellen Sharples, ca. 1793–1801. From the Collections of The New Jersey Historical Society, Newark, New Jersey.

6. Elias Boudinot

Portrait by Charles Willson Peale, from life, ca. 1782–1784. Courtesy of The Independence National Historical Park.

7. James Giles

General James Giles, ca. 1785. Oil on canvas by Joseph Wright. Courtesy of the Smithsonian American Art Museum, Washington, DC/Art Resource, NY.

8. Ebenezer Elmer

Silhouette by an unknown artist. Reprinted from Formation and Organization of the Society of the Cincinnati in the State of New Jersey *by Charles Martin Jones.*

9. Elias Dayton

Brigadier General Elias Dayton. Engraving by James Sharples. Courtesy of the Society of the Cincinnati, Anderson House, Washington, DC.

10. Marquis de Lafayette

Engraving by Hopewood. Courtesy of the Society of the Cincinnati.

11. Joseph Scott

Joseph Warren Scott. Courtesy of the Gloucester County Historical Society from a book in their collection, "The Flag of the Society of the Cincinnati"—Presidents of the Society of the Cincinnati in the State of New Jersey—rare etchings", *edited by James Campbell, Freehold, NJ 1926.*

12. John Hall

John Hall, D.D., LLD. Reproduced by permission of the Presbyterian Historical Society, 425 Lombard Street, Philadelphia, PA 19147–1516.

13. Luther Halsey

Luther Foster Halsey. Ca. 1890. Courtesy of Joseph Halsey Groff, III.

14. William Stryker

Adjutant General William Scudder Stryker. Oil on canvas by Henry Harrison, 1903. From the Collections of the New Jersey Historical Society, Newark, New Jersey.

15. George Washington

General George Washington. Oil on canvas by Edward Savage, 1790. Courtesy of the Harvard University Portrait Collection, Gift of Edward Savage to Harvard College, 1791.

16. Winslow Warren

1838–1938. Reproduced by permission of the Society of the Cincinnati.

17. Vincent C. De Baun

18. William Livingston

Ca. 1750–1760. Portrait by John Wollaston. Courtesy of the Fraunces Tavern Museum, New York City.

19. David Forman

Brigadier General David Forman. Oil by Charles Willson Peale. Courtesy of the Berkshire Museum, Pittsfield, Massachusetts, USA.

20. William Forman, Jr.
Lieutenant Colonel William H. Forman, Jr., LLB.

21. William B. Brown, III

22. Joseph Bloomfield

Portrait by an unknown artist, oil on canvas. Collection of The Society of the Cincinnati in the State of New Jersey at Anderson House.

Joseph Bloomfield (1753–1823), born in Woodbridge, New Jersey, was a lawyer, soldier, and public servant. He served during the Revolutionary War as a Major in the Third Regiment of the New Jersey Continental line from 1776 to 1778, and was wounded during the Battle of Brandywine. After the war he held several important positions within the state, including trustee of Princeton College (1793–1801), governor (1801, 1803–1812), and member of Congress (1817–1821). Bloomfield became an original member of the Society of the Cincinnati in the State of New Jersey and served as our second president from 1808 until his death in 1823. He is currently represented in our Society by his great-great-great-great-great grandnephew Anthony Allyn Monroe. This portrait of Bloomfield, donated to the Society of the Cincinnati in the State of New Jersey in 1959 by our late member Charles M. Jones, has not been attributed or dated, and presents a composition that is unlike other known portraits.

The honourable trust of dispensing this relief has fallen to us by descent from our fathers; by descent from better men than we are. O! Let not that sacred trust be violated in our hands.

Yes, with the swords we inherit, with the honourable names which have descended comes the irreversible injunction. The command accompanied the badge of honour, the trophy of renown. They are inseparable.

Do you cherish and value the latter in honest pride of heart? I know you do. The dying injunction of your fathers will not be forgotten.

The noblest example and the most virtuous precept are here held out in broad relief before the generous youth of our land. And shall not some gallant scion from this noble stock catch the inspiration? And shall he not at some future and perhaps not distant day, on the eve of expected battle, when his country shall need all his energy, devotion and love, exclaim in the fullness and elevation on his soul:

Spirit of my sainted sire
With success my soul inspire
Deeds of glory done by thee
In memory's mirror now I see
The inspiration now I feel
The ardent glow of patriot zeal
Spirit, spirit of my sainted sire
With success my soul inspire
And fame shall, when the battle's won
Declare–that I am all thy son.

Fellow citizens: It is an ancient law of our society. It was ordained by our fathers, and it has always been scrupulously obeyed, that the annual meeting shall be on the day of independence.

The principles of the institution are to be explained, and the duties enforced. And to that end the great charter of American Independence shall be audibly read by one of the members. At this assemblage we know no party but our country. Her glory is our pride. And this day brings with it those hallowed duties which our fathers have commanded: During our publick exercises that standard shall float and wave.

Flag of my country, Wave proudly and in
triumph wave.
Flag that bears on high the stripe and star shall
bear aloft the stripe and star.
Star-spangled banner, consecrated symbol of
virtue, liberty, and independence—Thou
that erst didst float and wave high on the
deck of glory, broadly over the field of
renown.
Wave and wave and wave in dignity and grace.

A world be thy realm, for a world be thy laws.
Enlarged as thine empire and just as thy cause.
On freedom's broad bases thine empire shall
rise.
Extend with the main and dissolve with the
skies.

Standard of our fathers, why art thou not here?
Standard of our fathers, sacred emblem of
their faithful, deep and undying devotion.
Standard of our fathers, 'twas thine in the din
of battle, thine on the breeze to point the
way where glory and our country call.
'Twas thine when the tempest raged to lead to
victory and renown.
Standard of our fathers, 'tis thine to evolve,
unfold, and wave in honour and in peace.
Wave glorious standard: wave, wave, still wave.
Long, very long unsevered may they wave, in
the land of the free and the home of the
brave.

NINE

THE ANNIVERSARY ORATION

Reverend Dr. John Hall, 1859

Reverend Dr. John Hall, 1829–1898, was of Scots-Irish descent and was born in Ballymorgan, County Armagh, Northern Ireland. He attended college and seminary in Belfast, Northern Ireland. After serving in several churches in Dublin, his fame as an orator spread, and he was sent as a delegate from the Presbyterian Church of Ireland to the Presbyterian Church of the United States. After several impressive sermons in 1867, he became well known. On his return to Ireland, he received and accepted an invitation to be pastor of the First Avenue Presbyterian Church at 19th Street in New York City. He was a masterful preacher. By 1875, the church congregation moved to its current location at Fifth Avenue and 55th Street. Reverend Hall served this church until shortly before his death, when he returned to Ireland in failing health and died in County Down, Ireland. He was Chancellor of New York University, Director of Union Seminary, Director of Princeton Seminary, and a Trustee of Princeton College (see illustration 12).

The Anniversary Oration of the Cincinnati of New Jersey, at Trenton, July 4, 1859

Gentlemen of the Cincinnati of New Jersey, and Fellow Citizens:

Thursday, the Fourth day of July, 1776, was a day of grave, of solemn, as well as of exciting interest. It was a small company of thoughtful, anxious men—not a crowd such as now fills the Capitol—which on that day was assembled in the old State House in Philadelphia. They were men of boldness and decision, of determination and courage, but they were MEN; men of deep-rooted, hereditary attachment to England and the English throne, men of families and of property; men of high honor; not actuated by selfish ambition; not seeking political independence from faction or for personal gain. All was at stake which such high-minded patriots knew how to value, more than the unreflecting who may have loved the occurrence of revolution for the sake of the excitement, and had less care for its results, because they had nothing valuable to lose, nothing sacred to abandon.

The very term *revolution* is a fearful one to such patriots as were presided over by John Hancock. Its ideas are those of changing what is established, overturning old foundations, innovating upon ancient institutions. The revolution of the heavens is their order; they revolve in regularity; their cycles, though in perpetual movement, are as fixed as the granite foundations of the everlasting hills. But when revolution is applied to civil government, it denotes disruption, confusion, discord, war; and the fear of change perplexes not monarchs only, but their best subjects. Such subjects had George the Third in those men who came to the old State House of the colony of Pennsylvania eighty-three years ago, to convert it into a Hall of National Independence.

But the gravity and solemnity of the day we celebrate have begun to disappear from our associations. The men who signed for themselves and us, for the mighty constituency which has only begun to show its extent, the Declaration of American Nationality, have disappeared from our sight, and every year that widens our distance from them diminishes the influence of their names and their examples. As long as any of the signers lingered among us, as long as their revolutionary contemporaries in the mass of citizens survived, the spirit of the great day of '76 was proportionately reverenced. The presence of those shadows of the past overawed the new generations. But when they were at length extinct, the Fourth began to be a common day, the Declaration to fall into the grade of a common State paper, and the signatures of the illustrious fifty-six, from Josiah Bartlett to George Walton, to represent comparative strangers to the new age of Americans.

Such is the result of time; of continued prosperity; such the effect of being accustomed to blessings without having first known what it was to be without them; such the effect of inheriting privileges without knowing, except historically, the cost at which they were procured.

The great object then, my fellow citizens, in keeping up the observance of the anniversary of Independence should be to keep up the memory and the influence of its Principles and its Men. The chief purpose of history, in all its forms, (and the anniversary is one of them,) is not to preserve antiquarian records, to transmit facts, to relate that such and such persons lived, and that such and such deeds were performed; or even to extol the deeds and eulogize the men. History is not an amusement, but a study. Its office is to instruct, to admonish, to show us the valuableness or worthlessness of what we find about us; to infuse, by the recital, the virtues we are made to admire in the past, and which are capable of being imitated in the present. We know very well that we are independent, without keeping the Fourth of July. The Declaration of Independence, as a document, is in our schoolbooks. But the day, as a monument to principles, the Declaration, as a grave moral sentiment, as a covenant and avowal binding us as well as the nation of that day, this whole reproduction of the scenes, the actors, and the purposes that make that day and its great deed so worthy of memory, these are the impressions which if not sought and declared, and readopted in our own names, turn our commemorations into mockeries, and make us guilty of dishonor to the graves of our Fathers. But, on the other hand, what a means of preserving our true position, of purifying our political sentiments, of maintaining the sound patriotism of the country, would it be, if, with the birth-day of our liberties, we could even annually revive the spirit in which they were engendered and born!

We are familiar with the designation of a period in intellectual history as the revival of learning; with other periods in economical history called revivals of trade and commerce; with others in moral history called revivals of religion. The same declensions which in these several departments of human interests necessitated the reaction that goes by this name, when they exist in political history, call for a revival of patriotism—of genuine politics. I say a revival; for it is not the necessity of our age to create—to originate American patriotism. We have it in its purest mold, in its perfect models, in the men who achieved our separation from an unsuitable and degrading connection abroad; who framed our constitution and laws; who inaugurated and administered the system; and who stamped on all they did the impress of their personal virtue. What greater blessing could we ask for our country than to be able to summon to the Capitol next December the men who founded our Republic? What part of the confederacy, which this day adds the thirty-third star to its flag, would not consent to submit the whole country to the legislation of such representatives as composed the first Congress? What American, native or naturalized, would hesitate to commit the entire executive power, this day or any day, to the first President? But the next thing after the impossible revival of the men, is the revival of their wisdom, their purity, their principles. All these survive. They are imperishably wrought into the fabric of our institutions. We have their debates, their essays, their correspondence, their enactments, their negotiations. Their personal history remains, attesting their sincerity and disinterestedness. Their success remains—attesting their sagacity, and indicating that there was a higher and more efficient guidance of their counsels and proceedings than unaided human wisdom. For I trust it will not be considered by this audience a mere professional sentiment on my part, when I say that the thirteen tribes of Israel (for thirteen was their actual number by the double tribe of Joseph) were not more obviously guided by Divine Providence, were not more distinctly placed under the instrumentality of men raised up and endowed for the accomplishing of high and far-reaching purposes for mankind, than were the thirteen American Colonies, when the time had come for the exodus from their vassalage to a land now for the first time truly their own. And the most profitable, and perhaps the least tedious discourse, that could be pronounced this day would be a selection of passages from the Books of Moses, setting forth the source and the principles of national prosperity, and the obligations of a free and religious people to abide by the Supreme Law of the King of Kings and Lord of Lords.

And this reminds us of the acknowledgments due this day, of the ecclesiastical independence effected by the revolution, which placed the church of the United States on the primitive basis of a spiritual body under a Divine head, requiring no "conformity," asking and accepting no identification with the powers of civil government. "Head and Supreme Governor of the Church," is one of the constitutional titles of the British monarch; and though religious liberty has made some progress in Britain since the great "dissent" of '76, so that the Jew and Roman Catholic sit in Parliament, and her Majesty is a

Presbyterian at Balmoral and an Episcopalian at Windsor, and I suppose, as a grandmother, a Lutheran at Berlin—yet enough remains, even in the glorious empire of Victoria, to make us content with our more free and voluntary system, as compared with her church establishments. We have the church. Our history, from the beginning, is full of proof that the ark of the covenant, as well as the rod of Moses, came over and remained with our fathers; and the continued presence of the Holy Spirit of God, in multiplying, extending and making effective His inspired word, has never ceased to accredit the genuineness of our free Christianity in the variety of its outward forms.

We are accustomed on the Fourth of July to hear more of the sword of the revolution, than of almost any other agency. Yet what particular day in all the annals of that epoch ought to be more suggestive of the power of the pen and of the tongue? The only sword drawn on the Fourth of July, '76, was the paper one adopted on the evening of that day, after a three days' debate. True, more material arguments had been already resorted to. The fields of Lexington and Bunker's Hill had anticipated, by more than a year, the calmer proceedings of Chestnut Street. But the battles prior to the Declaration were not the war. They were local resistances of some immediate aggressions. They were provincial, not national. The military acts of Congress had only been advisory and defensive. It was not till the signing of the Declaration that the Congress assumed, as we have just heard, on the ground of "free and independent states," "full power to levy war, conclude peace, contract alliances, establish commerce, and to do all other acts and things which independent states may of right do." In that paper, in its clear logic, its plain facts, its self-evident conclusions, lay the power which was to cast off tyranny, and justify to the world then and forever, all the consequences that might follow. The Declaration of Independence contains no declaration of war. The pen of Jefferson only wrote the final conclusions of what had already been discussed in the "Farmer's Letters" of Dickinson, the "Monitor" of Lee, Bland's "Inquiry," Nicholas's "Considerations," Paine's "Common Sense," and the writings of a host of coadjutors in newspapers and pamphlets. The pens of the signers only made the endorsement of the national sentiment in the name of the thirteen states they represented.

The same may be asserted of the contribution to the moral power of the act of independence, made by the arguments of the colonial statesmen and public speakers from New Hampshire to Georgia. They were not, as a general thing, inflammatory harangues, bombastic appeals to the ignorant. It was necessary to show the facts of the issue, and prove the legal right of the people to redress themselves in order to bring them to their proper position. We have a specimen of what was depended on as the true basis of success, in the fact that Congress sent two clergymen, one from his church in Newark, and another from his church in Trenton, to visit parts of Virginia, the Carolinas and Georgia, to give the people in certain remote settlements an intelligent understanding of the controversy, and of their rights and duties in relation to it. It was not yet the day when the patriotic sentiments of America, and the exercise of a free political choice, were to be turned about and guided as by a bit in the horse's mouth, or, by what is still more degrading, the bribes of office. Here is the political revival we need—a recurrence to the intelligence, the virtue, the trust in Providence which signalized the founding of our national fabric, and marked the personal character of its founders, including the great body of the people. That was no fanaticism which spoke in such terms as those employed by Chief Justice Drayton, of South Carolina, in April, '76, in his official charge to the grand jury, when, at the close of a cool constitutional statement of the question of rights between king and people, he said:

> *I think it is my duty to declare in this awful seat of justice, and before Almighty God, that in my opinion the Americans can have no safety but by the Divine favor, their own virtue, and their being so prudent as not to leave it in the power of the British rulers to injure them. . . . The Almighty created America to be independent of Britain. Let us beware of the impiety of being backward to act as instruments in the Almighty hand, now extended to accomplish his purpose. . . . In a word, our piety and political safety are so blended, that to refuse our labors in this Divine work, is to refuse to be a great, a free, a pious, and a happy people.*

I shall not undertake to draw the contrast between the politics of those days and the present. I will remember the inspired caution: "Say not thou, what is the cause that the former days were better than these? For thou dost not inquire wisely concerning this." There are many and natural reasons for the change, besides such as imply degeneracy; and perhaps, after all, our fathers were not so immaculate, nor are we so depraved, as Fourth of July speeches would make out. But still it well becomes us to take care that we do not exhaust our patriotism in the applause of the past, or in complacency with ourselves. There is a New American all the time developing; to adjust that development to the vital elements of our political existence is the trying problem of successive ages. We need to do something more than celebrate our Independence. We are independent, and by the Divine blessing mean to keep so. But to study how to use our nationality, how to preserve it sound and pure, how to recommend it and diffuse it, by the evidence of our welfare under it, over the rest of our American continent, and over the other hemisphere—this is the highest celebration of the great deed of '76. If to the mass of those who vote for legislators, representatives, governors, president, the only question is, whom does our party nominate? if to such the whole science and morals of civil government consist in succeeding with the nominee; if what a man's moral character, his capacity, his intelligence are, has little or nothing to do with supporting his election; if the money, whether of the party or of the candidate himself, buys his place; if men thrust themselves forward as seekers of place, and demand public positions as the reward of their partisanship; if intelligence and integrity become nothing in comparison with availability—if such signs as these should ever appear among us, then, in spite of all the cant about "progress," we cannot do better than go back to our beginning, four-score and three years ago, and sit at the feet of those honest men who signed the Declaration, and sealed it before God with the pledge of their lives, their fortunes, and their sacred honor.

These considerations show the importance of training American youth in a familiarity with the history and biography, as well as the constitution of their country. The mere chronicles of events will not do this. The battles show the practical force of the principles contended for, but the diplomacy, the debates, the writings, and above all, the personal qualities of the leaders of opinion, and the movers of the whole proceedings, contain the oil which is to revive and keep burning the true fire of the American altar.

In speaking thus of the training of our sons and of ourselves in the substantial doctrines of our nationality, I do not detract from the claims on the perpetual memory of the country, of that class of patriots who literally fought for the cause. On their account, in their honor, let monuments arise on every spot where they contended, whether with success or defeat; not raised as a memorial of the conflict itself, not to boast how many died, and how many suffered, or how deep the soil was wet with human blood, but to commemorate the spirit of devotion to justice, liberty, and humanity, which compelled those recruits of a day to defend their country and their homes against aggression. The battle monuments of a civilized and Christian people should honor first of all the cause of the warfare. As it is not the signature of the Declaration, but the Declaration of Independence itself, that is the chief object of our regard, and we honor the men for the sentiments they held, and the manner in which they avowed them, so we honor the parties in the battle according to the merits of their cause, more than according to the mere method or effect of their deeds in the field of contest. Who has thought of a monument to the thousands, whether of Austria or France, whose corpses fill the trenches of Montebello, Malegnano, and Magenta? The real heroes of those latest fields of carnage are the few who are scarcely heard of, except in some feeble echo of the name of Garibaldi, the Piedmontese, and other obscure, that is, weak subjects of Austrian oppression, with whose cause, as the "down-trodden peoples," our sympathy was awakened a few years since, in the very spot where I stand, by that great master of English eloquence (whatever he may be in European politics) Louis Kossuth. There are the Emperors, and their hundreds of thousands of slaves in regimentals, who flaunt before the world in this drama, and take all the glory, (excepting that the Irish General McMahon is metamorphosed into a French Duke;) but the humble Provinces, whose liberties are to be the prey of the successful power, the people whose are the fields and homes and churches invaded by the two great duellists, this is the party that must fill our thoughts, as spectators of the war, and they, because of the sentiments they represent. Yet let me not do the third Napoleon the injustice of omitting the acknowledgment that he wrote good doctrine on the 8th of last month, when in his address to Lombardy, dated at Milan, he said: "In the enlightened state of public opinion, there is more grandeur to be acquired by the moral influence that is exercised than by fruitless conquests, and that moral influence I seek with pride in contributing to restore to freedom one of the finest parts of Europe." Let us hope that his Imperial Majesty, in his zeal for the precedents of his uncle, has not adopted the theory of his great minister Talleyrand, that the political use of words is to say what is not meant. So (to return to our philosophy of monuments) when we keep our days, and build our obelisks, and buy Mount Vernon, in memory of the triumphs of our noble Continentals, Army, Congress, People, and of him who was head of all and the spirit of all—the great Commander-in-Chief and President—let it be in love and honor for the soul, rather than the outward body of the cause, and to give it the highest possible honor and reward—the perpetuation of that soul in the successive generations of our republican world. We want not only the memories of Washington, and the other men of '76—not only columns and statues—but new, living men, like them, to guide and adorn every era of our history.

Such, I have no doubt, are the most effective motives that actuate the enterprise of constructing, in our own town, a suitable memorial of the great incident of the 26th of December, '76, and its following week. And seldom has so truly appropriate a design for a patriotic monument been devised, as will be laid before the corporators to-day. That enterprise is in the best hands, and the impulse it is receiving is a worthy feature of the general celebration. I shall not trespass on ground so faithfully occupied by that company of our fellow citizens who are doing their best to eclipse us to-day; but in illustration of the general topic I may say, that, in commemorating the Battle of Trenton, the smallest part of the great subject is the skill of the tactics, the success of its manœuvre, the surprise of the German regiment, the victorious retreat, or the great aggregate of sagacity in the American leader, and fortitude in the troops, as evinced in every step of that week's work of mind and body from McKonkey's Ferry to Princeton. No heart, quicker than that of the Commander-in-Chief himself, would turn away from the mere details of the conflict. But the glory of the day, its monumental triumph, was its moral effect. The great victory of Washington on this ground was not over a few Hessians, but over the fears and despondencies of his own countrymen, and over the pride and *prestige* represented by Sir William Howe and Lord Cornwallis. The great honor which those days added to Washington's fame can never be told by any inscription, however minute in statistics of the battle-fields. That honor was but the development of the occasion. It showed what the man was, what he always was, equal to any emergency, prompt to every call of duty, faithful and fearless with many or with few, and having the trust of a Moses or a Joshua in the Providence whose favor to the just cause is stronger than armies.

These sentiments, gentlemen of the Cincinnati, ought to be, and I am confident are yours. They are both Roman and American. Our old friend Lucius Quintius—or Serranus (as he is called by Virgil[1] in allusion to his sowing his field, more appropriately for us, than Cincinnatus, from his curled hair)—is a hero, not because he conquered the Æqui and delivered the consuls, nor because he brought to terms the Senate and the people in the Agrarian conflict, (what care we for any of these parties?) but he is our hero and the hero of the world, because he was a soldier and a dictator, without ambition and without covetousness, coming out of retirement only from the necessity of serving his country in extremity, and returning as soon as that necessity ceased; refusing honors and riches as his reward, and content to have performed his duty. As Milton says of him, in connexion with Fabricius, Curius, Regulus, and other Romans of the same stamp, they were great, because men

> Who could do mighty things, and could
> contemn
> Riches, tho' offered from the hand of Kings.[2]

[1] "Te eulco, Serrane, serentem."—Æneid, *vi. 844.*

[2] Paradise Regained: *book ii.*

This is the immortality of Cincinnatus; this the quality of his patriotism you cherish by adopting his name. After the havoc that Niebuhr has made of the "Viri Romæ" of our school-days, we indeed hardly know whether we can certainly believe in the personal reality of our hero, more than that of Romulus and Remus; and the cautious Arnold gives the narrative in his legendary Æsop-like style, as "the story of Cincinnatus"; but, fable or fact, the moral is the same. It is such patriotism as this, such public men as he, that the United States and each State need, and never more than at this day. They were such men as he, who, when in 1783 they assembled, at the end of the "eight years' conflict," to form an Association of the officers of the late Army, to be perpetuated by their descendants, placed at the basis of the institution, not a celebration of their own deeds, but such "principles" as these: "An incessant attention to preserve inviolate those exalted rights and liberties of human nature for which they have fought and bled, and without which the high rank of a rational being is a curse, instead of a blessing"—"an unalterable determination to promote and cherish between the respective States that union and national honor so essentially necessary to their happiness and the future dignity of the American Empire." These, gentlemen, as your minutes show, were the expansive views taken by the founders of your Society. Though fresh from the actual warfare in which their names occupied so honorable a place, it was, as these extracts show, the cause of "human nature," of man as "a rational being," the "union and honor, happiness and dignity," of the whole "future" of their country, that they had in mind as the scope of the work. So the Declaration quotes "the laws of nature and of nature's God," as giving title to the separate and equal station of the new government. And so your diploma asserts one of the purposes of your Association to be, "inculcating the duty of laying down in peace arms assumed for public defence."

This largeness of view was eminently characteristic of those days. Our patriot fathers were not working for themselves alone. They would hardly have thought their own immediate and short-lived interest in the question sufficient to justify the sacrifices they personally made. Is this the spirit of our age? Is this the quality of our politics? Are such the aims and principles of our public men in and out of Congress, in and out of office?

Might not the confederate branches of the Cincinnati do something by pen and mouth to show that they are hereditary possessors of these enlarged and unselfish principles of their sires, and revive through the country the spirit of the times when American statesmen looked beyond themselves and the present moment, and remembered that their private reputations and their public acts were both to influence future ages, and to be judged by them? Might they not do something in imitation of the power of the pen of the revolution, to reform the political press of the country? What a noble protest against all spurious politics would that be which should emanate from the heirs and representatives of the signers and supporters of the Declaration of Independence, and its coincident manifestoes! The Cincinnati have long ago outlived and outlaughed the silly charge that they were contemplating a Patrician institution; but it would be a glorious order of American nobility, if the pure blood of the men—statesmen, soldiers, citizens—of the old north, south, east and west, not merely hereditary or exclusively native, but the true knighthood, in which should be found men like the signers of the Declaration of Independence and the members of the first Congress, of all trades and professions, rich and poor, if, I say, this true blood could be kept unmixed with the illegitimate line of men who, bearing the name of patriots, are simply and merely selfish jobbers. We want no aristocracy such as we understand from the idea of hereditary authority; but we want nothing more as a country than an aristarchy which is defined as "a body of good men in power," such men as were described so long ago as the book of Exodus, by the wise Jethro: "Moreover, thou shalt provide out of all the people, able men, such as fear God, men of truth, hating covetousness, and place such over them to be rulers."

The heroes of the pen and tongue, sword and musket, whom we honor to-day, were not only advocates of national independent men. Their politics was a science, a truth, a virtue. As the military character of their day was not made up of feathers and gilt wire, so its civic character was something else than hollow party names or a popular by-word, though that word were "Independence." They were men who could hold their own opinions without subserviency, and yet with fraternal regard to the compatriots who, with equal intelligence and sincerity, held opposite sentiments as to details, though identical in principle. They could be bitter enough, too, in their discussions, and sometimes in their personal animosities. Jefferson, Adams and Hamilton were not the most amiable persons to one another when the Federal and Democratic blood was fairly roused, or personal jealousies distorted their vision. But when men have something real to contend about under their party names, when every turn of opinion is shaped by diversity of views as to what is best in the inauguration of a government making a new experiment, and that not for a single country and a single generation, but for the world and for all time, we may well excuse high words and zealous proselytism. But when it comes, alas! to converting reason, principles, and lessons of history, the whole life and stability of a government into a scheme for bringing John Doe or Richard Roe into the Presidency for four years, and their respective hosts into the post offices, custom houses, and contractorships for the same term, then what is called *politics* comes down into the arena where "Tom Hyer" conquers, or the *area* where "Mike Walsh" breaks his neck.

And here I cannot help taking occasion, from the suggestion of what meets my eye as I look over this distinguished assembly, of congratulating the Society that New Jersey has determined to be represented in part, in the next Congress, by a member of the Cincinnati.[3]

But there are other lineal representatives here today of the virtues of '76, than you, gentlemen of the Cincinnati, who, according to the legal or romantic fiction, are supposed to have left your ploughs in the furrow this morning, and mean to go straight home to your cottages and frugal meals as soon as we have sung Hail Columbia and Old Hundred. Cincinnatus had a wife. Her name, according to some, was Attilia, according to others, Racilia. Perhaps, to be more like her husband, she would have her three names, and was Attilia Racilia Cincinnatus. The story is, that when the Roman deputies came to inform the farmer of his first election to the dictatorship, he took a "tender leave" of his wife, saying, "I fear, my Attilia, that this year our little fields must remain unsown." Whether the good man meant to attempt a little domestic dictatorship, and to insinuate that Attilia might attend to the farm while he was gone, and whether she thought that she had sewing enough of her own to do, we have only human nature to judge by; but (jesting apart) the "Roman woman," matron or maiden, is a proverb of patriotism and virtue. The story of Valeria, Volumnia and Virgilia, and the building of the temple to "Woman's Fortune," belongs to the age of Cincinnatus; and if the women of the American Revolution, who not only gave husbands and sons and brothers to the militia, but cheered the whole cause by their own courage and their actual help, were represented, as the men are, by a hereditary association, the Society of the Attiliæ would be as large as the Society of the Cincinnati. The wife of Cincinnatus has not been forgotten by his sons; for in the description of the order, or badge adopted in 1784, next to "the principal figure," is described "on a field in the background his wife standing at the door of their cottage." It is not required for the badge, as the history would warrant, that she should have her husband's coat in her hands; for it is said that as he was digging (as we should say in his shirt sleeves,) when the deputies came to salute him as "Master of the People," he called out to Attilia to bring him his coat to go to town in.

[3] *The Hon. William Pennington.*

I do not know that it would be a forward step in civilization to train our daughters to be doctresses of constitutional law, any more than of the practice of medicine, but perhaps some lessons from these old Roman and old American stories would be as profitable in our seminaries for "young ladies," as the modern curriculum of physiology and anatomy.

At all events we must look more to the domestic training of all our youth, for the political, as well as moral purity of our country. Politics and morals must never be separated. Falsehood, detraction, deception, peculation, bribery, perjury, are as criminal when perpetrated in the name of a state, or the United States, in a capitol or public office, behind a legislative desk, with a frank, or "stationery," or a ballot, or a job, as when the same offences figure in police reports, under the heads of pickpockets, swindlers, confidence men, mock auctions, and petty larceny. And so the crimes of drunkenness, licentiousness and homicide must be exhibited to our youth as neither screened nor palliated, in the sight of the God of law and purity, by the political or social position of the criminals. An immoral act is not the less wicked because committed at Washington or at Trenton; a gentleman forfeits his title, whether his vulgarity be only for the session, or all the year round.

Fellow-citizens: We have met on the day that reminds us of our privileges as a united, free religious nation: the day when, by the favor of Divine Providence, we were set apart for the high, broad, and long purpose in the designs of Him who does nothing without an object worthy of Himself. Our responsibilities, then, do not end with our country, with the day, with ourselves: our gratitude does not end with the tribute we render to the men whose names and memories are so precious in the associations of this anniversary. The Lord God Almighty is the Father, the Defender, the Saviour of our nation. He is its ruler. He is its king. There is no independence here. Eloquent praises, noisy acclamations, pompous boastings, solemn professions, make no impression on that mind which makes infinite holiness and infinite truth the standard of all moral virtue, in every relation sustained by man. Patriotism is a duty to God. To pass the test of His approbation it must be sincere, faithful and obedient. Like every other duty it should be performed religiously, that is, under the motives and sanctions implied in the fact that all our obligations begin and terminate in God. The political trust He has put into our hands is as sacred, as religious, as any other. It is to be used for His glory, and for the best welfare of His whole world.

This is the grand principle that we need to revive and purify our patriotism. This is the only security for the permanence of what we have acquired.

This is the ultimate end of what the Almighty has done for us, and therefore His voice to our country to-day is just what it was to our Jewish pioneers in independence, thirty-three centuries ago.

> *Because he loved thy fathers, therefore he chose their seed after them, and brought them out of his sight with his mighty power, . . . to drive out nations from before thee greater and mightier than thou art, to bring thee in, to give thee their land for an inheritance, as it is this day; know, therefore,* THIS DAY, *and consider it in thine heart that the Lord He is God in Heaven above, and upon the earth beneath; there is none else; thou shalt keep, therefore, His statutes and His commandments, which I command thee this day, that it may go well with thee, and with thy children after thee, and that thou mayest prolong thy days upon the earth, which the Lord thy God giveth thee, forever.*

TEN

THE REVOLUTIONARY WORTHIES OF THE MEDICAL STAFF

Luther Foster Halsey, M.D., 1890

Luther Foster Halsey, 1863–1895 (admitted 1884) was the grandson of Captain Luther Halsey (Original Member), Second Regiment, New Jersey Continental Line.

Captain Halsey participated in the Civil War as Assistant Surgeon, Seventh Regiment Infantry, New Jersey Volunteers, from 1862 to1863. He was transferred to the Second Regiment, March 9, 1863, and honorably discharged on May 31, 1864. He was a well-known physician who advocated strict cleanliness in his surgical procedures. Captain Halsey was credited with saving many limbs during the war at a time when most wounds required amputation because of the lack of aseptic treatment (see illustration 13).

Luther Foster Halsey is currently represented by Joseph Halsey Groff III of Elizabeth, Maine.

Read Before
The Society of the Cincinnati in the State of New Jersey
at Princeton, July 4, 1890

Mr. President and Fellows of the Society of the Cincinnati:

GENTLEMEN: I make this effort to bring to your notice some of the events connected with the Medical Department of the Army of the Revolution, as well as to call attention to many members of that noble profession who were important factors in that struggle.

I fully realize the magnitude of the undertaking and feel unequal to it, especially as a large country practice ties me very closely, and leaves me but little time that I am able to call my own. In this humble effort to rescue from the oblivion that time throws around all human actions, the names of those patriots of the Revolution who belonged to the medical profession, I only attempt to preserve and perpetuate the memory of those whose biographies have not yet been written.

That period in our history was one which demanded the aid of every citizen who had the intelligence to appreciate liberty and the courage to oppose tyranny.

From a review of the various actors on the stage of American affairs it appears that when the principles of free government were being evoked and matured no class of society or profession seemed to have deserved higher praise for their efforts to promote this result than the physicians: constant association with all classes makes the medical man acquainted with every shade of opinion of his day, and makes him the confidant and the counselor of the masses in questions of common interest.

Historians have over and over again eulogized the statesman, the orator, the soldier, the tragedian, and the clergyman, who took part in the efforts for independence, but the self-denying sacrifices and services of the physician have been almost entirely overlooked.

The Medical history of the Revolution properly begins with the casualties caused by the first collision between the British troops and the Colonists.

It is, however, exceedingly difficult now, to mark the exact period when petition ceased and protest began; when, from mere words of discussion tumults were excited and the Colonists came into collision with the troops.

The first blood shed was at the Boston Massacre, March 5, 1770, when the troops being insulted and pelted with stones fired upon the crowd killing three—

Samuel Gray, Crispus Attucks and James Caldwell; wounding Christopher Monk, Patrick Carr, John Clark, Edward Payne, John Green, Robert Patterson, David Parker and Samuel Maverick, the last mortally.

The first armed resistance to British encroachment was in North Carolina near the River Alamance on May 16, 1771. The citizens organized a force under the name of Regulators. Governor William Tryon, afterwards Governor of New York, commanded the Royal troops, about 1,100 strong, of whom he lost 63 in the engagement. The Regulators numbered about 2,000, very inefficiently officered, and were defeated with considerable loss. A number were taken prisoners, and were cruelly executed as traitors.

The excited condition of public opinion at the time, was aggravated by the want of tact of the military officials, and the controversy culminated at Lexington and Concord, in April, 1775, in engagement with the troops, the towns-people having been warned by Dr. Joseph Warren, who was ever vigilant, as a Son of Liberty, watching the movements of the British. The news was conveyed by Dr. Samuel Prescott. Thus we see that to the vigilance and sagacity of members of the medical profession were due whatever preparations the Americans had made to defend themselves.

At the battle of North Bridge the same day the forces were commanded by Dr. John Brooks. His loss was 4 killed and 8 wounded.

The militia were rapidly increased in number by new arrivals, and the retreat having begun about noon the British were pursued and attacked at every available point of the route back to Bunker's Hill, where they found safety under the guns of the fleet. The loss on the American side was 49 killed and 36 wounded and 5 missing. The British, 73 killed, 174 wounded and 26 missing.

The heroism displayed by the militia throughout the day was admirable, and the result in a military point of view highly creditable.

It will be remembered that the colony had no regular military establishment of trained and equipped soldiers, the militia gathered to defend themselves as best they could, and were, therefore, without commissioned officers.

I have been able to find the names of nine physicians who were in these first conflicts of arms or rendered medical service to the wounded on April 19, viz.: Drs. William Aspinwall, John Brooks, John Cumming, William Dexter, Eliphates Downer, Timothy Minot, Samuel Prescott, Joseph Warren and Thomas Welch. Dr. Joseph Warren was president of the Provincial Congress of Massachusetts, which was in session at this time, and was also chairman of the Committee of Public Safety; by virtue of this position and his widely recognized ability, he was one of the most influential of the patriots who shaped the course of the colony during the early days of the struggle.

In the Provincial Congress of Massachusetts in 1774 and 1775 there were 23 physicians, representing various districts of the State, many of whom by their devotion to the cause are well known in history—to wit, Drs. Joseph Batchelder, William Bayliss, Chauncey Brewer, Alexander Campbell, Benjamin Church, David Cobb, John Corbett, William Dinsmore, Isaac Foster, Ephraim Guiteau, Jeremiah Hall, James Hawse, Samuel Holton, William Jamieson, David Jones, Moses Morse, Richard Perkins, Charles Pynchon, Ebenezer Sawyer, John Taylor, Joseph Warren, William Whiting; and it is highly probable that there are other physicians who names deserve a place among these worthies.

The assemblies and conventions of the other colonies at this period also furnish us with the names of many leading medical men, so that the make up of the Congress of Massachusetts may be taken as the rule of such bodies and not as an exception.

After the battle of Lexington an army of over 3,000 men soon rendezvoused at or near Boston, forming a line of encampments from Roxbury to the Mystic River.

The necessity for establishing hospitals for the care of the sick and wounded soldiers now for the first time forced itself upon the consideration of the commanders as well as the Provincial Congress, which body took up the subject immediately after the assembling at Watertown, April 22, 1775. Thus far the colonels, and sometimes the captains, exercised the power of appointing surgeons to their commands.

To improve the medical service the Second Provincial Congress of Massachusetts, on May 8, 1775, at the instance of the Committee of Safety, created a committee to examine surgeons for the army—the first of the kind in America.

Dr. James Thacher, in his military journal of this period, has left a record of the character of those examinations. He was one of sixteen who were examined by the board. The business occupied about four hours. Ten were approved and accepted, receiving their appointments. The other six were privately rejected as being found unqualified. The examinations were considered very close and severe. At first it was hoped that there would be no war, but that an understanding would be reached which would prevent a resort to arms. The exigencies of the hour required the services of military leaders and medical men, otherwise failure would be inevitable.

The Congress and Council of Safety were naturally looked to by the patriots for guidance. Happily these bodies had in them men of marked ability and courage, who acted with rare wisdom, promptness and decision; selecting able generals to command who organized and disciplined the soldiers and collected supplies. Hospitals were established, and surgeons appointed to them, as well as to the regiments, and medicines and medical stores provided. Through the sagacity of Samuel Adams, committees of correspondence and of safety were established in nearly every town and county in the several colonies, by which means the different sections of the country were kept advised as to the feelings of the people as well as the movements of the enemy.

Drs. Warren and Church and John Hancock were appointed a committee to inspect all medical and hospital stores that were on hand, and what additional were needed, and to supply the deficiency by purchase and voluntary contributions of the people.

Diplomacy having failed, the Continental Congress, then in session in Philadelphia, realized more fully the determination of Great Britain to subjugate the colonies, and on May 20, 1775, passed resolutions that the colonies be put in a state of defence, and that 20,000 men should be immediately equipped.

The colony of Massachusetts had, through her Provincial Congress, on the 26th of October, 1774, recommended the organization of her militia into companies, and their equipment.

Most of the other colonies had only a theoretical military system, or *quasi* military organization, with but very few arms and no military stores.

The province of Massachusetts had, under the circumstances, made all the martial preparations possible for defending her rights, and which seemed, in the opinion of the commanders, to justify more active operations. The first movement, however, brought on the engagement, which is known in history as the battle of Bunker Hill, and the burning of Charlestown. In that engagement the Americans numbered, all told, according to the estimates of Gen. Washington, 2,200, of which, probably, not more than 1,500 were in action; while the British had not less than 4,000 trained and disciplined soldiers. The battle was closely contested, as is evinced by the losses on both sides, which were heavy, considering the forces engaged, with a more than ordinary proportion of officers. The British had 19 commissioned officers killed and 71 wounded. The Americans mourned the loss of Gen. Joseph Warren, Col. Gardner, Lieut.-Col Parker, Maj. Moore and Maj. McClancy.

There has been some question among historians as to whom belongs the honor of commanding the provincials. Dr. James Thacher, a surgeon of constant active service throughout the whole war, and who kept a journal of events, supposed to have been recorded at the time from day to day, says, on page 29:

> *On the American side, Gens. Warren, Putnam, Pomeroy and Col. Prescott were emphatically the heroes of the day, and their unexampled efforts were crowned with glory. The incomparable Prescott marched at the head of the detachment, and, though several general officers were present, he retained the command during the action. To these names should be added those of Gens. Ward and Joseph Warren. The latter fell in the engagement.*

The whole community mourned the heroic doctor's death, for all classes ranked him among the brightest and most self-sacrificing of their patriots.

If any disposition had been wanting, the events of the winter and the skirmishes at Concord and Lexington determined the necessity for the reassembling of Congress, which met in Philadelphia September 5, 1774, and remained in session about two months. Little was done beyond adopting a Bill of Rights, and again petitioning the King.

It reassembled in the same city May 10, 1775. The term United Colonies was first used officially in a resolution passed June 7, 1775, appointing July 20 as a day of prayer, to be observed by the twelve "United Colonies." Georgia at this time was not represented in the Provincial Congress.

It was characteristic of the chivalry of America that the colonies should declare themselves free and independent by the adoption of the Declaration of Independence, as they did July 4, 1776, before they would agree upon a definite union among themselves. Though Dr. Franklin had strongly urged in a convention held in Albany, June 14, 1754, a union for defence as well as for government, the articles of confederation between the provincial colonies were, however, only agreed upon July 12, 1776. So it will be seen that the battles of Lexington and Concord, the capture of Fort Ticonderoga, the capture of Crown Point, and the battle of Bunker's Hill were fought by the four New England colonies without treaties of union, but with perfect and earnest sympathy and interest, and in perfect accord.

The term "United States" was, by resolution of Congress, substituted in all commissions and official papers for that of "United Colonies" September 9, 1776.

The autonomy of a nation was created by the adoption of the Declaration of Independence and the recognition of the government in the Continental Congress.

The battle fought at Boston, which threw the whole country into the highest state of excitement and alarm—as in the instance of the Confederates firing upon Fort Sumter in the late civil war—was followed so naturally the next year by the Declaration of Independence as to give *éclat* and popularity to the latter measure, as it flattered the martial spirit and pride of the country.

It was a sad Saturday night and Sunday which followed the battle of Bunker Hill. The carrying of the wounded to their homes or to private houses and hospitals, the burying the dead, with all the scenes of private grief and camp excitement, gave a very mournful aspect to the day and to the religious exercises, which were well calculated to produce a profound impression on all who were capable of reflection.

The private houses could no longer accommodate the sick and wounded, so that additional hospitals had to be improvised. The wounded during the battle were removed to the west side of Bunker Hill, and from there to Cambridge. The army had no well-disciplined corps ready with convenient stretchers on which to convey the wounded from the field of action to the rear or comfortable ambulances to take them thence to the hospitals. The soldiers' blankets or quilts, with muskets or poles, improvised a sort of cot, and the common wagon, cart or sled was the precursor for the roomy and easy-motioned ambulance used in the army of to-day.

The Provincial Congress of Massachusetts on June 22, 1775, took further steps to secure a greater number of surgeons, so as to insure proper attention to the sick and wounded in the hospitals, as well as on the field. Greater surgical proficiency and a more regular system for the prompt care and treatment of sick and wounded soldiers had now become a necessity, and Congress was active in affording relief in every possible way. The surgeons then in service were instructed to improvise hospitals as best they could. The patriotism of all classes was so active and sympathetic that this was, for a time, an easy matter.

As might be expected, the demand for hospital accommodation was increasing.

On June 22, the Provincial Congress appointed Dr. Frank Kitredge to attend the hospitals until further orders of Congress, and instructed the colonies to nominate suitable physicians to act as surgeons to the regiments. One hospital was directed to be provided for the camp at Roxbury, and a committee appointed to carry the measure into effect.

Contagious diseases, the pest of armies, had actually made their appearance, and the Hospital Department was adopted by the Provincial Congress of Massachusetts, June 28, 1775. The same form was, with a variation as to the character of the service, used for surgeons' mates, who were also ranked among the commissioned officers.

On July 1, the Congress of Massachusetts directed a committee of three, with Dr. Taylor chairman, to report how the sick and wounded should be removed to the hospitals, and on July 3, a committee was appointed to prepare a letter to Gen. Washington, who had just assumed the command of the army, and inform him what provisions had been made for the sick and wounded.

On July 4, a list of the surgeons and surgeons' mates who had up to this time been examined and approved by the committee were reported to the Provincial Congress of Massachusetts, and warrants ordered to be made out for them.

We find that thirty-one medical men rendered service in the battle of Bunker Hill—most of them were at the time, or very soon after became, surgeons or surgeons' mates. A few of the physicians named served in this engagement as commanding officers, and a few as minute-men in the ranks. The physicians who were in this memorable battle are all worthy of being mentioned. Their names are hereunto appended:

Adams, Elijah.
Bacon, Jacob.
Blanchard, Samuel.
Brickett, James.
Brooks, John.
Crooker, John.
Dexter, William.
Downer, Eliphalet.
Durant, Edward.
Eustis, William.
Foster, Isaac.
Fridges, Harris Clasy.
Green, Ezra.
Hard, Isaac.
Hart, John.
Hastings, Walter.
Herrick, Martin.
Jones, David.
Kittredge, Thomas.
Putnam, Aaron.
Shepard, David.
Spofford, Isaac.
Tenney, Samuel.
Townsend, David.
Vinal, William.
Warren, John.
Warren, Joseph.
Watson, Abraham.
Welsh, Thomas.
Willard, Levi.
Williams, Obadiah.

Gen. Joseph Warren, who was the most eminent of the list, was killed, and Lieut-Col. James Brickett was wounded. Dr. Benjamin Church would no doubt have participated in the engagement, but he was absent, having been sent in May by the Provincial Congress of Massachusetts, of which he was a member, as a confidential agent to Philadelphia, to consult the Continental Congress convened in that city relative to such matters as were necessary for the defence of the colony and particularly the state of the army.

On July 7, Dr. Isaac Foster was commissioned surgeon of the hospital at Cambridge, and Dr. Isaac Rand as surgeon at the hospital at Roxbury.

The habit of naming military hospitals—like forts—after prominent and popular generals, obtained then as during the late civil war.

Misunderstandings about rank among the officers early showed themselves in different parts of the army, chiefly on account of the want of system or precision in the regulations. This was particularly true of the Medical Department, where they soon grew to be a source of much discontent and recrimination.

For some reason the rank of a hospital surgeon was at first esteemed higher than that of a regimental surgeon, which order the latter desired to reverse. This of course culminated in jealousies, discords, and unharmonious treatment of each other, as I have also seen many times instances of in the late civil war.

The Committee of Safety of the colony of Massachusetts made military appointments as well as the Provincial Congress, as this body commissioned Dr. John Warren, July 27, 1775, chief surgeon to the hospital at Watertown, and Dr. Isaac Foster was commissioned to remove all practicable cases to said hospital and draw on the commissary for funds and supplies.

Experience had already demonstrated the need of a surgeon-in-chief as a general head to the Medical Department. The Provincial Congress of Massachusetts had already discussed the matter, and was about to elect one for the troops of the colony of Massachusetts, when Gen. Washington arrived at Boston, on July 2, 1775, to whom, with great delicacy, they referred the whole subject.

The General on taking command, July 3, made an inspection of the fortifications and camps, and shortly after of all the hospitals. The condition of the latter he made the subject of a special letter to Congress.

Although Congress had on June 15, 1775, accepted the Colonial armies then in the field as Continental, and chosen a general-in-chief to command all the forces raised or to be raised, and provided for the appointment of generals and staff officers, yet no provision was made for the hospital department.

The first legislation by Congress touching the Medical Department then denominated Hospital service, was had July 19, 1775, which created a committee of three to report on a method of establishing a hospital. Messrs. Lewes of

New York, Paine of Massachusetts, and Middleton of South Carolina, constituted the committee.

On July 27, a report was made to the Continental Congress on the subject, which was adopted; this act gave authority and some system to the management of the Medical Department. It was designed for an army of only 20,000, but as experience proved, the law was not well digested, nor adopted in all its provisions for the best interests of a volunteer force; the force to consist of one director-general and surgeon-in-chief, his pay per day four dollars, four surgeons at one and one-third dollars, one apothecary at one and one-third dollars, twenty surgeons' mates at two-thirds of a dollar, two storekeepers at four dollars per month each, one nurse to every ten sick, at one-fifteenth of a dollar or two dollars per month. Dr. Church was elected as director, he to appoint the four surgeons. The mates to be appointed by the surgeons, the others to be appointed by the director. Although this act gave titles it bestowed no military rank.

The appointment of Dr. Church as director gave a head to the department, which hitherto had no unity of action or continental authority.

Dr. Joseph Warren could have had this position, but as it was understood that he preferred the more active and arduous duties of the field the commission of Major General in the army was given to him.

Dr. Church was a man of education, fine address, and skilled in his profession. From an early stage of the movements which led the colonists to independence he was an ardent and able patriot. He probably ranked as third or fourth in point of influence among the leading men of Massachusetts and would have been held in the highest esteem by his compatriots and by succeeding generations but for his own indiscretion. His administration of the Medical Department, during the few months that he held the position was not, however, marked by harmonious or successful management. Misunderstandings with the regimental surgeons led to very frequent complaints rather than to improvement of the Medical Department of the service. To a complete understanding of the doctor's position it should be borne in mind that he had rivals for his position among the medical men then in the service. That he suspended them for fomenting discontent is evident from his letter to Gen. Sullivan, September 14, 1775.

Able, accomplished and beloved as Dr. Church was by the leading patriots as well as the whole community, the weakness of human nature was painfully exemplified in him by his attempt to correspond secretly, by means of cipher, with parties within the enemy's lines, which being detected, he was arrested, tried by court martial of which Gen. Washington was president, October 3,

1775, and found guilty of "holding criminal correspondence with the enemy." The Provincial Congress of Massachusetts, of which body he was a member, by a unanimous vote expelled him November 4, 1775. A record of his trial and his answers may be seen in the American Archives, vol. iii, p. 958.

On October 17, 1775, Congress elected Dr. John Morgan director-general and physician-in-chief in the hospitals, in the place of Dr. Church.

Dr. Morgan's competitors for the position were Dr. Isaac Foster, surgeon of the hospital in Cambridge, and Lieut. Col. Hand, a resident of Pennsylvania, and at the time a surgeon in the army. Dr. John Morgan was a native of Pennsylvania, and had received his academic degree from the University of Pennsylvania, in Philadelphia, and his doctorate from the University of Edinburgh. He was a professor in the University of Pennsylvania, and the success which attended his administration in that institution gave him a prestige, and was of itself a first-class endorsement. His ability as a surgeon, his character as a man, his patriotism, and his influence as a citizen, were widely known to the public.

Therefore no more fitting appointment of chief medical officer could have been made.

Immediately after his commission was issued, he reported for duty to Gen. Washington at Cambridge. On his arrival, he found the hospitals crowded with sick, many of whom ought to have been treated in the camp, tents or barracks of the regiments. Reform in hospital management was at once commenced, which received the earnest sympathy and support of Gen. Washington. Dr. Morgan's displacement by Congress, early in 1777, was from nearly all quarters pronounced hasty and an undeserved censure upon his administration of the Medical Department.

The difficulties complained of arose from defects in legislation and other causes beyond the control of the medical officers. Dr. Morgan on entering upon his duties understood that he was expected to make the necessary medical appointments in the hospital department. This authority was also given to a limited extent to the surgeon in charge of the northern department and to the surgeon of the southern hospital in Virginia. The same view it would seem was at first held by Congress which on several occasions referred surgeons to him for appointment.

The practice, however, excited jealousies and had finally to be discontinued and all the appointments thenceforth came from Congress.

The separate command under Gen. Schuyler, operating in Canada, was at this time suffering greatly for want of surgeons, medical supplies, and particularly from inefficient medical management. Dr. Samuel Stringer, of Albany, was first employed by Gen. Schuyler, August 27, 1775, and commissioned by Congress September 14, 1775, director of the hospital and physician for the northern department of the army, and with authority to appoint a number of surgeons' mates, not exceeding four.

The doctor was a native of Maryland, and had studied medicine in Philadelphia, and had served as a surgeon in the British army in America, and was therefore presumed to be familiar with the duties and requirements of a medical director.

A misunderstanding of the powers and duties of the medical director, soon arose between Drs. Morgan and Stringer, so that Congress, August 20, 1776, passed the following among other resolutions:—That "Dr. Morgan was appointed director-general and physician-in-chief of the American hospitals. That Dr. Stringer was appointed director and physician of the hospital in the northern department only."

Gen. Washington had so fortified his position during the winter, that the British could no longer hold Boston; they therefore evacuated it Sunday, March 17, 1776. The theatre of active operations for the remainder of the war moved southward.

Armies had been collecting in the vicinity of New York. The British had other forces still farther to the south than those massed at the mouth of the Hudson, with a view of distracting the colonial sentiment, and to conceal from the Americans the real point of intended attack. Norfolk, Virginia, was burned January 1, 1776. A strong naval force also attacked Charleston, South Carolina, June 28, 1776, but was most gallantly repulsed.

The Declaration of Independence, the crowning political event of the age, had the effect of consolidating public sentiment and creating a permanent national policy in America.

The difficulty of transportation and of providing supplies for an army at that period can scarcely be realized by the present generation, accustomed as we are to bridged streams, good roads, to steamboats and railroads, such as we had and proved such a factor in the late civil war. Dr. Morgan received a special order April 3, 1776, for the removal of the hospital to New York. The minute details of this order show the great humanity and thoughtfulness of Gen. Washington, who expresses his full confidence in the zeal and ability of Dr. Morgan.

Dr. Morgan discharged this duty with promptness and fidelity, and reports to Gen. Washington in a letter from Cambridge, April 22, 1776.

The hospitals provided at New York, as well as the regulations for their management, were an improvement on those hitherto established. Experience was beginning to yield fruits. The surgeons and mates were becoming more familiar with their duties, and a rivalry for promotion began to develop.

But the jealousy of the regimental surgeons and hospital surgeons was growing more and more pronounced. The law relating to hospitals, passed by Congress July 17, 1776, it had been hoped would have promoted efficiency, allayed prejudices, and inspired confidence.

The battle of Long Island was fought August 27, 1776, which resulted in the loss to the Americans of nearly 1,000 men, and compelled Gen. Washington to retire from the city of New York.

Gen. Lee, in a letter to Congress from New York, February 9, 1776, suggests, that in consequence of the augmentation of troops there, a hospital be established at that place without loss of time. Upon the massing of both armies in and around New York, as a matter of course hospitals were provided, and the demand upon them constantly increased. These hospitals were chiefly in private houses, as the barracks, which had been provided for that purpose, had to be used for sheltering the troops. Queen's College was also used as a barracks.

Dr. Morgan, in anticipation of a great battle, made application to the New York convention in person, for the assignment of houses for hospitals. The failure of the Continental troops to hold New York against the British army, suddenly and violently deranged all previous plans for hospital accommodations in and about the city of New York. At Albany, a hospital was opened in July, 1776, in a building erected for a hospital during the French war, and which was capable of accommodating about 500 patients, besides quarters for the officers, store rooms, etc. To this the sick and wounded from Crown Point, Ticonderoga, and the northern army were generally removed. After the surrender of Gen. Burgoyne's army, Albany was overcrowded with sick and wounded soldiers and officers of both armies. Dr. Thacher in his journal draws a graphic picture of the hospitals at Albany. He says the British and Hessian troops were accommodated in the same hospital with our men. He further says that the British surgeons who took care of their own men were remarkable for their dexterity and skill, while on the other hand the Germans, with but very few exceptions, did no credit to the profession, but were uncouth and clumsy operators, and appeared utterly destitute of sympathy and tenderness of feelings for the suffering patients.

The fatigue and suffering of the troops in the battles which preceded the crossing of the American army into New Jersey, told severely on the health of the soldiers, so that the director-general and hospital surgeons were taxed to their utmost to provide cover and hospital supplies. Large hospitals were established during that winter at Peekskill, Fishkill, and other places in New York.

The vigilance and efforts of Gen. Heath to provide comfortable quarters for the soldiers, both sick and well, under his command, may be taken as a fair sample of the spirit with which the commanders executed their duties. The literature of the period is full of their appeals to Congress, as well as to local governments, and entreaties to quartermasters, hospital directors, etc., to discharge their trust with dispatch and fidelity. The response of Dr. Morgan to Gen. Heath shows how carefully he had considered the subject of his duties, and the promptness with which he replied to the general's letter shows how every one was awake to the necessity and vital importance of this matter. It is quite certain, from the action of the New York Committee of Safety, December 7, 1776, that Gen. Heath had also applied to that body for assistance to render the condition of the soldiers under his command, at Peekskill and at other points on the Hudson river, as comfortable as possible for the winter.

The British pressed the American army and forced the battle of Harlem Plaints, which was fought September 16, and on the 28th of the same month the battle of White Plains, the two without any special result on either side. But the loss of Fort Washington, November 16, and Fort Lee on the 18th, disheartened and greatly reduced the active strength of the army, which retreated into New Jersey and went into winter quarters.

Notice has been made of the provisions for the sick by the colonies of Massachusetts and Connecticut. All the others were equally solicitous on the subject, but the records on this subject, so far as I have had access to them, are on this point not well preserved, or are more difficult of access.

The southern people, too, at an early period of the struggle, made liberal provisions to establish hospitals and to procure competent surgeons and surgeons' mates for the army. Prior to the battle of Bunker Hill, or the Declaration of Independence, Virginia statesmen had discussed in convention the subject of establishing several hospitals at convenient points for the care and treatment of the sick and wounded soldiers, and had brought the subject to the attention of the Continental convention. The result of this deliberation was the establishment at Williamsburg, Virginia, of a large and well-appointed hospital, which was maintained to the close of the war. The compensation made by Virginia to medical men in pay and bounty far exceeded that of any colony.

December 8, 1775, Congress resolved that companies for two battalions be raised in New Jersey, and that a surgeon be allowed for each battalion. Dr. William Barnet, Jr., was elected surgeon to Lord Stirling's, the first battalion raised in New Jersey. Separate commands were multiplying, and, therefore, the necessity for separate and well-defined districts, with medical directors of good executive ability for each. The medical appointments by Congress, at this period, had probably this policy in view.

The exigencies of the war caused the collection of a very considerable militia, as well as Continental military forces, in and around Philadelphia during the winter of 1776 and 1777. With this concourse of troops, of course, came the demand for increased hospital accommodations. Congress passed a resolution looking to obtain the use of Pennsylvania Hospital for the use of the sick troops of the Continental army. The council of safety cooperated actively in the measure, and appointed a committee to confer with the board of war and to complete all needed arrangements for the accommodation and proper care of the sick and wounded. Dr. Thomas Bond, Jr., had charge of the hospital at Elizabeth Town, which he was directed to move to Philadelphia—which he did by placing his patients on a boat; no destination being at first determined upon. But the same day, in writing to his father, Dr. Thomas Bond, he says:

> *I have leave to carry my sick where I think proper, and have, therefore, determined to proceed with them to Philadelphia. I therefore request you will direct the bearer, John Long, in my employ, to wait on Gen. Mifflin and request him to issue orders for the reception of forty sick at some convenient place near the town, if such can be had. I should be obliged to you to consult Gen. Mifflin upon a proposal I have made of instituting hospitals for the sick at Darby, Chester, Marcus Hook, Wilmington and New Castle. I think the water carriage, from Trenton to these places, would save much carting and be more comfortable for the sufferers; and this plan is, I think, much better than the one now proposed of sending the sick to East Town (Easton), Bethlehem, Nazareth, Reading.*

The sympathy of many of the leading members of the profession was actively enlisted, not only for the cause of the colonies, but to the effort in lending their advice and aid for the relief of the sick and wounded soldiers. Besides the Pennsylvania Hospital, the poorhouse, some stores and many private houses were for a time used as hospitals. But, very properly, it was the desire of the medical directors to have the hospitals located at some distance from, or at least outside, the city. The largest were established at Bethlehem, Reading, Manheim, Lancaster and Bristol.

This was a season of great discontent and complaint, felt to be chargeable to the general management, or rather mismanagement, of the war, which—it was not prudent to criticize-could with impunity be indulged in against the hospitals, so that it became popular to decry their management.

This was aggravated by the fact that the American army had concentrated during the winter of 1776 and 1777, in the vicinity of Philadelphia, where Congress was then in session, so that all classes became familiar with the distress of the troops, which had the effect of exciting the philanthropists to make representations to members of Congress and persons influential with the military committee to secure greater comforts for the sick. Many suggestions were, in consequence, made to the generals and to Congress, but the scope of this paper will not admit of my noticing others than those in which the medical profession were interested.

The conviction was grounded in the minds of many that the organization of the Medical Department was defective and required some radical changes. This was, no doubt, the motive which induced a number of medical men to made suggestions to generals, to Congress, and to individual members of that body, looking to its improvement, and which finally led to radical changes in its organization. June 6, 1776, Dr. Jonathan Potts was appointed physician and surgeon in the Canadian department, or at Lake George, but not to supersede Dr. Springer.

The legislation in Congress at this time was, notably, in the direction of separate departments or divisions. On October 9, 1776, Dr. William Shippen, Jr., was appointed to provide and superintend a hospital for the army in New Jersey, leaving the hospitals on the east side of the North river under the control of Dr. Morgan.

The appointment of Dr. Shippen to a directorship in the hospital department, without any consultation, as far as we know, with Gen. Washington or Dr. Morgan, seems to have been brought about by the general discontent of the people and the army, and by the friends of Dr. Shippen who had influence in Congress, and, possibly, his own solicitation. The resolution of Congress, which enlarged his authority and power, would seem to give color to this hypothesis. His view of the duties of the position, assigned him by Congress, was not promptly acquiesced in or understood in the same way by commanders generally, and led him to write complainingly on the subject to Gen. Washington. The general's reply not proving satisfactory to him he wrote on the same subject and complained to Congress, and even reflects on the course pursued by Dr. Morgan and Gen. Washington. Dr. Shippen's letters are diplomatic, and show that he felt confident that he and Congress had come to an understanding on the subject of the future medical management of the hospital department. The further legislation, which required weekly reports from the hospital surgeons as to the condition and number under treatment, was an important step in securing efficiency in the medical corps. It was surprising that this had been so long neglected, but an examination of this particular phase of hospital management and military discipline makes it apparent that no good system of hospital returns ever came into use during the Revolutionary war.

Dr. Morgan, director-general of hospitals, made numerous appeals to Congress for more definite instructions as to his duties and powers over the hospitals in the northern division of the army, and particularly as to his furnishing them with medicines, and making medical appointments in the same. It seems that the medical director in that division of the army, made no report to Dr. Morgan or to Congress of the number sick, or of his hospital accommodations. No information was available on which could be based an exact judgment as to the medical management of that department. Believing it to be his duty, Dr. Morgan had always sent supplies and hospital stores when applied to, and had on one occasion appointed a medical officer, whose services, however, were not accepted. This loose and unsystematic management, Dr. Morgan foresaw must lead to unpleasant complications in the department, and dissatisfaction with the commanders and with Congress. The doctor, in his anxiety, and almost in despair, wrote to Samuel Adams a graphic account of the condition of the army in Canada, and suggested relief through additional legislation. It cannot, therefore be claimed, that Dr. Morgan was either ignorant of or indifferent to the condition and sufferings of the troops in the northern army. Indeed, it is evident on almost every page of the history of this period that he made frequent and urgent appeals to Congress upon the subject, and used his best endeavors to improve the management of the Medical Department in every division of the army. Much complaint of sickness and suffering on account of deficiencies of the medical stores in the northern department continued to be made to Congress. The physician-in-chief of that department would not concede that he was to receive orders from Dr. Morgan, who had on all occasions when applied to, promptly sent medical supplies, as was his duty, and he had also appointed suitable surgeons to attend the soldiers suffering in that region. But his appointees were not recognized, and their pay had been refused on technical grounds. Dr. Morgan's explanation of the condition of affairs was succinct and frank, and should have satisfied Congress. Under date July 18, 1776, Dr. Morgan communicated to Gen. Washington a plan for the better management of the hospital department.

The spirit of antagonism and jealousies existing between the regimental and hospital surgeons, extended in many instances to the corps and regimental commanders. The real source of the difficulty was defective legislative provisions, a want of reciprocal courtesies, and a spirit of accommodation of the different departments, and the impossibility on the part of the director-general to obtain supplies in sufficient quantities at all times, or to distribute them with that promptness desirable, which sudden emergencies and military disasters often rendered impracticable. Officers of all grades in the various departments were in the habit of writing exaggerated complaints to the council of safety and to Congress, and because sympathy could most certainly be excited in favor of the soldier, the hospital department was taken as the theme for denunciation and accused of most cruel neglect, and in some cases of absolute inhumanity, and the gravest charges were brought against the surgeons; a good illustration of the complaints, and the wholesale fault-finding indulged in on the part of correspondents, and the inconsiderate arraignment of the hospital management, as the sole cause of discontent, want of comforts, suffering among the troops, may be found in a letter of Gen. W. Smallwood, to the Council of Safety of Maryland—[See American Archives, vol. ii, p. 1099.]

The enthusiasm with which the people had at first rushed into the military service, began to be qualified by calmer reason, whilst in some, selfish propensities developed themselves, and influenced individual action. Gen. Washington, in a letter September 24, 1776, had expressed to Congress the view, that in order to secure the highest efficiency, there ought to be one recognized head to the whole Medical Department, in which he deprecated the indiscriminate appointment of surgeons, but that they should all be regularly examined as to their skill and proficiency by a regular government board of examiners, which would do away with appointments by favoritism; and often incompetent men were thus appointed and much mischief resulted therefrom. This was also Dr. Morgan's view, but he was at the same time anxious to conform to the wishes of Congress. That Gen. Washington entertained a high regard for medical men, and felt bound to secure them full justice in the army, is evidenced by his letter to Gen. Smallwood, January 13, 1778, relative to the British brig Symetry, which had been captured by Gen. Smallwood's forces in the Delaware, near Wilmington. The prize contained very many articles much needed by the officers and soldiers in camp; hence the feverish anxiety of all as to the regulations and principles which should govern the distribution of the cargo. The letter, so far as I know, has never been published.

It is still in a good state of preservation, and is now the property of Dr. James C. Hall, of Washington, D.C. A literal copy is given, as follows:—

HD. QTS., VALLEY FORGE, Jan. 13, 1778.

DEAR SIR:—Since writing to you this morning on the subject of the prize Brig Symetry, the Regulations of the First officers of the Division for conducting the Sale and disposing of the cargo was laid before me with a letter from the Regimental Surgeons and Mates to Doctor Cochran. These Gentlemen feel themselves so much hurt by the discrimination made by these Regulations between them and the officers of the Division that they have sent in their Resignations.

As the common Guardian of the Rights of every Man in this Army I am constrained to interfere in this matter and to say that by these regulations a manifest injury is intended not only to the Gentlemen in the Medical line but to the whole Staff, who, supposing the prize should be adjudged the sole property of the Captors (a matter in my opinion not easily to be reconciled on principles of Equity and Reason) have as good a right to become purchasers in the first instance and to all other privileges, as any Officers in the Division.

For these Reasons therefore I desire you will not proceed to a Sale or distribution of any of the Articles, Except the Vessel, till you have my further directions, and that you will as early as possible transmit me an inventory of the Baggage and Stores.

The letter to Congress is nevertheless to go on, and you will please to forward it by the first conveyance.

I am Dear Sir,
Your most Obt. Servt.,
G. WASHINGTON.
GENERAL SMALLWOOD

Growing out of the capture referred to in the foregoing letter was the following request, made by Gen. Washington, January 22, 1778, of Gen. Smallwood, which furnishes additional evidence of his consideration for medical men and the medical profession, in his desiring to return to a British surgeon books and manuscripts taken in the prize Symetry. "A few days ago," he says,

> *I received a very polite letter from Dr. Boyer, surgeon of the Sixteenth regiment, British, requesting me to return [to] him some valuable medical manuscripts, taken in the brig Symetry. He says they are packed in a neat kind of portable library, and consist of Dr. Cullen's lectures on the Practice of Medicine, thirty-nine or forty volumes; Collin's lectures on the Institute of Medicine, eighteen volumes; anatomical lectures, eight volumes; and Dr. Black on Chemistry, nine volumes, the whole in octavo. If they can be found, I beg that they may be sent to me, that I may return them to the Doctor. I have no other view in doing this, than that of showing our enemies that we do not war against the sciences.*
>
> —*Spark's Life and Writings of Washington, vol. v, p. 223.*

Gen. Washington's views, which were substantially those of Dr. Morgan, as to hospital management, were at a later period adopted. In the interest of good management and immediate improvement in the Medical Department, with the approval of Gen. Washington, a conference was had early in July, at the request of Dr. Morgan, between the regimental surgeons and mates and himself, at which regulations for the government of the Medical Department were adopted, the first of which we have any record. [See American Archives, 5th series, vol. 1, p. 108.]

Congress was steadily assuming a more complete supervision of all the military operations (see Jour. Congress April 7, 1777); yet the spirit of independence in the colonies, and indeed the necessity of their home defences, rendered it necessary to maintain a colonial as well as a continental army. A proper subordination was often difficult, but with good will as a basis, system and order, and therefore, strength, were gradually developing in all the departments.

With a view to further improve the Medical Department, Congress, September 3, 1776, passed resolutions requiring examiners to be appointed to determine upon the qualifications of those applying to enter the medical service, and requiring their approval before appointments should be confirmed.

The General Assembly of Connecticut, whose soldiers had been largely employed in the Lake region, where there had been much suffering from sickness and possibly inefficient management on the part of the medical officers, passed October, 1776, a resolution to create a committee of medical gentlemen to examine applicants for admission as surgeons and mates into the army and navy belonging to the colony. The form of an oath was at the same time prescribed, which all were required to subscribe to; both examiners and applicants being required to take this oath.

The leading men of Connecticut were patriotic, vigilant and well informed in what was essential in raising and properly equipping an army. The soldiers were brave and among the earliest to take the field and win distinction by their prowess; they were poorly supplied for a long campaign, however. The comfort of the soldier and his care and skillful treatment when sick or wounded was held to be a paramount duty of the officers and the State government. Connecticut was the first to suggest and put in operation convalescent hospitals; which no doubt prevented much suffering, and assisted in restoring many to health and future usefulness in the army, who, if longer neglected, would have sunk beyond recovery. Perhaps the largest of the general hospitals in this State was at Stamford, of which Dr. Philip Turner was the surgeon in charge.

To meet the requirements of the service in supplying and distributing medicines and hospital stores to the army, Congress, in August, appointed Dr. William Smith, of Philadelphia, a druggist to the army, with a salary of $30 per month. Dr. Stringer, having failed to give satisfaction, notwithstanding the strong personal friendship to Gen. Schuyler for him, was dismissed January 9, 1777, and Dr. Potts appointed to succeed him in authority.

The strenuous efforts of Dr. Morgan to place the hospital department on a better footing had caused many interested and some incompetent parties to oppose him.

This clamor against the doctor increased as the troops and officers collected in Philadelphia and mingled in society, and it was so pressed by his opponents, that he was at length summarily dismissed January 9, 1777, without a hearing; his reputation sacrificed, and his eminent abilities lost to his country, and this too in a very unjust manner. The doctor presented to Congress a defence of his official course while medical director of the Continental army, and asked that an inquiry be made into his official conduct. The subject was referred to a committee, but a report was not made until June 12, 1779. This report fully exonerated him from all blame, but did not restore him to the service, and placed the cause of removal on the ground of public policy. This committee consisted of Messrs. Drayton, Hoovie and Witherspoon.

Congress, on April 7, 1777, resumed the consideration of a report on the hospitals. Plans had been proposed by Dr. John Cochran and Dr. William Shippen, patterned after those of the British army, which received the endorsement of

Gen. Washington, and were adopted. These regulations were more explicit in prescribing the duties and powers of the department of medicine, and it divided the country into military districts, viz.: Eastern, Northern, Middle, and, inferentially, a Southern division; also making appointments of medical officers for each. Dr. James Tilton, in his little work on hospitals, says, that there were in 1781 thirteen divisions of military commands under major generals. New hospital regulations were also presented and adopted by Congress September 10, 1780. The following physicians were elected by Congress for their several positions;—

Dr. William Shippen, Jr., director-general of all the military hospitals; Dr. Walter Jones, physician-general of hospitals in the Middle department; Dr. Benjamin Rush, surgeon-general of hospitals in the Middle department; Dr. John Cochran, physician and surgeon-general of army in the Middle department; Dr. Isaac Foster, deputy director-general of hospitals in the Eastern department; Dr. Ammi Ruhamah Cutter, physician-general of hospitals in the Eastern department; Dr. Philip Turner, surgeon-general of hospitals in the Eastern department; Dr. William Burnet, physician and surgeon-general of army in the Eastern department; Dr. John Potts, deputy director-general of hospitals in the Northern department; Dr. Malachi Treat, physician-general of hospitals in the Northern department; Dr. Forgue, surgeon-general of the Northern department; Dr. John Bartlett, physician and surgeon-general of army in the Northern department.

The surgeons and mates had from 1776 been petitioning Congress for an increase of pay. In May, 1778, it was raised for surgeons $60, and mates $40 per month.

The depreciation in Continental currency increased, so that even this increase of pay became inadequate to their support. August 24, 1780, as an inducement to officers to continue in the service to the end of the war, Congress had devised and established a system of half-pay and commutation at the end of the war, which was so amended as to benefit widows and orphans, but in none of these acts was the hospital department or surgeons and mates included.

The schedule of pay adopted by Congress, in 1780, therefore but very slightly improved the Medical Department and did not, as was expected it would, include medical officers among those entitled to half-pay, etc. But on July 17, 1781, a law was passed placing surgeons and surgeons' mates upon an equal footing with other officers of similar grade.

Virginia with her immense territory of unoccupied lands, early made liberal provisions for disposing of it as a bounty or as land grants to her soldiers, including surgeons and mates who served to the close of the war either in her army or navy. The State finally ceded all her western lands to the United States. About 70 surgeons and surgeons' mates received land from Virginia for services in the Revolutionary war.

From this time forward the Medical Department had fewer annoyances, because of the better defined rules and greater familiarity with their duties; the higher standard of qualifications demanded for surgeons and mates in the regimental and hospital departments also added greatly both to the efficiency and harmony.

There was, however, much suffering in the army and also in the hospital department, during the year, or rather winter, of 1777 and 1778, chiefly from the scarcity of funds and deficient supplies of all kinds. Those were without exaggeration the dark years of the Revolution. But the fortitude and determination of the people were equal to the crisis. Nothing is so difficult as the beginning. The machinery for recruiting and supporting armies in the field was now getting into full operation, so that final success depended upon good generalship and the wisdom of Congress. If any army and country ever possessed these America was favored with them to an unexampled degree; all subsequent legislation upon hospital matters was in the direction of perfecting plans already inaugurated, the details of which are fully set forth in the journals of Congress. The separation of the purveying from the hospital management, was an important step in giving confidence to this branch of the service.

From what has been said, as I have been enabled to glean from a multitude of sources, I trust you all may be able to gather some idea of the difficulties that at first surrounded the surgeons of the Revolution, and the steps that led up to the systematic organization which even now exists, though somewhat improved upon in the United States army and navy. Of course in the hundred and more years past there have been many amendatory enactments and changes to bring the latter body up to its present efficiency, which is not now excelled by any similar organization in the wide world, and which has received repeated and well-deserved compliments from the profession and governments in Europe.

Large hospitals were established in the vicinity of New York, and a continental hospital was established at Providence, Rhode Island; the college building being used. A general hospital under the direction of Dr. John Warren, was opened at Long Island. After the battle of August, 1776, it was removed to Hackensack, New Jersey. One had already been established at Albany. We find in a report of Dr. Shippen to the board of war, November 1, 1776, that there were in New Jersey, two hospitals at Amboy, one at Elizabethtown, one at Fort Lee, one at New Brunswick and one at Trenton. In Pennsylvania, there were a number of hospitals in and near Philadelphia. A large general hospital was established at Bethlehem, in which Dr. Tilton says that one of the hospital surgeons, Dr. Joseph Harrison, died of typhoid fever, contracted in the discharge of his duties. A severe form of this disease had prevailed in the hospital at Trenton. The poorhouse at Philadelphia was used as a hospital during the time the army lay in the vicinity of that city. There was also a general hospital at Alexandria, and another at Williamsburg, Virginia. The dates when all these hospitals were established seem somewhat muddled. There were other general hospitals established at other points in the South.

It is greatly to be regretted that so few of the surgeons left any records of their observations and experiences. The number who have done so can be readily counted on the fingers, viz.: Thacher's Military Journal, Tilton on Military Hospitals, Rush's Observations on Diseases in Military Hospitals of the United States, and Dr. Ebenezer Beardsley's History of Dysentery in the Twenty-second regiment, Connecticut Troops.

The surgeons of that war had better results, considering their means and hospital facilities, by far than we could expect, wedded as they were at that time to salves, lint, and the cumbersome poultice dressings.

Dr. Tilton comments quite critically on the general management and condition of the hospitals in that critical and fatal period, 1777, and of the very large percentage of deaths-dwelling mainly upon the discords and mismanagements under the then existing regulations and legislation, together with the great lack of supplies, and of the necessary appliances as well as suitable quarters.

I could readily fill quite a large book, were I to discuss the career and noble traits and deeds of all the physicians and surgeons in the different departments, said departments numbering 23 at the close of the war, under the charge of the following medical gentlemen: John Bartlett, James Brown, William Brown, Nathaniel Brownson, William Burnet, Benjamin Church, John Cochran, James Craik, Ammi R. Cutter, Peter Fayssoux, Isaac Foster, Walter Jones, Adam Kuhn, Charles McKnight, John Morgan, David Oliphant, Jonathan Potts, Benjamin Rush, William Shippen, Samuel Stringer, Malachi Treat and Philip Turner. There was also a Dr. Bartlett, of Newburyport, who, November 4, 1776, had charge of the sick belonging to the fleet. This may be the same gentleman, as I find no other record of him. In the reorganization of the medical corps in 1780, this name does not appear, and it is probable that he did not enter upon the duty, or did not remain long in the service. There was a surgeon in Capt. James Keats' company of Maryland

(February 3, 1776), minute men, who marched from Queen Anne's county, Md., at this date, by the name of James Brown—possibly the same who was appointed subsequently by Congress as physician-in-chief of the Southern army. It would be useless, or rather almost impracticable, for me to enter into a full biographical sketch of each and all these worthies in my profession who took such a wholehearted and earnest part in the Revolutionary war. I will simply dot down a few of the most worthy of note to us, in our beloved State of New Jersey.

Dr. William Burnet, son of Ichabod Burnet, a distinguished physician of Elizabethtown, graduate from Nassau Hall, 1749, studied medicine with Dr. Staats, of New York City, and practiced in New Jersey; at the outbreak of the war he relinquished his very large and lucrative practice, and entered actively into the political movements of the day; was chairman of the committee of public safety; in 1776 was superintendent of a military hospital, which he established on his own responsibility at Newark; in 1776, was a member of the Continental Congress; October 11, 1777, he was appointed by Congress to be physician and surgeon general of the army in the Eastern department, whereupon he resigned his seat in Congress, and entered upon the arduous duties which he continued to discharge till the close of the war in 1783. He dined with Gen. Arnold on the evening that Maj. Andre was captured. After the war he was presiding judge of the court of common pleas, appointed by the legislature of New Jersey; was also the second president of the State Medical Society, 1767, as was also Dr. John Cochran, 1768; Dr. Nathaniel Scudder, 1770; Dr. Isaac Smith, 1771; James Newel, 1772; Absolom Bainbridge, 1773; Thomas Wiggins, 1774; and Hezekiah Stiles, 1775; after which date there was no meeting of the State Society till 1782, when John Beatty was president, Thomas Barber, in 1783; Lawrence VanDerveer, 1784; Moses Bloomfield, 1785; William Burnett, 1786; Johnathan Elmer, 1787; James Stratton, the father of Governor C.C. Stratton, 1788; Robert McKean being the first president of the society at its organization, 1766.

For notice of other medical gentlemen of New Jersey, who served or rendered aid and assistance to the Colonial government during that ever memorable struggle, which culminated in the establishment of the independence of our beloved country, and the taking its place among the nations of the world, with whom it now stands second to none, see the list taken from History of Medicine and Medical Men in New Jersey, by Dr. Stephen Wickes, of Orange, New Jersey, who was in 1883 president of the New Jersey Medical Society.

ELEVEN

THE AFFAIR AT EGG HARBOR

William Scudder Stryker, 1894

William Scudder Stryker, 1838–1900 (admitted 1876) was the great-great-grandnephew of Colonel Nathaniel Scudder.

Born in Trenton, New Jersey, Stryker was educated at Princeton College and was graduated in 1859. During the Civil War, he served as Major and aide-de-camp to Major General Quincy A. Gillmore, United States Volunteers. He was brevetted Lieutenant-Colonel for faithful and meritorious services during the war. According to *The Stryker Family History*,

> *Later due to illness, he was transferred to the Paymaster's Office at Columbus Ohio. On the way he stopped at Washington, D.C. to deliver some messages to President Lincoln. During their conversation William fainted from fever. Lincoln caught him in his arms, laid him down on a couch and helped him recover until he could return to his hotel.*

Stryker resigned his commission on June 30, 1866, and was appointed to various positions in the Adjutant-General's Office of New Jersey over the next eight years ending as a brevetted Major-General for long and meritorious service. General Stryker was a well-known historian and an authority on New Jersey history. He wrote an extensive reference of lists of the officers and men on the New Jersey rosters in the Revolution as well as lists of New Jersey soldiers in the Civil War. The General was President of the New Jersey Society of the Cincinnati from 1896 to 1900 (see illustration 14).

Strtyker is not currently represented in the Society.

Read July 3, 1894, at the dedication of a memorial tablet, erected on the field of the massacre by the Society of the Cincinnati in the State of New Jersey, and at the annual meeting of theSociety on the following day

The annals of the war for independence in America are replete with pages of fearful suffering, of cruelty and of bloodshed. The British soldiers' reputation for chivalry was stained again and again by acts of brutal passion and by the malignant butchery of an unprotected foe. Even as early in the war as the battle of Long Island, they record it as "a fine sight to see with what alacrity they dispatched the rebels with their bayonets, after we had surrounded them so they could not resist." The barbarities in the prisons and on the prison ships at New York fill the legendary history of the Revolutionary War, and the atrocious conduct of the army in the Southern States has left a stigma on the soldiery of the crown never to be effaced. The Tory marauder, the Indian ally and the Hessian hireling led the way in these deeds of blood-thirstiness, but the Highlander, the British dragoon and the British foot followed rapidly in the path of plunder, of rapine, and of murder. The year 1778 is particularly noted as being that period in the conflict during which most of these inhuman crimes were committed in the middle colonies. The massacre at Wyoming, the malicious attack on Andrustown, the brutality at German Flats, the bloody work at Old Tappan, all preceded the merciless affair which we are about minutely to describe. The brutish assault at Cherry Valley fitly closed a year conspicuous for its record of cruelty.

It is asserted by Stedman, the British military historian—and he was in a position to be correctly advised—that the predatory advance of Lord Cornwallis' division in New Jersey on the west wide of the Hudson River in September, 1778, an incident of which advance was the massacre at Old Tappan, and the change of position made by General Knyphausen and his Hessian troops on the east side of the river, was part of the general plan to divert the attention of General Washington from the expedition which had been fitted out to make an incursion on the Jersey coast at Little Egg Harbor. This movement of the British forces was certainly a correct military proceeding to successfully create a diversion of the patriot army.

During the early years of the war, Little Egg Harbor, a bay lying east of the main shore of old Burlington county, and separated from the ocean by a narrow sand dune, was, as the British officers called it, a "nest of rebel pirates." The sea-faring patriots of that section of the State were accustomed to slip out of the bay and capture many of the rich-laden cruisers which sailed between New York harbor and Delaware bay. The prizes taken were brought into Little Egg Harbor, and a vast amount of stores and other property was thus distributed among the daring sailors of that part of New Jersey.

Local tradition says that in this resort for American privateers, as many as thirty armed sloops at one time have been lying in wait for some heavy laden vessel which had been signaled off the shore-land. Late in the summer of 1778, two very valuable and important prize ships, the Venus and the Major Pearson, both under manifest from London, were towed into the harbor by these bold seamen. It became necessary, therefore, for the British commander, Sir Henry Clinton, to take speedy and sure measures to stop this business, which seriously menaced the commerce of the old country.

In the last week of September, a fleet of vessels was collected and placed in commission in New York harbor for the purpose of suppressing the work of these patriots. The vessels assigned for this duty were the sloops Zebra, Vigilant and Nautilus, with two galleys and four other armed boats—nine sailing vessels in all. Captain Henry Collins, of the Zebra, was ordered in command of the fleet. On these vessels were placed a detail of three hundred men of the Fifth Regiment British Foot and one hundred men of the Third Battalion New Jersey Volunteers. The former organization was an old regiment of the British Line and the latter a force of Loyalists. Captain Patrick Ferguson, Seventieth Regiment British Foot, was placed in command of this detail of soldiery.

A brief sketch of Captain Ferguson, the master spirit of this affair, will not be inappropriate. He was born in Aberdeenshire, Scotland, in the year 1744. At the age of fifteen, he purchased a commission as Cornet, dated July 12, 1759, in the Second Regiment British Dragoons and served in that command during the war in Flanders, where he distinguished himself greatly by his courage and ability. On September 1, 1768, he bought a commission as Captain in the Seventieth Regiment British Foot and with this command he took part in quelling an insurrection on the Island of Saint Vincent. Just before the opening of the war in America, he invented a new military rifle, and in the completion of his invention, he became very expert in the practice of this new weapon. He was soon afterward regarded as the best marksman in the British army. In the spring of 1777, he was sent to America and with a select corps of riflemen, he participated in the battle of Brandywine. In this battle, he was severely wounded in his right arm, from which disability he never fully recovered. On October 25, 1779, he was made the Major of the Second Battalion Seventy-first Regiment British Foot, which was commonly called the Highland Light Infantry. He was promoted to the rank of Lieutenant-Colonel on taking command of the American Volunteers in 1779, and setting out with the expedition against Charleston. He took a conspicuous part in the fight at McPherson's Plantation where he received a bayonet wound in his left arm, but this did not deter him from taking an active part in the massacre at Monk's Corner. In the latter part of April, 1779, he captured a fort at Haddrell's Point, near Charleston. In the fight at Cedar Springs, he distinguished himself by the skillful management of his troops. He entered on the fight at King's Mountain with a profane boast that he could not be dislodged from that natural defence, but the mountaineers of the surrounding country proposed to destroy his force; and at the close of the terrific fighting on the hillside, when first retreat and then flight was the desperate order of the British commander, several of Colonel Sevier's men took deliberate aim at Lieutenant-Colonel Ferguson and he fell from his horse pierced with six or eight bullets. He wore that day a light hunting shirt, and carried his sword in his left hand, but when he fell both garment and sword were soon covered with his blood. He died very soon after receiving these wounds and was buried in a hastily made grave on the side of the mountain.

On September 30, 1778, the fleet of Captain Collins weighed anchor and passed outside of Sandy Hook, but the weather soon became boisterous, and it was with some difficulty, owing to contrary winds, that they could sail down the Jersey coast. It was not until quite late in the afternoon of October 5th that the fleet appeared off the bar at an inlet, about a mile below what is now called Long Beach, the inlet then being designated as Little Egg Harbor Inlet. It was closed by the shifting sand in the year 1874.

The fact of the sailing of this expedition and its destination was immediately made known to General Washington, and he sent Count Pulaski and his Legion to the little village on Pohatcong creek, called "Middle of the Shore," now known as Tuckerton, to defend that part of the State. Governor William Livingston heard of it on the evening of September 29th, and at three o'clock the next morning called a meeting of the Council of Safety to take measures to defeat the enterprise. He immediately sent express riders into all that section of

Burlington county to arouse the inhabitants that they might be on their guard against this incursion and prepare to defend their homes.

The village, as we have said, was known as "Middle of the Shore," but the Orthodox Quakers, who lived in this section, generally spoke of the district as "Little Egg Harbor Monthly Meeting." Another name, however, had been given it, probably in derision, possibly from the toothsome bivalves found in the bay—"Clam Town." Judge Ebenezer Tucker, in 1786, named the place Tuckerton, giving, at the time, a great feast to his neighbors. It is said that after partaking of his bounty to the full, they left his house with an ungrateful cheer for "Clam Town."

Before the arrival of the British fleet, on the morning of October 2nd, three captured privateers, with six or eight guns each, and a strong, well-armed pilot boat had been sent out of the harbor to sea. All the other vessels, which could not be prepared quickly for ocean service, were sent some twenty miles up the creek to the small village of Chestnut Neck.

On the morning of October 6th, Captain Collins found that, owing to the winds, he was still unable to get his fleet inside the harbor, and Captain Ferguson, knowing full well that the whole neighborhood would soon be prepared for his attack, and waiting not for the passage of the sloops through the inlet, filled the galleys and armed boats with his soldiers and started up the creek in all haste.

Captain Ferguson had been informed by the Loyalists that Chestnut Neck was the nearest wharfage and store house for prize vessels and their goods, and he immediately ordered his party to row up the creek to that place. When they came near the village, which was obscured by a thick fog, they discovered the shipping, and instantly prepared to make a landing and an attack. As they reached the shore they were greeted with some little show of resistance from a small body of militia behind a breastwork [embankment] near the landing, and from another battery on a little piece of high ground behind it. Neither of these works, however, was provided with artillery. The landing of the British troops was effected under the fire of the galleys, and the only casualty was the wounding of one man of the Fifth Regiment. A charge was then made on the militia, driving them from the breastworks and compelling them to take refuge in an adjoining woods. Returning to the shore, the British found two large prize ships scuttled and dismantled, and these they destroyed.

They also burned eight other sloops and schooners, with some periaguas [skiffs] and large whaleboats. The twelve houses which constituted the little town were plundered and destroyed, as well as several barns belonging to the villagers. The store house near the wharf was stripped of all the goods it contained, and fired. The breastworks, which had afforded some scanty protection to the militia, were demolished. This completed the destruction of Chestnut Neck.

The day was well advanced when they had finished this work of plunder and devastation, and it was with great regret that Captain Ferguson obeyed the dictates of prudence and retired his force under the protection of the guns of the Zebra, the Vigilant and the Nautilus. It would have afforded him much pleasure to have pressed on about twenty miles up the creek to "The Forks," where he knew from the Tories that the principal depot for the captured goods had been located for many months. It was said that this place was but thirty-five miles from the Quaker city of Philadelphia, where, through the last long winter, the officers of the Fifth Regiment of British foot had reveled in routs, and in balls, in gaming, in masquerades and in cockfighting. But Mullica's creek was too shallow for their galleys, and forty miles was too far to push out from their supplies and from their fleet into a country aroused and excited. The eager desire to undertake this part of the expedition was, therefore, abandoned.

Before the British commander left Chestnut Neck on his return to the convoy, he was notified of the contiguity of three small salt works on Bass River. Orders were then given to steer the barges to the landing place of Eli Mathis, near the mouth of the river. Here the party again disembarked, and tradition says they were welcomed with a feast at a Tory farmer's, nearby. It is said that having heard that the British were in the vicinity, he concluded that the salt works would attract them, and that a generous table would perchance save intact both his property and his life. His hospitality and his loyalty to the crown availed him well, for having eaten of his banquet they left him unharmed. Not so did they serve the patriot Eli Mathis, for they destroyed his dwelling house and farm buildings, with all their contents. The salt works were then demolished, a saw mill burned, as well as twelve houses of well-known patriots near the banks of the Bass River.

It was not until the following day, Wednesday, October 7th, that Ferguson's party reached the inlet at the mouth of the harbor, and here they found the Zebra and the Vigilant aground on the bar. It took them all that day and night to lighten up the sloops, so that it was not until the next morning that the vessels were again afloat.

On the evening of the same day, October 8th, the force of Count Pulaski entered the little village [of] "Middle of the Shore," and proceeding down the Island Road, encamped on the farm of James Willets. This Legion of the distinguished Pole had arrived at Trenton on October 4th. The next evening,

Pulaski had heard of the anticipated descent on Little Egg Harbor, and on October 6th had started across the State "with all his troops in high spirits and with great alacrity." The command consisted of three companies of light infantry, a detachment of light artillery, but equipped with but one brass field piece, and three troops of light horse.

Brigadier-General the Count Casimer Pulaski was born in Podolia, March 4, 1748. He commenced his military life in the guard of Duke Charles of Courland. Afterward, he joined his distinguished father in the struggle for liberty in Poland as one of the Eight Associates of the Confederation of Barr. In the year 1770, he was elected Commander-in-Chief of the insurgent army, and, on its defeat, he was outlawed and fled to Turkey. With a heart full of sympathy for the cause of freedom everywhere, he came to America in March, 1777, and offered his sword to the Continental Congress. He was first temporarily attached to the Staff of General Washington, and in that capacity acted well at the battle of Brandywine and also took an active part in the fight on the streets of Germantown.[1]

At this time, the Congress of the United States placed Pulaski in charge of the cavalry of the army, and on September 15, 1777, commissioned him a Brigadier-General. He resigned the command of the cavalry on March 28, 1778, but later, under the order of Congress, began with the same rank to recruit a legion to consist of sixty light horsemen and two hundred foot soldiers. He was allowed to enlist deserters from the British and Hessian armies, and also prisoners of war. This he did principally in and around the city of Baltimore. In February 1779, having a second time recruited his Legion, he went to the South and took part in the siege of Savannah. In this fight, October 9, 1779, he was mortally wounded by a ball in the upper part of his right thigh and died two days later on the United States brig Wasp. Some reports say he was buried at sea, but a more probable statement is that he was interred on Saint Helena Island, South Carolina. Count Pulaski was accounted the finest swordsman and one of the best horsemen in the army, and frequently astonished his men by his marvelous feats of horsemanship. Tradition informs us that when his horse was at full gallop he would discharge his pistol, throw it in the air, catch it as it descended, again hurl it with all his power in front of him and with but one foot in the stirrup, pick it up from the ground and resume his position in the saddle. On the formation of his Legion, it is said that the Moravian Sisters, at Bethlehem, made for his command a beautiful flag of crimson silk, with neat designs embroidered in yellow silk

[1] *His conduct in this affair was the subject of an acrimonious controversy. An Associate Justice of the Supreme Court of the United States, Judge William Johnson, opened the subject in his life of General Nathanael Greene, and in 1826 a paper by him appeared in the North American Review in answer to a pamphlet entitled "Pulaski Vindicated," by Captain Paul Bentalow, of Baltimore, formerly an officer of the Legion.*

and surrounded with a deep green bullion fringe. The flag was twenty inches square, and the Legion carried it attached to a lance. It is now in possession of the Maryland Historical Society at Baltimore. Longfellow wrote a hymn in commemoration of this gift, the last stanza of which runs thus:

> "Take this banner, and if e'er
> Thou should'st press the soldier's bier,
> And the muffled drum should beat
> To the tread of mournful feet,
> Then this crimson flag shall be
> Martial cloak and shroud for thee!"
> And the warrior took that banner proud,
> And it was his martial cloak and shroud!

To return to the narrative. The Legion had encamped on the James Willets' farm, which is now owned by the heirs of the late Nathan Andrews. The present Andrews house stands on the old foundation, and some of it once formed a part of the Willets' farmhouse. From the front of the homestead—a fine old farmhouse still standing, with cedar-shingled roof and sides—a good view could be taken of the harbor and of the English fleet at anchor there. Pulaski had his headquarters in this house. A few hundred yards from the doorway, and nearer to Little Egg Harbor Bay, but concealed from the bay by a close growth of timber, which still remains, the troops of horse, the artillery and a portion of the infantry of the Legion were encamped. Farther down the Island road, and nearer to the lowlands and Osborn Island, was a picket post, occupied by about fifty infantrymen under the command of Lieutenant-Colonel the Baron de Bosen, the second in rank in the Legion. This post was the then untenanted farmhouse of Jeremiah Ridgway. The farm was afterwards sold to the Hubbs family, and subsequently came into the possession of Joseph Parker, whose daughter married the present owner, George S. Courtney, of Philadelphia. Mrs. Blackman in her interesting narrative says that the site of the house is still indicated by a hollow place in the ground and a cluster of trees.

On the afternoon of October 13, Lieutenant Gustav Juliet, of the Legion, organized a fishing party to go out on the bay, and having reduced three of their number to a state of helpless intoxication, and compelled two others to submit to their disgraceful proceedings, they signaled and were taken on the British fleet as deserters from the Americans. This renegade poured into the willing ears of Captain Ferguson a complete account of the strength and the position of Pulaski's force. Captain Ferguson always spoke of this man by the name of Bromville, but returns [his reports] show that it was as herein given. Juliet falsely informed Captain Ferguson that Pulaski had directed in orders that no quarter should be given to any of the British soldiery if at any time a fight ensued. This man Juliet had in 1777 belonged to one of the Landgrave regiments of Hessian troops, had deserted from them, and without a commission had been sent by the Board of War to do duty in the Legion as an acting Sub-Lieutenant. Lieutenant-Colonel the Baron de Bosen did not admire that style of a man who would desert his colors after once enrolling himself, and he did not show him any respect whatever. This it was that made Juliet seek to avenge himself, especially on De Bosen. When Juliet did not return from his fishing party that evening, it was supposed that he had been drowned in the bay, but it did not once occur to his comrades that he would a second time become a deserter.

In Vol. IV, Historical Magazine, page 136, a letter appears dated Newport, Rhode Island, January 11, 1779, saying, "In the fleet from Long Island arrived several Hessians, among them Lieutenant Juliet, of the Landgrave Regiment, who deserted to the Provincials when the island was besieged by them and then went back to New York. He is under an arrest."

From this letter it is apparent that even the great services of Juliet at the affair at Little Egg Harbor did not shield him from Sir Henry Clinton's wrath.

Soon after Captain Ferguson had returned from his Chestnut Neck expedition, and had relieved the war vessels which had been aground, Captain Collins, who on September 23, had been placed in chief command of the British fleet on the American station in the place of Lord Howe, received from Admiral Gambier a letter which had also the concurrence of Sir Henry Clinton directing him to return immediately to New York. But again the winds were contrary. As at first they had successfully foiled his attempt to enter the harbor promptly, so they would not now allow him to leave it. The British army no longer held any portion of New Jersey, from whence any aid or succor could be rendered, and the British commanders of both sea and land forces agreed that it was unwise to remain in that part of the State any longer. So day after day passed with the idle soldiers on board the wind-bound fleet. But Juliet's arrival and the information he brought determined Captain Ferguson to make an attack on that part of Pulaski's corps which had been cantoned [encamped] on the road leading to Osborn Island. He fully believed he could thus occupy his time to the advantage of the royal cause and could make good his retreat when it became necessary.

At an hour before midnight on October 14, 1778, Captain Ferguson, accompanied by the renegade Juliet, left the fleet with two hundred and fifty men, detachments from the British regulars and the Jersey Loyalists, and a number of marines attached to the war vessels. They proceeded somewhat over ten miles in their row-galleys to what in English reports is called Monhunk Island, but was then, and is now, better known as Osborn's Island. This little tract of land has been in a Quaker family of that name as far back as the first settlement of the country. The hostile force effected a landing between three and four o'clock in the morning of Thursday, October 15,[2] and Captain Ferguson immediately sent a party to guard the inmates of the dwelling house of Richard Osborn, Junior, and to force some man therein to guide them on the mainland to the picket post of the Americans. Mr. Osborn's son Thomas was instantly threatened with a drawn sword and compelled thus to accede to their will. He readily saw the outcome of this demand and begged that they would spare the lives of his neighbors. It does not appear in the sequel that any of the Ridgway family were injured. Marching across the island, they came first to a narrow defile and then to a bridge over what was called "The Ditch" on Big Creek. Here they found no sentinel, a criminal neglect of De Bosen, when he knew the enemy were so near. The British Commandant left fifty men at the bridge to secure his retreat. Then silently proceeding about a mile over a rough corduroy road across the salt meadows north of the bridge, they came suddenly at the bend of the Island Road, on the upland, upon a single sentry, whom they captured before he could discharge his firelock. This soldier being secured, and some accounts say he was killed, and the three houses nearby, which contained the picket guard, being descried, a rush was made by the whole command of Ferguson, and they succeeded in surrounding the entire party. In the meantime, Thomas Osborn, the unwilling guide, had concealed himself in the low meadow, and from his hiding place, he could distinctly hear the massacre which followed. The American infantry, awakened by the shouts of the British party around their houses, hastily seized their weapons and prepared to make a defence. Lieutenant-Colonel de Bozen led his men from the houses in their desperate charge to break the cordon of their captors. He was a large, soldierly man, of great personal bravery, and with both sword and pistol he vigorously fought the ranks of his foe. Juliet spied him and called out, "This is the Colonel; kill

[2] *Doctor Theodore T. Price, of Tuckerton, has ascertained by calculations that the moon was in the last quarter and rose about one o'clock A.M., and that high water in the harbor was between three and four o'clock* A.M.

him!" and instantly his body was pierced with many bayonets. The men cried out for quarter, but, as at Old Tappan, their appeals for life were disregarded. Some forty men, including the Lieutenant-Colonel in command and a subaltern officer, Lieutenant de la Borderie, were overpowered by the numbers of the enemy and cruelly butchered. Some British reports also add that two Captains were killed. Five men only were taken prisoners, and very few escaped. As Ferguson reported, they were "almost entirely cut to pieces." The British destroyed also some baggage and equipments of the Legion. Captain Ferguson implies in his report that he did not destroy the houses used by the infantry as quarters, for he wrote that "the injury that would have been done to the enemy would not have compensated for the sufferings of these innocent people." History, however, in many places informs us that he burned these houses of the Quaker settlers.

The first discharge of firearms at this encounter was heard at Pulaski's headquarters and at the camp of the cavalry of the Legion, scarcely more than a half mile distant. The General was instantly in the saddle, and while his command was "mounting in hot haste" he plunged spurs into his horse and dashed down a short wood road to give aid to De Bozen. But he was too late. The British after their cruel deed made a hasty retreat to the bridge and toward the island.

Pulaski and his troopers soon came up to the picket post, saw the dead bodies of his murdered officers and men lying near the burning houses, and without halting they dashed down the rough road in the track of the hurrying foe. On they way thither, they cut off a few of the straggling party who took to the low ground, but the mounted men were stopped at the creek where the planking had been torn up on the bridge. The stream, at that time, was not fordable by horses, but a little detachment of riflemen and a few light infantry, which had followed as closely as possible in the wake of the troopers, succeeded in getting across and in firing first on the upper and then on the lower side of the creek at the retreating enemy. In these volleys, they succeeded in doing some little damage. It was thought safer, however, to recall the men when it was found that the cavalry could not in any way support them.

On their return to the scene of the massacre, they hastened to succor the wounded, and they buried the dead on a knoll on the southern end of the lot on which the farm house stood.

The reluctant guide, Thomas Osborn, had come out of the low meadow as soon as he had seen the American force pushing down the Island road after the fugitives. He came up to Count Pulaski and told his story. The excitement of the hour was so great no one believed the tale he told of his compulsory service, and the angry soldiers fastened him to a tree and commenced to flog him. Had it not been for the timely interference of the officers he might have been killed. They sent a party over to Osborn Island and took his father a prisoner and had them both conveyed to Trenton and lodged in the jail at that place. Some two weeks after this event, these two Quakers, against whom no treason could be proven, were released from jail and allowed to return to their home under the protection of the following pass:

> *"Permit the bearers, Richard and Thomas Osborn, to pass to their homes at Egg Harbour; they being examined before the Judges at Trenton, and not found guilty, are therefore discharged and at liberty.*
> *"By order of Gen. Pulaski.*
> *"LE BRUCE DE BALQUOER,*
> *"Aide-de-camp.*
> *"WILLIAM CLAYTON,*
> *"Justice of the Peace.*
> *"HUGH ROSSEL,*
> *"Jailer.*
> *"TRENTON, Oct. 30, 1778."*

The British loss in this affair was two soldiers of the Fifth Regiment British Foot killed, and two men of the same Regiment slightly wounded; Ensign John Camp, of the Third Battalion New Jersey Volunteers, stabbed in the thigh, and a private soldier of the same command wounded. Some sketches of this affair speak of a Captain in the British line being pinned to the door of the house by a patriot bayonet, but I find no account of such a wound in the British records.

The British force left the south side of Osborn Island about ten o'clock in the morning of the same day, and in their hurry of retreat lost several arms, accoutrements and some clothing. As they were crossing the island, a Tory informant told them that Colonel Thomas Proctor, the Pennsylvania artillerist, with a detachment of artillery, armed with two brass twelve-pounders and one three-pounder, was hotly pursuing them and was now but two miles in their rear, being well supported by the fully aroused militia of the neighborhood. Having no artillery to oppose the coming force of patriots, Captain Ferguson concluded that he would not remain longer and risk another encounter with men rendered desperate by the thought of the butchery of their comrades. In the middle of the afternoon, therefore, they rejoined the fleet, which immediately weighed anchor in the harbor and put to sea.

As the flagship Zebra was a second time passing over the bar at the inlet, she again struck on the sand bar. After trying in vain to get her off, the men on board of her were transferred to the Nautilus and the Vigilant, and Captain Collins, with great reluctance, ordered her to be fired. He then feared greatly that she would fall into the hands of the Americans. Much amusement was created in Pulaski's camp, and indeed in all the neighborhood, as the shotted guns were heard to discharge when the flames enveloped the vessel.

The fleet arrived in New York on Thursday morning, October 22.

For his cruelty of the previous night, Captain Ferguson attempts to excuse himself in his report—"it being a night attack, little quarter could, of course, be given." Hearing falsely from Juliet that Pulaski had ordered no quarter to be given, he thought he could do no less than pursue the same method.

In the history of the Fifth Foot, it is said that the commanding officer of the expedition reported:

> *It is but justice to inform you that the officers and men, both British and Provincials, behaved on the occasion in a manner to do themselves honor. To the conduct of Captain William Cox, Lieutenant Thomas Littleton and Ensign Edward Cotter, of the Fifth Regiment, and of Captain Peter Campbell, of the Third New Jersey Volunteers, this little enterprise owes much of its success.*

Of this affair Judge Jones, the Tory historian, speaks as follows: "They plundered the inhabitants; burnt their houses, their churches and their barns; ruined their farms; stole their cattle, hogs, horses and sheep, and then triumphantly returned to New York." Washington Irving says of it that it was "a marauding expedition worthy of the times of the buccaneers." Admiral Gambler, however, called it "a spirited service," and to Sir Henry Clinton, it was "a success under the direction of that very active and zealous officer, Ferguson."

Appendix.

Report of Captain Collins, British Navy—
ZEBRA, in Little Egg Harbour, October 9.

SIR—The King's ships, galleys and armed vessels, appointed to act under my orders, having all joined at Staten Island the evening of the thirtieth of September, and the troops being embarked on board the transports, I got under weigh and stood to sea, with the wind northerly, but it shifting the day following to the southward, and blowing strong, together with some severe weather, which afterwards ensued, prevented our getting off this place before the afternoon of the 5th of this month, when the tide proving favourable, I ordered the Halifax brig, together with the Dependence and Cornwallis galleys, to proceed into the harbour and take a position to prevent the escape of any of the enemy's vessels. The wind being at N.W. and continuing to blow fresh the next day, made it impossible to get the King's ships or transports over the Bar. I, therefore, ordered the troops to be put on board the armed vessels, and it proving a little more moderate in the evening, we had the good fortune to get them all safe into the harbour. As we found, by some information we received, that intelligence of our intentions had reached the rebels several days preceding our arrival (which enabled them to get four privateers to sea), no time was to be lost in proceeding up the river: we, therefore, embarked as many of the troops as was possible on board the galleys and armed vessels (previously taking everything out of them which could be done to lessen their draught of water), and the rest I ordered into the flat and gunboats, and proceeded with the whole at daybreak the next morning up the river; our progress was attended with great difficulty, owing to the extreme shoalness of the water and the want of pilots: the Grandby and Greenwich, armed sloops, grounded off Mincock Island, and could not be advanced farther; we, however, got up with the galleys, and Nautilus and Experiment's tenders [small boats], about four in the afternoon, to Chestnut-neck, where the rebels had several vessels and storehouses. They ranged themselves in numbers, in a breastwork they had erected on an eminence, and showed themselves in a battery (which, as we afterwards found, had no guns) on the beach, but were soon disordered by a well-managed fire from the galleys, the troops landing immediately under the protection of the gunboats and cannonade of the galley, soon drove them from their works, and made them disperse in the woods without any loss. The vessels at this place, amounting to ten in number, we found were mostly British, which had been seized upon by the rebel cruisers; amongst them was the Venus, of London, and others of considerable size, which they could not carry higher up; as all of them were scuttled and dismantled, and some sunk, it was impossible (notwithstanding my solicitude and wishes to recover the property of the King's subjects) to get them down here; I, therefore, ordered them to be fired and destroyed. The storehouses and settlements here, which seemed so particularly adapted to the convenience of this nest of freebooters [pirates], I was also of opinion, with the commanding officer of the troops, should be destroyed; which was accordingly done, also the battery before mentioned, and the work on the hill. About noon this day all the King's ships and the two transports got safe over the Bar, and anchored in the harbour.

Had the weather admitted of our arriving more opportunely, we had it in view to attempt penetrating to the Forks, where the rebels have some small privateers and a few other inconsiderable trading vessels; but as the country had been long alarmed, the natural difficulties attending the bringing [of] the galleys and armed vessels, unprovided with pilots, up so shoal and narrow a channel, through a commanding country, would have been so much increased by the efforts of a prepared enemy, that we could not entertain much hopes of success, particularly as we had intelligence the rebels had collected all their strength to that point, consisting of Proctor's artillery and some other regular force from Philadelphia, in addition to a large body of militia provided properly with cannon; we, therefore, thought it most prudent to abandon that enterprise.

The 7th, at noon, I got under weight with the galleys, armed vessels, etc., and stood down the river; the Greenwich and Granby, armed sloops, being still aground, I brought to anchor in the evening, to assist in getting them off, which was effected by taking everything out of them the next morning: during this delay of the vessels, the troops under the command of Captain Ferguson were employed, under cover of the gunboats, in an excursion on the north shore, to destroy some principal salt works, also some stores and lodgments belonging to the people the most notorious for being concerned in the privateers, and destroying and oppressing the peaceable and moderate part of the King's subjects, which was likewise accomplished without any loss.

The morning following I got under weight with all the vessels, and came down here with the Cornwallis galley and two of the armed sloops; the Greenwich having again got aground in her way down, has obliged me to leave the Dependence galley at some distance from here, for her protection.

I shall take the most early opportunity of the wind to leave this place, and (if the weather proves so favourable as to admit of it), we have it in view to employ ourselves, on our return to New York, in looking into Barnegat and Cranbury inlets, and to destroy or bring off any vessels that may happen to be there, and demolish the salt works, which are very considerable, on the shores of those recesses.

I think it my particular duty to inform you, the officers and seamen I have had the honour to command on this service, have manifested their best endeavours in their duty. I should also think myself wanting, if I omitted to acquaint you, that Captain Ferguson, the commanding officer of the detachment of the army, as well as every officer and man under his command, have shown the utmost zeal and forwardness to co-operate in every thing for the advancement and benefit of his Majesty's service. I have the honour to be, with great respect, Sir, your most obedient, humble servant,

HENRY COLLINS.

P.S..—This will be delivered by lieutenant Quarme, of the Halifax brig, who, being on a cruise on this station, and thinking his vessel might prove useful, I took the liberty to bring on with me. Besides the vessels I have before had the honour to inform you were destroyed at Chestnut Neck, we have taken a brig here, laden with lumber; but as she is stripped of most of the material of her rigging, and all her sails, and being besides very old and unfit to bring around, I have ordered her cargo to be put on board the two transports, knowing how serviceable such a supply will prove to the dock yard.

Report of Captain Ferguson, of the Seventieth Regiment, to his Excellency, Sir Henry Clinton, dated

LITTLE EGG HARBOUR, October 10th

SIR—I have the honour to inform you that the ships, with the detachment ordered to this place, arrived off the bar on the evening of the 5th instant, when captain Collins sent in the galleys, but the ships could not enter before the 7th.

Three privateers of six or eight guns, with an armed pilot-boat, had escaped out of the harbour before our arrival, in consequence of advice received on the second from Mr. Livingston, warning them of our destination.

As it was from this evident that preparations had been made against us for several days, it was determined to allow no further time, but to push up with our galleys and small craft, with what soldiers could be crowded into them, without waiting for the coming in of the ships; accordingly, after a very difficult navigation of twenty miles inland, we came opposite to Chestnut-neck, where there were several vessels and about a dozen of houses, with stores for the reception of prize goods, and accommodation for their privateers' men.

The rebels had there erected a work with embrasures for six guns, on a level with the water, to rake the channel, and another upon a commanding eminence, with a platform for guns en barbette, in which, however, it afterwards appeared that they had not as yet placed artillery.

The banks of the river below the works being swampy, rendered it necessary for the boats with the troops to pass within musquet shot, in order to land beyond them, previous to which captain Collins advanced with the galleys to cover our landing, and as he came to very close to the works, and the guns of the galleys were remarkably well pointed, the fire from the rebels was effectually stifled, and the detachment, landing with ease, soon drove into the woods the skulking banditti that endeavoured to oppose it.

The seamen were employed all that evening and the next day till noon in destroying ten capital vessels, and the soldiers in demolishing the village, which was the principal resort of this nest of pirates. Had we arrived by surprize, we meant to have pushed forwards with celerity to the Forks, within thirty-five miles of Philadelphia. But as the alarm had been spread through the country, and the militia there had been reinforced from Philadelphia by a detachment of foot, five field pieces and a body of light horse, our small detachment could not pretend to enter twenty miles further into the country to reach the stores and small craft there; and the shallowness of the navigation rendered it impracticable for the galleys to co-operate with us; it was, therefore, determined to return without loss of time and endeavour to employ our force with effect elsewhere: but some of our vessels having run aground, notwithstanding the very great diligence and activity of captain Collins, and the gentlemen of the navy, an opportunity offered, without interrupting our progress, to make two descents on the north side of the river, to penetrate some miles into the country, destroy three salt works, and raze to the ground the stores and settlements of a chairman of their committees, a captain of militia, and one or two other virulent rebels, who had shares in the prizes brought in here, and who had all been remarkably active in fomenting the rebellion, oppressing the people and forcing them, against their inclination and better judgment, to assist in their crimes.

At the same time, be assured, Sir, no manner of insult or injury has been offered to the peaceable inhabitants, nor even to such, as without taking a lead, have been made, from the tyranny or influence of their rulers, to forget their allegiance.

It is my duty to inform you that the officers and men have cheerfully undergone much fatigue, and everywhere shown a disposition to encounter any difficulties that might offer.

I have the honour to be, with the greatest respect, etc.

PAT. FERGUSON,
Captain Seventieth Reg.

P.S.—One Solider of the Fifth was wounded through the leg at Chestnut-neck, but we have neither lost a man by the enemy nor deserting since we set out.

Report of Captain Collins, British Navy—

ZEBRA, Little Egg Harbour, October 15.

SIR—Since closing my letter of the 9th, I have had the honour to receive your orders of the 10th, by a sloop from New York, to which I shall not fail to pay due attention. The weather having proved exceedingly bad since that time, and the wind having been continually foul, has prevented me dispatching the Halifax, as I first intended, and put it totally out of my power attempting any movement from hence with the fleet, which cannot be undertaken but with a good opportunity to pass the Bar, which is dangerous and difficult. This delay of the vessels has given captain Ferguson and his detachment an opportunity of performing a very gallant and meritorious piece of service. A captain, sergeant and four men came down to us the evening before last from the rebels, and gave us some very satisfactory intelligence of the legion of Pulaski (to which they belonged), being posted about ten miles from hence; and captain Ferguson being of opinion, with myself, that a safe attempt might be made

You must know that one Juliet, an officer, lately deserted from the enemy, went off to them two days ago with three men whom he debauched, and two others whom they forced with them. The enemy, excited, without doubt, by this Juliet, attacked us the fifteenth instant, at three o'clock in the morning, with four hundred men. They seemed, at first, to attack our pickets of infantry with fury, who lost a few men in retreating; then the enemy advanced to our infantry. The Lieutenant-colonel Baron de Bose, who headed his men and fought vigorously, was killed with several bayonet wounds, as well as the Lieutenant de la Borderie, and a small number of soldiers and others were wounded. This slaughter would not have ceased so soon, if, on the first alarm, I had not hastened with my cavalry to support the infantry, which then kept a good countenance. The enemy soon fled in great disorder, and left behind them a great quantity of arms, accoutrements, hats, blades, etc.

We took some prisoners, and should have taken many, had it not been for a swamp, through which our horses could scarcely walk. Notwithstanding this, we still advanced, in hopes to come up with them, but they had taken up the planks of a bridge, for fear of being overtaken, which accordingly saved them. However, my light infantry, and particularly the company of riflemen, got over the remains of the plank and fired some volleys on their rear. The fire began again on both sides. We had the advantage and made them run again, although they were more in number.

I would not permit my hunters to pursue any farther, because I could not assist them, and they returned again to our line without any loss at that time.

Our loss is estimated, dead, wounded and absent, about twenty-five or thirty men, and some horses. That of the enemy appears to be much more considerable. We had cut off the retreat of about twenty-five men, who retired into the country and the woods, and we cannot find them. The general opinion is that they are concealed by the Tories in the neighborhood of this encampment.

In Congress, seventeenth of October, 1778.

Ordered to be published.

HENRY LAURENS,
President.

Extract of a letter from Rear Admiral Gambier to Mr. Stephens, dated on

October 20—

You will please to acquaint their lordships that having, in conjunction with the commander-in-chief of the army, judged it expedient to annoy the rebels at Egg Harbour, situated near the mouth of this port, from whence their little privateers sally to intercept the trade bound hither, I ordered captain Collins, of the Zebra, with the Vigilant, Nautilus, some galleys and small armed vessels of little draught of water, on this service, the army furnishing 300 men under the command of captain Ferguson, on board small transports. The little squadron sailed on the 30th of September, but, by unfavorable winds, could not get off the bar until the 5th following. I have this moment received the accompanying letters from captain Collins, which I enclose for the information of their lordships, of the particulars of that spirited service; which, we have reason to believe, has sensibly annoyed the rebels.

The Raleigh, a very fine rebel frigate, has been taken and brought in here by the Experiment and Unicorn.

Extract of a letter from General Sir Henry Clinton, Knight of the Bath, to Lord George Germain, dated October 25th—

In my letter of the 8th inst., I mentioned that my move into Jersey was partly to favour an expedition sent to Egg Harbour. I have now the honour to enclose copies of two reports made to me by captain Ferguson, of the 70th Regiment, who commanded the troops employed upon that service, to which I beg leave to refer your lordship for an account of its success, under the direction of that very active and zealous officer.

TWELVE

A Study of George Washington

William Scudder Stryker, 1897

William Scudder Stryker, 1838–1900 (admitted 1876) was the great-great-grandnephew of Colonel Nathaniel Scudder.

Born in Trenton, New Jersey, Stryker was educated at Princeton College and was graduated in 1859. During the Civil War, he served as Major and aide-de-camp to Major General Quincy A. Gillmore, United States Volunteers. He was brevetted Lieutenant-Colonel for faithful and meritorious services during the war. According to *The Stryker Family History*,

> *Later due to illness, he was transferred to the Paymaster's Office at Columbus Ohio. On the way he stopped at Washington, D.C. to deliver some messages to President Lincoln. During their conversation William fainted from fever. Lincoln caught him in his arms, laid him down on a couch and helped him recover until he could return to his hotel.*

Stryker resigned his commission on June 30, 1866, and was appointed to various positions in the Adjutant-General's Office of New Jersey over the next eight years ending as a brevetted Major-General for long and meritorious service. General Stryker was a well-known historian and an authority on New Jersey history. He wrote an extensive reference of lists of the officers and men on the New Jersey rosters in the Revolution as well as lists of New Jersey soldiers in the Civil War. The General was President of the New Jersey Society of the Cincinnati from 1896 to 1900 (see illustration 14).

Stryker is not currently represented in the Society.

Read before the Society of the Cincinnati in the State of New Jersey, on February 22, 1897

The study of the life and character of General Washington is a pleasant and instructive work to every true American scholar. To one who loves to search among the records, letters, documents and contemporaneous biographies of the Revolutionary period, nothing is more interesting than to picture to oneself in strong outlines the grand personality of the great commander. It is a most delightful pastime on a winter evening, surrounded by a library rich in Americana, to read what has been said of him by officers of his own army, by distinguished members of the French contingent and by the common people—how he appeared to them, how he impressed them from the time he drew his sword on the common at Boston until he bade them farewell at Frances Tavern in New York. I shall give you the result of my own searches on this line in as brief a sketch as possible, and in this way, on his natal day, we will to some degree, I trust, form a conception of what manner of man he was.

In a letter from John Adams to his wife, dated June 17, 1775, we find the following paragraph, descriptive of the young soldier who had just been selected to lead the fortunes of the cause of independence: "I can now inform you that the Congress have made choice of the modest and virtuous, the amiable, generous and brave George Washington, Esquire to be General of the American Army."

And the next day, the same great statesman wrote to Elbridge Gerry,

> *There is something charming to me in the conduct of Washington. A gentleman of one of the first fortunes upon the continent leaving his delicious retirement, his family and friends, sacrificing his ease and hazarding all in the cause of his country! His views are noble and disinterested!*

After the disastrous battle of Long Island, in August, 1776, the Abbe Robin said that the men of the American Army "were rivals in praising him, fearing him when he was silent and retaining their full confidence in him after defeats and disgrace."

His bravery in conflict is clearly evinced when at Princeton in 1777, his officers said, "Our army love their General very much, but they have one thing against him, which is the little care he takes of himself in any action."

The battles of Brandywine and Germantown had been fought, nearly three months of that awful winter at Valley Forge had slowly passed, the countenance of Washington had become more grave and careworn, his stately bearing still more dignified, his manner still more reserved, when Peter S. Du Ponceau came to America with General the Baron von Steuben and gave us, February 23, 1778, his impressions of the chief:

> *I could not keep my eyes from that imposing countenance,—is grave, yet not severe! affable without familiarity! Its predominant expression was calm dignity, through which you could trace the strong feelings of the patriot and discern the father as well as the commander of his soldiers! I have never seen a picture which represents him to me as I saw him at Valley Forge. Perhaps that expression was beyond the skill of the painter, but while I live it will remain impressed on my memory.*

The cold of that terrible winter encampment on the Schuylkill had given way to the warmth of June when the race began between the British and the American forces across New Jersey to the plains of Monmouth. The night after the battle, the gallant General Lafayette, who had slept by the side of General Washington under the same military cloak, said of him, "During this affair which ended so well, although begun so ill, General Washington appeared to arrest fortune by one glance and his presence of mind, valour and decision of character were never displayed to greater advantage than at that moment."

Later on in the year, Doctor James Thacher, a Surgeon of Colonel Henry Jackson's Massachusetts Continental regiment, gives us in his military journal a very graphic description of Washington:

> *The personal appearance of our Commander-in-Chief is that of the perfect gentleman and accomplished warrior. He is remarkably tall, full six feet, erect and well proportioned. The strength and proportion of*

> *his muscles appear to be commensurate with preeminent powers of his mind. The severity of his countenance and majestic gracefulness of his deportment impart a strong impression of that dignity and grandeur, which are his peculiar characteristics, and no one can stand in his presence without feeling the ascendancy of his mind and associating with his countenance the idea of wisdom, philanthropy, magnanimity and patriotism. There is a fine symmetry in the features of his face indicative of a benign and dignified spirit.*

And at the close of the year, Major-General the Marquis de Chastelleux, a noted French officer under the Count de Rochambeau, when he saw the leader of the American troops for the first time said,

> *It is not my intention to exaggerate; I wish only to express the impression General Washington has left on my mind. Brave without temerity, generous without prodigality, noble without pride, virtuous without serenity; he seems always to have confined himself within those limits where the virtues, by clothing themselves in more lively, but more changeable and doubtful colors, may be mistaken for faults. It will be said of him* at the end *of a long civil war he had nothing with which he could reproach himself.*

On the 3rd day of May, 1779, John Bell, Esquire of Maryland, in a letter to the Reverend Doctor Charles Henry Wharton of Worcester, England, says,

> *General Washington is now in the fifty-seventh year of his age; he is a tall, well-made man, rather large boned, and has a tolerably genteel address; his features are manly and bold, his eyes of a bluish cast and very lively; his hair a deep brown, his face rather long and marked with the small pox; his complexion sunburnt and without much colour and his countenance sensible, composed and thoughtful; there is a remarkable air of dignity about him, with a striking degree of gracefulness. . . . Candour, sincerity, affability and simplicity seems to be the striking features of his character, till an occasion offers of displaying the most determined bravery and independence of spirit.*

Again on November 23, 1780, the Marquis de Chastelleux met General Washington at Pompton in our State and he remarked,

> *The goodness and benevolence which characterize him are evident from everything about him; but the confidence he gives birth to never occasions improper familiarity; for the sentiment he inspires has the same origin in every individual, a profound esteem for his virtues and a high opinion of his talents.*

On the 10th of January, 1781, the gallant General Nathanael Greene, second only to Washington in soldierly ability in the Continental Army, wrote to Colonel Alexander Hamilton, who knew him equally well,— "I always thought him exceedingly popular, but in many places he is little less than adored and universally admired. His influence in this country might possibly effect something great."

And again in August of the same year the Abbe Robin Chaplain of the Regiment Soissonnais of the French contingent, said,

> *I have seen General Washington that most singular man the soul and support of one of the greatest revolutions that has ever happened or can happen. He is of tall and noble stature, well proportioned, a fine, cheerful open countenance, a simple and modest carriage. . . . In all these extensive States they consider him in the light of a beneficent God, dispensing peace and happiness around him. Old men, women and children press about him when he accidentally passes along, and think themselves happy once in their lives to have seen him. The Americans are roused, animated and inflamed at the very mention of his name; and the first songs that sentiment or gratitude has dictated have been to celebrate General Washington.*

When in September 1782, the Count de Segur, the Colonel of the same French regiment as Chaplain the Abbe Robin, gives us in his "Recollections" this description:

> *His exterior disclosed, as it were, the history of his life; simplicity, grandeur, dignity, calmness, goodness, firmness, the attributes of his character were also stamped upon his features and in all his person. His*

> *stature was noble and elevated; the expression of his features mild and benevolent; his smile graceful and pleasing, his manners simple, without familiarity.*

In these quotations we can, as with the pencil of an artist, picture to ourselves the singular majesty of his figure and the peculiar expression of his countenance. We are impressed with his grave dignity, his unconscious sincerity, the reverent awe his appearance and mind created, the pureness of his motives, the simple qualities of his patriotism. And as we feel the warm blood pulse through our veins, the same strain of blood that flowed in the comrades of Washington, we greet him in the words of Light Horse Harry Lee as "first in war, first in peace, and first in the hearts of his countrymen!"

THIRTEEN

The Beginnings of the Society of the Cincinnati

William Pennington, 1897

William Pennington, 1866–1922 (admitted 1887), was the great-grandson of Captain William Sandford, Pennington (Original Member), Second Regiment, Continental Artillery.

Pennington was born in Newark, New Jersey, and resided in Morris Plains, New Jersey. He was Vice President of the New Jersey Society from 1909 to1922.

Read before the Society of the Cincinnati in the State of New Jersey on July 5, 1897

The creation of an honorable order, as well as its bestowal, is usually associated with brave and worthy deeds.

In many instances, achievement or sacrifice has been the corner stone upon which the foreign institution has been built, and the very essence of an order is that it shall have endured from the historical period which gave it birth directly to the present time, freighted with the intervening years that hallow a nation's history.

Age is a necessity; it tempers and it tries; it is the crucible that purges and refines, and that which has successfully withstood the test of a century deserves the most dignified consideration.

As I find myself to-day about to give a sketch of the "Beginnings of the Ancient and Honorable Order of the Cincinnati," there comes upon me an earnest sense of the responsibility of the undertaking, coupled with the thought of many a distinguished wearer of the ribbon to whom these words of mine may come, and I sincerely hope that the honor of preparing this paper may prove to have been not altogether unworthily delegated.

The beginnings of the Society! What a vast amount of interesting history envelopes the institution of this order. There must have been the sincerest kind of enthusiasm among the soldiers of the American army at the close of the war. A consciousness of victory, most acute and significant, throbbed in the heads and hearts of those glorious patriots.

Here, not merely some comparatively petty right had been preserved by force of arms; no local embroilment had been quelled; not even as happened nearly a hundred years later, an established order of things assailed had been maintained, but now, a grand, independent nation and country had been reared, practically upon the shoulders of these sturdy American warriors, and the sacred, inspiring thought that they had been building for all time came into the minds of these heroes of the long ago; and, aside from the priceless legacy of a free country, handed down by them to posterity, the thought of a union of hearts and hands, in which should be perpetuated for all time the animating and ennobling deeds that made free and independent a great people, prompted our ancestors to found this glorious order of peace and patriotism, the Society of the Cincinnati.

But, curiously enough, the institution of this Society evoked from the master minds of the Fathers of Liberty most varied and interesting arguments for and against its establishment; and the preponderance of opinion was of that sturdy, fearless kind, that showed above all else a jealous love of country swaying and influencing every material consideration.

We see in these very views appearing the germs of individual strength of thought and character that rightly belong to builders of a country and founders of a new common wealth—solidity and honesty of purpose—the conservatism of the diplomat and the intrepidity and assurance of the soldier. These phases of mental and moral caliber were reflected in the expressions of approval and disapproval that were called forth during the early existence of the Society.

And, after all, the institution of this order was a most important innovation, a something that might not be properly understood and appreciated, and following directly upon such a victory as this just over had been, it is a matter of small surprise that Benjamin Franklin, the careful, level-headed diplomatist, expressed in no uncertain tone his grave doubts as to the advisability of forming a society who methods and principles might be misconstrued.

Masonry was thoroughly represented in the American army, and the Masonic element were anxious that General Washington should be made the head of the fraternity in this country at the close of the war.

But the Masonic brethren, as such, acting fraternally, were perhaps not as decisive in their actions as they had been as soldiers, and before any steps were taken toward the consummation of their patriotic wishes, General Knox had communicated a plan of brotherly organization, distinct from Masonry, to Baron Steuben; and the Baron, who was thoroughly familiar with orders in their most exclusive and beneficial sense, immediately set about the formation and organization of a fraternal society, to be recognized by an order or insignia; and at the general meting of the officers on the 13th of May, 1783, with the earnest approval of the commander-in-chief, "the Society of the Cincinnati" was formally instituted, and had the honor of electing as its first President, Gen. George Washington, who soon after became also the first President of the United States.

Surely, our ancestors have handed down to us a priceless treasure in this sacred order. Let us guard it jealously and worthily maintain it.

There had been for some time previous to the creation of this order of ours, an evident leaning toward some original form of fraternal organization, and that something more ambitious in design than mere fellowship was covertly desired, would appear from the fact that an association to be called "The New Order of American Knighthood" was seriously considered and actually planned, and in March, 1783, two months before the institution of the Society of the Cincinnati, it was stated in a Philadelphia paper that "On the next anniversary of Independence, the 4th of July, a new order of Knighthood, called the Order of Freedom, will be established, and the institution take place in the city of Philadelphia."

One can scarcely be surprised at any style of criticism which so daring an announcement as this might call out.

A new order of Knighthood! Think of it! We can imagine the sturdy minds of Robert Morris and of Benjamin Franklin pondering over the pomp and circumstance of glorious Knighthood, and we can picture the shudders that possessed these stern patriots in consequence. But this same order of Knighthood was nevertheless the earliest effort to form a social institution founded upon civic distinctions of Society in Europe, and as such deserves particular mention here.

That this was a direct attempt to establish what might really become in after years a serious menace to the social order of things in the new country's government, there can be hardly a doubt. In the first place, the patron of the order was St. Louis, and the members were to be decorated with the order of St. Louis. Foreign enough, all this.

Gen. Washington was to be the Grand Master of the Order, and poor Dr. Franklin, who seems to have come in for a good deal of uncoveted glory, was most innocently elected as its Chancellor. Dr. Franklin's acknowledgment of this distinguished perspective honor does not appear upon the records.

There were to be ushers, heralds, and "twenty-four Knight companions, consisting of the Governor of each State of the time being, which they reckon nineteen." (I quote from the Philadelphia newspaper before referred to or rather quoted.) "The robe to be scarlet and blue, with ermine, etc."

All these glittering promises, however, came practically and literally to naught; but the seeds of organized fellowship were sown, and taking root, grew and waxed strong, and spread their sacred branches over many places, guarding a love of country and keeping sacred a brotherly affection and esteem that cannot die as long as the Society of the Cincinnati shall exist to nourish this vital patriotic growth.

"The beginnings," so called of the Society, practically date from that wonderfully interesting meeting in the house once owned by Gulian G. Ver-Planck, one of the old Colonial Governors of New York, at Fishkill, upon the Hudson, on the 13th of May, 1783.

At this meeting, Gen. Knox, Brig. Gen. Huntington and Captain Shaw reported a form or plan of organization which was adopted, and the dear old Society had formally begun its honorable career.

You may be sure that the Baron Steuben was at this meeting. He was, indeed, and acted, moreover, as its chairman, and doubtless the business was conducted with much ceremony.

Speaking of ceremony, it is curious to see the modernizing effect of the years, even upon such an institution as this, wherein it would seem one of the greatest legacies bequeathed through it to us, would be a close and jealous observance of the ancient tradition and forms that gave to it a particular distinction in the first years of its history.

Let me read here the description of the formalities attending the admission of new members in the year 1786; and I beg to acknowledge my indebtedness for this following interesting item to a most attractive paper written upon the Society by our loved and lamented brother and former President, Col. Clifford Stanley Sims, than whom no one could be more truly an ornament to any society or organization that had for its principles and purposes the maintenance of a true patriotism, and the furtherance of all patriotic enterprises.

"The audience being prepared," so the quaint description reads,

> *and the kettledrums and trumpets having already occupied their places, the standard bearer of the Society, in his continental uniform, escorted by four members also in full uniform, took his position on the right of the dais. Then entered the masters of ceremony, the members, two by two, the Secretary, carrying the original institution, bound in light blue satin, the Treasurer and Deputy Treasurer, bearing white satin cushions, on which were displayed the eagle and diplomas of the new members, the Vice-President, and last of all, the President, who on this occasion was the Baron de Steuben.*
>
> *At his entrance, the Standard saluted, and the Kettledrums and trumpets gave a flourish until he had taken the chair of state on the dais, when the standard was again raised, and the members, who till now had remained standing, seated themselves.*
>
> *The candidate, having been then introduced and duly admonished, the President and all the members arose, and the former, covering with neat form and ceremony, admitted the new comers into the Society and introduced them to their brother members.*

Of course, in this practical day and generation, such elaborate formalities seem almost absurd, and doubtless such some of them would prove to be were they revived in the year of grace, 1897, but while our honored President, Gen. Stryker, does not need the rattle of kettledrums nor the blare of trumpets to assure him of the dignified respect and esteem in which he is held by us all, and while, too, blue satin cushions and white satin cushions are somewhat suggestive in the abstract of societies widely different from ours, there yet is much in these ancient customs that it would be well for us in these latter days to infuse into our meetings and councils.

I will not say that all our members should be equipped on meeting days with side arms and cocked hats, which were once the "outward and visible signs" of the true Cincinnatian; but surely, when a new member comes amongst us for the first time, there would seem to be a difference [distinction] directly due the patriot he represents, aside from the respect which attaches personally to him as a Cincinnatian, and how could these duties be better displayed than that the stranger, coming, it is true, among those to whom he is affectionately linked by very precious traditional memories and associations, should be formally presented to each of his fellow members, so that he may feel in his heart that he is indeed "in the house of his friends."

Yes, the Society was practically a struggling one for a short time after its conception. That this is so, is evidenced by the fact that Pennsylvania, Massachusetts and Connecticut openly and formally declared the institution unjustifiable, and it is said that little Rhode Island threatened to annul the civic privileges of all the citizens who should become members of it.

Washington heartily approved of the Society itself from the very outset; but he felt that the prejudices of the people might be disturbed if it continued to claim hereditary distinctions for its members, and it is to his characteristic prudence and timely advice that at the next or second regular meeting all unnecessary social pretentions were disclaimed, the funds put under the cognizance of State Legislatures, the Society retaining only the right to indulge in acts of friendship and patriotic benevolence, which are today its distinguishing attributes.

When these modifications became known, the Society immediately took a renewed hold upon those who had before opposed its early institutions, and its exalted position since then is now and forever will be, part of this great nation's history.

From the mass of letters written at this early period, in which mention is vigorously made of the Society, I have selected a few sentences from the pens of those great statesmen, John Adams and Benj. Franklin, for the purpose of showing what the most educated opinions really were against the institution of the Society of the Cincinnati.

After reading from this correspondence I shall give an extract from a letter from Gen. Washington, which will have a most grateful ring to the ears of the latter-day Cincinnatians, and will serve as a sort of benediction uttered for us all by our first President.

But first let us listen to the words of John Adams, then Minister to the Hague, and let me say here that both Adams and Benj. Franklin were almost unconditional opponents of the Society from the outset, and therefore we should not be surprised at the style and spirit of the following remarks.

Adams, in the course of his masterly defence of the Constitution of the government of the United States, says, speaking of titles and nobility in Italy:

> *The family Del Pecora was the principal one of cavaliers, and they enslaved their country, of course, just as the Medici did in Florence.*
>
> *Perhaps it may be said that in America we have no distinctions of ranks, and therefore shall not be liable to those divisions and discords which spring from them. . . . All that we can say in America is that legal distinctions, titles, powers and privileges are not hereditary, but that the disposition to artful distinctions, to titles and ribbons, and to the hereditary descent of them, is ardent in America, we may see by the institution of the Cincinnati. There is not a more remarkable phenomenon in universal history nor in universal human nature than this order. The officers of an army who had voluntarily engaged in a service under the authority of the people, whose creation and preservation was upon the principle that the body of the people were the only fountain of power and honor, officers, too, as enlightened and virtuous as ever served in any army, the moment they had answered the end of their creation, instituted title and ribbons and hereditary descents, by their own authority only, without the consent or knowledge of the people or their representations or legislatures.*

Adams was decidedly contra, but at this time the Society's aims were absolutely misunderstood, and in a foot-note to this very letter just quoted, Jared Sparks, the eminent historian and biographer himself says: "The moderation of Washington in recommending a modification of the objectionable features of the institution, and the wisdom of the Society in yielding at once to public opinion smoothed all difficulties, etc."

That hardy, powerful soul, Benjamin Franklin, deals rather more summarily with our beloved Cincinnati. "In this view," he says,

> *perhaps I should not myself, if my advice had been asked, have objected to their wearing their riband and badge themselves according to their fancy, though I should to the entailing it as an honor on their posterity. For honor, worthily obtained (as that, for example, of our officers), is in its nature a personal thing, and incommunicable to any but those who had some share in obtaining it.*

The doctor then goes on to speak of ascending honors and descending honors, the latter institution being to him "not only groundless, but absurd. I wish, therefore," he adds, "that the Cincinnati, if they must go on with their project, would direct the badges of their order to be worn by their fathers and mothers instead of handing them down to their children. It would be a good precedent, and might have good effects."

Doctor Franklin, then turning his attention to our order, and referring to the eagle, which he thinks looks particularly like a turkey, adds that he is glad of the resemblance, "for, in truth, the turkey is in comparison a much more respectable bird, and withal, a true, original native of America."

I might continue to quote indefinitely, perhaps, concerning the Society of the Cincinnati from the correspondence of every public man who lived and swayed thought in these cradle days of our Republic and our Society, but I have preferred here to give an example of the style of antagonistic criticism the Society at first provoked.

We know already the sentiment prevailing in the army, and the powerful support the order received from many influential patriots, both soldiers and citizens; but it has seemed to me that the above quoted sentiments of Adams and Franklin are particularly interesting to us nineteenth-century Cincinnatians, seeing that in this year, 1897, our Society has so firm a hold upon the hearts of the true American nature that neither fear for her welfare nor doubt as to her continuance ever enters the public mind.

I will close this little sketch or story of our Society's beginnings by quoting from a letter of General Washington to James Madison: "When the Society of the Cincinnati was first formed," the General says,

> *I am persuaded not a member in it conceived that it would give birth to those jealousies, or be charged with those ills, real or imaginary, with which the minds of many and of some respectable characters in these states seem to be agitated. The motives which induced the officers to enter into were, I am positive, truly and frankly recited in the institution, one of which, and the principle, was to establish a charitable fund for the relief of such of their compatriots, and the widows and descendants of them, as were fit objects for such support, and for whom no provision had been made by the public.*

In these words, the great General speaks of our dear Society. What better authority for continuance than his sanction and approval? More than ever before I realize that this Society is an inheritance of unusual value and significance. We practically have in our keeping traditions and principles that were born with this blessed country of ours, and that were part of its infancy and early growth.

Let us try to feel more and more the richness of the legacy we possess, and may we bear in mind the largeness of soul that prompted the institution of the Order, so we may come to feel and know the depth and strength and noble significance of our Society, and of those glowing words: "Omnia Reliquit Servare Rempublicam."

FOURTEEN

CAMPAIGN IN CANADA, 1775

Timothy Matlack Cheesman, M.D., 1898

Timothy Matlack Cheesman, 1853–1919 (admitted to the Society, 1889) was the great-grandnephew of Jacob Cheesman, First Regiment, New York Continental Line.

Cheesman was educated at Columbia College and received a Master of Arts degree in 1877. He then was graduated with a degree in medicine in 1874. He was an instructor in bacteriology at the College of Physicians and Surgeons, Columbia University, New York City. He transferred to the Connecticut Society on July 4, 1912.

Read before the Society of the Cincinnati in the State of New Jersey, at Princeton, N.J., February 22, 1898

The Campaign in Canada seems to have had its conception in the applications made by Col. Ethan Allen and Col. Benedict Arnold for troops to hold that country in the interest of the United Colonies.

Arnold petitioned the provincial congresses of New York (2nd June) and Massachusetts (6th June) and later appeared before the Continental Congress, while Allen sent his petition directly to the Continental Congress (13th June, 1775).

On the 27th June, Major General Philip Schuyler was directed by Congress to repair to Crown Point and Ticonderoga, take such steps as were necessary to insure these posts to the United Colonies, and if he found it practical "to take possession of St. Johns, Montreal, and any other parts of the country and pursue any other measures in Canada which may have a tendency to promote the peace and security of these colonies."

General Schuyler arrived at Ticonderoga on the 18th July and found that Colonel Hinman, who was in command, had done nothing either for offence or defence; the guards slept on their posts with impunity, and everything was in dire disorder. Within a week of his arrival, however, an agent was sent into Canada to learn how the inhabitants were disposed towards the proposed expedition, to discover the number and condition of the Royal troops and to gain such other information as was obtainable.

Through delays in receiving reinforcements and supplies, no advance was made until the 31st of August, when General Montgomery, with troops under Cols. Waterbury, McDougal, Parsons and Wooster, numbering about 1,200 men, set out to attack St. Johns, and a few days later was joined by General Schuyler and his remaining force.

St. Johns was forced to surrender on the 2nd November, but not until after many attempts had been made to subdue it. Bad weather, sickness among the troops, scantiness of both provisions and ammunition, all played a part in the delay and this was supplemented by insubordination among the men, especially among the troops from New England, who resented being under the command of a New Yorker; and charges of cowardice were made, which, as General Schuyler states, led many of the men to resort to strange devices to obtain their discharges from the army, such as burning their tongues with hot chocolate to produce the evidences of disease, and swallowing tobacco to bring on obstinate vomiting.

On the 16th September, General Schuyler, on account of illness, was obliged to return to Ticonderoga, leaving General Montgomery in command.

While the Colonial troops were in the neighborhood of St. Johns, several officers with small bodies of troops were employed as scouts, and endeavored to induce the inhabitants to join them. On the 24th September, two of these parties met at Longueil, one consisting of 100 men under Colonel Allen, the other of about 200 men under Major Brown, and without authority, planned an attack on Montreal.

General Carleton, in command of the British forces, at first prepared to retire, but, upon learning the weakness of the attacking force, determined to resist. Major Brown, when the critical time arrived, failed to render support; Colonel Allen was repulsed, and he and forty-five of his men were taken prisoners. To Montgomery, Schuyler and Washington, this unauthorized attack was the subject of great anxiety, illustrating, as it did, the insubordination that existed among the troops. At the surrender of St. Johns, Major André and Captain Aubury were taken prisoners, both of whom subsequently became well known in the history of the Revolution. General Montgomery was unable to persuade his troops to advance on Montreal until after he had promised an honorable discharge to all who desired it on reaching that city. After further delay by bad weather and bad roads, Montreal was reached on the 12th November, but the city had been abandoned, General Carleton, with the garrison and civil officers and with all the ammunition, having embarked on ten or eleven small vessels which had been reserved for this purpose.

The retreating forces were intercepted, however, through the foresight of General Montgomery, who had sent Colonel Easton with some artillery, to a point at the mouth of the Sorel River, and the whole force under General Prescott surrendered, General Carleton having escaped in disguise.

In the meantime, General Montgomery, immediately on his arrival, addressed a letter to the Governor and inhabitants of Montreal, urging the propriety of a surrender, expressing his friendliness towards them and relating the damage which would ensue from a forced entrance into the city, which was, if possible, to be avoided at that season of the year. On that same day the inhabitants formally surrendered, and on the day following the army entered the city.

At about the time General Schuyler returned to Ticonderoga, leaving the forces encamped about St. Johns under command of General Montgomery, Colonel Benedict Arnold set out (15th September) on a secret expedition, with a detachment of about 1,100 men, by way of the Kennebec and Chaudiere Rivers to attack Quebec. He was accompanied by Colonels Greene and Enos,

Majors Meigs and Bigelow, Captain Daniel Morgan and Aaron Burr, then only nineteen years of age, who accompanied the expedition as a volunteer.

The route pursued by this force was through practically an unknown wilderness, and the obstacles they met with and the sufferings they endured are said to be unrivalled in history. (See letters of Colonel Arnold, Journals of Colonel Arnold and Major Meigs, and narrative of Judge J. J. Henry.)

On the 8th November, however, about the time of the surrender of Montreal to General Montgomery, Colonel Arnold reached Point Levi, opposite Quebec, but his coming had been heralded through the treachery of an Indian to whom had been entrusted letters to General Schuyler. On the morning of the 13th, however, his forces were drawn up on the Heights of Abraham, having scaled the heights during the previous night. He at once sent a flag to the gate of the city, demanding a surrender, but the officer bearing it was fired upon and narrowly escaped with his life. This summons was repeated two days later with a like result.

Colonel Arnold having an ineffective force of but a little over 500 men, and finding that much of his ammunition was useless from having become wet, withdrew his forces from before the city. General Montgomery arrived on the 3rd December, with 300 men, some artillery, and the vessels captured near Montreal, and on the following day the whole force took up a position before Quebec, preparatory to an attack upon the city. It was determined eventually to make two feints upon the upper town, with forces under Major Brown and Colonel Livingston, and two attacks upon the lower town under command of Colonel Arnold and General Montgomery. This attack was made at five o'clock on the morning of the 31st December, during a terrific snow storm.

The feints of Colonel Livingston and Major Brown failed to draw the attention of the garrison to such degree as to weaken the defences of the lower town; and the death of General Montgomery and his aides McPherson and Cheesman by a single shot, as they were passing the second barrier, so demoralized the force under his command that they were withdrawn. The force commanded by Colonel Arnold, and after he was wounded, by Captain Morgan, successively stormed two barriers, but were then overpowered by superior numbers and forced to surrender. After this disaster, the fragments of the American forces, under Colonel Arnold, withdrew from the city until April, when the siege was renewed under General Wooster, who had arrived from Montreal. In May, Major General Thomas was placed in command, but powerful reinforcements under General Burgoyne having reached Quebec, the continentals hastily retreated "leaving their stores and sick behind them," and shortly afterwards returned to the Colonies.

I have in my possession two letters written by Major Cheesman about one week before his death. The one to his father, dated "Saint Foys before Quebec, 23rd December, 1775," I have brought a photographic copy of, reads as follows:

The man-of-war brigantine, Gaspé, to which Major Cheesman refers, is the one in which his Company and General Montgomery came down the St. Lawrence from Montreal.

Lossing, in his *Pictorial Field Book of the Revolution*, in a footnote referring to Major Cheesman, says, Volume I, page 198:

> *This officer had a presentiment that he should not survive the battle. When preparing to go forth on that stormy December morning, he dressed himself with more care than usual, and putting a considerable sum of money, in gold, in his pocket, remarked, with a smile, "this will insure me a decent burial." A sergeant and eleven men fell with him. He was not instantly killed, but arose to press forward to charge the battery. It was a feeble effort, and he fell back a corpse in a winding sheet of snow.*

FIFTEEN

SPRINGFIELD, 1780—AND AFTER

William Nelson, 1900

William Nelson was a lawyer and historian who lived from 1847 to 1914. He was the Corresponding Secretary for the New Jersey Historical Society.

Read before the Society of the Cincinnati in the State of New Jersey at its annual Washington's Birthday dinner at the Waldorf Astoria Hotel in New York City, February 22, 1900, at 7:00 P.M.

This is a story of A Red, Red Rose, an Incident of Springfield, 1780—and after. It has nothing to do with the battle itself. At least, I shall not speak of that. What is the use of the rest of us bothering ourselves to store our minds with useless misinformation regarding Revolutionary events, when we have with us your President, the attractive and most delightful gentleman, the accomplished scholar and the profound student, who has all these facts in his head, and who is as ready to impart them to others as he is successful in acquiring them.

And yet this story hinges upon that dashing raid of Gen. Knyphausen, on June 23, 1780, from Staten Island toward Morristown, whose audacious aim it was to surprise Washington, crush his little army, and capture the paltry stores of his starving men. What need to remind you how the beacon fires leaped luridly, and the old cannon sounded the rude alarm from Short Hills, arousing the country, and summoning the sturdy militia to the defence of their homes and their dear ones? Nor need I speak of the stubborn resistance of the Continentals and the Jersey Blues as they checked the British advance across one bridge, and then another, until the baffled Hessians and redcoats, angered at the unexpected halt, vented their mad rage and lust for beauty in the burning of the church and nearly every house in the little village; and then, crestfallen, beat an ignominious retreat before the foe they had so rashly despised in the morning, and were fain to hurry back by night across the sullen waters to Staten Island. Of all this you have read, and of how Parson Caldwell, still crazed with grief over the dastardly shooting of his wife at Connecticut Farms by these same alien soldiery but two weeks before, rushed into the burning church at a critical moment, and gathering up an armful of hymn books, ran out among the patriot troops and cried, "Put Watts into 'em, boys! Put Watts into 'em!" But all this has naught to do with my story of a Red, Red Rose.

Among the British officers who participated in the affair at Springfield was one Colonel Cosmo Gordon. He was of a noble Scottish family, a brother of the Duke of Gordon, and had served as a Lieutenant in the 78th Regiment in America and elsewhere for eighteen years. As a Scotchman, he naturally felt that blood was thicker than water, and when winsome Kitty Alexander went on a lark to New York, Col. Gordon assiduously sought her acquaintance, on account of her father, the doughty American Major General, who laid claim to the title of Earl of Stirling in the Scottish peerage. At least, that is what Kitty dutifully wrote to her father. We may well believe that the gallant Scottish Colonel put it differently to her with lips and eyes.

Now, you will recollect that Kitty Alexander was a cousin of Gov. William Livingston's daughters. It is to be supposed that when she returned from that famous frolic in New York to her quiet home at Baskingridge, where Mrs. Livingston and her two unmarried daughters spent much of the time, she did not tell her cousins all about the gallant Scottish Colonel. Nay, when the Livingstons returned to Liberty Hall, only a mile or two out of Elizabethtown, would it be strange if, in the racing to and fro, the curious Scotchman made a polite call at the hospitable mansion to inquire after the fair young maid he had met in New York?

And so it came to pass that when Gen. Knyphausen's troops began their march on the morning of June 23, 1780, Col. Gordon joined his command of the First Battalion of the Guards at three o'clock, and went with them until they were within a quarter of a mile of Livingston's house. Solicitous for the safety of the fair inmates, he cantered on ahead with three fellow-officers, and made an unceremonious call upon the ladies there. The stay was brief, "but five minutes," *he* says, but the ladies were evidently on the qui vive, for Miss Susan Livingston bargained with him for a written safeguard to protect the premises from his rude soldiery. And with what, do you suppose, did she buy this precious document? Why, forsooth, with a Red, Red Rose! Moreover, this was to be *his* protection against any prowling patriot, in his venturesome foray amid a hostile populace. Surely, this fair Jersey girl must have exercised no common witchery over that quartette of British officers to wheedle out of them such a valuable bit of paper, and all for a paltry Rose! But was not Gordon equally successful in winning from her not only a Red, Red Rose, but the symbol therein of a friend to certain fair Americans, despite his cruel, avowed mission? Moreover, he says he received from the ladies, "the intelligence he wished for," whereupon the officers made their bow, and rejoined their column, that by this time was passing nearly opposite the house.

In the meantime, the Brigade of Guards had marched from Elizabethtown, and reached Springfield at or before daybreak. The Brigade was under command of Col. Howard; the First Battalion was commanded by Col. Cosmo Gordon, whose First Company was under Lieut. Col. Frederick Thomas. This Company led the column when the flanking companies were sent detached, as they were during the greater part of the day, so that the First Company remained under arms and under the fire of the American troops until the latter retreated. When he had won the heights, Thomas sent to Col. Gordon for further orders, but the gallant and susceptible Colonel was not to be found. An hour or two after the firing had ceased, he rode up the hill, with the Red Rose flaunting its beauty on his breast, where dainty hands had pinned it before daylight that morning. Lieut. Col. Thomas hotly asked where he had been, and declared that *he* had commanded the Guards during the fighting. It is easy to imagine the jealousy and the scorn with which he pointed at the Red, Red Rose of him who had been more fortunate on another field than that of Mars—a field where not improbably they had been rivals. This would explain Gordon's declaration that the charge of cowardice, subsequently brought against him, had proceeded from "the bitter fountain of rancor and private animosity."

On the retreat that night, in the darkness, the brilliancy of the Red Rose was obscured. It no longer served as a talisman for the protection of the wearer, and he was struck by a stray bullet. By a curious coincidence, this befell just in front of the Livingston house, and there the stricken Colonel tumbled from his horse. Did he hope that the fair maid who had smiled upon him in the morning would take compassion on his plight in the dire mishap? And did he see before him visions of tender nursing in that hospitable mansion? Alas! when he was disabled, his scornful junior, Col. Thomas, assumed the command, just as he had in the fighting, and Gordon was carried on to the British camp, where he was laid up for a month or more.

When Col. Gordon reappeared for duty, he saw that there was a coldness toward him in his mess. He soon learned that Col. Thomas had been repeating what he said to his face at Springfield—that *he* had commanded the Guards when the Heights were taken. His fellow-officers refused to "roll" with him. He was sent to Coventry. There was nothing for him to do but to prefer charges against Thomas. This he did, accusing him of "secretly and scandalously aspersing his character, in a manner unlike an officer and a gentleman." A general court martial was held in New York, September 15–25, 1780, to try the accused. Thomas proved that he had charged Gordon *to his face*, on the field of battle, with having neglected his duty; that he had repeated the declaration openly and often, and that on August 2, 1780, a day or two after Gordon had resumed duty, he had, in the presence of a meeting of the officers of the Brigade of Guards, assembled in the camp on the Heights of Fordham, *openly* accused Gordon of "not doing his duty before the enemy on the 23d of June, 1780." As the charge against Thomas was that he had *secretly* aspersed his Colonel, and as it appeared beyond question that his aspersions had been made in the most public manner, he was acquitted.

But Col. Cosmo Gordon still had at least the memory of that stolen interview before daybreak with the witching little Rebel, and there lingered yet in his recollection the intoxicating perfume of that Red Rose.

On the other hand, there was the stinging denunciation of the contumacious Thomas, and the ill-concealed contempt of the mess. His accuser had sailed for England, without waiting for the verdict of the court martial. Thither Gordon followed him, and challenged him to mortal combat. Thomas declined his challenge on the ground that "he did not stand in a proper situation to be answered." At last, another court-martial, which sat in New York, August 22d–September 4, 1782, to try him on the charge of "not having done his duty before the enemy on the 23d of June, 1780." In other words, he was charged with cowardice, meaning that he had preferred to encounter the shafts from the eyes of a certain fair girl at the Livingston house, to the bullets of the soldiery on the Heights of Springfield; that he preferred a Red Rose from beauty's bower to the gory battlefield. The court found him *not guilty*, and two months later, the finding was approved by the King.

He at once sought anew a meeting with his accuser, Lieut. Col. Thomas. That gentleman still considered him attainted, [condemned by a sentence of attainder] and avoided an encounter, even ordering his servants not to deliver to him any letters from Col. Gordon. Finally, a challenge was smuggled into the house, and reached the hands of Col. Thomas. It was in the most violent terms, and declared that if he did not agree to give Col. Gordon the satisfaction of a gentleman, he would attack him wherever they met. Col. Thomas, with great reluctance, accepted the cartel. He made his will that same night, committing his soul to Almighty God, "in hopes," he said, "of his mercy and pardon for the irreligious step I now (in compliance with the unwarrantable customs of this wicked world) put myself under the necessity of taking." He had no wife nor children, and so left a legacy to his servants, and the rest of his modest estate to his brother. As he wrote this farewell to the world, his mind naturally reverted to that day at Springfield, three years before, when his superior officer arrived on the field—after the fighting—jauntily wearing a Red Rose; and who can say what thoughts were his of that witching maiden, who unwittingly had been the cause of this fatal bitterness between brother officers?

The two men met at six o'clock on the following morning, Thursday, September 4, 1783, in Hyde Park, London. The lush grass was still besprinkled with dew that sparkled like jewels from heaven. The soaring larks were yet warbling their sweet melody in the sky. The rays of the early sun shone pure and bright through the foliage, as though murder had never entered the hearts of men. In a few minutes it was all over. The "rancor and private animosity" of Col. Thomas was expiated in his heart's blood. Col. Gordon fled the field and the country, an outcast, accused by the Coroner's Jury of "willful murder." The Red Rose had become the Mark of Cain. Col. Thomas lingered for just twenty-four hours. "Death was kinder to him than life, for as the rosy dawn looked in upon him, it touched his pallid countenance with a crimson tinge, and as he expired, his hand moved over his wound, the blood welled forth, and lo, he clasped a Red, Red Rose!"

Just three months later, there appeared in Rivington's *New York Gazette*, the third and last canto of Andre's famous "Con Chace," wherein that connoisseur of female beauty paid his tribute to this same winning maid, predicting:

> And all the land around shall glory
> To see the Frenchman caper,
> And pretty Susan tell the story
> In the next Chatham paper.

SIXTEEN

COMMENTS ON CUSTOMS OF THE SOCIETY OF THE CINCINNATI

Wessel Ten Broeck Stout Imlay, 1901

Wessel Ten Broeck Stout Imlay, 1850–1910 (admitted 1885) was the great-grandson of Captain Wessel Ten Broeck Stout (Original Member), First Regiment, New Jersey Continental Line. Imlay was born in New York City and spent his entire professional life there. For many years, he was a grammar school principal in Brooklyn, New York. He was Assistant Secretary of the New Jersey Society in 1894 and Secretary from 1895 to 1901. Imlay is currently represented in the Society by Jack Stevens Jordan.

Taken from the Minutes
of a Meeting
of the Society of the Cincinnati in the State of New Jersey,
held on February 22, 1901,
in the Waldorf-Astoria Hotel in New York City

Introduction by President Frank Landon Humphreys:

According to the Institution of the Society just read by your Vice President, this Society is pre-eminently a society of friends, formed, first of all, to keep alive the friendship of our fathers, and to perpetuate that friendship in us, their sons; a friendship born in the old days—of a common peril & a life of hardship—a friendship kept alive in us their sons today by a common realization of the necessity of keeping ever before us, especially in these days of the flood tide of foreign emigration, American principles. To this end we meet; to this end we bid you welcome to our board tonight.

In the hurry of modern life we have lost a good deal of the repose and dignity of the old days. The impatience of the day has swept away a great many of the old customs because they take up a little of our time. The world moves on apace. The old customs are forgotten; & there is nothing to take their place. We are just beginning to awaken to this fact today. Men everywhere are going back to the old days for their best models in matters of art and manners. There has been serious talk of the revival of some of our old customs here in the Society of the Cincinnati. We of the Cincinnati should be of the very first to welcome the return of any of those old ceremonial customs that can add gentleness or dignity or beauty to the acts of men. Our Secretary has in his keeping the ancient book describing many old ceremonials of this Society. He will read to us from it tonight and give us an idea of what some of those old customs were. I call upon Mr. Imlay.

Talk by Mr. Wessel Ten Broeck Stout Imlay:

I have sometimes thought that the term, "Society of the Cincinnati," for our Society was a misnomer. We are looked upon as representing perhaps the City of Cincinnati, and being gathered together in the State of New Jersey to celebrate the founding of that city, whereas we celebrate the founding of the United States of America. The thirteen stars in that flag do not represent thirteen states or parts of the Cincinnati, for we have but one order of the Cincinnati, for convenience divided into thirteen separate societies,—not separate societies of the Cincinnati, but societies in the states of the original colonies.

Our ancestors possibly may have been fond of ardent spirits, for in 1828 I find a memorandum to the following effect, to which I wish the Chairman of the Committee of Arrangements would listen with attention. [Reads] "Resolved that the Society of the Cincinnati agree to abstain from the use of ardent spirits at dinner this day."

Question: "What is the date of that?"

Mr. Imlay: "1828"

Questioner: "I knew it was obsolete."

Mr. Imlay: In 1795 the Society took two days to attend to the business of the meeting. They assembled at two o'clock on the third of July, did a little business, adjourned until evening. On the fourth of July attended church, to which they marched, listened to the Declaration of Independence and an oration, came back, ate dinner, transacted business and went home. If a member was absent he was fined four dollars. If he attended later on he was paid ten dollars. [Laughter].

In 1794 we find that there was manifested a fear that some of the members of the Society would attain to greater dignity and have more titles to their names than others, and as we were a band of friends, of brothers, those who were more fortunate were told that in future the members would be recorded in the minutes and called upon in the Society by their names, with the appellation of Mr., any forms or rules to the contrary notwithstanding. And therefore, gentleman, to return to the old customs, I call the reverend doctors, the learned doctors, and generals &c. plain Mr.

In 1791 I find it was unanimously resolved that mourning, consisting of crepe or ribbon on the left arm should be worn for thirty days in memory (Secretary will please supply the names of two members) of late members of this Society, deceased, and that in case of the death of any member the presiding officer give public notice that mourning will be worn by the members of the Society during the time above mentioned; and I think Mr. President, that the custom could be revived with credit to the Society.

In 1801 I find that we are told who shall be invited—"Resolved that invitations to dine with the Society be confined to the principal officers of the general and state governments and clergy, and that they be made by or under the direction of the President only."

In 1807 I find a resolution that every member of the Society be at liberty to dine with the Society at Anniversary Meetings [with] the person whom he expects will represent him after his decease, provided there be nothing improper in the character of the person to be introduced, of which the Committee of Arrangements shall be the judge. [Laughter.]

I am delighted that our Committee of Arrangements shall have something to do.

In 1828, and mark you this is the time the use of ardent spirits was to be abolished, an orderly sergeant was appointed. [Laughter.]

The Society proceeded to appoint an orderly sergeant, when Albert Voorhees, a sergeant of the Revolution was appointed orderly sergeant of this Society.

In 1831 honorary members were distinctly said to be life members, not in the sense that there are honorary members of other societies where they are admitted and meet with, but do not take part, but as the founders of our order banded together those who had fought for their country, and as they recognized that in future there were many others who would do the same, or contribute in some manner to the growth of the country, these were deemed worthy to become members of the Order of the Cincinnati. As such members they were to meet with, take part, preside and hold office, as we have had many honorary members in our Order and in the general society. When they die, their membership lapses; when we die our membership descends. That is the only difference between an hereditary and an honorary member. And, Mr. President, I believe that New Jersey today has a gentleman whom we could safely elect a year or six months hence to the position of honorary member. During the late war the advisor of the President, the Attorney-General of the United States came from this State, and therefore, I will give notice that at the next meeting of the Society, I shall propose for honorary membership the Hon. John W. Griggs.

I could go on and quote from nearly every page of this book, but it is getting late, there are others to take part, and therefore I beg to be excused from going further.

SEVENTEEN

ELIAS DAYTON, BRIGADIER GENERAL, CONTINENTAL LINE

Hughes Dayton, M.D., 1901

Hughes Dayton, 1873–1944 (admitted 1895) was the great-great-grandson of Lieutenant Colonel Elias Dayton (Original Member), Commander, New Jersey Brigade, Continental Line.

Hughes was a graduate of Yale University and the College of Physicians and Surgeons at Columbia. He was Assistant Treasurer of the New Jersey Society from 1901 to 1908 and Vice President from 1926 to1944 (see illustration 9).

Hughes Dayton is currently represented in the Society by Samuel Gray Dayton III of Chadds Ford, Pennsylvania.

Read before the Society of the Cincinnati in the State of New Jersey, at Atlantic City, N.J., July 4, 1901

Elias Dayton, the son of Jonathan Dayton, was born at Elizabethtown, N.J., May 1, 1737. His great-great-grandfather, Ralph Dayton, came from England to Boston, and thence, in 1639, to New Haven, Conn. Soon after this he moved to South Hampton, L.I., where he remained for ten years, changing his residence in 1650 to East Hampton. Here he died in 1658, leaving two sons, Robert and Samuel. Robert, born in 1628, married Elizabeth Woodruff, had three children, and died April 16, 1712. His son Samuel was born in 1665 and died January 30, 1746. Samuel's wife, Dorothy Miller, was the mother of seven children, one of whom, Jonathan, was born in 1700. Jonathan left East Hampton about 1720, settling at Elizabethtown. He was twice married. His first wife, Mary, gave birth to three children, Mary, Samuel, and Jonathan. His second, Patience, was the mother of Elias, Patience, Daniel, Robert, and Sarah. He has left "An Account of the Bearth of My Children:

> *Mary was born September the 5 day: 1726. Samuel was Born Febewary the Nineteenth Day: 1727–8. Jonathan was Born June the 24: 1731. Elias Was Born May the first: 1737. My daughter Patience was Born Febewary the 14: 1738–9. My Son Daniel was Born Jenewary the 17: 1741. Robert was Born June the 3 Annoy Domney: 1743.*

He is said to have had another daughter, Sarah, though this name does not appear upon his own record. Brought up in this large family, Elias is said to have followed "a mechanical profession" after reaching manhood until the outbreak of the French and Indian War.

His first military training was received during this war. His commission "to be Lieutenant of a Company of New Jersey troops in Colonel Peter Schuyler's Regiment," was signed by Governor Bernard on March 19, 1758, four days after the passage of the law authorizing the formation of the regiment.

His book, containing the orders for the day for part of this campaign, reveals many of the characteristics of the military life at that time. The first entry, "Camp at Fort Edward, June 11, 1759. Parole Norfolk," is followed by the list of officers for the day and directions for construction of paths by which the troops might advance "if in any Case of an Allarm in the Night, that the Regiment Shall be Ordered out." The same order contains the following provision for the material wants of the soldiers:

> *Spruse Beer will be Brewed for the health and Conveniency of the Troops, which will be Served out at prime cost; five Quarts of Malasious will be put in each Barrel of Said Beer; each Gallon will cost three Coppers. The Quartermaster of the Regiment, Regulars and Proventials, is to give Notice this Evening to Lieut. Colonel Robinson of the Quantity of each corps is desirous to receive, for which they must give a Receipt, and pay the Money before the Regiment marches. Each Regiment to Send a Man Acquainted with Brewing, or is best capable of Assisting the Brewr, to the Brewry to morrow morning, at 6 Oclock on the Revalet, a Lieutenant of Montgumaryes Regiment. Their Men are to remain, and are to be paid at the Rate of Eighteen Pence per Day. The Sergeants of the Regulars, and one of the Proventials to be Supported by the Brewry, who will be paid one Shilling & Sixpence per Day. Spruse Beer will be delivered to the Regiment on Tuesday morning or Evening.*

The orders for June 13 state: "All the Provision Barrels to be returned to the Quartermaster to put Indian Corn in, and every one encamped to take Care and not break them. The Whole Regiment to turn out to Prayers This Evening."

The orders overflow with notices of court-martial and regulations relating to matters of discipline. On the 16th of June they give the warning: "The Centry on the Bastions, or any part of the Ramparts, not to Smoak Tobacco, on any pertence, whoever is found Guilty in Disobeying these Orders, will be confined and severely punish'd." That evening we find "For Guard to morrow Lieutenant Dayton." On June 19 the orders are dated at Half Way Brook, where a detachment was left after departure of the main body for Lake George. The men stationed at Half Way Brook seem to have been difficult to control, for we find the warning:

> *Whosoever is found Guilty of making any Disturbance in Camp or Stockades after the Retreat beating either by Singing, or Cursing, or Swearing or any noise [by] which the Guard may be disturbed, and the Centries not well able to distinguish any approach of the enemy, if any should be looking in Order for a prisoner he shall be severely punish'd for the same.*

Silence is repeatedly enjoined and the men are ordered "to ly on their Arms and to be ready to Turn out on the least Alarm in the Night." A few days later, the troops are reminded that it is necessary to awaken when called and are warned

> *that if they dont out with calling upon, so much as has been they may expect to be confin'd for such neglect; an they must be sent to the Lake at head Quarters Guards for Tryal. Whosoever in this Camp is Guilty of Card playing after the publication of these Orders must expect to suffer for disobeying the Orders, of this Camp.*

Having regulated the morals of the detachment, the commanding officer directs the next day that "every Captain or Commanding Officer of Companys will fetch every Man of Duty to wash their Clothes, as perhaps this will be the only Time they will have at this post." They are further ordered "to see that all their Men of Duty to draw their Charges, and wash their pieces Clean, and have them very dry before Loading."

The main body, including Colonel Schuyler's regiment, in camp at Lake George after June 26, also found it necessary to enforce discipline. On the 29th the orders require "The Serjeants and Corporals to Turn out every Morning to exercise their men at the parading place, and the absent shall be Broke immediately. And it is Standing Orders, that the first Serjeant or Corporal, who is found Drunk at the Exercise, or any other Duty, shall be Broke, and punish'd imediately." The question of payment of the troops appears to have been a secondary matter and one left to discretion, as we read on July 1:

> *The General Directed the payment to be made in the following manner viz. a Serjeant 6 shillings, a Corporal 4 shillings, a Drum 4 Shillings. Private Men 3 Shillings per Week, York Currency; Eight Shillings that Currency being 1 Dollar.*

On July 4 it is ordered that "All the Men yet are now in Camp, are to turn out with Captain Schuyler imediately to go and cut bark and Brush for the Regimental Hospital. They are to take one half their Arms and Accoutrements and the other half without, Axes and Tomahawks." The record suddenly ends on July 5 at Lake George with: "For Working party Jersey Regiment." Then followed the expedition up Lake George, with the skirmish before Ticonderoga and the evacuation of that fortress and Crown Point by the French. Lieutenant Dayton is reported as being with the "Jersey Blues" under Wolfe at Quebec on September 13, 1759; but there seems to be no record of his movements after the encampment at Lake George in July. It is uncertain whether he remained with the army under Amherst, who, after the destruction of Fort Ticonderoga, moved down Lake Champlain, driving the French from the lake and then ignominiously settled for the winter at Crown Point instead of moving on Montreal and joining Wolfe in the attack on Quebec.

On March 29, 1760, Lieutenant Dayton was made Captain in Colonel Schuyler's regiment. This year was also marked by the birth on October 16 at Elizabethtown, of his first son, Jonathan, who became a Captain in his father's regiment during the Revolution.

In 1760, he was ordered to Albany by General Amherst.

His next military service was performed in 1764, when he commanded a successful expedition against the Indians near Detroit.

From this time Elias Dayton, living with his wife Hannah and an increasing family, was engaged in mercantile life at Elizabethtown, an occupation which was interrupted by the breaking out of the Revolutionary War. In 1774, we find him a member of the Corporation of Elizabethtown; and on December 6th of that year, the Freeholders of the town met at the Court House and appointed a committee, of which he was one, to organize the town for vigorous support of the measures recommended by the General Congress for resisting British oppression. From the beginning of the troubles which led to the final outbreak, he was placed in one of the most active centers of patriotic effort, and his personal history is closely linked with that of the town, which early began military preparations. In July and August, 1775, they were able to forward to Washington several tons of powder, and it is recorded that on October 3 "Sixteen Companies of Foot and one of Horse, belonging to this Borough, were reviewed on the Parade, went through their Military Exercises with Alertness and Regularity, and made a very handsome Appearance."

Elias Dayton is mentioned as one of four Muster Masters for two battalions recommended by the Continental Congress to be raised and authorized by the Provincial Congress held at Trenton, October 26, 1775.

One of the first active steps taken was the capture of the British ship, Blue Mountain Valley on January 22, 1776, by 100 volunteers from Elizabethtown in 3 or 4 boats under the command of Elias Dayton, now Colonel of the Militia of Essex County, acting in conjunction with another boat containing 40 men under Lord Stirling. The Provincial Congress ordered the sale of the ship and its cargo of provisions, coal, and other stores, and the division of the proceeds among its captors.

On February 5, Elias Dayton was recommended by the Provincial Congress, and on February 9 received his appointment from the Continental Congress, as Colonel of the Third Battalion of the "Jersey Line" of Continental Troops; and took part in all the battles in which the Continental Line of New Jersey was engaged during the war. At the Second Establishment on November 28, of the same year he retained the position of Colonel of his battalion, and at the time of the Third Establishment in 1780, became Colonel of the Third Regiment.

He has left a brief summary of his Revolutionary career, beginning: "February 1776 Warrants Issued to raise the Third Regiment Jersey in April following I marched the Regiment compleet out of the State in to New York & in May marched to the northward."

A letter from Major Barber to Mr. Caldwell, dated July 17, 1776, describes the reception of the news of the Declaration of Independence by Colonel Dayton's New Jersey troops at Fort Schuyler. The Declaration was read, cannon were fired, huzzas given, and the battalion formed in a circle with three barrels of grog in the center. Colonel Dayton took a cup and drank to the toast "God Bless the United States of America." The other officers and troops then drank the same toast with loud signs of approbation.

A touch of humor is given to this portion of Elias Dayton's career by a letter addressed to "Mr. Jno. Dayton" by six prisoners, and dated "September 18, 1776." It reads:

> *The Humble Address of the several Persons now confined for their several crimes in the Main Guard House*
>
> *Humbly Sheweth*
>
> *That we entirely rely on your*
>
> *Interest and Goodness.*
>
> *Humbly Hoping that you will Interest yourself in our behalf and plead with Your Honourd Father for to Relieve us out of a Miserable prison as we hope you of your Goodness can & entreat of him to Mitigate our punishment & as he feels Joy at the Meeting of his beloved Son. I hope he will feel the same Joy at the Returning of several of his sons by Adoption to their duty. this done we shall be for ever bound for to pray &c.*

The diary of Elias Dayton continues:

> *the last of October marched from Fort Schuyler for Ticonderoga on my way & at G. Schuyler's Quarters I received a letter giveing an account of the death of my Father & my presence being very necessary to settle the estate as Executor G.S. gave me permission to return which I declined doing untill the enemy gave over their attempts against Fort Ticonderoga. In December I returned to Jersey where I found the enemy had almost over run the State. Mrs. Dayton with her children had just escaped them & got back into Morris County, leaving behind her great part of our cloaths, household goods &c. &c. all which were totally lost. instead of*

> *going to my famely I immediately upon my arrival in the State Joyned the Melitia I found in arms & continued with them until I march into El. Town made prisoner of a Lt. Jno. McDonald & 30 highlanders with a Schooner loaded with the baggage of the 71st Regiment; the baggage was sold by way of vendue at Springfield.*
>
> *March 1777 I joyned the army Morris Town marched with them to Middlebrook, in the action Short hills and my horse wounded, was never absent from this time until December '77 was at Brandwin & Germantown & at the last place had a horse killed under me, in December was sent by G. Wishington into Jersey to collect cloathing of any kind for our naked men. I suffered near one hundred pounds by this business.*

This was during the winter at Valley Forge. Then came the news of the French alliance, and Clinton's movement from Philadelphia to New York with the battle of Monmouth in June 1778. Elias Dayton writes: "I was in front of the enemy & again had a horse wounded at Crosswick's bridge. After the enemy went to New York I was stationed in El. Town where I have frequently command but never lost a single man taken from me by the enemy."

The "Massacre of Wyoming" and the tragedy at Cherry Valley had aroused Congress, and a punitive expedition was sent, in 1779, against the Indians in Western New York. The diary says:

> *I was upon the Western expedition with G. Sulivan where my conduct meet with the fulest approbation of the General, at this time I was apointed member of Congress but as I had an acquaintance among the Indians I thought I might render the most essential service to my country in the field.*

After the successful completion of this expedition, Colonel Dayton returned to Elizabethtown and was stationed there in June 1780 when Knyphausen attempted his invasion of New Jersey. He met him in the engagements at Connecticut Farms and Springfield. Here it was that the pastor, Mr. Caldwell, distributed the psalm books for wadding for the muskets, shouting to the soldiers "Now put Watts into them, boys!" Of this campaign Colonel Dayton writes: "When G. Kniphausen came out to El. Town with all the British army I was their and was so very fortinate as to have my conduct with the enemy at Connecticut Farms & Springfield approved of by General Washington which I then thought one of the most happy events of my life."

On July 25, 1780, General Maxwell resigned and Colonel Dayton as senior officer succeeded to the command of the New Jersey Brigade, Continental Line, which he held during the remainder of the war.

In October he wrote:

> *I was sent by General Green who commanded the right wing of the army in Bergen County, to Eliz. Town in order to gain some particular intelligence from the enemy in New York. in October I fell sick & did not recover perfectly in twelve months, notwithstanding which, I undertook the long march to Virginia & was at the taking of Ld. Cornwallace.*

Early in the year 1781 came the meeting of the New Jersey troops which he aided in suppressing.

On the 21st of September the Jersey Brigade landed on the James River in Virginia, and the story of the siege of Yorktown with its triumphant conclusion is told by Colonel Dayton in two letters to his son. The first reads:

> *Camp before York Town October 12, 1781*
>
> *Sir*
>
> *I wrote you last about the time we came on this ground since which time we have been busily employed in making preparation for & carrying on our approaches against the enemy the 9th we opened our batterys against the town in ten hours time the enemies guns were almost totally silanced, our cannon about 30 in number and 15 mortors have been incessantly fireing night & day ever since, the night before last the Charon of 44 guns was burnt by our shels & yesterday morning two other large ships (names unknown) were burnt in like manner. Ld. Cornwallis has got into a cave to be out of the way of our shels, both shels and shot we are informed by deserters do great execution in the town the first shot we fired killed two officers, our loss has been very trifeling about six men killed & 10 or 12 wounded. amongts the former is Colonel Scammel, late Adjutant General, an excellent officer & a good man he was wickedly murdered by the brittish some time after they had taken him prisoner he was taken by imprudently advanceing too near their works to reconitre them, at 12 Oclock this day my Brigade goes into the trenches & this night we shall advance our lines within musket shot of the enemies,*

& if no actident hapens I hope & believe that before this reaches you his Lordship will be our prisoner. Enclosed I send you a rough draft of our situation and that of the enemy I have done it without any regard to distances just to give you an Idea of our aproaces since writeing the above I am informed that our troops began a second line last night within musket shot of the Enemies lines, which second line the Jersey Brigade must compleet this Night, the british killed only one of our men last night.

I have received two letters from you for which I thank you I hope to receive a third this day as the post is hourly expected. I am very sorry to hear your Mama continues so much indisposed but hope by proper assistance she may be recovered, and that you may inform me of it in your next—

And now my dear son take the advice of a fond father it may be the last you will ever receive from him. Attend to your Studies & prepair yourself to be usefull to your fellow men and if possible an ornament to the Society in which you live. Above all I pray you to do justice love mercy and to walk humbly with your God, & then I am sure happiness will attend you through all eternity.

The drums are just going to beat to parade for the march to the trenches So fare well and God bless you—remember me most effectionately to your dear brothers & sisters. The drum beats to arms.

Farewell & God bless you
Elias Dayton

P.S..—*Seven deserters came from the enemy last night, a number comes every night.*

The second letter continues:

Camp York Town October 19, 1781
10 Oclock A.M.

Sir

I have this moment returned from head Quarters wher I saw the General sign the articles of capitulation with Ld. Cornwallis, his Lordship is to give us possession of the redoubts or horn works at 12 Oclock & at one Oclock is to march out at the head of his troops his drums are forbiden to play eighter a french or American march & another very mortifying circumstance to the british their Colours are to be

Cased *At 3 Oclock the troops at glocester march out in like manner, they are all to pile their arms in presents of the french & American Army who are to be paraded upon this glorious ocasion, this parade differs very materially from the one I was going to when I wrote you last—*

The number of prisoners is not yet exactly ascertained but estemated at about 5000 A very considerable number of Horse & near one hundred topsail vessels must fall into our hands beside a very large number of cannon &c. &c. The night after we opened our second paralel the british guards passed the french lines under pretext of being americans by which mean before the imposition was discovered they killed one french officer three men & spiked eight of their cannon, but as soon as they were known to be british three companies french granidiers (although not half their number) charged them with baynets killed ten upon the spot & took 8 prisoners, the remainder run to their works with precipitation—The 17th in the after part of the day Ld. Cornwallis beat a parlay and offered to surrender on certain conditions which our General would not grant, the whole time has been taken up since in settling the tirms, the enemy are all prisoners of war to be sent to any part of Virginia, Maryland or Pennsylvania that G. Washington chooses. In six or eight days I hope to begin our march northward, but a suffitient number from this army to reduce Charles Town will march southward—I received your letter by last post & thank you for it. After recept of this you will write to me and send it under to Lary & Stockholm apoligise to them for the trouble you give them by my order & beg them to keep the letter untill they see me, or certainly know where to send it to me. In your letter inform me of the prices with you of Rum, wine, Loaf Sugar, brown Do.[ditto: (brown) sugar], Tea, coffee, chocolat, molasses &c. &c. Mention any sort of dry goods that may be wanted desire your Mama to send particular word what she would wish should be brought from Philadelphia look out for plenty of good Apples & turnips, let no Indian corn be lost as it will be most wanted if you can put the little mere any place to earn her keeping until I want her it will be well, as I fear your pasture will be short—

The drums are now beginning to beat for parade I must break off and hast to receive, a haughty cruel, unjust but now crest fallen foe

I am yours

Affectionately

Elias Dayton

General Washington's friendship for Colonel Dayton is shown by one of his letters:

Head Quarters January 15, 1782

Sir

I have the pleasure to congratulate you on your late promotion to the rank of Brigadier General which took place in Congress the 7th Inst.

Your Commission arrived here yesterday and I shall keep it until I can have the pleasure to deliver it to you in Person—which I must request may be as soon as possible and that you come prepared to remain with your Brigade the remainder of the Winter.

If Captain Schaack is not yet gone to New York I must desire you to take measures to oblige him to go in—

I am
Sir
Your Most Obedt. Servt.
G. Washington

The date of his promotion is usually stated as 1783 (See "Jerseymen in the Revolutionary War") and it is possible that being early in January 1782 was carelessly written instead of the former date.

General Dayton's diary closes with the words: "1782. At Verplanck's point I was taken very ill and the Doctor who attended me thought best I should get to my famely as soon as possible." That he was in Elizabethtown in March may be inferred from a letter which is addressed to him by General Knox, which also substantiates the view that his promotion did not occur until 1783 as it is directed to Colonel Dayton.

Boonton, March 21, 1782

Dear Sir

We have received an answer from General Sir H. Clinton, informing us that he will direct his commissioners to meet us at Elizabeth-Town on the 28th instant. We have to request you will be so good as to have the seal at that place at the above mentioned time.

I am Dear Sir
Your Humble Serv.
H. Knox.

On April 19, 1783, the news of the signing of the treaty of peace with Great Britton was announced in the camp of the New Jersey Brigade. On May 13, the Society of the Cincinnati was instituted. On June 11, General Dayton called together the officers of the New Jersey Line before they returned to their homes. They subscribed the Institution and General Dayton was elected the first President of the State Society, a position which he occupied until the time of his death in 1807. One of the orders upon the Treasurer, which he signed in his official capacity, calls for the payment of $32. to a Mr. Drake in settlement of the expenses of the annual dinner of the Society on July 4, 1792.

After the close of the war, General Dayton returned to Elizabethtown where he carried on a mercantile business under the name of "Elias Dayton and Son." Like others of his time, he was a slave owner. In his will, we find a bequest to his wife Hannah of a "Negro wench named Lem," and to his son Elias, a "negro boy named Michael." He has left also a bill of sale for $200, dated November 14, 1803, for a negress named Phillis and her infant aged sixteen months, signed by Alexander C. M'Whorter.

His will and two codicils contain as names of his children: Jonathan, Elias B., William, Horatio, Aaron, Polly Barber, Hannah, and Sarah. In addition, Jonathan refers in a letter to his sister Molly.

Elias Dayton's warm friendship for Lafayette is demonstrated by letters which show the existence of business relations as well.

In form and carriage, he was said to resemble General Washington so closely that when their backs were turned it was difficult to distinguish them.

After the close of his active military career, Elias Dayton served his native town and state as well as the general government. For several years, he was a member of the New Jersey House of Assembly. In 1787, he declined an appointment to the convention that framed the Constitution of the United States, in favor of his son Jonathan, then only twenty-seven years of age. However, he spent the years 1787 to 1788 as a member of the Continental Congress. In 1789, he was Recorder of Elizabethtown; he served also as a member of the Corporation [governing body of Elizabethtown]. From 1796 to 1805, he was Mayor of the Borough except for one year. In 1793, he became Major General of the Second Division of New Jersey Militia, an appointment which he retained until his death. For many years, he was a member and president of the Board of Trustees of the Presbyterian Church of Elizabethtown, where he was buried with "military honors" and where the

> *assemblage of citizens was more numerous than we ever knew on the like occasion in this town. . . . The whole proceedings were marked with*

> *uncommon solemnity, and evinced the unfeigned affliction felt by all classes of citizens. In this solemn dispensation of Providence, we behold the uncertainty of sublunary things, a fellow-mortal, in health in the evening, and a corpse before the next rising sun.*

The "American Register" for 1807 thus comments upon his death, which occurred on October 22, of that year:

> *Very Suddenly, of the gout in the stomach, Major-General Elias Dayton, in the 71st year of his age; the corpse was removed to the Presbyterian church where a funeral sermon was preached by the Rev. John M'Dowell.*
>
> *At the commencement of our revolution, General Dayton, though possessed of a competency of* this world's goods, *and in the fruition of every domestic enjoyment, he balanced not between which side he should take, but with a patriotic ardor devoted himself to the service of his country in the times which tested true patriotism, and never quitted the tented field until the consummation of our Independence.*
>
> *General Dayton was open, generous and sincere; ardent in his friendship, and scrupulously upright in all the moral duties; in manners easy, unassuming and pleasant; his charity prompt and diffusive; a warm and zealous supporter of the gospel. Few excelled him in the relative duties of husband and parent; and as a neighbor he was pre-eminent in that virtue.*
>
> *This venerable patriot of '76 had been engaged in active life ever since he was 19 years of age, and a greater part of it in the service of his country.*

EIGHTEEN

TALK ON THE FOUNDATION OF THE NATIONAL SOCIETY, ORIGIN OF THE NAME, AND SOME DISTINGUISHED NEW JERSEY MEMBERS, PAST AND PRESENT

Wessel Ten Broeck Stout Imlay, 1908

Wessel Ten Broeck Stout Imlay, 1850–1910 (admitted 1885) was the great-grandson of Captain Wessel Ten Broeck Stout (Original Member), First Regiment, New Jersey Continental Line. Imlay was born in New York City and spent his entire professional life there. For many years, he was a grammar school principal in Brooklyn, New York. He was Assistant Secretary of the New Jersey Society in 1894 and Secretary from 1895 to 1901. Imlay is currently represented in the Society by Jack Stevens Jordan.

The members, upon the adoption of this memorial of organization all signed it, and General Heath, General Baron de Steuben, and General Knox were selected as a committee to wait on His Excellency General Washington, the Commander-in-Chief, with a copy of the Institution, and request him to Honor the Society, by placing his name at the head of it. The various States were requested to immediately form their State Societies and send a delegation from each to represent them in the first general meeting to be held on the first Monday in May 1784.

Another meeting was held at the Cantonment of the American Army on the 19th of June, 1783, at which the Baron de Steuben, reported on the question of the Insignia of the Society, and it was adopted, as designed, by that famous French engineer, Major L'Enfant, who made an immortal name for himself by designing the city of Washington, D.C., and the National Capital building. Major L'Enfant's history was a sad one, but recently his services have been recognized; his grave long neglected and unmarked has been reopened, and his remains interred with honor, in the Arlington National Cemetery, and his grave appropriately marked.

At this Convention, a resolution was passed

> *that the thanks of this Convention be transmitted, by the president to Major L'Enfant, for his care and ingenuity in preparing the aforementioned designs, and that he [be] acquainted that they cheerfully embrace his offer of assistance, and request a continuance of his attention in carrying the designs into execution, for which purpose the president is desired to correspond with him.*

Thus was the insignia and diploma of parchment adopted.

Origin of the Name

Who shall say that the name of Washington was not in the minds and hearts of the founders of this honorable Society?

Many indeed, there were, who probably would have liked to have called the Society for their illustrious chief "the Society of Washington," for all historians agree that not only did he inspire the respect and fidelity of his officers and men, but their ardent love as well.

He had already won undying fame in the arts of war, and was yet to win still greater renown in the arts of peace. His well-known modesty would probably have compelled him to decline the honor had it been tendered to him. That these gallant men had him in mind, is demonstrated when they selected the name of his Roman prototype, Cincinnatus, for the name of their Society. Both were farmers, both were called from the plough to save the state from enemies from without, both accomplished gloriously their missions, and both returned again to the field and the plough to finish out the measure of their days. It does not take a great effort of the imagination to picture this noble Roman clad only in his tunic or shirt, drawing his plough in the quiet fields of the Campagna, and thus receiving the deputies of the Senate, who announced to him his elevation to the dictatorship, and his wife, Racilia, placing upon his shoulders his toga and sending him forth to victory—to save the state, and returning to Rome, in twenty-four hours, after he had quitted it, in triumph, after saving the whole Roman army from destruction. So, too, can we picture Washington, called from his fallow fields of fair Virginia, from beautiful Mount Vernon, and the sainted wife, Martha, placing upon his fine, firm brow, the well-known three-cornered red hat and placing in his hand the sword of authority, to go forth to save the young republic, and subsequently to head it, young and feeble for eight years to a firmer foundation and a stabler existence.

His record of sixteen long years of earnest effort is unequalled in history. Fortunate indeed is the Society in its name, and it has given it to one of our great cities on the banks of the Ohio, of which there is a bit of interesting history. Congress gave lands in the territory northwest of the Ohio to many of its members for services in the Revolution, as the result of a petition and on April 7, 1788 Marietta was the first place in Ohio to be settled. All of the civil officers and most of the settlers were members of the Society.

It was, therefore, very appropriate for the Honorable Major General Arthur St. Clair, president of the Pennsylvania State Society, and Governor of the Northwest territory to change the name of the little hamlet of log huts, subsequently erected on the banks of the Ohio, and known as Losantiville, to "Cincinnati," in honor of the Society, and thus leave an enduring mark of its existence in the settlement which has now become one of the great cities of the Union. So much for its name. What a wealth of glorious achievement and illustrious self-sacrifice cluster around it! It is a far cry from 458 B.C. to A.D. 1776, but great deeds always deserve great honor.

The National Society is made up of the delegations from the State Societies, and meets every three years.

There are two classes of members—Hereditary members, which now number about seven hundred and fifty, and fifty-three Honorary members, divided among thirteen State Societies.

GENERAL ELIAS DAYTON, the first President, served in the French and Indian War, and during the entire revolution on active duty, and was a member of the Continental Congress. His descendents have been members in an unbroken line and his great, great grandson, Mr. Hughes Dayton, now represents him.

GENERAL JOSEPH BLOOMFIELD, the Second President, served until badly wounded at the Battle of the Brandywine, September 11, 1776. In 1801, he was elected Governor and Chancellor of New Jersey, and again from 1803 to 1812. He was a Member of Congress from 1817 to 1821. He was one of the founders of the Trenton Banking Company, and a Director, until his death in 1823.

MAJOR AARON OGDEN, the third President, was a graduate of Princeton College, served actively all through the war, and afterwards in the regular army. He served as a United States Senator from 1801 to 1803, Governor of New Jersey in 1812 and 1813, and President General [of the General Society] from 1829 to the date of his death in 1839. He was a very distinguished and able man and has been represented in the Society by two sons, a grandson, and now a great grandson, Mr. Henry Ford Ogden of Hoboken, New Jersey.

DR. EBENEZER ELMER, the fourth President, was a surgeon from the beginning to the end of the war, commanded a brigade in the War of 1812. He was a Member and Speaker of the New Jersey House of Assembly from 1791 to 1795 and a Member of Congress from 1801 to 1807. Dr. Elmer was the last surviving revolutionary officer of the Original Members and died at the age of ninety-one, October 18, 1843.

CAPTAIN WILLIAM SHUTE, the fifth President, was a Captain and Paymaster, served three years, resigned and was out two years, and then returned for three years, the balance of the war. His son and now his grandson, Mr. James Davies Shute of Mississippi, represents him.

DR. EBENEZER ELMER, the sixth President, again served as president for one year and until his death.

COL. JOSEPH WARREN SCOTT, the seventh President, was a son of Surgeon Moses Scott, who served during the first five years of the war. Col. Scott was a graduate of Princeton College, 1795, and served for a long time in the State Militia. He was a Presidential Elector in 1825. The present representative is Prof. William Earle Dodge Scott, a great grandson, long a Professor of Princeton College, and now residing at Saranac Lake, New York.

HON. L.Q.C. ELMER, the eighth President, was a distinguished lawyer, Member and Speaker of the New Jersey Assembly and of Congress, a United States

Attorney, a State Attorney General, a Member of Congress, and a Justice of the Supreme Court. He died at the age of ninety years. His grandson, Mr. Enoch Anson More Jr., of Denver, Colorado now represents the family of Dr. Ebenezer Elmer.

COL. CLIFFORD STANLEY SIMS, the ninth President, was a great grandson of Major John Ross, who entered the service in February, 1776, and served actively until he was retired in 1781. Col. Sims served both in the Army and Navy during the Civil War and was for some time an officer of the Pennsylvania Railroad Company. He died in Trenton, N.J. very suddenly, while in the discharge of his duties as Judge of the Court of Errors and Appeals. As President of the New Jersey Society, he was most energetic and faithful, and did much for its welfare and upbuilding.

GEN. WILLIAM SCUDDER STRYKER, the tenth President, of Trenton, New Jersey, was descended from Col. Nathaniel Scudder, who was graduated from Princeton College in 1751, and entered the Army at the beginning of the war and served until he was killed in action, October 15, 1781 at Black Point near Shrewsburg, Monmouth County, New Jersey, not many miles from his birthplace and home. He was buried with military honors in the old Tannant Church graveyard. He was the only member of the Continental Congress killed in battle during the Revolutionary War. General Stryker served with distinction during the Civil War and was many years thereafter and until his death, Adjutant General of New Jersey, and filled many positions of trust and honor. He wrote many books and pamphlets as the result of his historical studies of the revolutionary times, notably the "Battle of Trenton" upon which he spent many years of conscientious labor in this country and in Europe. Mr. William Bradford Stryker, of Trenton, succeeded to his father's membership in 1908.

REV. FRANK LANDON HUMPHREYS, the eleventh President, is descended from Lt. Col. David Humphreys, of the Connecticut line, who served on the staffs of General Putman and General Greene and was aide-de-camp to General Washington from 1780 to 1783. He received the thanks and a sword from the Continental Congress, when he presented the standards captured at Yorktown, Virginia, at the time of the surrender of Cornwallis. Rev. Mr. Humphreys is Chaplain of the General Society and has been recently transferred from the New Jersey to the Connecticut Society.

MR. JAMES WALL SCHUREMAN CAMPBELL, the twelfth and current President of the Society, is a resident of Freehold, New Jersey, and is a descendent of Surgeon George Walker Campbell, who served faithfully from 1777 to the close of the war.

Many men, distinguished in various walks of life have been members of the New Jersey Society.

Rev. James Francis Armstrong was a chaplain in the Continental Army and for many years thereafter pastor of the First Presbyterian Church of Trenton, there closing an honorable and useful career. He has been represented in the New Jersey Society by a son, a grandson and namesake who was a distinguished officer of the Navy during the Civil War and now by a great grandson, Mr. Ogden Armstrong of Harrisburg, Pennsylvania. General David Hunter, a famous soldier of the Civil War, who was born near Trenton, New Jersey, was a son of Chaplain Andrew Hunter, a Virginian, a graduate of Princeton College, a Professor of Astronomy there, and although once a prisoner of war for a time, was released and served during the entire war. General Hunter was a member of the New Jersey Society and is now represented by a son, Mr. Richard Stockton Hunter of Philadelphia. The late president of the Pennsylvania Railroad Company, Mr. Alexander Johnston Cassatt, was also a member and a great grandson of Ensign James Johnson of the Pennsylvania Continental Line. A son of President Cassatt, Major E. B. Cassatt of Chesterbrook Farm, near Philadelphia, succeeded to membership upon the death of the former.

Two distinguished citizens of Newark, New Jersey, have been honored members of the Society, the late F. Wolcott Jackson and Thomas Talmage Kinney. The former was a great grandson of Lt. Col. Joshua Huntington, a valiant officer of the Connecticut Continental Line. Mr. Jackson was Treasurer General of the National Society and his son, Mr. Philip Nye Jackson, has succeeded to his membership. Mr. Kinney was a grandson of Lt. Abraham Kinney of the Pennsylvania Line, and also great grandson of Surgeon General William Burnet, of the American Army, and from whom are descended the famous New Jersey family of Hornblower. Mr. William Burnet Kinney of Newark, a great grandson of Lt. Abraham Kinney, now represents this lineage.

General Peter D. Vroom of Trenton, a retired officer of the United States Army, and a member of the New Jersey Society is a great grandson of Captain Jonathan Rhea of the New Jersey Line, who served throughout the entire war, and was Quarter Master General of New Jersey from 1813 to 1815, in which year he died in Trenton. General Rhea was one of the founders and second President of the Trenton Banking Company until his death. A younger brother of General Vroom, Judge G.D.W. Vroom of Trenton, has been an honorary member of the New Jersey Society since 1888.

General Edward Burd Grubb of Edgewater Park, New Jersey, is a member and is a great-grandson of Captain Peter Grubb. From 1861 to 1865, General Grubb served in the Civil War, entering the service when only nineteen years of age. He was United States Minister to Spain and once Republican candidate for Governor of New Jersey.

These brief bits of family history will serve to recall many deeds of valor and useful services to State and Nation and it is fitting that we, of the present generation should keep them alive and fresh in memory, as an incentive to patriotic effort and enthusiasm. The archives of the New Jersey Society are full of most interesting and valuable data covering the lives and records of original and subsequent members. To attempt to reproduce them fully would be a task quite beyond the limits of this article. There are now eighty hereditary members scattered from Maine to California, and nine honorary members, whose rights are not transmittable, and whose membership has been conferred for distinguished services. Some thirty-six original members are not now represented in the Society, and in some cases, the families have died out or disappeared and cannot be located. Those who read history might agree that England underestimated the strength of the American revolt, and that a larger force would have crushed it out completely. The patriots or war party were but a little band at first, and grew in members and power as the struggle was prolonged through eight long years until finally those immortal words of Patrick Henry "give me liberty or give me death" awoke an echoing response in every American heart.

NINETEEN

THE MISSION OF THE CINCINNATI

William Pennington, 1909

William Pennington, 1866–1922 (admitted 1887), was the great-grandson of Captain William Sandford, Pennington (Original Member), Second Regiment, Continental Artillery.

Pennington was born in Newark, New Jersey, and resided in Morris Plains, New Jersey. He was Vice President of the New Jersey Society from 1909 to1922.

Read before the Society of the Cincinnati in the State of New Jersey on February 22, 1909 at the Hotel Plaza in New York City

In that Yule Tide Classic of Charles Dickens, "The Christmas Carol" one of the three spirits which upon as many occasions appear to old Scrooge is asked by him upon being shown an unhappy future state of things if these results *must* be, are accomplished facts, or whether they may be averted.

To this the spirit replies: "Men's courses will foreshow certain ends, to which, if persevered in they must lead, but if the courses be departed from the ends will change." Then says Scrooge, "Say it is thus with what you show me" etc. etc.—

I have always thought of this passage in the Carol when considering the ultimate achievement in any enterprise, individual or collective; and when trying to fathom the outcome of endeavor along any given lines wherein much good is hoped for or some misfortune feared, these lines of Dickens rise as upon the printed page before me and I, in my turn speculate upon the changes and chances of the future.

And so, while discussing the future of our Society, I am not emphasizing the pessimistic refrain of the spirit's admonition, nor am I adopting a gloomy or dubious view as to the Society's tendencies, I am about to direct your thoughts to a serious consideration of the duties and responsibilities of this Order, a duty first to the country, second to the Society itself, and third to the individual members thereof. Basing my remarks now upon our Society as a National Order, I shall speak of conditions as they seem to be at this time.

Ours is the original Society of its kind, and constitutes the foundation principle upon which like patriotic structures have since been built.

We are all familiar with the circumstances under which the Cincinnati grew into being and we know the impulses, ripe and seasonable that actuated its formation.

The Institution of this Society is its Creed, and our forefathers in framing it outlined for themselves and for us their descendants a rule of action and a kind of a Common Law which terms, according to Sir William Blackstone are identical in meaning, under which rule and law we should direct our deliberations and without obedience thereto we are not fulfilling our duties as trustees and custodians of a sacred inheritance.

The tendency at present in our Society—I am speaking more particularly of New Jersey, but doubtless my words will apply elsewhere—is toward an evasion—or perhaps I ought to say the non-performance of some of the inherited duties of membership.

This Society has within this State a hereditary membership of about 80 persons, and an honorary list of 7 members.

The average attendance at our regular meetings in July is less than 25, and in February less than 16.

True, many members reside at comparatively remote distances, and where the circumstances appear to warrant it absence should not be criticised, but some sacrifices must be made for a mutual and good cause, and there should be a pleasure and satisfaction in such self-denial.

Our ancestors, those great sturdy men who founded this Order did so in a spirit of commendable pride of brotherhood "through a common danger" and this Society is based upon victories won through the exercise of sacrifices manifold in themselves, the memory of which, as much as any other thing is the blessed heritage of the members of this Order.

There is but small excuse for the limited attendance of late years at our meetings, provided the true Cincinnati spirit lives within us. If this spirit is dead—then an ample but most unworthy reason is apparent, but this last cannot be. We believe the inherited nobility of patriotism resides forever within the being of every member of this Order in New Jersey, and elsewhere, but there must be an awakening of that spirit an "evidence of things hoped for and unseen."

And so, in the first place the indifferent attendance should be improved upon, and to this end let some of us exercise a little self-denial by leaving home upon the Fourth of July—let each one of us be "minute men" in this regard, responsive to our Society's call, remembering that there are patriotic duties devolving upon us as members of this fraternity, and let us show by rallying around our standard as did the loyal citizenry of 1776 that the spirit which animated our forebears is still afire within our own bosoms.

For some time this Society has ceased publishing, there being apparently nothing in our transactions calling for such an edifying proceeding.

Formerly a paper written and read by a member upon some Revolutionary subject, about which frequently the individual association largely and interestingly figured has occasionally been a feature of our meetings, and I can recall one or more of these occurrences and the pleasure they gave to those present.

One redeeming accomplishment, however, must be acknowledged; the compilation of the Excerpts from the Minutes of this State Society:—this book elegant in its form, will be a lasting credit to the Society, and an hereditary treasure to our membership.

Let us encourage "native talent" along these literary lines, and welcome any act of ours distinctly in keeping with patriotic enterprise.

Whenever, too, an occasion, or historic spot may be commemorated by tablature or otherwise, let us try to show the citizens of this State that our Society stands for definite purposes and objects and is not merely a quiescent social organization.

There are many ways in which our Society can not only interest and instruct the busy public mind of to-day, too much bent upon commercial and selfish purposes, and in habitually so doing fulfill the destiny of the Order, and do justice to the State in which it resides, thereby honoring the Society and the impulses and patriotic spirit of its members.

There has been, and there still is quite too much complacency in this State Society of ours; satisfied with ourselves, and all that has already been vested in us as members of this Order we have, while not let us hope becoming "rusted in ignoble sloth," yet failed to produce within recent years tangible evidence of our active accomplishment as members of an organization committed to certain enterprises.

It is true that simplicity of manner and form in our annual meetings should not be overshadowed by profitless ostentation, but, to those who would disapprove of efforts made with the utmost sincerity by a few of our brothers to make memorable a certain meeting of this Society, it would be proper to say that with the year 1889—when the writer became a member and for several years thereafter our July meetings were most distinguished events. A dinner worthy of the Society was then furnished,—no buffet lunches such as our ancestors would have considered almost a breach of propriety were served in those days,—but Banquets, with the old fashioned toast lists and leisurely discussion of the viands and respectful attention given to the speakers—distinguished men. Then there was no haste to catch certain trains, and in the doing of this to turn one's back upon the honorable Society while still in session!

This I may say was the order of events some years ago; let this order return again,—let our banquets *be* banquets, and our speakers worthy of the function, and honored by the elegance of the event aside from every other distinction.

I am not to be taken to mean that the patriotic system must be fed upon the dainties in order to live, nor that the spirit of '76 must be nurtured by the material delights of the table that it may thrive,—I have already, I think, made myself clear on this point, but I *do* say that a centre of attraction must exist to draw into communion and fellowship our members, and this need is supplied by more elaborate ceremonial on July 4th and the presence of distinguished personages as guests of the Society.

To make these meetings memorable, to make the Society the medium of patriotic revival in sentiment is the duty each one of us owes the country; to in every way promote the dignity of the Order and further the objects [purposes] for which the Society calls in its Institution is the duty we owe our ancestors, and the Society itself, and to engender feelings of fellowship, brotherhood and sincerity and harmony in endeavor is the duty we owe each other in our fraternal relations.

These happy conditions can be brought about and sustained only by a unity of action, and with the hearty cooperation of all, or a great majority of the membership.

A fraternity like this, linked by personal representation with the noble past through such names as were originally associated with the Order, many of which appear to-day upon our roster, should be one of the proudest possessions of New Jersey, herself one of the original thirteen states, that glorious nucleus of freedom banded together irrevocably to secure the independence that we now enjoy.

And so, to sum up in this short and quite imperfect argument for improvement in society conditions I suggest—more interest in our Society's doings which of itself will beget better attendance; a thoughtful realization of what the Order really is; a publication now and then, to stimulate our recollection, and to give us a "realizing sense" as it were; an entablature when the proper cause therefore appears by the Society, and the funds thereof warrant it; Historical reminiscence; and our 4th of July meeting as orthodox and elegant as possible, with gentlemen of national repute as speakers and guests, and in these ways drawing about us the attention of all persons interested in the perpetuity of patriotic impulse, and thus recognizing, too, the Society of the Cincinnati in the State of New Jersey as not only one of the early supports of the cradle of liberty, but the careful guardian of the infant therein laid, from those cradle days on and through the 126 years that intervene, as let us hope she will continue to be beyond us and our time on—forever and forever!

TWENTY

ADDRESS

Winslow Warren, 1910

Winslow Warren, 1838–1938 (admitted 1870) was educated at Harvard with an A.B. in 1858 and an LL.B. in 1861.

He practiced law in his own office most of his long career. He was a United States Commissioner in Boston from 1864 to 1894, Collector of the Port of Boston from 1894 to1898, Counsel for the Boston and Providence Railroad for many years, and one of the founders of the Dedham Water Company in 1884. He was active in many hereditary organizations and served long and well as an officer in the Society of the Cincinnati. Winslow was President of the General Society from 1902 to 1930 (see illustration 16).

Address
Delivered at a banquet given by the Society of the Cincinnati in the State of New Jersey at the Hotel Plaza New York City on February twenty-second nineteen hundred and ten to Commemorate the One hundred and seventy-eighth birthday of General George Washington and in Honor of The Hon. William Howard Taft President of the United States

Mr. Vice-President of the New Jersey Society, Mr. President of the United States, and Brethren of the Order of the Cincinnati of New Jersey: This seems like Alice in Wonderland, we move down one seat after each speech. I esteem it a great honor at any time to be invited to attend a meeting of the Society of New Jersey, but as a special honor to attend at this time and to greet the President of the United States. My first meeting with the Society of New Jersey was at the Triennial meeting in Princeton in 1884, which was presided over by the Honorable Hamilton Fish, then President-General of the Society. There were but six Societies represented, which may account for the rather sobering fact that in looking over the list of delegates present upon that occasion, I can find but three living members: Richard Dale, the President of the Pennsylvania Society, Secretary-General Gardiner and myself, but Gentlemen, I shall not soon forget the pleasure that I then had in making the acquaintance for the first time of such interesting members of your Society as Clifford Stanley Sims, the then President, who afterwards presided at the Triennial meeting in Boston, and if he had lived might well have occupied the place that I now hold; that singularly attractive gentleman, General Stryker, William B. Buck, Francis B. Ogden, and others whom if time allowed I might well mention. Their places are doubtless well filled in this Society, but their memory will ever be fragrant in the minds of those who were privileged to know them. A few weeks since at a banquet in Boston, after replying to the toast to the Cincinnati, as I sat down a prominent gentleman of the Loyal Legion said to me, "While you have been speaking I have been wondering whether a hundred years hence there will be the same feeling towards the original members of the Loyal Legion and their descendants as there now is towards the Cincinnati." I could not but feel, Gentlemen, that that was a somewhat complicated question to answer, for although the American people will never forget, and never cease to honor the men who sacrificed all for their country, it could not be still complicated with the thought that from its name and origin the Loyal Legion must of necessity represent but one section of the country, and recall a civil war which future generations may feel desirous to keep somewhat in the background. There is an important difference between that Society, honored and honorable as it is, and this Society of the Cincinnati. Although we are restricted (the Cincinnati represents no section) by our Institution to the thirteen original States and to maintaining only that brotherly love and friendship which existed between the leaders from all the States, and principles which are the common heritage of every citizen of the United States, of every State in this Union to-day, and of every State to come. To the Society of the Cincinnati was entrusted no special mission to support those principles which was not equally the mission, the right and the duty of all lovers of their country. Whatever prestige may come to this Society, and it is not small, comes from the fact that Washington was our first President-General, that Hamilton succeeded him, that many of the original members of the Society of the Cincinnati were prominent in the Constitutional Convention and in the first Congress; that this Society has kept its organization intact from the Revolution to the present day and that it has been the fount from which have sprung very many large and influential patriotic associations which are now invigorating American principles and keeping before the people the truths which our fathers vindicated. You will remember, Gentlemen, that at the time that this Society was first founded, many eminent patriots of the Revolution bitterly opposed it. They were obsessed with the idea that this might be a step towards founding an Order of nobility oblivious of the fact that in a democratic republic, with no primogeniture, and with no privileged classes, a Society, although it might be hereditary, was bound to become as this has become, the most democratic Society in the world, and I do not except another Society which was founded as you may remember as an offset to the Cincinnati Society termed originally, "The Columbian Order," now Tammany Hall. It was created because it was supposed that it would be more democratic than this Society, and it has remained more democratic from that time on. (Laughter.) If any gentlemen prefer membership in that Society to membership in the Society of the Cincinnati, we have no reason to complain. The only kind of nobility that this Society can represent is the most republican and the safest and the most desirable Order of nobility in the world because it is simply nobility of character and high citizenship. That kind of nobility I do not think that our patriot friends of the Revolution would really have objected to, and that that has been the result of this Society's formation can be seen nowhere better than at one of our Triennial meetings. At the last Triennial at Charleston, a distinguished guest who was not a member of the Society, said to me, "This body of gentlemen before me is the most imposing body that I have ever looked upon," and I was proud to believe that those men there bearing the names of the great leaders of the Revolution also maintained all those high patriotic instincts of the fathers and in their own communities were filling high and responsible positions and devoting themselves to the good of their country. We have, Gentlemen, before us to-day—no one knows it better than our distinguished guest of the evening—intricate, perplexing, important questions, equal to any questions that the men of '76 had to deal with. To solve them, to solve them rightly, will require all the patience, all the wisdom, all the skill and courage that could have been asked of the men of the Revolution, and you, Gentlemen of the Cincinnati, have your own duties so far as in you lies to devote yourselves to aid in the solution of these great questions and in that way to faithfully and patriotically serve your country. The Society of the Cincinnati is to-day a small body, but it is not without its influence. You men here may be pardoned if at times you are inclined to boast of the blood that flows in your veins, of your ancestral descent, you may be pardoned, I say, but only in case you have shown by your own accomplishments that you have a right to such pride. The eagles that you wear to-night are as nought unless you are ready with equal faithfulness and equal devotion as the men who gave you the right to wear them, to serve your country to the extent of your ability. An incident which seems to me to show the patriotic feeling towards the country instilled by the Institution of the Cincinnati was exhibited most remarkably in an unexpected place and is still fresh in my mind. Some years since, while driving over the battlefields at Concord and Lexington with Col. Simons, the President of the South Carolina Society of the Cincinnati and our honored Vice-President-General, he said to me, "It may surprise you to know that in the midst of the Civil War I stood up in Confederate uniform at a meeting of the Society of the Cincinnati in Charleston, South Carolina, upon the anniversary of the battle of Yorktown, and there read the Institution of the Cincinnati." I could not but feel that the old Cincinnati spirit was there, some lingering love for the old flag in the midst of the terrible war, and it may well be that the old associations clustering around the Cincinnati meetings, the spirit of brotherly love, and a common inheritance may have kept alive even then some latent Union feeling which after the war was closed helped to bring on that era of good feeling which in less than half a century is so remarkably manifested throughout the whole of the United States. (Applause.) That to me, Gentlemen, was a striking and a touching thing, and if I interpret it as somewhat a credit to the Society of the Cincinnati, I think I may be pardoned in view of the fact of the intense good feeling now existing between the South Carolina Society and the Societies of the Cincinnati in other States. (Applause.) And now, Gentlemen of New Jersey, coming from a State which was the broad highway of the Revolution, blessed with the glorious memories of Trenton and Princeton and Monmouth and Morristown, a State that suffered with the reverses and rejoiced in the victories of Washington, you have everything to inspire you to make your Society a strong and influential body—numbers are as nothing—all depends upon the character of the individual members of your Society. Cultivate in every way good feeling and harmony among yourselves and cordial feelings towards all your sister Societies. Remember that you are but carrying on the work of former generations, and it is for you to hand to your successors the name and fame of the Cincinnati untarnished.

It has given me a great deal of pleasure to be with you to-night. I wish that it was in my power to remain the whole evening, but I have made a previous engagement which I can hardly break, and so, Gentlemen, in closing I can only in the words of Tiny Tim say to each and all, "God bless us, everyone."

TWENTY-ONE

AN INTERPRETATION OF THE INSTITUTION OF 1783

Wessel Ten Broeck Stout Imlay, 1910

Wessel Ten Broeck Stout Imlay, 1850–1910 (admitted 1885) was the great-grandson of Captain Wessel Ten Broeck Stout (Original Member), First Regiment, New Jersey Continental Line. Imlay was born in New York City and spent his entire professional life there. For many years, he was a grammar school principal in Brooklyn, New York. He was Assistant Secretary of the New Jersey Society in 1894 and Secretary from 1895 to 1901. Imlay is currently represented in the Society by Jack Stevens Jordan.

Delivered at a banquet given by the
Society of the Cincinnati
in the
State of New Jersey
at the Hotel Plaza
New York City
on February twenty-second
nineteen hundred and ten
to Commemorate the
One hundred and seventy-eighth birthday of
General George Washington
and in Honor of
The Hon. William Howard Taft
President of the United States

At a meeting of the Standing Committee held last October, I was directed to prepare for publication a paper upon The Interpretation of the Institution of the Cincinnati, the paper to be read at the meeting of the Society on February twenty-second, 1910. Neither the time nor your patience would allow me to inflict such a paper upon you this evening, but with your permission I will give you an outline of the Institution of 1783.

When we look back at the history of our country, we find that it is filled with trying critical periods. Periods that required the wisdom and tact of those in charge of the Ship of state, to pilot it safely through the breakers that seemed to surround it, and bring it into smooth waters. Among all of these, the one that stands out in bold relief, is that between the cessation of hostilities in 1781 and the adoption of the Constitution in 1788. Well has it been said that this period was preeminently the turning point in the development of political society in the western hemisphere. It was the work done in the years between 1783 and 1789 that created a federal nation capable of enduring the storms and stress of future years. It was in the earlier crises that the pliant twig was bent; and as it was bent so has it grown; until it has become a goodly and sturdy tree.

We, viewing the past through the lapse of years, are prone to imagine that the several colonies were enthusiastic in their support of the American Army during the Revolution. Yet such was not the case. It was the courageous men few in number, who being insistant in season and out of season, by their strength of character forced enthusiasm and secured success.

But the war was over. The dangers of battle field and the fear of failure were things of the past. The colonies had ceased to exist and in their place were free, independent states. States that claimed sovereign rights and that owed allegiance to none. A law unto themselves they were jealous one of the other. Their very freedom from Great Britain was the rock upon which there was danger of being wrecked.

The credit of the country was practically gone. Money was difficult to borrow at home or abroad. Congress, which in the past had made promises to the army it had called into being, now found itself unable to keep these promises. It asked the states to honor its acts and it was met with refusals on every hand.

Schism and distrust were everywhere rampant. The army, finding itself deserted by Congress and feared by the people, who imagined that it would seek to establish a military form of government, became a hotbed of plots and counterplots. In this condition of public affairs, feeling ran high. A slight overt act would set the whole country aflame. Here among many strong men, the personal magnetism of Washington was manifest. Acting as a pacificator, he, to a great degree, smoothed out the differences and allayed the disquietude that existed between the army and the people of the several states. As the army had but little to do, Washington granted furloughs and by two's and three's the men returned to their homes. Then came the order to disband. Those who were left in the Cantonments on Hudson's River were saddened at this order. Soon they who for eight long years had been comrades, comrades amidst scenes that draw men closer together than any thing else can, would be separated. They were to return to the dear ones at home, but what of the friendship formed on battle field and by camp fire, were they to be forgotten? Could they forget how they stood shoulder to shoulder while shot fell thick and fast about them? Could they forget the dangers they had been through together? They were not that kind of men. Comradeship formed as theirs had been, must not, could not be forever lost.

This condition caused General Knox with others whose counsel he sought to bring into being a plan whereby there would be one Society of Friends to endure as long as they should endure or any of their male posterity, and, in failure thereof the collateral branches who may be judged worthy of becoming its members. Not a society for the present alone but one that was to endure through all time and grow in strength with each succeeding year.

It has been said that as early as 1776, General Knox in a conversation with John Adams expressed the wish for some ribbon to wear in his hat or button-hole, to transmit to his descendants as a badge and proof that he had fought in defense of their liberties. Such being the case, it is not too much to claim for him the honor of being the originator or founder of our Order when in addition there has been found in the hand-writing of this general the first draft of a constitution dated April 15, 1783.

This draft formed the basis of the proposals that were formerly submitted to the officers of the American Army May 10, 1783. These proposals were not adopted at that time but were considered and amended and then referred to a committee to report at a subsequent meeting.

When the second meeting was called on May 13, the committee reported to the officers there assembled an Institution which was accepted by them and adopted. As there were very few of the officers present at this meeting, no attempt was made to effect a temporary organization. A resolution was passed which directed that a copy of the Institution be given to the senior officer of each State line. He was to request the officers of the respective state lines to sign their names to the same.

The members of the several State Societies were to assemble as soon as possible for the choice of president and other officers; and the presidents of the State Societies were to appoint a meeting of the officers who might be chosen from each state, in order to pursue such further measures as might be judged necessary.

As yet the Institution had not been signed by any officer. This was a condition necessary to membership in the order. A committee was appointed at this meeting to wait on his Excellency, the commander-in-chief, with a copy of the Institution, and request him to honor the Society by placing his name at the head of it.

The officers of the Southern Army as well as those of Rhode Island were not present at this time, for General Heath, second in command, was desired to transmit to the senior officer in each state from Pennsylvania to Georgia inclusive, and to the commanding officer of the Rhode Island line the Institution.

On June 19, of the same year, the Baron de Steuben called a meeting of the officers, letters were read and the suggestions relative to the medal and to the order to be made for the society were accepted. General Washington was requested to act as president until the first general meeting. General Knox was elected Secretary-General and General McDougall, Treasurer-General. The principal objects being accomplished, the members of the convention thought fit to dissolve the same and it was dissolved. Thus you see that this

left it to each state society to determine for itself what action it would take in the matter.

During the period from 1784 to 1800, the unsettled condition of the Cincinnati as to what was its basal law brought about a state of affairs that was anything but conducive to its growth. Apathy was soon manifest, and it was not long before several State Societies became dormant, until only six had a continued existence, among which was that of the State of New Jersey. Now all this has changed; renewed interest exists and each of the original thirteen states has its active state society. The uncertainty as to what would become of the Order caused State Societies to establish diverse rules for the admission of members, some under the provisions of the Institution of 1783, some under those of 1784 and some under provisions made up of a compromise between the two, until today there is but little uniformity in the rules of admission of the several states.

The Institution of our Order antedates the Constitution of the United States by five years. It was the men of the Cincinnati who solemnly pledged their sacred honor to uphold the principles as laid down in the Institution, that made it possible for the several states by mutual concessions to accept the Constitution and make it the law of the land, and the United States an actuality.

They recognized that the immutable principles they had accepted which made them bound to preserve inviolate the rights and liberties of human nature as well as a determination to promote and cherish between the States Union and National honor, must be the keynote of the Union of States.

This, gentlemen of the Cincinnati is our heritage. Greater than that held by any man or body of men in this or any other country. This insignia is not only an emblem of an Order as orders are understood in the courts of the old world, but it is a patent of noble deeds handed down to us by those who by their acts made it possible for the United States to be. It shows that we are not only the representatives of the past, but also the custodians of the present by a trust imposed upon us by those whose representatives we are. This trust is sacred and imposes something upon each member that cannot be cast aside. We may not have the ability to carry it out, as did our sires of old, yet each Cincinnatus must recognize that it becomes his duty to see to the best of his ability that the principles of our Institution are not empty words. The Union of States is now assured, but what about the rights and liberties of human nature without which the high rank of a rational being is a curse instead of a blessing?

As we gaze down the corridors of time, we find its walls filled with the names of those who have helped to make this country of ours great. The men of 1783 recognized that these men would have the same ideals as they and under the Institution of 1783, they gave to us of today the privilege of enrolling them as members of the Cincinnati.

Honorary members of our Order, we are conscious of your having done noble deeds, of being the noble few who have stood out bold and true when duty called. Tonight another name is added to our number. It is not in the hazy past that we must look to find his deeds spoken of. No musty tome must we pore over to bring to light some new fact about him. Around the world is he known as diplomat, pacificator, statesman. It is not as President of these United States alone that we welcome William Howard Taft to our number, but as the worthy associate of the men of 1783 who brought our Order into being.

TWENTY-TWO

AN AWAKENING ADDRESS

William Pennington, 1911

William Pennington, 1866–1922 (admitted 1887), was the great-grandson of Captain William Sandford, Pennington (Original Member), Second Regiment, Continental Artillery.

Pennington was born in Newark, New Jersey, and resided in Morris Plains, New Jersey. He was Vice President of the New Jersey Society from 1909 to1922.

Delivered at Allenhurst, New Jersey, July 4, 1911 upon the occasion of the Annual Meeting of the Society of the Cincinnati in the State of New Jersey

The Society of the Cincinnati was instituted directly after the close of the war of the Revolution by the Officers of the Continental Army. The truth of that statement is the absolute foundation of this organization, the original of all patriotic societies, and the base upon which subsequent orders of a like nature have since been reared. It is well that not only members of the Cincinnati, who should need no emphatic reminders of this, but those belonging to kindred societies be impressed with a fact of such supreme importance. Let us consider for a moment what all this means; a war undertaken to right wrongs that cried aloud in their extreme injustice for remedy or abolition; a war that ultimately became a struggle for absolute freedom of individual and institution, and in its ultimate result brought into existence the greatest Republic upon this earth, had just come to a close. The English possessions known as the American Colonies were now freed from the overbearing and insolent domination of Great Britain's King and Ministry, and belonged to the liberty-loving people whose cause had triumphed along with their victorious armies. These armies were at the outset of the struggle motley aggregations, grotesque, one might say, if such a word could be applied to that which was so noble in motive and exalted in incentive as this citizen army that found itself in pitiful array against the trained soldiers of His Majesty King George III, in the year A.D. 1776. Is it possible for us in this advanced day and generation to realize what living in these wonderful times meant? Can you imagine what the daily life of an active patriotic man must have been then? The terrific importance of a combat at arms wherein the physical odds were so painfully against the success of the principles involved must have so taken possession of the hearts and brains of the patriots of that day, that they literally and absolutely resolved to die; to give up their lives in real earnest fact ere they would falter or bend the knee in surrender of either individual or principle. We talk and read lightly about sacrifices, the giving of life for life, in ancient and in current affairs, but do we Americans living now ever put ourselves in the place of these founders and heroes of one hundred and thirty-five years ago and grant to their memories in silence and in awe their meed of reverence. In the hurly-burly of to-day, we fail to recall as often as would be for our own good these facts, that this nation, one of the greatest in existence, is but a baby in years as Empires are reckoned, and all that we see about us—that which compels a world—wide wonder and admiration, had its inception and inspiration in those first rude struggles between the farm hands and defenders of their rural homes with scarlet-coated soldiers from across the sea, and rising like incense from the smoke of these early unequal conflicts has come the apotheosis of power, dignity, wealth and independence, which today we call with pride the United States of America. But what could those earnest, loyal, liberty-loving men accomplish, unofficered and undisciplined? Could courage unfostered and unhusbanded accomplish aught without hardship and a dominant directing will? And so even as the householders rushed to arms and filled the ranks, rare souls with the Divine gift of command took their exalted stations at the head of these untried troops and the war went on through alternate elation and depression, but always with a dogged determination, to its triumphal close.

At the time of these soul-stirring happenings, and under these rare conditions, the Society of the Cincinnati came into being. Can you imagine a more responsible heritage than you as a member of this Society possess? Linked by ties the most sacred in life's experience, you were by an inversion of inheritance represented in that famous gathering at the Verplanck House, whereat the Society was formally organized; your ancestor, whatever his rank, spoke at that time for you through his representatives in that assembly, and pledged you to a faithful fulfillment of the duties of this choice brotherhood. What do you think was uppermost in the minds of these great men when they came to realize the importance of these principles? I believe they saw in the long vista of the future a nucleus for such love of country and mystic binding together their posterity in a hallowed fraternity ever deepening, no matter whether the actual membership increased or fell away, as would exert a positive and incalculable influence for good upon the destinies of their country, and they had the belief because they could not find it in their hearts to doubt, that a strong reciprocal sentiment would bind close together for all time as nothing else could, this one Society of Friends. See what was given to us to treasure and emphasize; a permanent membership for our posterity in an organization whose founders were also the founders of the Republic in which we live. Can you parallel this happening? Do you realize this privilege? And what is asked of you latter day Cincinnatus? Attention, reverence, and an intelligent and scrupulous performance of the duty you owe to your Country, your Society and your ancestors, and I may add to yourself. I fear and I dislike to acknowledge it, but I greatly fear that a lack of knowledge which tends to chill realization is to blame for the lapse of devotion now and then in this

State Society and elsewhere within the order at large. But, call to mind the remarkable proprietary interest which we rightful inheritors of Cincinnati membership hold in a fellowship founded upon and co-existent with this great Republic of which we are citizens. Do we appreciate the significance of this? I most respectfully maintain that members of the order of the Society of the Cincinnati, whose title thereto is complete and flawless, are in their own persons more closely identified with the birth and early nurture of this great Republic than any other sentient being—and as such stand alone in all the confusion and multiplicity of patriotic societies and kindred movements of the present day. Do you think every member of this order realizes this fact as he ought? Do you believe that if these truths were taken to heart and believed as experiences in life are realized that there would be as much indifference in Society matters as there is? I know there would not be. And so in an attempt to awaken a life conception of our duties as members of this order and to outline what was transpiring when this wonderful Society was given life,—a life co-existent with the Government its founders helped to create, I have written this brief paper.

Brothers let us in our solitary hours dwell in memory upon the past, but emerging from this reflective mood let us bestir ourselves as active patriots. The chief negligence in Society matters is through non-attendance at meetings. I beg of you, gentlemen, to let nothing but death or serious illness or too great a distance stand between these meetings and yourselves. Your ancestor has pledged you to keep alive sentiments of patriotism, and you must obey these mandates if you are to be a worthy member of this Society. If you wish inspiration, conjure up as by the wand of Wizardry, the last scenes at Yorktown, where our allies the Duc De Rochambeau and the beloved Lafayette, helped us to victory in the final scenes; going back a little let us call to mind Valley Forge and the blood-stained snow—stained with the blood of patriots.—Then we in New Jersey—brothers all, should call to mind, Princeton, Monmouth and above all, that "Unhappy affair at Trenton," these are scenes in which by an inverse scheme of representation we participated. Were we not nobly represented there in the thick of the conflict, with the liberties of individuals and the fate of nations at stake? How do we fulfill *our* duty as representatives of these noble sires in this year of grace 1911?

The following principles shall be immutable and form the basis of the Society of the Cincinnati.

An incessant attention to preserve inviolate those rights and liberties of human nature for which they have fought and bled, and without which the high rank of a rational being is a curse instead of a blessing.

> *An unalterable determination to promote and cherish, between the respective States, that union and national honor so essentially necessary to their happiness, and the future dignity of the American Empire.*

That is what is asked of us—is it much compared to what was done for us? Oh let there be a richly awakened interest in this great order, the noblest on earth, let us in New Jersey show to the Country and to each other, that the Divine spark still lives undimmed and undiminished and let there be no excuse for non-attendance at our meetings, so shall we go from strength to strength individually, and collectively, as members of the Society of the Cincinnati—and prove to all mankind the propriety of our beloved order and make its accomplishments for good evident unto all, thus justifying by our acts the intent of those glorious characters gone before, and fulfilling as men the duties so honorably entrusted to us.

TWENTY-THREE

GEORGE WASHINGTON STAYED AWAKE HERE

John T. Cunningham, 1968

John T. Cunningham was born and raised in New Jersey, where he graduated from Drew University in Madison, New Jersey, in 1938. For many years, he was a feature writer for the *Newark News,* where he was known as "New Jersey's popular historian," and he was a past president of the New Jersey Historical Society.

Before the Triennial Luncheon Meeting of Delegates of the Society of the Cincinnati May 30, 1968 Morristown, New Jersey

It must be difficult for today's youngsters to assess George Washington's positioning in history. They have been exposed to the ceaseless dedication of American merchants and publishers of American newspapers to the assurance that Washington lived only as an excuse for an annual clearing of surplus merchandise. I am sure that many of our children think that Washington kept a store, like Mr. Macy and Mr. Gimbel.

However, these children at least are spared the silly gilded nonsense of Parson Weems that was popular a generation or two ago. I know that the fables about Washington that I was fed as a boy did as much to push him into my subconsciousness as any proliferation of annual sales do to today's youngsters.

I am equally sure that the status seekers, who perpetuate the legends that Washington slept here, there and everywhere, do little to enhance his memory. Washington's much-acclaimed proclivity for napping may make old houses more expensive, but I have never been impressed by sleeping generals.

Fortunately, not all children grow up unaware of George Washington's character and ability. Last spring, a fifth grader in a New Jersey school emphasized for me the role of Washington in history as well as any scholar ever has done.

That boy drew an outline map of New Jersey; it was rough and irregular, but at least it was his, unlike most of the other exhibits that were shown. On the map, he pasted crude figures made from pipe cleaners to show the places in the State where Washington had campaigned or where he had stayed. Then he captioned his project in a manner to remember: "George Stayed Awake Here!"

George stayed awake here! How simple, how direct, how vividly in contrast with the ridiculous, if time-honored, Washington slept here!

That boy has a beginning to understanding Washington that was denied most of us in this room. He approaches history with a sense of perspective, plus the sense of humor that is almost always missing whenever historians get together. Most historians forget that history is a matter of human beings who once lived—not people who have always been dead. We forget that people of two centuries ago laughed and lived and loved; these things were not invented in the twentieth century.

That New Jersey boy has had another advantage; he has learned in the fifth grade that New Jersey was one of the original thirteen states—a fact that constantly seems to escape most adults who studied the Revolution. If you wish an underscoring of this, consult any standard history of the Revolution. If New Jersey gets more than ten pages out of four hundred, that historian will be read out of the lodge.

I am firmly convinced that none of the thirteen states was more important to the cause of American Revolution than New Jersey. Our colonial history has been written so long from the viewpoints of Massachusetts and Virginia that historians have come to neglect automatically other areas. I plead today the cause of New Jersey. I submit that this was the single most important strategic area of the war. My thesis is simple. New Jersey lay between the first and second American cities: Philadelphia and New York. Whoever controlled New Jersey controlled both Philadelphia and New York; whoever controlled both won the war.

I am aware of Lexington, of Concord, of Bunker Hill and Ticonderoga. I know of that October day when Cornwallis surrendered at Yorktown.

Certainly, I do not demean the spirit and pride of other states, especially Massachusetts and Virginia, but I am speaking about New Jersey. I wish that we could muster similar pride. Three years ago, my family and I revisited Concord and Lexington. We met a pleasant, elderly man—about eighty, I judged—in the Concord business center, who made himself our unofficial host and informal guide. Eventually, he asked where we were from. We replied, "Morristown, New Jersey." He admitted, "I have heard of it."

"Have you ever been there?" I asked.

"Good heavens, no!" He answered in a bit of a shock, "Why I have not seen all of Massachusetts yet!"

I tell you that Longfellow was wrong. There is many a Concord man still alive who remembers that day in '75. They may not have stood personally by the rude bridge that arched the flood. They may not have heard directly the "shot heard 'round the world," but that shot echoes for them down through their years—and they are tuned to listen.

Yet, from the standpoint of hard military value, Concord had little meaning. It provided emotional shock, it provided symbolic beginning. The war could not be won or lost there—or at Boston or Charleston. It had to be won in the heartland of economic power and population density.

You will admit that it takes mixed amounts of courage and foolhardiness to discuss Washington and the Revolution before this group. You have been hearing of these things for years. You all should know as much about these subjects as I. That I accept, but my purpose today is not to instruct, but to arouse enthusiasm for this state's role in forming a nation.

I begin with facts, scarcely a way to arouse enthusiasm, but these set my pace.

Consider this fact: Washington spent a total of more than 730 full days and nights on New Jersey soil—and 730 days total two full years!

If we agree that the war began at Lexington and Concord and ended at Yorktown, that means that Washington was in New Jersey for one-third of the entire war. ONE-THIRD OF THE ENTIRE WAR! This was no place for sleeping.

New Jersey was a place for major battles at Trenton, at Princeton, at Monmouth, at Springfield. This was a place for eternal vigilance on the Watchung Mountains, a place for watching New York, a place for endless maneuverings of an underfed, ill-equipped, miserably paid army in the face of King George's might.

New Jersey was a place of revolutionary zeal. It was also a place where Tories were almost as numerous as patriots. It was a place of privateers and minutemen; it always comes as a surprise that minutemen neither began nor ended at Concord.

This was a place of heroes and scoundrels. This was a place of guerilla warfare and determined stands. New Jersey was, indeed, everything that the war could bring.

New Jersey's role in the war has been scorned. On the sad retreat across the state in November of 1776, General Nathanael Greene declared that Jerseymen acted "scurvily." On this march, the melting army caused Thomas Paine to write his brilliant words: "These are the times that try men's souls. The summer soldier and sunshine patriot will, in this crisis, shrink from the service of the country."

It is true that on the last day of November, a brigade of Jersey men left the ranks when their enlistments expired—but it is equally true that a brigade of Marylanders left the same day. New Englanders and Southerners also left when their enlistments expired—and with far less impending reason. After all, if the main army collapsed, the Jerseymen had homes to defend against an invader. This region was where the action was. I observe that patriotism usually shines most brightly when the enemy is on someone else's doorstep.

Washington knew well the strategic importance of New Jersey. His choice of the Watchung Hills for three of the first four winters of the war was no whim. He did not turn north at that bridge in Princeton in January 1777 because he thought the scenery was good.

Fortunately for the course of our history, British commanders never had a similar awareness. Suppose, for example, that General William Howe had decided to swing westward into New Jersey after his troopship appeared off Sandy Hook late in July 1776.

The war might well have ended in a month, since possession of this peninsula at that early stage would have split New York from Philadelphia and New England from the South. Conquest of New Jersey would have been a simple matter. Howe could have moved westward easily. The main force of Americans in the so-called Flying Camp at Perth Amboy was undermanned, poorly armed and so low in morale that soldiers pillaged the countryside. Abraham Clark of Elizabethtown, one of the signers of the Declaration of Independence, declared: "We have not had the enemy among us, but Staten Island hath not suffered from the British troops scarcely the tenth part this town hath from the militia."

Howe did not invade New Jersey. Instead, he pursued Washington into Long Island and New York and let him slip away to the north. Washington swung around into New Jersey and began the dismal march from Hackensack to Newark to New Brunswick to the eventual westward crossing of the Delaware on December 7, 1776.

Foes sneered that Washington was a "master of defeat and retreat," but before he reached the river bank, the general had ordered all boats commandeered up and down the river for miles. Cornwallis could not possibly follow him.

Nothing indicates that Cornwallis cared. He had packed his bags and was preparing to embark for England to spend the winter. He had agreed to return in the spring if, as he said, "There is another campaign, which we doubt."

Everyone knows of the battle of Trenton, but one of the major little-known stories of the war is what happened in New Jersey between December 7 and December 25.

This was occupied country, filled with enemy troops. Lord Howe offered amnesty. Loyalists streamed in, along with others of lukewarm spirit who hoped that their property might be protected. Instead, the British and Hessians turned savage, looting and pillaging and ravishing in the classic way that occupying troops use to make friends of the natives. Lord Howe had America in his hand. He preferred to spend his time and energy with a blonde widow in New York. It is axiomatic that when the fat cats play, the mice in the ranks run wild.

Shocked Tories saw their belongings pilfered and their houses burned. Overnight, they too became revolutionists.

Slowly, and without plan, the counterattack began. Small bands of Americans prowled in the night, slipping up behind sentries and killing them in the darkness. Every bush, every tree, every stone fence, was feared by the enemy, for there death might lurk. Hessians in Trenton complained, "We have not slept one night since we came to this place." By December 18, British troops were forbidden to move anywhere out of New Brunswick without armed escort.

Across the river, Washington's army was melting away. Soldiers went home when enlistments expired. What had been called the Grand Army seemed likely to shrivel away to fourteen hundred men at most by January 1. If Washington had fallen asleep on that gloomy river bank, the war would have ground to a halt before February.

Congress would not have helped; Congress could not have helped. General Charles Lee could not help; he had been captured in his nightshirt on the morning of December 13, while he dallied at the Widow White's in Basking Ridge. Washington and his men had to help themselves.

Need I tell this audience of Christmas Day in 1776—a day that I believe was the second most important Christmas Day in history? You know the story of the crossing, of the delays, of the sleet storm, of the bloody footprints in the snow, of the strike at a bewildered enemy at eight A.M.

I say bewildered enemy—not a sodden, drunken playboy army of Hessians. Usually, the Hessian troops at Trenton are written off as having tasted too heavily of the wassail bowl. To say that Washington's army downed a drunken foe is to demean the grandeur of the triumph. It is also to ignore the known facts. The truth is that Colonel Rall, the Hessian commander, knew that a strike was coming.

Ironically, in one of the strange twists of historic fate, a sizeable, wandering band of Americans fired on a Hessian outpost at twilight on Christmas night. Rall raced to the scene and concluded that the expected attack had come—and had been repulsed. Tension in the camp relaxed, and so did watchfulness. If Hessians had been patrolling the river road that night as they should have been, the Revolution would have ended outside of Trenton.

I hasten along with a thoroughly wakeful Washington. He returned across the river immediately, then came back December 30—exactly what conservative military leaders would have insisted he should not have done. Cornwallis by then had unpacked his bags and was hurrying to deal death to this "fox," as he called Washington.

Here again, a classic incident occurred. Cornwallis tried three frontal attacks, then fell back, as he said, to "bag the fox in the morning." Washington stayed awake, left fires burning and a few men to man wooden cannon. He slipped northeastward with the bulk of his army toward Princeton, with cannon wheels bound with bagging and bits of clothing to muffle the sound. Then there ensued the sharp, short clash at Princeton and the struggles outside Nassau Hall. Washington moved again. There was no question where he was going, he was headed for Morristown. There he could regroup his forces in safety, protected by the Watchungs to the east and south and by the bogs of the Great Swamp between. To the northwest lay the iron mines and forges.

This was a perfect military capital—the very place where an alert Howe should have headed in December. But it is doubtful that his girlfriend would have wintered well in that village.

Quickly, now, let history hasten on. Winter melted into spring, and Washington moved his army to the rim of the Watchungs, the better to watch the valley. Lord Howe ended his New York hibernation, kissed Mrs. Loring farewell, took charge at New Brunswick and tried to lure Washington out of the hills. He pushed the paw of the British army forward; the Americans nipped off the toenails and the paw drew back.

Tiring of that cat and mouse game, Howe withdrew from New Jersey late in June and took his army around Cape May by ship to Philadelphia. This is vital; he did not dare cross New Jersey. The long water voyage and American defenses on the Delaware River brought Howe into November before supplies came to Philadelphia unobstructed. By then, Washington was firmly in Valley Forge, ready to move when Howe took his annual spring tonic. Before spring came, the lady-loving Howe was replaced by Clinton.

Clinton moved in June, headed across New Jersey for New York. Washington broke camp and followed, determined to keep between the enemy and the direct roads to New York.

Once again, you know the story: the clash at Monmouth, the dreadful heat, the reluctance, possibly even the outright treachery of Charles Lee. You know of Washington's rally of the Americans, of the day-long battle that proved for the first time that the supposed rag-tag American army could stand up to the vaunted British on an open battlefield. Clinton escaped in the night to New York, but he had lost New Jersey again. I skip blithely along to the winter of 1778–79, when Washington returned to this state, taking up quarters in Somerville for seven months. This was a relatively pleasant interlude, filled with gaiety and fun—at least for the officers. That was the time of the grand party at Pluckemin to mark the first anniversary of the French alliance.

That was also the winter of what was called "a pretty little frisk" at Nathanael Greene's headquarters in Finderne. Tradition says that Washington that night "evinced such interest in young Mrs. Greene that he danced with her for three hours without once sitting down." That showed both his ability to stay awake and his fortitude in the face of what Mrs. Washington was certain to say as soon as they reached the privacy of their boudoir. I have a hunch that General Greene might have spoken to his spouse, too. Unfortunately, such things never get into the footnotes of history.

Then there was the third New Jersey winter; OUR winter, we Jerseymen in this room might say. That was the winter of 1779–80, the winter that Washington spent in Morristown.

That was a dreadful time. It was snowing when Washington arrived on December 1. It snowed and snowed—twenty-eight separate times that winter. It snowed so hard between the third and fifth of January 1780 that an eyewitness wrote of soldiers who died in collapsed tents, "buried like sheep in the snow." A regimental clothier wrote of soldiers "as naked as Lazarus." An officer in Stark's brigade noted "many a good lad with nothing to cover him from his hips to his toes save his blanket." Washington himself wrote that the enlisted men ate "every kind of horse food but hay," and he gave tacit approval to the illegal foraging that spread outward from the camps.

That was the winter when Benedict Arnold was tried—in Morristown—on a charge of favoring Tories in Philadelphia. He was found guilty, given a mild reprimand and soon after defected to the British. Consider the awesome impact of that trial on American morale. Arnold was second only to Washington in the esteem of his country.

Despite the air of depression and gloom, that winter offered some contrasting cheer to Morristown. Alexander Hamilton wooed Miss Betsy Schuyler, just down the street. Lafayette returned from France in the spring with the bright news that a French fleet was on the way. In the Ford mansion, Mrs. Ford and her four young children had the thrill of sharing their house with General and Mrs. Washington and the greatest military leaders of the day.

The tide was turning, but on June 6, 1780, Washington could only write: "One year rolls over another and without some change, we are hastening to our ruin."

You know me as a dedicated Jerseyman. You would expect me to say stoutly that the winter of 1779–80 was the worst of the war. Don't take it from me alone, take it rather from a distinguished Virginian, the late Douglas Southall Freeman, who wrote in *American Heritage* in February 1956:

> *There is a mass of evidence to show that the winter of 1779–80 at Morristown and Jockey Hollow was a period of far worse suffering than the corresponding months of 1777–78 at Valley Forge. This evidence is*

> *not going to upset tradition. Valley Forge has become emotionally the symbol of patient suffering during the Revolution, and it will remain so, though one finds it somewhat perplexing to know why the hunger and shivering of Morristown have been so nearly forgotten while the miseries of the gloomy camp on the Schuylkill are known to every child in the fifth grade.*

That New Jersey winter did not roll peacefully into a New Jersey summer. There were the two June smashes by the British in the direction of Springfield, a searching for a way to Morristown. That Springfield story is too broad for this afternoon; suffice it to say that the ability of major American historians to overlook a battle in which eight thousand British and Hessians opposed five thousand American regulars and militia is beyond my senses. The battle of Springfield gets far less attention than the clash at Lexington. The Massachusetts people have simply been more aware of good public relations—and they had Longfellow!

In these few minutes I have tried to sketch a basis for my point—that Washington stayed awake in New Jersey. He stayed awake here for two full years. Here, on our soil, the cause of revolution was kept alive. Here men fought and died. Here men spoke bold words. Here men suffered in the wretchedness of Middlebrook and Jockey Hollow.

And here we have largely forgotten our role in the brainwashing by generations of national historians. We ought to remember. We must remember. We ought to stir Jerseymen into pride.

Pride! Where was pride when announcement was made in 1955 that Route 287 was to be slashed through Morristown—and still will be sliced through this town despite protests? It will cross a corner of Washington's Headquarters grounds.

I have been told that only a tiny corner of the headquarters property will be taken. Only a tiny corner of one of America's top ten or a dozen great historic shrines! Imagine the anguish that would ensue in Texas if only a tiny corner of the Alamo were snatched away for any purpose!

But I am especially pleased to see a definite stirring of spirit and energy in the New Jersey Society of the Cincinnati. This is good; such Societies ought never to be closed corporations, more interested in the "society" than the history. History does not belong to the fortunate few or to the descendants of heroic figures; history belongs to all the people—and those who are blessed ought to be using their good fortunes to see that all the people can share in the glory of America.

There is much to do and little time to do it. We are approaching the two hundredth anniversary of the Revolution—the two hundredth anniversary of everything from the first shot fired at Lexington to the mournful fifers and drummers playing "The World Turned Upside Down" at Yorktown. The United States Government has taken due note of this. Last year the president appointed a twenty-five-member committee to plan the bicentennial.

The committee is headed by the president of Colonial Williamsburg. I accept that easily. Three of the eight members from the Senate and the House are from Virginia; two are from Massachusetts with others from New Hampshire, Rhode Island and Pennsylvania. I accept that but with lessening grace. It does seem a bit too much Virginia and Massachusetts. I even accept a bit disgruntled, the fact that five members representing the public are from New York City. What disturbs me is that there was no room for even one member from New Jersey, much less Delaware, Maryland, South Carolina, Connecticut or Georgia.

There was room, however, for a representative from Houston, Texas; from Toledo, Ohio; from the University of Chicago; from New Mexico; Los Angeles and Nebraska. You all know how vital Houston, New Mexico, Los Angeles, the University of Chicago, Toledo and Nebraska were to the American Revolution.

I submit that New Jersey ought to be represented and so should all the original thirteen states.

Time fleets by. We bulldoze; we rip; we destroy. But don't criticize today's destroyers unduly. Our ancestors let the Arnold Tavern be moved from its place on the Morristown Village Green and destroyed. Destruction is not alone a twentieth-century preoccupation.

I urge the Society of the Cincinnati and all similar groups to become active, to become involved, to take stands. I think of the great good that patriotic organizations could do—and were founded to do—even as they too often dissipate their time, their purpose and their energies seeking out enemies under the bed.

A rebirth of American patriotism will not come from bemoaning that the alleged good old days have gone. It will not come by denying the full rights of citizenship to all fellow Americans. It will not come by being suspicious of all those whose opinions are different from our own.

We do not honor bold ancestors by becoming timid descendants. We do not preserve the past by demeaning the present. We do not further the cause of history by keeping it to ourselves. History is too exciting, too vibrant, too worthy to wear the dim cloak of nobility.

We can only regain our sense of national proportion, our sense of heritage and our sense of honor if we become enthusiastic about history rather than by holding it in reverential awe. We ought to be able to laugh at history as well as to learn from it. Our emphasis ought to be this: George Washington stayed awake here.

I rest my case.

TWENTY-FOUR

THE BATTLE OF MONMOUTH

Jack Hite Gilbert, 1973

Jack Hite Gilbert was admitted to the Society in 1951. He was born July 25, 1900, in Louisville, Kentucky, and married Edith Porter. He graduated from the Georgia Institute of Technology with a B.S. in 1922, served as Assistant Secretary of the New Jersey Society from 1963 to 1968, as Treasurer from 1968 to1971, and as President from 1971 to 1974. He was a retired captain in the United States Navy.

The Battle of Monmouth June 28, 1778 As officially reported by General George Washington and General Sir Henry Clinton

Presented to the Society of the Cincinnati in the State of New Jersey at its Spring Meeting Freehold, New Jersey May 19, 1973

Foreword

To Monmouth—so rich in history and inspiring in future hopes—the New Jersey Society of the Cincinnati pays grateful homage.

Here it was on an unbearably hot Sunday, June 28, 1778, George Washington, who later became the first President of the Society of the Cincinnati, led his aides and citizen soldier forces against the greatest military power in the world.

Now, almost two hundred years later, we dedicate this booklet to all Americans who took part in the landmark Battle of Monmouth and unveil a monument in old Tennent Church Yard to the memory of five original members of the Society who are buried here, and a sixth who lies in a nearby family burial ground. With gratitude, we wish to honor all who won America for us.

In those nearly two hundred years that have elapsed since the Battle of Monmouth, legends have been handed down, fact has been embellished with fiction, and historians have given a varied assortment of accounts as to just how and what they think took place.

To get the true account, certainly there can be no greater authorities on the actual events of the battle than the opposing commanding generals—George Washington and Sir Henry Clinton. Each general wrote an official account of the battle within a week of the event. These reports were submitted to their respective governments—Washington's to the President of the Congress, and Clinton's to Lord George Germaine.

This booklet contains both reports just as they were written in July 1778. There are also the casualty lists of both armies and General Washington's commendation of the conduct of his army and the New Jersey militia. Also included are his congratulations to them on the victory "obtained over the arms of his Britannic Majesty."

As you read these reports written so many years ago, may you renew your appreciation of the American heritage we all so fortunately share today.

—*Jack Hite Gilbert*
President
The Society of the Cincinnati
in the State of New Jersey
Freehold, New Jersey
May 19, 1973

General Washington's Account of the Battle of Monmouth

Englishtown, July 1, 1778

SIR: I embrace this first moment of leisure to give congress a more full and particular account of the movements of the army under my command, since its passing the Delaware, than the situation of our affairs would heretofore permit.

I had the honor to advise them, that on the appearance of the enemy's intentions to march through Jersey becoming serious, I had detached General Maxwell's brigade, in conjunction with the militia of that state, to interrupt and impede their progress by every obstruction in their power, so as to give time to the army under my command to come up with them, and take advantage of any favorable circumstances that might present themselves. The army having proceeded to Coryell's ferry, and crossed the Delaware at that place, I immediately detached Col. Morgan, with a select corps of 600 men, to reinforce Gen. Maxwell, and marched with the main body toward Princeton.

The slow advances of the enemy had greatly the air of design, and led me with many others to suspect that Gen. Clinton, desirous of a general action, was endeavoring to draw us down into the lower country, in order by a rapid movement to gain our right, and take possession of the strong ground above us. This consideration, and to give the troops time to repose and refresh themselves from the fatigues they had experienced from rainy and excessive hot weather, determined me to halt at Hopewell township, above five miles from Princeton, where we remained until the morning of the 25th. On the preceding day I made a second detachment of 1,500 chosen troops, under Brigadier-general Scott, to reinforce those already in the vicinity of the enemy, the more effectually to annoy and delay their march.

The next day the army moved to Kingston, and having received intelligence that the enemy were prosecuting their route toward Monmouth Courthouse, I dispatched 1,000 select men under Brigadier-general Wayne, and sent the Marquis de Lafayette to take the command of the whole of the advanced corps, including Maxwell's brigade and Morgan's light-infantry, with orders to take the first fair opportunity of attacking the enemy's rear. In the evening of the same day the whole army advanced from Kingston, where our baggage was left, with intention to preserve a proper distance for supporting the advanced corps, and arrived at Cranberry early the next morning. The intense heat of the weather, and a heavy storm unluckily coming on, made it impossible for us to resume our march that day, without great inconvenience and injury to the troops. Our advanced corps being differently circumstanced, moved from the position it had held the night before, and took post in the evening on the Monmouth road, about five miles from the enemy's rear, in the expectation of attacking them the next morning on their march. The main body having remained at Cranberry, the advanced corps was found to be too remote, and too far upon the right, to be supported either in case of an attack upon, or from the enemy, which induced me to send orders to the marquis to file off by his left toward Englishtown, which he accordingly executed early in the morning of the 27th.

The enemy, in marching from Allentown, had changed their disposition, and placed their best troops in the rear; consisting of all the grenadiers, light-infantry, and chasseurs [skirmishers or scouts] of the line. This alteration made it necessary to increase the number of our advanced corps, and in consequence of which I detached Major-general Lee, with two brigades, to join the marquis at Englishtown, on whom of course the command of the whole devolved, amounting to about 5,000 men. The main army marched the same day, and encamped within three miles of that place. Morgan's corps was left hovering on the army's right flank, and the Jersey militia, amounting at this time to about 700 or 800 men, under Gen. Dickinson, on their left.

The enemy were now encamped in a strong position, with their right extending about a mile and a half beyond the courthouse, in the parting of the road leading to Shrewsbury and Middleton, and their left along the road from Allentown and Monmouth, about three miles this side of the courthouse.

Their right flank lay on the skirt of a small wood, while their left was secured by a very thick one; a morass running toward their rear, and their whole front covered by a wood, and to a considerable extent toward the left with a morass. In this situation they halted, until the morning of the 28th.

Matters being thus situated, and having had the best information, that if the enemy were once arrived at the heights of Middletown, 10 or 12 miles from where they were, it would be impossible to attempt any thing against them with a prospect of success, I determined to attack their rear the moment they should get in motion from their present ground. I communicated my intention to Gen. Lee, and ordered him to make his disposition for the attack, and to keep his troops constantly lying upon their arms, to be in readiness at the shortest notice. This was done with respect to the troops under my immediate command.

About five in the morning, Gen. Dickinson sent an express, informing that the front of the enemy had begun their march. I instantly put the army in motion, and sent order by one of my aids to Gen. Lee, to move on and attack them, unless there should be very powerful reasons to the contrary; acquainting him at the same time that I was marching to support him; and for doing it with the greatest expedition and convenience, should make the men disencumber themselves of their packs and blankets.

After marching five miles, to my great surprise and mortification, I met the whole advanced corps retreating, and, as I was told, by Gen. Lee's orders, without having made any opposition, except one fire, given by the party under the command of Col. Butler, on their being charged by the enemy's cavalry, who were repulsed. I proceeded immediately to the rear of the corps, which I found closely pressed by the enemy, and gave directions for forming part of the retreating troops, who, by the brave and spirited conduct of the officers, aided by some pieces of well-served artillery, checked the enemy's advances, and gave time to make a disposition of the left wing and second lines of the army upon an eminence and in a wood a little in the rear, covered by a morass in front. On this were placed some batteries of cannon, by Lord Stirling, who commanded the left wing, which played upon the enemy with great effect, and seconded by parties of infantry detached to oppose them, effectually put a stop to their advance.

Gen. Lee being detached with the advanced corps, the command of the right wing was given, for the occasion, to Gen. Greene. For the expedition of the march, and to counteract any attempt to turn our right, I had ordered him to file off by the new church 2 miles from Englishtown, and fall into the Monmouth road, a small distance in the rear of the courthouse, while the rest of the column moved on directly toward the courthouse. On intelligence of the retreat, he marched up, and took up a very advantageous position on the right.

The enemy, by this time finding themselves warmly opposed in front, made an attempt to turn our left flank; but they were bravely repulsed, and driven back by detached parties of infantry. They also made a movement toward our right, with as little success; Gen. Greene having advanced a body of troops, with artillery, to a commanding piece of ground, which not only disappointed their design of turning our right, but severely enfiladed [gunfire that swept the length of a target] those in front of the left wing. In addition to this, Gen. Wayne advanced with a body of troops, and kept up so severe and well-directed a fire, that the enemy were soon compelled to retire behind the defile where the first stand in the beginning of the action was made.

In this situation, the enemy had both their flanks secured by thick woods and morasses, while their front could only be approached through a narrow pass. I resolved, nevertheless, to attack them—and for that purpose ordered Gen. Poor, with his own and the Carolina brigade, to move round upon their right, and Gen. Woodford upon their left, and the artillery to gall them in front; but the impediments in the way prevented their getting within reach before it was dark. They remained upon the grounds they had been directed to occupy, during the night, with intention to begin the attack early the next morning; and the army continued lying upon their arms in the field of action, to be ready to support them. In the mean time, the enemy were employed in removing their wounded, and, about 12 o'clock that night, marched away in such silence, that, although Gen. Poor lay extremely near them, they effected their retreat without his knowledge. They carried off their wounded except four officers and about forty privates, whose wounds were too dangerous to permit their removal. The extreme heat of the weather, the fatigue of the men from their march through a deep, sandy country, almost entirely destitute of water, and the distance the enemy had gained by marching in the night, made a pursuit impracticable and fruitless. It would have answered no valuable purpose, and prove fatal to numbers of our men—several of whom died the preceding day with heat.

Were I to conclude my account of this day's transactions without expressing my obligations to the officers of the army in general, I should do injustice to their merit, and violence to my own feelings. They seemed to vie with each other in manifesting their zeal and bravery. The catalogue of those who distinguished themselves, is too long to admit of particularizing individuals. I cannot, however, forbear mentioning Brigadier-general Wayne, whose conduct and bravery during the whole action deserve particular commendation. The behavior of the troops in general, after they recovered from the first surprise occasioned by the retreat of the advanced corps, was such as could not be surpassed.

All the artillery, both officers and men, that were engaged, distinguished themselves in a remarkable manner.

Enclosed, congress will be pleased to receive a return of our killed and wounded. Among the first, were Lieut. Col. Bunner, of Pennsylvania, and Maj. Dickinson, of Virginia,—both distinguished officers, and much to be regretted. The enemy's slain of the field, and buried by us,—according to the return of the persons assigned to that duty,—were four officers, and 245 privates. In the former was the Hon. Col. Monckton. Exclusive of these, they buried some themselves,—as there were several new graves near the field of battle. How many men they have had wounded, cannot be determined; but, from the usual proportion, the number must have been considerable. There were a few prisoners taken.

The peculiar situation of Gen. Lee at this time, requires that I should say nothing of his conduct. He is now in arrest. The charges against him, with such sentence as the court-martial may decree in his case, shall be transmitted, for the approbation or disapprobation of congress, as soon as it shall have passed.

Being fully convinced, by the gentlemen of this country, that the enemy cannot be hurt or injured in their embarkation at Sandy Hook, (the place to which they are now moving,) and unwilling to get too far removed from the North river, I put the troops in motion early this morning, and shall proceed that way,—leaving the Jersey Brigade, Morgan's corps, and other light parties, (the militia being all dismissed,) to hover about them, countenance desertion, and prevent depredations as far as possible. After they embark, the former will take post in the neighborhood of Elizabethtown, the latter rejoin the corps from which they were detached. I have the honor, &c.

—*G. WASHINGTON*

Return of the killed, wounded, and missing, of the American army, in the battle of Monmouth, on the 28th day of June 1778

Killed—1 lieutenant-colonel, 1 major, 3 captains, 2 lieutenants, 1 sergeant, 52 rank and file.

Wounded—2 colonels, 8 captains, 4 first lieutenants, 2 second lieutenants, 1 ensign, 1 adjutant, 8 sergeants, 1 drummer, 120 rank and file.

Missing—5 sergeants, 126 rank and file. Some of the missing, dropped through fatigue and hardship, since come in.

ARTILLERY—*Killed*—1 first lieutenant, 7 matrosses [rank and file or private soldier], 1 bombardier. *Wounded*—1 captain, 1 sergeant, 1 corporal, 1 gunner, 10 matrosses. *Missing*—1 matross. Six horses killed, and two wounded.

Extract from the General Orders Head-quarters, Freehold, New Jersey, June 29, 1778

The commander-in-chief congratulates the army on the victory obtained over the arms of his Britannic Majesty, and thanks most sincerely the gallant officers and men who distinguished themselves upon this occasion, and such others as, by their good order and coolness, gave the happiest presage of what might have been expected had they come to action.

Gen. Dickinson, and the militia of this state, are also thanked for their nobleness in opposing the enemy on their march from Philadelphia, and for the aid which they have given in embarrassing and impeding their motions so as to allow the continental troops to come up with them.

It is with peculiar pleasure the commander-in-chief, in addition to the above, can inform Gen. Knox, and the officers of the artillery, that the enemy have done them the justice to acknowledge that no artillery could have been better served than ours.

Sir Henry Clinton's Account of the Battle of Monmouth

New York, July 5, 1778

MY LORD: I have the honor to inform your lordship that, pursuant to his majesty's instructions, I evacuated Philadelphia on the 18th of June, at three o'clock in the morning, and proceeded to Gloucester Point, without being followed by the enemy. Every thing from thence being passed in safety across the Delaware, through the excellent disposition made by our admiral to secure our passage, the army marched at ten o'clock, and reached Haddonfield the same day. A strong corps of the enemy having, upon our approach, abandoned the difficult pass of Mount Holly, the army proceeded, without any interruption from them, except by what was occasioned by their having destroyed every bridge on our road. As the country is much intersected with marshy rivulets, the obstructions we met with were frequent; and the excessive heat of the weather rendered the labor of repairing the bridges severely felt.

The advanced parties of our light troops arriving unexpectedly at Crosswicks, on the 23d, after a trifling skirmish, prevented the enemy from destroying a bridge over a large creek at that village; and the army passed it the next morning. One column, under the command of his excellency Lieut. Gen. Knyphausen, halted near Imlay's town; and as the provision train and heavy artillery were stationed in that division, the other column, under Lieut. Gen. Earl Cornwallis, took a position at Allen's town, which covered the other encampment. Thus far, my lord, my march pointed equally toward Hudson River and Staten Island, by the Raritan. I was now at the juncture when it was necessary to decide ultimately what course to pursue. Encumbered as I was by an enormous provision train, &c., to which impediment the probability of obstruction and length of my march obliged me to submit, I was led to wish for a route less liable to obstacles than those above mentioned.

I had received intelligence that Gen. Washington and Lee had passed the Delaware, with their army, had assembled a numerous militia, from all the neighboring provinces; and that Gates, with an army from the northward, was advancing to join them on the Raritan. As I could not hope that, after having always hitherto so studiously avoided a general action, they would now give in to it, against every dictate of policy, I could only suppose his views were directed against my baggage, &c., in which part I was indeed vulnerable. This circumstance alone would have tempted me to avoid the difficult passage of the Raritan; but when I reflected that from Sandy Hook I should be able, with more expedition, to carry his majesty's further orders into execution, I did not hesitate to order the army into the road which leads through Freehold to the Navisink. The approach of the enemy's army being denoted by the frequent appearance of their light troops on our rear, I requested his excellency Lieut. Gen. Knyphausen to take the baggage of the whole army under the charge of his division, consisting of the troops mentioned in the margin.[1] Under the head of baggage was comprised not only all the wheel-carriages, of every department, but also the bat-horses; a train which, as the country admitted but of one route for carriages, extended near twelve miles. The indispensable necessity I was under of securing these is obvious, and the difficulty of doing it, in a most woody country, against an army far superior in numbers, will, I trust, be no less so.

I desired Lieut. Gen. Knyphausen to move at daybreak, on the 28th; and that I might not press upon him, in the first part of the march, in which we

[1] *17th Light Dragoons, 2d battalion of Light Infantry, Hessian Yagers, 1st and 2d brigades British, Stern's and Loo's brigades of Hessians, Pennsylvania Loyalists, West Jersey Volunteers, Maryland Loyalists.*

had but one route, I did not follow him with the other division[2] until near eight o'clock. Soon after I had marched, reconnoitering parties of the enemy appeared on our left flank. The Queen's Rangers fell in with and dispersed some detachments, among the woods, in the same quarter. Our rear-guard having descended from the heights, above Freehold, into a plain near three miles in length, and about one mile in breadth, several columns of the enemy appeared likewise descending into the plain; and about ten o'clock they began to cannonade our rear. Intelligence was this moment brought me that the enemy were discovered marching in force on both our flanks. I was convinced that our baggage was their object; but it being in this juncture engaged in the defiles, which continued for some miles, no means occurred of parrying the blow, but attacking the corps which harassed our rear, and pressing it so hard as to oblige the detachments to return from our flanks to its assistance.

I had good information that Gen. Washington was up with his whole army, estimated at about 20,000; but as I knew there were two defiles between him and the corps at which I meant to strike, I judged that he could not have passed them with a greater force than what Lord Cornwall's division was well able to engage; and had I even met his whole army in the passage of those defiles, I had but little to apprehend but his situation might have been critical.

The enemy's cavalry, commanded, it is said, by M. Lafayette, having approached our reach, they were charged, with great spirit, by the Queen's Light Dragoons. They did not wait the shock, but fell back, in confusion, upon their own infantry.

Thinking it possible that the event might draw to a general action, I sent for a brigade of British, and the 17th Light Dragoons, from Lieut. Gen. Knyphausen's division; and having directed them, on their arrival, to take a position of attack on the plain. But before I could advance, the enemy fell back, and took a strong position on the heights above Freehold courthouse. The heat of the weather was intense, and our men already suffered severely from fatigue. But our circumstances obliged us to make a vigorous exertion. The British Grenadiers, with their left to the village of Freehold, and the Guards on the right of the Grenadiers, began the attack with such spirit, that the enemy gave way immediately. The second line of the enemy stood the attack with greater obstinacy, but was likewise completely routed. They then took a third position, with a marshy hollow in front, over which it would have been scarcely possible to have attacked them. However, part of the second

[2] *16th Light Dragoons, 1st battalion of British Grenadiers, 2d ditto, 1st battalion of Light Infantry, Hessian Grenadiers, 3d, 4th, 5th brigades British.*

line made a movement to the front, occupied some ground on the enemy's left flank, and the Light Infantry and Queen's Rangers turned their left.

By this time our men were so overpowered with fatigue, that I could press the affair no further; especially as I was confident the end was gained for which the attack had been made.

I ordered the Light Infantry to rejoin me, but a strong detachment of the enemy having possessed themselves of a post which would have annoyed them in their retreat, the 33d regiment made a movement toward the enemy; which, with a similar one made by the first Grenadiers, immediately dispersed them.

I took the position from which the enemy had been first driven, after they had quitted the plain; and having reposed the troops until ten at night, to avoid the excessive heat of the day, I took advantage of the moonlight to rejoin Lieut. Gen. Knyphausen, who had advanced to Nut Swamp, near Middletown.

Our baggage had been attempted by some of the enemy's light troops, who were repulsed by the good dispositions made by Lieut. Gen. Knyphausen and Maj. Grant, and the good countenance of the 40th regiment, whose piquets alone were attacked, and one troop of the 17th Light Dragoons. The two corps which had marched against it (being, as I since learn, a brigade on each flank) were recalled, as I had suspected, at the beginning of the action.

It would be sufficient honor to the troops to barely say, that they had forced a corps, as I am informed, of near 12,000 men, from two strong positions; but it will, I doubt not, be considered doubly creditable when I mention they did it under such disadvantages of heat and fatigue, that a great part of those we lost fell dead as they advanced.

Fearing that my order had miscarried, before I quitted the ground I sent a second, for a brigade of infantry, the 17th Light Dragoons, and the 2d battalion of Light Infantry, to meet on the march, to which additional force had Gen. Washington shown himself the next day, I was determined to attack him; but there being not the least appearance of an enemy, I suspected he might have passed a considerable corps to a strong position, near Middletown; I therefore left the rear-guard on its march, and detached Maj. Gen. Grant to take post there, which was effected on the 29th. The whole army marched to this position the next day, and then fell back to another, near Navisink; where I waited two days, in the hope that Mr. Washington might have been tempted to advance to the position near Middletown, which we had quitted; in which case I might have attacked him to advantage.

During this time the sick and wounded were embarked, and preparations made for passing to Sandy Hook island, by a bridge, which by the extraordinary labors of the men was soon completed, and over which the whole army passed, in about two hours' time; the horses and cattle having been previously transported.

Your lordship will receive herewith a return of the killed, wounded, missing, &c., of his majesty's troops, on the 28th of last month. That of the enemy is supposed to have been more considerable, especially in killed.

The loss of Lieut. Col. Monckton, who commanded the 2d battalion of Grenadiers, is much to be lamented.

I am much indebted to Lord Cornwallis for his zealous services, on every occasion; and I found great support from the activity of Maj. Gen. Grey, Brig. Gens. Matthew, Leslie, and Sir William Erskine.

I beg leave to refer your lordship, for any other particulars which you may wish to be informed of, to Col. Patterson, who will have the honor of delivering these dispatches, and whose services in this country entitle him to every mark of your lordship's favor.

I have the honor to be, &c.

—*H. CLINTON*

Return of the killed, wounded, missing, &c. of the troops under command of Gen. Sir Henry Clinton, in an engagement with the Rebel army, on the heights of Freehold, Monmouth County, New Jersey, the 28th of June 1778.

TOTAL BRITISH.—1 lieutenant-colonel, 1 captain, 2 lieutenants, 4 sergeants, 56 rank and file killed; 3 sergeants, 45 rank and file died with fatigue; 1 colonel, 1 lieutenant-colonel, 1 major, 7 captains, 5 lieutenants, 7 sergeants, 137 rank and file wounded; 7 sergeants, 61 rank and file missing.

TOTAL GERMAN.—1 rank and file killed, 11 rank and file died with fatigue, 11 rank and file wounded.

GENERAL TOTAL.—1 lieutenant-colonel, 1 captain, 2 lieutenants, 4 sergeants, 57 rank and file killed; 3 sergeants, 56 rank and file died with fatigue; 1 colonel, 1 lieutenant-colonel, 1 major, 7 captains, 5 lieutenants, 7 sergeants, 148 rank and file wounded; 7 sergeants, 61 rank and file missing.

PLAN
OF
THE BATTLE OF MONMOUTH,

Where General Washington commanded the American army, and General Clinton he English army, June 28, 1778

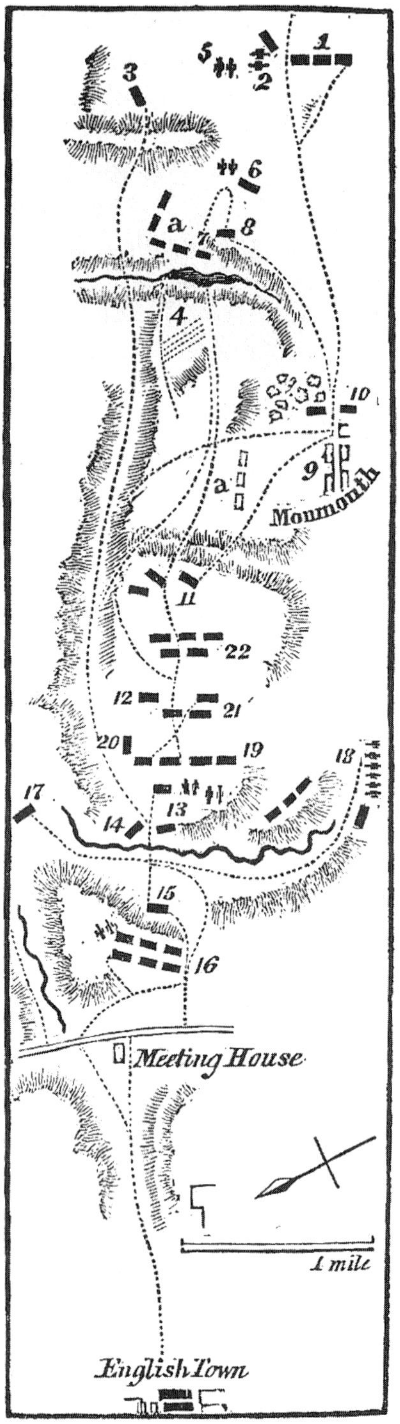

a. Position occupied by the English on the eve of the battle.

1. English column deploying itself to the left, from which were detached the dragoons, to take a position on the right of the American columns, which were debouching (or emerging) from the woods.
2. First battery of the English, which discharged while deploying.
3. Debouchement [starting out] of the 1st brigade of the detachment of Gen. Lee, stationed in the woods, where the rest of the detachment debouched in four columns.
4. Debouchement of the four columns.
5. Second battery of the English.

6.-7. First and second batteries of the Americans.

8. Troops formed at the right of the batteries 6 and 7, which were ordered to retire without discharging.
9. Village of Monmouth, containing the courthouse.
10. Troops formed before Monmouth, which withdrew without waiting for the enemy.
11. First position occupied by all the troops under command of Gen. Lee, where they did not wait for the attack, and from which they threw themselves into the woods on the left.
12. Fierce attack of the English on the troops thrown into the woods during the retreat from position 11.
13. Second position occupied by the rest of the troops, and from which they withdrew when charged by the English dragoons, which were afterwards dispersed by Col. Stuart.
14. Point from which debouched a body of English, having fired on the rest of the troops which still occupied position 13.
15. Position taken by the troops on retiring from point 13, and from which Gen. Washington took them behind the line which he had just formed at point 16.
16. Position which Gen. Washington occupied by the troops which came to support Gen. Lee's detachment.
17. English column which advanced to attack the left, and withdrew after reconnoitering.
18. Battery of six pieces, commanded by Chevalier du Plessis Mauduit, and supported by 500 men.
19. Position occupied by the English troops withdrawn from points 14 and 17, and from which they were repulsed with great loss.
20. Station occupied by the English after having been driven from point 19.
21. New position taken by the English when Washington attacked them, and from which they were also repulsed.
22. Final position of the English, where they passed the night.

PLAN
OF THE
BATTLE OF MONMOUTH,

Fought Sunday, June 28, 1778

REFERENCES.

S. Road to Shrewsbury.
M. Road to Middletown.
A. Briar Hill.
C. Road to Allentown
E. Washington's main body.
H. Comb's Hill
W. Advanced corps of Americans under Wayne.
P. Parsonage.
G. Fence.
F. British main army.
I. Encampment of do. on the night after the action.
L. Forest now standing.

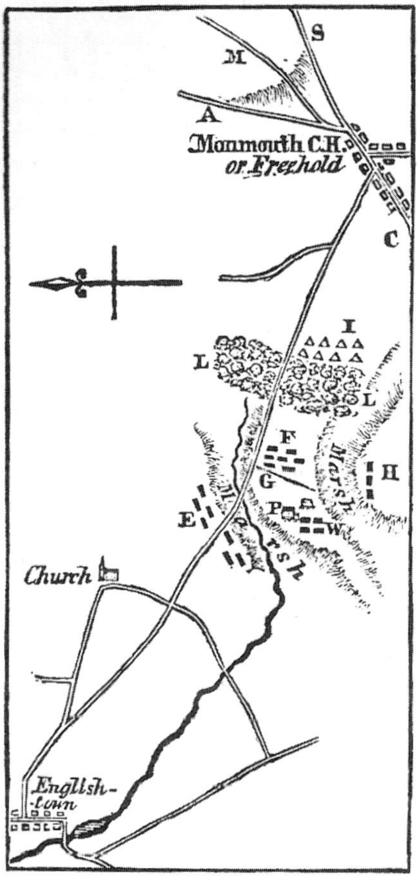

Grateful acknowledgment is made to Grandin Ward Schenck, member of the Society of the Cincinnati, Little Silver, New Jersey, for making the historical documents reprinted in this booklet available from his private library.

TWENTY-FIVE

PASSIONATE PATRIOTS

Richard P. McCormick, Ph.D., 1980

Richard P. McCormick (1916–2006), who made a distinctive contribution to American colonial history with a series of finds, crafted essays on early New Jersey history and spent virtually his entire career at Rutgers University. He earned a BA in History at Rutgers College in 1938 and a Master's in 1940. He earned his Ph.D at the University of Pennsylvania. He returned to Rutgers in 1945, and remained there for the rest of his career, except for a wonderful year (1961–62) as a Visiting Professor at Cambridge University.

Professor McCormick's paper was read to the Society of the Cincinnati in the State of New Jersey On May 10, 1980 in New Jersey. This paper inaugurated the new series of annual prize lectures by illustrious academics which has continued since that date.

You have been generous enough to invite me to offer some brief remarks related to my present research interest, and I am glad to respond. I am presently engaged in writing a book on what I call "The Origins of the Presidential Game." Looking at developments from the creation of the presidency at the Constitutional Convention down to the events associated with the election of 1844, I am trying to explain how we came to elect our president the way we do.

In the early period of my study, dealing with the years between 1789 and 1800, I was deeply impressed by the extraordinary passion that the leading men brought to their politics. At first, my inclination was to discount their inflammatory rhetoric, their uncompromising attitude toward their opponents. But as I came to understand the depth and vigor of their convictions, I was obliged to take their assertions seriously. In their perceptions, the political issues of their day involved a clash between good and evil, between virtue and corruption, and nothing less than the fate of the nation was at stake.

Today, as we approach another presidential contest, we scarcely feel that whether our country founders or survives hinges on a choice between Carter and Reagan, or even between Kennedy and Bush. Whatever misgivings we may have about particular candidates—and some of us may have such misgivings about all of them—we do not see the election of one as portending the establishment of a monarchy, or of another as ushering in a reign of terror, followed by lawless anarchy. Yet such were the awful choices that were envisioned in lurid colors during the first decade of our national experience.

I shall defer, for the moment, a full explanation of why the statesmen of that era were so passionate, so vehement, in their political views. Suffice it to say now that they were very sensitively aware that our new nation was embarked on an extremely hazardous experiment. We were venturing forth on the world scene as a republic. Not since ancient times had men attempted to provide themselves with order and liberty under such a form of government, and the lessons of history were not heartening. All of the early republics had met a dire fate; they had succumbed either to the forces of anarchy or of tyranny. So the overriding fear was that America would not be able to defy what seemed to be a historical law, and their passion was rooted in that fear.

Everywhere they saw lurking dangers, any one of which could subvert the experiment in republicanism.

In the eyes of many ardent patriots, one of the earliest menaces to their hopes was the founding of your illustrious Society. When it was learned that the officers of the Continental Army had met on May 13, 1783, to found the Society of the Cincinnati, there were immediate expressions of apprehension and alarm. Had we not fought a war to overthrow monarch and end hereditary distinctions? Must we then be confronted with a new hereditary order, which surely constituted the first step toward the creation of an American nobility? The Society, it was understood, would have a large treasury, resulting from the contribution by each officer of a full month's pay. To what sinister purposes would such a fund be applied? And there was the provision in the Society's constitution that the several state organizations would correspond with one another through circular letters. Recalling the previous effective use by the revolutionaries of committees of correspondence to bring about the end of British rule, it was not difficult for the alarmists to conjure up visions of the Society taking over political control of the nation.

So violent, widespread, and damaging were the attacks that some politically ambitious members of the Society found it expedient to withdraw. Sam Adams expressed a common view when he said he thought the Society represented "as rapid a Stride towards an hereditary Military Nobility as was ever made in so short a Time." The furor soon convinced concerned members of the Society—and especially the President General, George Washington—that steps must be taken to disarm the critics. Accordingly, when the Society held its first general meeting in May 1784, its constitution was amended to abolish hereditary descent, honorary memberships, and regular correspondence among the state societies. However, four state branches refused to ratify these changes, and because unanimity was required, the amendments did not become effective. Washington was so distressed at this failure that he attended only one other meeting of the Society.

Gradually, popular suspicion of the Cincinnati moderated. But when, in the course of the debates in the Constitutional Convention, a proposal was made that the President should be elected by popular vote, Elbridge Gerry of Massachusetts expressed a latent fear. "A popular election in this case is radically vicious," he declaimed. "The ignorance of the people would put it in the power of some one set of men dispersed through the Union & acting in Concert to delude them into any appointment." He observed that such a Society of men existed in the Order of the Cincinnati. "They will in fact," he prophesied, "elect the Chief Magistrate in every instance." We can readily attribute such apprehensions about the Cincinnati to paranoia, but to do so would be to miss the key point. Republicanism was a fragile system; its defenders must ever be on their guard against any threats to its integrity.

Concern about the fate of the nation was magnified early in Washington's administration as controversies arose over the implications and tendencies of the policies advanced so forcefully by Alexander Hamilton. Soon Jefferson and Hamilton were at one another's throats, with President Washington attempting without success to moderate their differences.

By September 1792, Jefferson was expressing to Washington his abhorrence of his fellow Cabinet member. "That I have utterly, in my private conversations, disapproved of the system of the Secretary of the Treasury, I acknowledge and avow. . . . His system flowed from principles adverse to liberty, & was calculated to undermine and demolish the republic," he wrote. He referred to Hamilton as "a man whose history, from the moment at which history can stoop to notice him, is a tissue of machinations against the liberty of the country. . . . " Insisting that the "Monarchical federalists" had never liked the constitution, he charged: "That the ultimate object of all this is to prepare the way for a change from the present republican form of government, to that of a monarchy, of which the English constitution is to be the model." These were not statements made in the course of a political harangue but in serious correspondence with the President.

Hamilton was no less vehement in condemning Jefferson. He described him as "a man of sublimated and paradoxical imagination, cherishing notions incompatible with regular and firm government." Jefferson, abetted by Madison, was "at the head of a faction decidedly hostile to me," said Hamilton, "and actuated by views in my judgment subversive of the principles of good government and dangerous to the union, peace and happiness of the Country." What was Jefferson's ulterior objective? "'Tis evident beyond a question, from every movement," Hamilton wrote in 1792, "that Mr. Jefferson aims with ardent desire at the Presidential Chair." He was, in short, "a man of profound ambition and violent passions."

Faced with such a bitter quarrel between his two chief advisers, Washington could only deplore the "internal dissensions . . . harrowing and tearing our vitals." He pled in vain for "liberal allowances, mutual forbearances, and temporizing yieldings on all sides." Attorney General Edmund Randolph urged Washington to serve a second term. "Should a civil war arise, you cannot stay at home," he explained. "And how much easier it will be to disperse the factions which are rushing to this catastrophe, than to subdue them after they shall appear in arms."

Even Washington was not spared. Journalists such as Benjamin Franklin Bache, James Duane, and Philip Freneau—the Poet of the Revolution—vied with one another in heaping abuse on the President. He was charged with stealing government funds, with creating an aura of aristocracy around his office, even with lending his enormous influence to a movement to establish a monarchy. On one memorable occasion, Washington let loose his thunderous temper at a Cabinet meeting and launched into a fervent denunciation of "that rascal Freneau." Senator Maclay of Pennsylvania excoriated the President, "If there is treason in the wish I retract it," he exploded, "but would to God this same General Washington was in heaven. We would not then have him brought forward as the constant cover to every unconstitutional and unrepublican act." Thomas Paine, who had served the cause so powerfully with his stirring pamphlets, was even more vicious. "As to you, sir," he wrote Washington in 1796, "treacherous in private friendships . . . and a hypocrite in public life, the world will be puzzled to decide whether you have abandoned good principles or whether you ever had any." You will readily agree that strong language was the order of the day, and it voiced passionately held opinions.

This intensely heated political environment persisted through the decade. During the presidency of John Adams, tempers rose even higher as war with France threatened and efforts were made to repress dissent by the enforcement of the Alien and Sedition Acts. Adding to the dangers of a fratricidal confrontation was the emergence of organized political parties—the Republicans and the Federalists—each hurling anathemas at the other. As the election of 1800 approached, offering a choice between Jefferson and Adams, it seemed that we had arrived at Armageddon.

A typical Federalist pamphlet, warning against the dangers of Jefferson's election, portrayed him as "an avowed Deist, an enemy to pure morals and religion, and consequently an enemy to his country and his God. Whoever, therefore, furthers the election of this man to the Presidency of the United States, insults his maker and redeemer. . . . What can screen such wretches from the just vengeance of insulted heaven!"

On the other side, the Republicans were no less vehement. "Thomas Jefferson first drew the declaration of American independence; he first framed the sacred political sentence that all men are born equal," read one tract. "John Adams says this is all a farce and a falsehood, that some men should be born Kings, and some should be born Nobles. Will you, by your votes, contribute to make this avowed friend of monarchy President?"

Within the Federalist camp, discord appeared. Hamilton circulated a lengthy pamphlet attacking Adams. "I will never more be responsible for him by my direct support," Hamilton wrote with some bitterness, "even though the consequence should be the election of Jefferson. If the cause is to be sacrificed to a weak and perverse man, I withdraw from the party and act on my own ground." Adams retaliated in kind. He told one of his Cabinet members: "Hamilton is an intriguant—the greatest intriguant in the World—a man devoid of every moral principle—a Bastard, and as much a foreigner as Gallatin."

A genuine crisis arose when the election produced a tie between Jefferson and his running mate, Aaron Burr, and it fell to the Federalist-controlled House of Representatives to make the choice between the two. Extremist Federalist leaders, determined to go to any lengths to prevent the accession of Jefferson, schemed to set aside the election or, failing that, to install Burr as President. For nearly a week, the House proceeded through thirty-five ballots without reaching a decision. There were rumors of military preparations in Virginia and Pennsylvania to back Jefferson's rightful claim to the presidency.

Jefferson became convinced that the Federalists intended to maintain the deadlock and then designate a President by law. "But we thought it best," he later revealed, "to declare openly and firmly, one and all, that the day such an act passed, the middle States would arm, and that no such usurpation, even for a single day, should be submitted to." Faced with such an ultimatum, enough Federalists yielded to permit the election of Jefferson. But the possibility of civil strife had been real; the nation nearly foundered in its infancy because of the passion with which men held opposing political views.

James Monroe expressed it succinctly: "There is a conflict of principle, and either democracy,—that is, the government of the people,—or royalty, must prevail. The opposing parties can never be united . . . because their views are as opposite as light and darkness." This was his perception of the issue facing the nation. John Adams voiced a different view. "If we had been blessed with common sense," he wrote after his defeat, "we should not have been overthrown by Philip Freneau, Duane, Callender, Cooper, and Lyon, or their great patron and protector [referring to Jefferson]. A group of foreign liars, encouraged by a few native gentlemen, has discomfited the education, the virtue, and the property of the country. The reason is, we have no Americans in America."

We are not obliged to accept either Monroe's analysis or that of Adams. Both believed sincerely that the other's party represented the forces of evil. Neither was in the least prepared to acknowledge the legitimacy of the opposition. Each party saw the other as threatening the success of the republican experiment. Their differences, they would insist, admitted of no compromise. From our vantage point, both Adams and Monroe were in error; their common passion for republicanism drove them to exaggerate their differences and to magnify the dangers to the republic.

It was their very commitment to republicanism, along with their fears that it would be subverted, that made these patriots so passionate in their disagreements. Paradoxically, it was because they shared the same basic faith that they were so suspicious of one another. They all saw lurking dangers. These took the forms of demagoguery, corruption, foreign intrigue, the influence of a monied interest, or assaults on property by the mob. Some were appalled by what they thought was a concentration of excessive power in the hands of the executive; others deplored such outbursts as the Whiskey Rebellion. What some termed liberty, others branded as licentiousness. They all used the same vocabulary, but one side emphasized those evils that seemed to be transforming the government into a monarchy, while the other side focused its concern on those tendencies that were productive of democracy, which they equated with mob rule.

But the greatest danger of all, both agreed, was faction. Citizens of a republic should share a common concern for the general welfare; they should, therefore, be united in political sentiments. The rise of faction—or political parties—created special anxieties, because in a properly constituted republic of virtuous citizens and disinterested statesmen, there was no justification for factions or parties. Greatly alarmed by the appearance of parties and convinced that their very existence foretold the destruction of the republic, the political leaders of the period were caught in a terrible dilemma. Jefferson and Hamilton each felt that *his* party must be mobilized to save the republic, but both shared the awful sense that parties were evil. Thus, to the feelings of patriotic concern, there were added those of guilt and despair.

It was these sentiments, then, that made the patriots so passionate. Like parents who share the same deep love for their children but quarrel over their upbringing or like different sects of Christians who revile one another in the name of the same God, the founding fathers, because they shared the same faith, and were so zealous to defend it, arrayed themselves in hostile factions.

Today, whether because the ardor of our republican faith has cooled, or whether we have become relatively secure in it, we are less passionate in our political quarrels. We can contemplate with some equanimity the low-keyed contests between Republicans and Democrats and resign ourselves to the victory of either party. Only on very extraordinary occasions—as in 1860, 1896, 1932, or 1952—are our passions strongly aroused. Thus, we need to be reminded of what a very different aspect politics bore when the republic was young and its destiny was uncertain.

TWENTY-SIX

THE "SPIRIT OF SEVENTY-SIX": PRESCRIPTION FOR REPUBLICANISM

Larry R. Gerlach, Ph.D., 1981

Larry R. Gerlach received his M.A. in 1965 from the University of Nebraska and his Ph.D. in 1968 from Rutgers University. He is Professor of History at the University of Utah in Salt Lake City, and his most recent book was published in 2004, entitled: *The Winter Olympics: from Chamonix to Salt Lake City.*

Professor Gerlach's paper was read on May 23, 1981, in New Jersey to the Society as the second in the new series of prize lectures.

I am deeply honored to be recognized by the Society of the Cincinnati in the State of New Jersey "for distinguished achievement in promoting the knowledge, understanding, and appreciation of the history of the State of New Jersey in its early years." And I am appreciative for the opportunity to share with you today some personal reflections on the creation of the American republic with special reference to New Jersey.

I have spent considerable time during the past eighteen years—more time than a supposedly sane man ought to admit—with the archival and historiographical remains of the Revolutionary generation in an attempt not only to acquire a better understanding of the American Revolution as a historical event but also to assess its meaning for subsequent American history. Most of my time has been devoted to the history of individual states, particularly New Jersey, believing as I do that state and local history are the wellsprings of national history: The history of a nation is, after all, the composite of its communities. While rummaging through mountains of manuscript material and piles of books and articles I have become aware of a serious discrepancy in our knowledge of Revolutionary America. As our comprehension of the American Revolution as a chapter in American history increases, our appreciation of what the Revolution meant to those who put their lives, honors, and sacred fortunes on the line in 1776, decreases: We know a great deal about the causes and consequences of the Revolution but relatively little about the hopes and fears of the Revolutionary generation.

Illustrative are the political histories of America from 1765 to 1800. Historians who have studied the political course of the Revolution and the creation of the new nation have been concerned overwhelmingly with constitutional theory and governmental organization, with suffrage qualifications and electoral procedures, with the formation of political parties and the nature of partisan politics. While enlightening and informative, this preoccupation with procedures and practices, institutions and legal codes, is unfortunate for it has obscured the fundamental political truth articulated so poignantly by Thomas Paine in *Common Sense:* Good government is *"wholly owning to the constitution of the People, and not to the constitution of Government."*

Jonathan Elmer, prominent rebel physician from Cumberland County, New Jersey, knew as much. Addressing a gathering at Bridge-Town on August 7, 1776, to celebrate the adoption of the Declaration of Independence and the

New Jersey State Constitution, Elmer observed that "with the independency of the American states, a new era in politics has commenced. . . . No people under Heaven, were ever favored with a fairer opportunity, of laying a sure foundation for future grandeur and happiness than we." But, he warned, "our future happiness or misery . . . will depend entirely upon ourselves":

> *If actuated by principles of virtue and genuine patriotism, we make the welfare of our country the sole aim of all our actions; If we entrust none but persons of abilities and integrity, with the management of our public affairs; If we carefully guard against corruption and undue influence, in the several departments of government; If we are steady and zealous in putting the laws in strict execution; the spirit and principles of our new constitution . . . may be preserved for a long time; but if faction and party spirit, the destruction of popular governments, take place, anarchy and confusion will soon ensue, and we shall either fall an easy prey to a foreign enemy, or some factious and aspiring Demagogue . . . will spring up among ourselves, who, taking advantage of our political animosities, will lay violent hands on the government, and sacrifice the liberties of his country to his own ambitious and domineering humour.*

Elmer's optimism was tempered by apprehension because the American Revolution was an audacious political gamble. More than the first anticolonial war for independence in modern history, the Revolution was also a bold attempt to establish a unique mode of government—a democratic-republic based wholly upon the sovereignty of the people.

The Revolutionary generation was dedicated to government of, by, and for the people. They believed in the ability of people to govern themselves. The basic credo was that canonized by Thomas Jefferson in his first inaugural address:

> *Sometimes it is said that man cannot be trusted with the government of himself. Can he, then, be trusted with the government of others?*

To facilitate self-government, the Revolution brought about fundamental changes in the structure and operation of government and politics in America. State constitutions increased the authority of the legislature and decreased the power of the executive, provided for frequent and regular legislative sessions, made elective many government posts that had been previously appointive, and reduced the property qualifications for holding office. Electoral laws liberalized voting requirements, substituted balloting for voice voting, and permitted multiple polling places to bring the ballot box closer to the people. In short, the Revolutionary generation devised a constitutional-legal environment that would not only make government more representative of and responsible to the people but also encourage popular participation in the political process.

But state constitutions merely provided blueprints for government and legal codes merely determined the mechanics of politics. The Revolutionary generation understood all too well that checks and balances, separation of powers, electoral laws, and two-party systems alone would not secure the experiment in republicanism. The novel experiment in republican government would rest not on statutes and constitutional provisions but upon a new system of popular politics in which both the governors and the governed were actuated by a spirit of civic virtue and responsibility. In short, the greatest political challenge of the Revolution was attitudinal rather than institutional, for it was the collective political attitudes of the American people that would transform institutions of representative government into organs of democratic self-government.

Alas, it is much easier to delineate laws and constitutional prescriptions than to define the attitudes and assumptions of a people. Nonetheless, it seems to me that the Revolutionary generation did embrace a public vision, a prescription for republicanism if you will, that we might designate, for want of a better term, the "Spirit of Seventy-six."

Distilled to its basic ingredients, the "Spirit of Seventy-six" consists of a pursuit of honor, a quest for fame, a sense of history, a dedication to reform, and a commitment to posterity.

The Revolutionary generation was obsessed with honor. "Honor" was realized by adhering to a code of *ethical conduct* that merited approval in one's own mind *as well as* in the eyes of contemporaries. There was no distinction between ethical *private* and *public* behavior; the one was impossible without the other. Hence Thomas Jefferson's admonition to his nephew, Peter Carr, always to "ask yourself how you would act if all the world were looking at you, and act accordingly"; hence the incessant discussions about the virtuous conduct of good rulers and good citizens. Listen to William Livingston address in 1776 the members of the first state legislature in New Jersey:

> *As it is our indispensable Duty, may it be our invariable Aim, to exhibit to our Constituents, the brightest Examples of a disinterested Love for the common Weal; and be inflexible in our Resolution, to know neither Friend nor Favorite, whenever his Solicitations appear incompatible with*

> *the general Good. In our publick Capacities, we ought to rise superior to all private Attachment or Resentment, and make the intrinsic Merit of every Candidate for an Office, our sole Rule for his Promotion. Let us, Gentlemen, both by Precept and Practice, encourage a Spirit of Economy, Industry, and Patriotism; and that publick Integrity and Righteousness which cannot fail to* exalt a Nation: *Setting our Faces at the same Time like a Flint, against that Dissoluteness of Manners, and political Corruption, which will ever be the* Reproach of any People. *May the Foundation of [the] Infant State be laid in Virtue and the Fear of God; and the Superstructure will rise glorious, and endure for Ages.*

Political leaders do not talk like that today, and we do not expect it of them. That, of course, is why terms such as *Watergate* and *Abscam* have become part of our political lexicon.

The Founding Fathers strove for fame. To them, "fame" meant recognition by peers *and posterity* for deeds performed in the *public interest.* The spur of fame was a noble passion that transformed personal ambition and self-interest into unselfish, disinterested public service. It may have been extreme to assert, as did Benjamin Rush, the Philadelphia physician who was the son-in-law of New Jersey's Richard Stockton, that "every many in a republic is public property—his time and talents—his youth—his manhood—his old age—nay more, his life, his all belongs to his country." But without question public service was life's highest calling in the minds of the Revolutionary generation. Thus the Jeffersons, Livingstons, and Washingtons repeatedly abandoned private pursuits to take on yet another position of public service. Thus, on his deathbed, the man who had served as a state legislator, governor, congressman, ambassador, secretary of state, and president of the United States ordered inscribed on his tombstone "the following inscription and not a word more

> Here was buried
> Thomas Jefferson
> Author of the Declaration of American Independence,
> Of the Statute of Virginia for Religious Freedom,
> And Father of the University of Virginia

because by these, as testimonials that I have lived, I wish most to be remembered." Today, we have substituted private for public enterprise, personal aggrandizement for public leadership. That, of course, is what accounts for political scandals and the recent resignation of a president and vice president in shame; that is why corporate boards of directors boast more talented memberships than state legislatures.

The men and women who lived in the last third of the eighteenth century were imbued with a sense of history. They were historically conscious not only in that they paged through the annals of history to discover precepts and "lessons" to guide their conduct in the present, but also in that they were keenly aware of their ability to *make* history. The Revolution, wrote South Carolina's rebel physician David Ramsay,

> *called forth many virtues and gave occasion for the display of abilities which, but for that event, would have been lost to the world. . . . In the years 1775 and 1776, the country being suddenly thrown into a situation that* needed *the ability of all its sons . . . a vast expansion of the human mind speedily followed. . . . It seemed as if the war not only* required *but* created *talents. Men whose minds were warmed with the love of liberty . . . spoke, wrote, and acted, with an energy far surpassing all expectations, which could be reasonably founded on their previous acquirements.*

Every generation can "make history," revolution or no, but not all strive to do so. Today, we seem preoccupied with nostalgic "Happy Days" devoid of Watergates and Vietnams. That, of course, is why voters turn out at the polls in embarrassingly small numbers, why inefficiency and ineffectiveness pervade the halls of government.

As revolutionaries, the Founding Fathers were committed to ongoing innovation and reform. They were American Adams living in a new paradise called the United States. With a stroke of Thomas Jefferson's pen, they philosophically loosed themselves from the sins of their fathers—the tyranny of tradition, class, ignorance, churches, armies, and kings was gone. But they knew the future would hold more conflict and change, continual creation and re-creation, for the battle for human freedom and dignity was never ending. Hear Mr. Jefferson:

> *Some men look at constitutions with sanctimonious reverence, and deem them like the ark of the covenant, too sacred to be touched. . . . But I know also that laws and institutions must go hand in hand with the progress of the human mind. As that becomes more developed, more enlightened, as new discoveries are made, new truths disclosed, and manners and opinions change with the change of circumstances, institutions must advance also, and keep pace with the times.*

Today, Americans preach the virtues of the status quo and practice the politics of apathy or self-interest. That, of course, is why it has not yet become a universally self-evident truth that "all men are created equal," and that for some Americans "Life, Liberty, and the pursuit of Happiness" remain elusive "unalienable Rights."

Last, those who brought forth the new nation had a fiduciary sense of obligation to posterity. Theirs was an extraordinary contribution to American philosophy: They substituted the future for the past. If they looked to the past for wisdom, they looked to future generations as the primary beneficiaries of the new order. Indeed, John Dickinson voiced the watchword of the day when he exhorted his comrades: "Remember your ancestors *and* your posterity." They knew, as Thomas Paine declared in *Common Sense,* that "the cause of America is in a great measure the cause of all mankind. 'Tis not the concern of a day, a year, or an age; posterity are virtually involved in the contest, and will be more or less affected even to the end of time by our proceedings now." Believing as did Jefferson that "the Creator has made the earth for the living" and that "every age and generation must be as free to act for itself, in all cases, as the ages and generation which preceded it," they worked to devise political, social, and economic systems that would enable succeeding generations, unrestrained by mortgages from the past, to maximize the "pursuit of happiness" in what was hoped would be an unending cycle of progress. Today, we are concerned mainly with our own presence, thinking, perhaps, that this land was in fact "made for you and me." That, of course, is why our children as well as generations yet unborn will pay a heavy price for our exploitation of natural resources, pollution of the environment, social insensitivity, and fiscal mismanagement.

To "secure the Blessings of Liberty to ourselves and our Posterity," the Revolutionary generation did more than establish the constitutional-legal foundations of a republican government; they also formulated the philosophical principles of *republican society.* In the final analysis, however, the success of the new republic depended not upon institutions and ideology but upon the willingness of the people to assume the responsibilities of self-government.

The Revolutionary republicans had indeed, as Abraham Clark of Elizabeth, a signer of the Declaration of Independence, observed, "embarked upon a most Tempestuous Sea" with "dangers Scattered thick Around." They were not certain that a man would in fact seek office "for the sole purpose of rendering his country all the service in his power" and thus place public affairs and the common welfare above personal and private interests. They were not certain that citizens would in fact become knowledgeable about public affairs and active in the political process. They were certain only of the consequences of corruption and apathy for the republic: They knew, as Thomas Jefferson put it, that "once the people become inattentive to the public affairs" government leaders "shall all become wolves." Or, as an anonymous Jerseyman observed: "Whenever our public virtue decays, our government, which owes its origin to and was founded upon public virtue, will languish."

The challenge was self-evident. How to transform the rhetoric of republicanism into the reality of American politics? How to convert pre-1776 constitutional monarchists into postindependence democratic republicans? Responsibility for creating a civic-minded, politically conscious citizenry imbued with republican principles became the primary charge of two institutions elevated to unprecedented importance in American society by the political imperatives of the Revolution—the press and the public school.

The American Revolution was accompanied by nothing less than a communications revolution. The impact was especially profound in New Jersey: Although some forty newspapers were published in America in 1775, New Jersey was the only colony without a newspaper in the colonial period. The appearance of Isaac Collins's *New-Jersey Gazette* (Burlington) in December 1777 heralded the beginning of a publication boom; a decade later four major weeklies were being published in the state.

The impetus behind the profusion of newspapers and magazines published in New Jersey during and after the Revolution was clearly political. That the press was filled with political news and partisan views is a reflection of the belief that a public informed about the issues and events of the day was essential in a democratic republic. It was through newspapers and periodical literature that Jerseymen not only obtained the information and opinions necessary to render intelligent decisions about the issues of the day, but also were apprised of the deeds of their elected representatives. The press and the ballot were thus inexorably linked in republican government: representative government turned on an informed electorate determined to hold public officials accountable at the polls. As a Jerseyman admonished the readers of the *New-Jersey Gazette* in 1778:

> Electors watch with careful eye,
> Nor ever let New Jersey die,
> Peruse the minutes, there you'll see,
> By persons' conduct, what they be,
> At next election then appear,
> And do your country service there.

Thus was a free press considered to be "the grand palladium of freedom, and scourge of tyrants"; thus did Thomas Jefferson aver that "were it left to me to decide whether we should have a government without newspapers, or newspapers without a government, I should not hesitate a moment to prefer the latter."

The second pillar of the republic was the public school. John Witherspoon, the president of the College of New Jersey (Princeton) and the foremost educator in the state, emphasized that education must be viewed in "a political light" because of "the unspeakable importance of a liberal education to civil society." He declared, "The superior advantages derived to the community from men of letters, in the various offices of government, and especially in the character of legislators and magistrates are too numerous to be recounted." While Witherspoon was concerned principally with the college-trained elite, he also understood the crucial role to be played by the public school: Only an educated people could truly understand their political rights and civic responsibilities as well as properly assess public issues. According to Jefferson, who wished to be remembered as much for being the founder of the University of Virginia as for authoring the Declaration of Independence, the only "sure foundation" for the "preservation of freedom and happiness" was the "diffusion of knowledge among the people." Thus public education, confined almost exclusively to New England before 1776, became an article of national faith after the Revolution. Because of the perceived link between schooling and citizenship, the United States became the first (and to date only) nation committed to the concept of a free, public, democratic education for all citizens.

If Thomas Jefferson, William Livingston, and the other progenitors of the republic could assess America today, they would, I am confident, approve of much that has happened over the course of two centuries and accept with understanding and compassion the less admirable chapters of our history. But they would likely be most disturbed—as am I—that somewhere, somehow, the "Spirit of Seventy-six" has been diluted.

The Founding Fathers were not demigods, pure in thought, consistent in action. There was then, as now, often a discrepancy between words and deeds, principles and practices. But they at least established an exalted public vision, formulated lofty goals, and maintained high expectations. Would that modern Americans were so concerned with honor, fame, history, progress, and posterity as were their Revolutionary forebears.

Perhaps my perspective is skewed, my historical faith stubborn and wrong-headed. Perhaps it is preferable to extend the terms of elected officials and turn over the business of government to "experts" instead of insisting upon frequent elections and government by the "common man." Perhaps it is preferable for the modern communications media to transmit innocuous wire-service reports and peddle goods and services instead of providing in-depth commentary and partisan opinion. Perhaps it is preferable for modern schools to emphasize "socialization" and "job training" instead of rigorous academic instruction in the liberal arts and humanities. Perhaps it is preferable that modern Americans "do their own thing" and equate fame with notoriety and honor with personal achievement instead of subordinating private interests and ambitions to public service. Perhaps, in short, the Revolutionary generation's prescription for republicanism is an antiquated political formula, no longer relevant to modern American government.

But I don't think so. At least I hope not, for if what I have called the "Spirit of Seventy-six" is politically irrelevant, then it follows that the mode of government established by the Founding Fathers—a democratic-republic based upon the sovereignty of the people—is also obsolete.

Wither America? I do not know. Historians are far better at probing the past than forecasting the future. But I do know that Thomas Paine was correct when he admonished:

> *It is at all times necessary that we frequently refresh our patriotism by reference to first principles. It is by tracing things to their origin that we learn to understand them, and it is by keeping that line and that origin always in view that we never forget them.*

TWENTY-SEVEN

THE HERITAGE OF A CINCINNATIAN

Vincent C. De Baun, Ph.D., 1982

Vincent C. De Baun is a graduate of Union College and holds his Ph.D. from Rutgers University. After teaching English at Union, Rutgers, the University of New Hampshire, and Wells College, he became president of Lasell College and Cazenovia College and then director of development at M.I.T. He served as an officer in the U.S. Navy in World War II and the Korean War. He was president of the Society of the Cincinnati in the State of New Jersey from 1982 to 1986. He is a collateral descendant of Captain Cornelius Hennion, Third Regiment, New Jersey Continental Line (see illustration 17).

Remarks
delivered at the
One hundred and ninety-ninth Annual Meeting
of the
Society of the Cincinnati in the State of New Jersey
Anderson House, Washington, D.C.
October 23, 1982

Last spring, when Craig Colgate called on me to write a brief article for the fall issue of *Cincinnati Fourteen*, I accepted the task matter of factly; it was just one of those missions we all undertake from time to time out of loyalty, because a friend has asked. Craig suggested I might find some interesting ideas in a book[1] he sent me—and he was quite right, as he usually is. Indeed the book was not merely interesting, it was fascinating.

It is an imposing volume, clad in red, with lettering stamped in gold that is still bright after all the long years since it was first privately published in a limited edition in 1908. Its pages offer an extensive collection of excerpts from the minutes of all the meetings of the Society of the Cincinnati in the State of New Jersey, from its founding in 1783 through 1906. No, let me correct that. It is more than a collection of excerpts. It is a series of glimpses of men and their problems, men and their aspirations, men and their memories, striving to preserve what was good and honorable in their lives even as they sought to work out a new form of government in a kind of nation that the world had never seen before. It is moving to me that, in the beginning, these men were our propositi and their friends: and that in the generations that followed, their sons, the lines of descent that lead to us gathered here this evening, shaped and nurtured the brotherhood of which we are a part, and preserved unbroken its principles in time of trial.

Let me here enter a personal note. It should be said that I believe, along with William Faulkner, "The past is never dead. It is not even past."

If that's too mystical for you, let me try to explain. I believe that all of us, as members of this Society, are somehow committed to history. If our membership has meaning, it grows out of the blood and honor of men long gone—but they live in us yet. And as long as we keep faith with them, as best we can, in our decisions and plans, they will not die. To paraphrase the old hymn: The faith of our Fathers will be living still.

---

[1] *Excerpts of the* Proceedings of the Society of the Cincinnati in the State of New Jersey from May 13, 1783, to July 4, 1906, *published by the Society, 1908.*

Those were some of the thoughts that crowded my mind as I read that book, with its deep concern for accuracy and fairness as membership claims were judged, its charity for the widows and orphans of brothers in arms, its passionate dedication to these United States.

In the beginning, and for many decades thereafter, membership questions occupied major attention. The Committee of Claims, as it was called, dealt with the matter of admitting members who technically ought to have belonged to Societies in Pennsylvania, New York, or Connecticut, and it accepted them on the sensible grounds that they had "removed into and now reside within this State." It debated the admission of second sons and nephews and brothers and those descended through daughters. There is a certain mild air of vexation to this entry in the minutes in 1847:

> *As there have been some doubts arisen among some members of our Society whether persons claiming to be admitted members thereof through a female line, are not entitled to membership, the Committee would therefore prefer to leave this question to the judgment of the Society, trusting that they will adopt measures to put at rest this ever agitating and interesting subject.*

I am delighted that in this matter the decision was affirmative, else I would not be here.

Throughout the century, there is a determined independence in New Jersey's view of the General Society. It never failed, of course, in its support (as in 1811) of the position that all should work at "the most efficient means of restoring that harmony which ought forever to subsist" among those who "as faithful comrades in honour and misfortune" founded the General Society "in solemn engagement on the banks of the Hudson." But that loyalty did not prevent New Jersey (as in 1878) from standing on its "dignity and rights" when the General Society questioned the validity of one membership. New Jersey declared stiffly that it had made its decision "by virtue of certain rules and regulations which this Society has seen fit and proper to adopt, and therefore this Society denies the right of any other body to question its action in the premises. Resolved, that the Secretary is directed to transmit copies of these resolutions to the Secretary General."

Among all the debates about membership, I think none is more absorbing than the case of Surgeon Alexander Ross, which in various ways kept surfacing from 1868 to 1884. The right of Surgeon Ross to be a propositus was complicated by the fact that records of the Medical Service were, as one account put it, "exceedingly imperfect prior to 1781, more so indeed, than as to any other branch of the service." There was also the question of his possibly being confused with his son, John Ross, also a doctor, who was Brigade Major of the New Jersey Brigade, Continental Army, and one of our original members. Further, Alexander had died in 1780 and thus had never entered his own claim.

Reconstructing that case was a fine bit of creative historical scholarship. It involved establishing Dr. Ross's distinction as a graduate of the University of Edinburgh and finding this extract, which tells much of what practice must have been like in those days, in an old history of medicine in New Jersey:

> *[Dr. Ross] was one of the most prominent and skillful medical men of South Jersey, at the time in which he lived. He rode over a large extent of country, on an old black mare, with his saddle bags stuffed with medicines, and required two weeks, generally, to make each of his patients a visit.*

Among other pieces of evidence is the fact that both his son and son-in-law were army officers. I find it especially delightful and possibly even clinching that his son was married to the only daughter of a minister famed for having preached a fiery patriotic sermon based on a text from Psalm CXLIV "Blessed be the Lord my strength, which teacheth my hands to war and fingers to fight."

This is not the right time or place to tell Dr. Ross's story in detail, but I think it is worth at least quoting excerpts from a passage from Asa Bird Gardner's statement on his behalf as the case was put to rest:

> *The history of the Medical Department of the Continental Army points directly to the time when Surgeon Ross must have served. . . . The winter of 1779-80 was one of unexampled severity, and the soldiers being ill supplied with clothing and their subsistence being scanty and of poor quality, sickness and disease increased in an alarming ratio. . . . The demand for medical attendance became most urgent, and the few Whig practitioners in New Jersey were called upon and could not decline to serve. Hospitals were opened in many parts of the State. Private practice was almost at a standstill. The deep snows and prevalence of gangs of marauders prevented any itinerant practice, and medical men, unless they had other resources, were then unable to support themselves by their profession. . . .*
>
> *The campaign of the Continental Army during the year of 1780 was exclusively conducted in the Jersies. . . . During the year, all business*

> *in that unfortunate state was at a standstill, and no private medical practitioner could, with personal safety, practice his profession for a living and make itinerant medical visits. General Knyphausen made his raid into the Jersies, and the Battle of Springfield was fought, in 1780. The militia were under arms, and the farmers who had sown their crops were in many instances unable to reap them, or else the invading or Continental armies did it for them.*
>
> *There can be no reasonable doubt that Dr. Alexander Ross served. . . . I therefore express it as my opinion and belief, after mature deliberation, that Dr. Alexander Ross entered the Continental Service as a hospital physician and surgeon on or about December 1, 1779, and continued in service until the close of the campaign in 1780.*

So the case of Dr. Ross was brought to a happy conclusion, and his right to membership in our Society continues to be held to this day.

The care that was evident in this judgment of the Society, the obvious determination to do the right and honorable thing, was also clear in decisions made about charity. The early minutes are filled with references to gifts like these: 1793—$50 to the widow of Captain Pike; 1795—$50 for the widow and orphan children of Captain William Piatt, with special instruction to "pay particular attention to the education of the eldest son"; 1798—$40 to Lieutenant Abraham Stout, then "in very indigent circumstances," with the stipulation that it "be applied to the education of his children"; 1804—$100 to the widow of the late Governor Richard Howell, who suffered "unpleasant circumstances as to the means of supporting and educating her family"; and so on.

For those of you with feminist convictions, it may be worth noting that in the beginning, all these donations were sent not to the widows concerned, but to men who were charged with being trustees. By the 1830s, however, that narrow-minded practice had been done away with, and the sums went directly to the ladies.

Instead, a new issue came forward: namely, the hard choice of determining the size of individual grants. In 1833, the Standing Committee issued the plaintive statement that

> *they are unable, from delicacy and feeling, to make any discrimination. The sacred fund of benevolence created by the sympathies and nurtured by the care of the officers of the Revolution and their descendants and successors was intended to relieve the distresses and the feelings of their*

> *widows and children in all tenderness and delicacy; and in this sense of delicacy, the committee shrink from the investigation into the comparative extent of their wants.*

And so five of the six recipients that year received a flat $30 each, and the last received a double portion of $60, for reasons not explained.

The practice of responding to individual pleas for assistance continued well through the nineteenth century, but then the grants began to shift to objectives that were perhaps less personal: the purchase of what is described as "a piece of colonial furniture: which was to be contributed to the Washington's Headquarters Association at Rocky Hill; participation in the erection of a monument to mark the spot where Washington crossed the Delaware; and in 1894 the purchase of a tiny plot of land and raising of what the minutes called

> *a monument of granite with a bronze historical tablet, on the scene of the massacre of Pulaski's troops at Egg Harbor, a few miles south of Tuckerton. . . . The deed of the property on which the Pulaski Monument was placed has been presented by the President, and the bills of the Monument Committee, $234.12, are recommended to the Society for payment.*

Perhaps at this point it would be worth looking at the context, as it were, of those early meetings and the decisions that were reached within them. In the beginning, the meetings must have been colorful, and they were taken seriously. Members were directed in 1783 to wear "the proper uniform of the Jersey line," and if they "absented themselves without leave," they were subject to "the penalty of four dollars." The latter regulation apparently caused considerable dissent, because by 1787 it was voted that the resolution "be repealed and the moneys heretofore paid be reimbursed."

Another directive, even shorter-lived, was passed in 1828—namely, that the members "agree to abstain from the use of ardent spirits at dinner." It is not clear whether this resolution was the result of undue boisterousness or whether it was pushed through by temperance enthusiasts; what is clear is that at least some of our ancestors took vigorous countermeasures. The minutes of the following year record sternly that

> *of the sum paid at the last meeting for the expenses of the Society, the sum of $24.87-1/2 was improperly charged and paid for the Tavern Bills of certain of the members. The Committee have with reluctance paid*

> *so much of this bill at this time, and they take occasion to announce that except by the instructions of the Society, they will not allow such bills in time to come.*

My imagination is wonderfully tickled by this incident, which seems to me to manifest a splendid sense of American independence. No more was heard of the "ardent spirits" issue, and indeed the account books later show many expenditures for wines, liquors, cigars, and even, in 1843, "for a band of music." That must have been a good year.

But all was not jollity by any means. Throughout the first half of the nineteenth century especially, there are mentions of the members' meetings, usually on February 22 and July 4, at some convenient place and then marching solemnly with a military escort to a church—most often Presbyterian, occasionally Methodist—to hear an oration, which, according to a resolution of 1820, would have

> *the purpose of inculcating those principles which form the basis [of the Society], as of tracing the causes which led to the American Revolution, and which attended and preceded that vast event, and showing the influence which it has had and probably will have on the morals, religion, and politics of the Society in general.*

In the years that followed, such orations were variously described as "very eloquent and truly patriotic," "very pathetic," "instructive," "excellent and appropriate," and "appropriate to our circumstances and grateful to our recollection of the piety and valor of the soldiers of the Revolution."

In addition there was a reading of the Declaration of Independence and hymns rendered by what the Secretary for a number of years called "an efficient choir." That adjective "efficient" is certainly not one to make the heart leap in expectation.

As I have said, a major activity of our Society since its inception was a contributions program, and you may wonder how our ancestors found the means. The early records all seem to be about bills paid—some of my favorites among them being 57 pounds, 7s, 10p for the expenses of members attending a meeting at the General Society in 1784, and 20s paid General Dayton for postage in 1792. The latter, by the way, is the last reference to the old British monetary system. There are other references to payments of $150 for the State's share of the debt to Major L'Enfant, presumably for his design and execution of the President-General's eagle; $80 for diplomas on parchment; $6 for two "facsimiles" of the Declaration of Independence, to be put "in a frame or other state of preservation"; and so on.

Of course there had been the original shares of a month's pay which the first members had put forward, and as the years wore on, new entrants paid $500 or $250. (I am not entirely clear on this point, but I believe the former were to establish new lines of right, while the latter were successors in lines already confirmed.) The important point in my mind was that the funds were wisely invested and developed, and indeed the investment policies as the generations unfolded offer a special perspective on American history.

In 1808, a special appropriation of $166.66 was ordered so that the "capital stock" of the Society—that is, its principal, or its endowment, if you like—could stand at exactly $10,000. This amount was invested in "the permanent stock of the United States," paying 6 percent. In 1811, for unexplained reasons, $7,600 was diverted to "the stock of the Masonic Loan," and the Treasurer was instructed that he could invest "in whole or in part in any other public stocks, provided always that in no case they lessen the annual income of $600 per annum if it can be done without diminishing the capital sum of $10,000."

In succeeding years, at various points the Society's investments were put into New York Life Insurance stock, bonds of the State of Pennsylvania, the City of Philadelphia, the City of New York, and the State of New Jersey. In 1863, in a dazzling maneuver that fills me with admiration, they did the following. They sold a $10,000 U.S. bond that was payable in gold, took the gold and disposed of it at a premium of 34.52 percent, used an uncommitted $48 that was in the hands of the Treasurer, and converted the resulting $13,500 into another U.S. Bond paying 6 percent. In other words, in one transaction they realized a profit of 35 percent, with income flow to match.

By the time the decade of the 1880s opened, principal had climbed to more than $15,000, and in keeping with the financial wisdom of the time, it was invested variously in the West Jersey Rail Road; the Pemberton & Hightstown Rail Road; The Pennsylvania Car Trust; The Susquehanna Coal Company; The Pittsburgh, Cincinnati & St. Louis Railway; and other companies that now could be no more than footnotes in the dissertation of some economics graduate student, but all vigorously profitable.

So the investment group was, as we would say, "on a roll." Its success was brilliant, and "the permanent fund of the Society" moved up year after year from $15,000 in 1883 to $16,800 in 1885, to $18,500 in 1887, to $19,700 in 1889, and to slightly more than $24,000 in 1894.

For us to have kept even with this record, we ought to have a principal of at least $240,000 on hand today, instead of something more than $100,000. We clearly have a task ahead of us if we want to come even once again.

Mind you, this was sound business practice conducted wisely not just by hard-headed businessmen, but by friends who felt deeply and warmly for one another. One cannot read those minutes without being struck by the pain and sense of loss that followed the deaths of fellow members, as in the following excerpts:

> *1862, of George Cumins Thomas: "With grief of heart, I am compelled to announce to you that death since our last anniversary has visited our ancient Society with an unsparing hand. . . . For seventeen years consecutively, [Mr. Thomas] was our Vice-President. He was a good man, and all who knew him loved him and now lament his death. . . . We were school boys together more than seventy years ago. An intimate and warm friendship was then formed [and] it continued through youth, manhood, and old age. I take pleasure and pride in saying that in that long lapse of years it was not interrupted by a single discordance."*
>
> *1872, of Colonel James Walter Wall: [He] occupied an honored seat in the Senate of the United States. . . . A man of rare culture and ability. . . . A writer correct, elegant, and forcible. An orator, brilliant and distinguished. A man respected by all, and beloved by those who knew him best; he was true to all convictions of right, fearless in their maintenance, and of undeviating fidelity to every principle."*
>
> *1883, of Charles Clinton Beatty: "We remember that although living at a distance, his attendance was regular even at an advanced age, and that for some time when blind from an infection of the eyes he was not absent from our councils, albeit he had to be led to them by the hand. Yet, while animated by sentiments of respect and fraternal regard for his memory, we feel no longer or more elaborate eulogy would be in place. . . . Therefore, of him let it be briefly regarded in the words of the Apostle Paul, that 'after he had served his own generation by the will of God, [he] fell upon sleep, and was laid unto his fathers.' "*

So I add that sentiment, too, to the others that are so simple and pervasive throughout those pages—the abiding sense of justice, the quiet commitment to charity and patriotism, the penetrating judgment that built a sound financial base for the future—all are founded in the deep affection they felt for one another: not merely the original members, but the generations that followed them.

As I look back on my remarks this evening, I realize that I have not touched at all on the dramatic high points in that history: the threat posed by Napoleonic France in 1798; the death of Washington in 1799; the return of La Fayette for his final visit in 1824; the assassination of President James Garfield in 1881; the tumult that followed the news of the Battle of Santiago in 1898.

I regret that I seem not to have given you a coherent, consecutive picture. Rather, I seem to have given a series of unevenly lighted, flickering scenes like out-takes from an old movie in the imagination. For one who was trained as a scholar, that should be an embarrassing admission. And yet . . . and yet . . . I am willing to risk that. For I am secure in the hope that most of you, my brother Cincinnati and friends and guest, found your thoughts focusing at last as mine did, on something like the closing lines of that splendid poem by Stephen Spender, "I Think Continually of Those Who Were Truly Great." They go like this:

> Near the sun, in the highest fields
> See how their names are feted by the wavering
> grass,
> And by the Streamers of white cloud,
> And whispers of wind in the listening sky;
> The names of those who in their lives fought
> for life,
> Who wore at their hearts the fire's center.
> Born of the sun they traveled a short while
> towards the sun,
> And left the vivid air signed with their honor.

TWENTY-EIGHT

WILLIAM LIVINGSTON: THE TRIALS OF A REVOLUTIONARY WAR GOVERNOR

Carl E. Prince, Ph.D., 1983

Carl E. Prince received his B.A. in 1956, his M.A. in 1958, and his Ph.D. in 1963, all from Rutgers University. He was Assistant and Associate Professor at Seton Hall University, 1963–1968, and Associate Professor 1968–1974, and Professor of History and Editor, *Papers of William Livingstone,* 1974 to present at New York University.

Read to the Society of the Cincinnati on May 8, 1983 in New Jersey as the third paper in the new series of prize lectures

William Livingston may well have been the best state executive in the thirteen states during the American Revolution. It was not merely his grasp of administration and use of executive authority that made him a strong leader. More subtly, his success derived as well from his unity with the people of the state. A patrician by birth himself, he was able to establish a close rapport with a population of farmers, artisans, and shopkeepers at war. That he was able to do so in a state racked for five years by invasion, the internal divisions triggered by widespread loyalism, enemy occupation, and devastation of the land was all the more remarkable.

Yet as the real William Livingston emerges from the shadows of history, he appears increasingly as an amalgam of the cold, austere, private person he was on the one hand, and the witty, compassionate, accessible and human public person he also proved himself to be, on the other. In short, what the Livingston Papers project has discovered behind the mass of historical documents brought together for the first time is a complete human being. He had all the foibles, internal contradictions, weaknesses, and inconsistencies of any person. We have also learned a great deal about New Jersey in the American Revolution along the way.

Born in 1723 to a patriarchal family headed by the Lord of Livingston Manor in New York State, he knew instinctively and by early training how to exercise authority. As governor, he disdained due process under law for the many loyalists in New Jersey. Occupation of the state's soil by the enemy, and internal harassment by these same loyalists for more than five years, did not permit him to do otherwise. Between 1777 and 1779, he was perfectly capable of using the New Jersey Council of Safety. The council was a revolutionary tribunal with powers to prosecute individuals even suspected of loyalism and "aiding the enemy." As president of this revolutionary tribunal, he would order the arrest, interrogation, and jailing of hundreds of suspect Jerseymen in the name of order and endangerment of the state's precarious internal security.

That precariousness was underscored by the fact that, as governor, he lived his life on the run. He rarely spent a week in one place for more than five years between 1776 and 178l. As a result, he came to know his constituency with an intimacy borne of that experience, an experience probably unique or nearly so, for an American political figure at any time in any place. Because he was so visible in so many places so often, it appears most Jersey residents were comforted by his austere, strong, energetic presence among them, looking on him with ever-deepening paternal feelings. And the contact made by Livingston caused him slowly to shed his inherited prejudices against the great mass of middling, anonymous Jerseymen, prejudices ingrained in the course of a half century of patrician life.

Almost in spite of himself, Livingston came to respect and admire the stolid citizenry of New Jersey. These people were the farmers whose harvests were threatened, the townsmen and women undermined and harassed intermittently by a strong loyalist presence and British and Hessian occupiers. He moved almost weekly from one place to another; from Newton in Sussex County to Morristown, Elizabethtown, and on to Woodbridge and Princeton, then perhaps southward to Trenton, Burlington Pittstown, Haddonfield, and a dozen other places scattered across the New Jersey landscape. In the course of his travels, he came to know and observe an ever-widening number of people. Most of these formed a class he had had only limited contact with heretofore, in the segregated society of eighteenth-century America. And as he came to know these people, he came to respect them. For the first time in his life, Livingston perceived these farmers and artisans in ways that were more than one-dimensional.

The rapport that grew out of this growing mutual respect manifested itself in several ways. Livingston was elected governor annually fourteen times in as many years, designated by a legislature highly sensitive to the moods of its constituents, and itself elected annually. Nobody in New Jersey, with the exception of Abraham Clark, "the poor man's counsellor," pressed harder for revolutionary democratic reform that did William Livingston. He shed most of his elite predilections. In advanced middle age, the governor pressed successfully for many of those political reforms that help characterize the American Revolution as a real revolution, one that radically transformed both the political and social structure of state and fledging nation.

Livingston helped pioneer in the extension of the suffrage to all taxpayers, not merely landowners; he was a moving force behind the concept of frequent popular elections, and of accountability of officeholders to the public. Under his tutelage, New Jersey became one of the first states to adopt laws confiscating and redistributing loyalist property. This was a leveling policy that in New Jersey and elsewhere may well have been among the most meaningful ways in which the American Revolution displaced an existing elite that had dominated the colony for a century.

The governor came face to face with tough, bitter experiences. Most notably, he had several narrow escapes from assassination attempts by either loyalists or British agents. In 1778, two attempts were made to either kill or kidnap him from Liberty Hall, his Elizabethtown estate. Once, he had departed only minutes before the loyalists arrived. On another occasion, the home was looted and his daughters harassed. Livingston wrote wryly to a friend that "I am not often so near home as they [the British] imagine." That was true. His administration-in-motion was so well known to the loyalists press he was dubbed "the Invisible Governor." Loyalists chided, "Your agility in New Jersey has been proverbial."

Livingston wrote of these assassination attempts to his friend Henry Laurens, president of the Continental Congress as follows:

> *The Enemy have lately tempted me to consider myself in a point of light in which I should never have had the vanity to consider myself but for their most gracious opinion of me, that is as a Man of Consequence. I hope they will never succeed in killing me, as I should by that means most certainly lose the honor of being hanged in Company with some of you more illustrious Rebels.*

As a result of these experiences, as well as his life on the run, Will Livingston developed an appreciation for both the responsibilities and anguish of power. He learned to use it well. This, as we know too well, is not a common characteristic of American politicians in general, or so history would indicate. He was one of the earliest public figures in revolutionary America to openly appose black slavery. As governor he pioneered, much to the distress of many in the Continental Congress, in successfully pressing for reform of the military hospitals in the new nation. Many of these hospitals were located in New Jersey. He recognized that these pestilential holes killed more enlisted men and officers than they saved. He always spoke out eloquently on the Continental Army troops' behalf.

When the British and Hessians periodically swept through parts of New Jersey, they left in their wake, among many other tragedies, a series of brutal rapes. The governor demanded justice from his enemies under the rules of war, law, and humanity. At the same time, he demonstrated great compassion for both the victims of rape and their families and exposed the whole hidden issue to public censure. He protected the anonymity of the victims at all costs. Indeed, he went beyond the mores of the era in finding ways of providing whatever meager compensation and justice there could be for the women and families so victimized.

As both a militia general and governor, he tried hard to order the activation of Jersey militia for duty so as to best protect the harvests of the state's marginal farmers. These families made up the bulk of the Jersey militia force. These men were invariably torn between their land and family obligations on the one hand, and their wartime military obligations on the other. He helped make the New Jersey militia one of the best and most active in the nation.

In sum, as patrician and arrogant as he was by nature and background, neither vanity nor smugness was part of his character. As a result, he never stopped learning from his wartime experiences. Over the years, compassion replaced arrogance and a commitment to social and political reform tempered his ingrained conception of a nation ruled by the upper class.

This last aspect of his character was borne out by an ability not to personalize political disagreement. He gracefully accepted criticism from those who generally wished him well and fought in the same cause. Thus, political enemies remained personal friends, and critics found they could engage him in extended dialogue. Two examples can illustrate this point.

Over the years, Will Livingston and his neighbor Abraham Clark, at various times a member of the Continental Congress or the New Jersey Legislature, had serious political disagreements, often of a highly public nature. Yet they maintained a mutual respect. They praised each other's motives and character and rarely ever personalized their myriad differences.

Samuel Allinson, a South Jersey Quaker who opposed the Revolutionary War on religious grounds, wrote Livingston many ten-page letters. In them, he took issue with the governor on a wide variety of matters, ranging from the chief executive's persecution of loyalists to government tax policies burdensome to Quaker consciences. Any tax, after all, that Quakers interpreted as supportive of war, became a matter of conscience for them, and they formed a large part of the population of West Jersey in the eighteenth century. Livingston invariably responded with ten-page letters of his own explaining his feelings and positions. The governor raised questions of his own for Allinson to comment on. In an era of heightened political emotions and chasm-like ideological differences among Americans, these letters constitute a remarkable display of political sensitivity and maturity. They tell us a good deal about Livingston's ability as a political moderator. This receptivity to views inherently distasteful and troubling to him, helped make the transplanted New Yorker a better war governor.

Because of these human qualities, Livingston survived under the toughest of political conditions. He shared major responsibility for holding the state's civil government together at a time when its role in the American war effort was crucial. This personally taciturn, austere, aristocratic, and judgmental figure actually came to be revered by most of the Whig civilians of the state. "You are the father of us all," one Jersey farmer wrote him. His popularity among the rank and file was testimony to his personal indefatigability and political and administrative good sense. Although he would remain governor throughout the Confederation era, indeed until his death in 1790, the war years proved the toughest in his life. The Revolutionary War called forth all the great intelligence and ability to communicate he possessed. It would be too much to claim he was beloved by all, nobody ever is that. But he was respected by most, and no political figure can ask for more than that.

Perhaps, in closing, the public tribute paid him by the Trenton Committee of Correspondence, delivered at a public ceremony marking the close of the war in 1783, can stand as a synthesis of the feelings he called forth from Jersey men and women:

> *We recollect, with pleasure and veneration, that when the helm of state was committed to your hands, at an early period of the revolution, you accepted, with firmness, the perilous station; and when the storm increased and raged with the greatest violence, we have seen you persevering in the face of every danger and discouragement, till we happily arrived at the haven of Peace, Liberty, and Independence.*

Will Livingston ended his career having earned the gratitude of his constituents, the least advantaged among them included. In so doing, he himself was able to come half circle. He developed a deep admiration for those he governed—all of them. Little more can ever be asked of any political figure at any time.

TWENTY-NINE

NEW JERSEY'S REVOLUTIONARY WAR DAMAGE CLAIMS

Peter O. Wacker, Ph.D., 1985

Peter O. Wacker is Emeritus Professor, Department of Geography, at Rutgers University. He received his B.A. from Montclair State College in 1959, and his M.A. and Ph.D. from Louisiana State University in 1961 and 1966, respectively. He was a University Fellow at Rutgers University, a Guggenheim Fellow and a Fellow of the New Jersey Historical Society. He was also Chairman of the Department of Geography at Rutgers University and the New Jersey State Review Board for Historic Sites.

Read to the Society on May 8, 1985
in New Jersey
as the fifth paper in the series of prize lectures

Let me begin my talk today by thanking you all again for your generosity and for adding my name to the distinguished group of historians you have honored on previous occasions. Because of this organization's very particular tie to the American Revolution, I have decided to discuss a unique data source concerning the Revolution, which is in the possession of the Bureau of Archives in Trenton, New Jersey.

New Jersey provides an especially fine "laboratory" to study the impact of distinctly different cultures on the landscape. As is well known, in British North America, the Middle Colonies of Delaware, Pennsylvania, New Jersey, and New York possessed the greatest cultural diversity. New England was overwhelmingly English, as were the southern colonies, except for ethnic islands here and there—the Carolina Piedmont and the Shenandoah Valley, for example.

I would contend that New Jersey was the most culturally diverse of the Middle Colonies. It shared in Swedes, English Quakers, Scots-Irish, and Germans with Pennsylvania and Delaware. Admittedly it had few Welsh, but it did have ethnic Scots. With New York, it shared the Dutch of the Hudson Valley and Long Island and the expanding sphere of New England settlement. Large numbers of blacks were also on the scene, especially in Dutch-settled areas.

New Jersey's cultural groups were very much regionalized during the eighteenth century, and we can especially identify their locations by mapping (a particularly useful geographic technique) the locations of churches of different denominations. Extreme northeastern New Jersey was dominated by Dutch culture (old Bergen County, Figure1). The "Dutch" included many people of non-Holland origin who had become "Dutch" through intermarriage and acculturation.

Beginning with old Essex County, just south of the Dutch culture area, were New Englanders who dominated most of Essex County and extended into adjacent Morris and Middlesex counties. Southwestern New Jersey was dominated by English Quakers with some New Englanders in the extreme south and a few Swedes largely in the Outer Coastal Plain. North of Trenton could be found the thrust of Pennsylvanians into New Jersey, many of them of Scots-Irish and German origin.

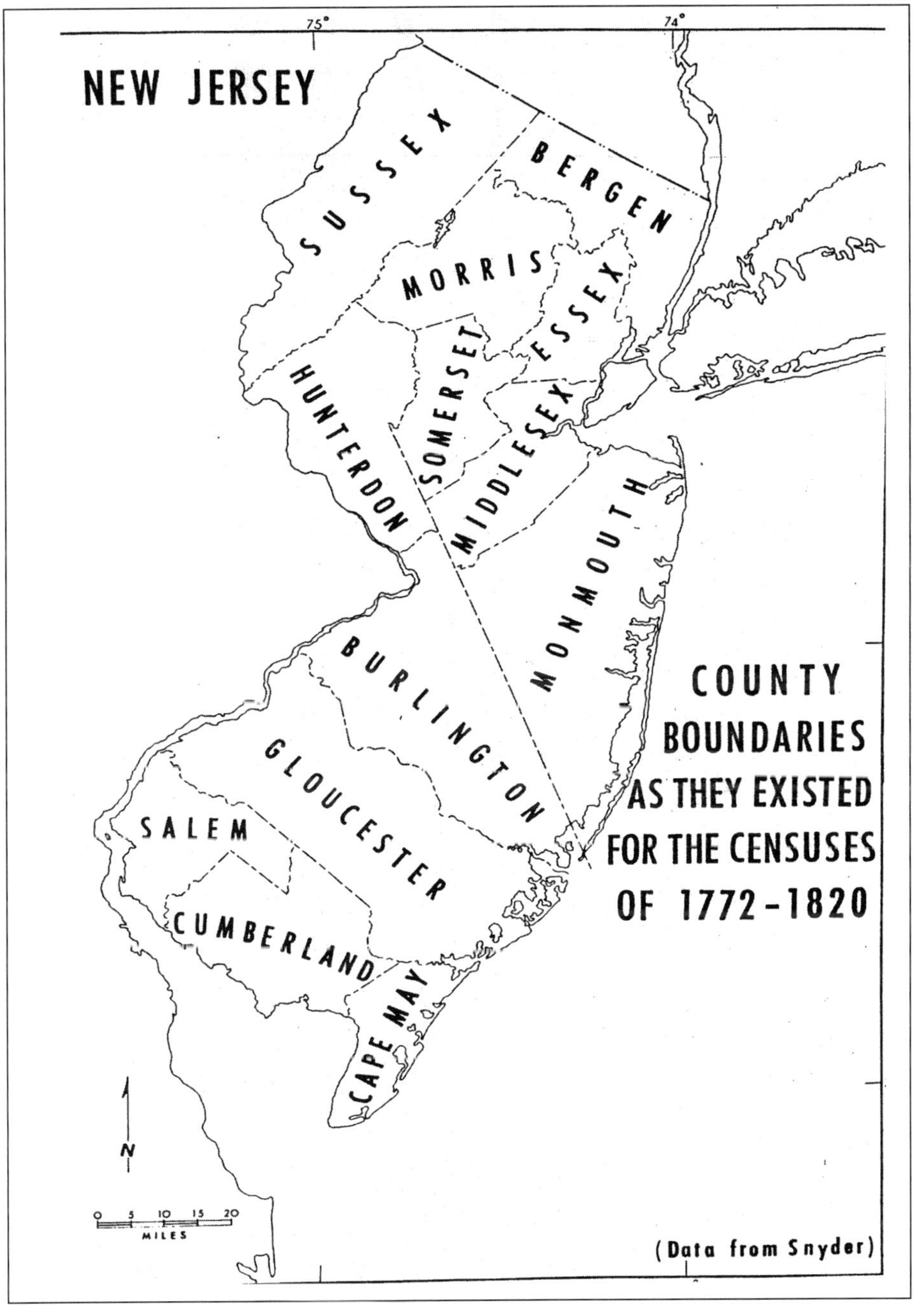
75°
74°
NEW JERSEY
SUSSEX
BERGEN
MORRIS
ESSEX
SOMERSET
HUNTERDON
MIDDLESEX
MONMOUTH
BURLINGTON
GLOUCESTER
SALEM
CUMBERLAND
CAPE MAY
COUNTY BOUNDARIES AS THEY EXISTED FOR THE CENSUSES OF 1772-1820
N
0 5 10 15 20
MILES
(Data from Snyder)

Figure 1

The Raritan Valley and northern Monmouth County was a zone of cultural heterogeneity where New Englanders, Scots, and Dutch elements could be found. Somerset County was especially dominated by the Dutch. The Outer Coastal Plain, or Pine Barrens, and the northern Highlands were sparsely populated, male dominated, and quite heterogeneous, devoted largely to extractive industries and not permanent agricultural settlement.

I have used many different sources to elucidate the similarities and the differences among New Jersey's cultural regions. One unique and useful source is what I would like to tell you about today. These are the Revolutionary War Damage Claims. As this organization well knows, the state of New Jersey was a major theater of activity during the Revolution and a great deal of damage was done by the armies during battles and skirmishes as well as by foraging, especially on the part of British troops and Loyalists (Figure 2).

On December 20, 1781, New Jersey passed legislation entitled

> *An Act to Procure an Estimate of the Damages Sustained by the Inhabitants of this State from the Waste and Spoil Committed by the Troops in the Service of the Enemy and their Adherents, by the Continental Army, or by the Militia of this or of the Neighboring States.*

The purpose of collecting information on the damages was that "it is necessary that an Estimate be made of the same in order to enable the Legislature to devise Ways and Means for the Relief of those who have suffered, that equal Justice may be done to all the Inhabitants of this State." The claims were to be solicited by three appraisers in each county, two of whom had to be present at public places where the claimants were to appear after proper notice had been given and posted. This was to be at least four weeks in advance of the arrival of the appraisers. Claimants were to produce inventories of the damages

> *which Inventories shall contain a List of the specified Goods, Chattels or Property of what Nature or Kind soever, so damaged, wasted, spoiled, plundered, burned or destroyed, expressing the time when and the troops by whom the same was done.*

The appraisers were to value the damages "as nearly as may be, agreeably to the current Prices such Articles would have borne respectively in the Year One Thousand Seven Hundred and Seventy-five." Each inventory, after being proved to the "Satisfaction of the said Appraisers" was to be entered in

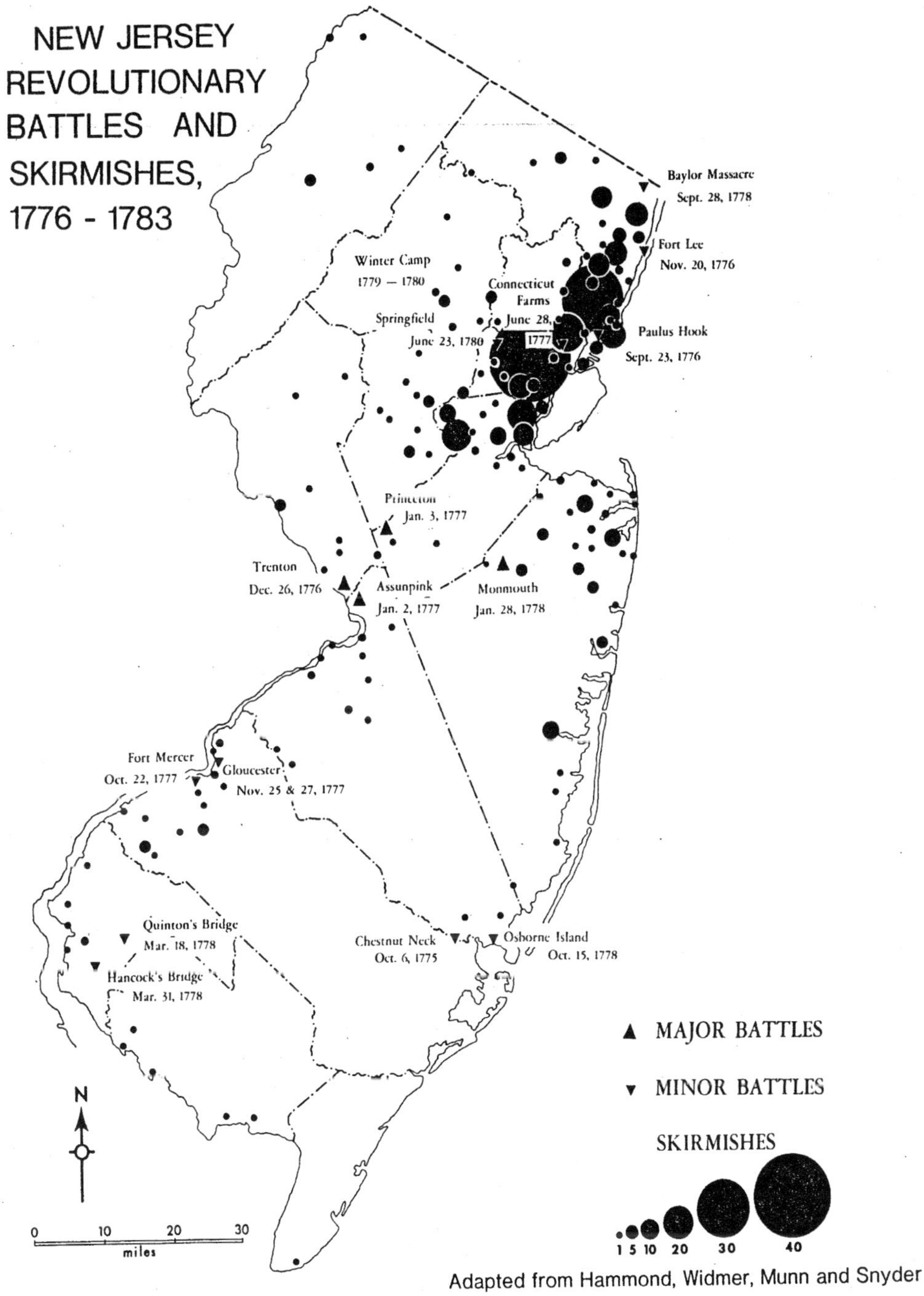
NEW JERSEY REVOLUTIONARY BATTLES AND SKIRMISHES, 1776 - 1783
Baylor Massacre Sept. 28, 1778
Fort Lee Nov. 20, 1776
Winter Camp 1779 — 1780
Connecticut Farms June 28, 1777
Springfield June 23, 1780
Paulus Hook Sept. 23, 1776
Princeton Jan. 3, 1777
Trenton Dec. 26, 1776
Assunpink Jan. 2, 1777
Monmouth Jan. 28, 1778
Fort Mercer Oct. 22, 1777
Gloucester Nov. 25 & 27, 1777
Quinton's Bridge Mar. 18, 1778
Hancock's Bridge Mar. 31, 1778
Chestnut Neck Oct. 6, 1775
Osborne Island Oct. 15, 1778
MAJOR BATTLES
MINOR BATTLES
SKIRMISHES
1 5 10 20 30 40
N
0 10 20 30
miles
Adapted from Hammond, Widmer, Munn and Snyder

Figure 2

a book to be kept for that purpose. Part of the proof to be demanded by the appraisers was an oath or affirmation by one or more reliable witnesses who were neighbors of the claimant and knew that the damages in fact had been incurred. Penalties were established for witnesses refusing to answer a summons to appear and also for any fraud associated with the claim:

> *Persons so offending shall forever thereafter be excluded from deriving any benefit from this Act, and shall moreover be liable to the same Pains and Penalties as are by Law inflicted upon Persons guilty of willful and corrupt Perjury.*

From this quote, I think we can ascertain that at least in theory the appraisals of damages were to be taken seriously, that responsible neighbors were to corroborate the losses, that accurate records were to be kept, and that the values placed on damages were to reflect prices current in 1775. Even if we were to be skeptical of the veracity of the claimants and their neighbors in regard to the amounts claimed, I think we would accept the notion that *what* they claimed they lost or was destroyed actually existed in that area. What I mean is that if the claim were for a Dutch barn damaged or destroyed, it is reasonable to suppose that Dutch barns were at least common in that area.

At this point, it is important to mention that the data for some counties are better than for others in both quality, numbers, and location (Figure 3). For Bergen, Essex, Middlesex, and Somerset counties, for example, claims are listed by township or often by nucleation within a township. In the case of Morris, Hunterdon, and Burlington counties, we do not have specific locations but can generally guess, from our knowledge of military activities, which areas were involved. Luckily for comparative purposes, Bergen and Somerset at the time were dominantly Dutch, Essex dominantly New England, and Middlesex mixed.

We could spend the day talking about the patterns revealed by analysis of the damage claims. As I have been asked to limit my time to about twenty-five minutes, I have to be selective. Thus, I have chosen to present to you briefly what can generally be learned from claims for the loss of farm buildings, agricultural products, and fences.

With regard to farm buildings, we have a fair knowledge of distributional patterns from contemporary newspaper advertisements. Unfortunately, New Englanders and the Dutch, especially those of Bergen County, appear to have advertised very little. Thus, the damage claims are especially useful for these areas. One conclusion I have drawn from these claims, for example, is that

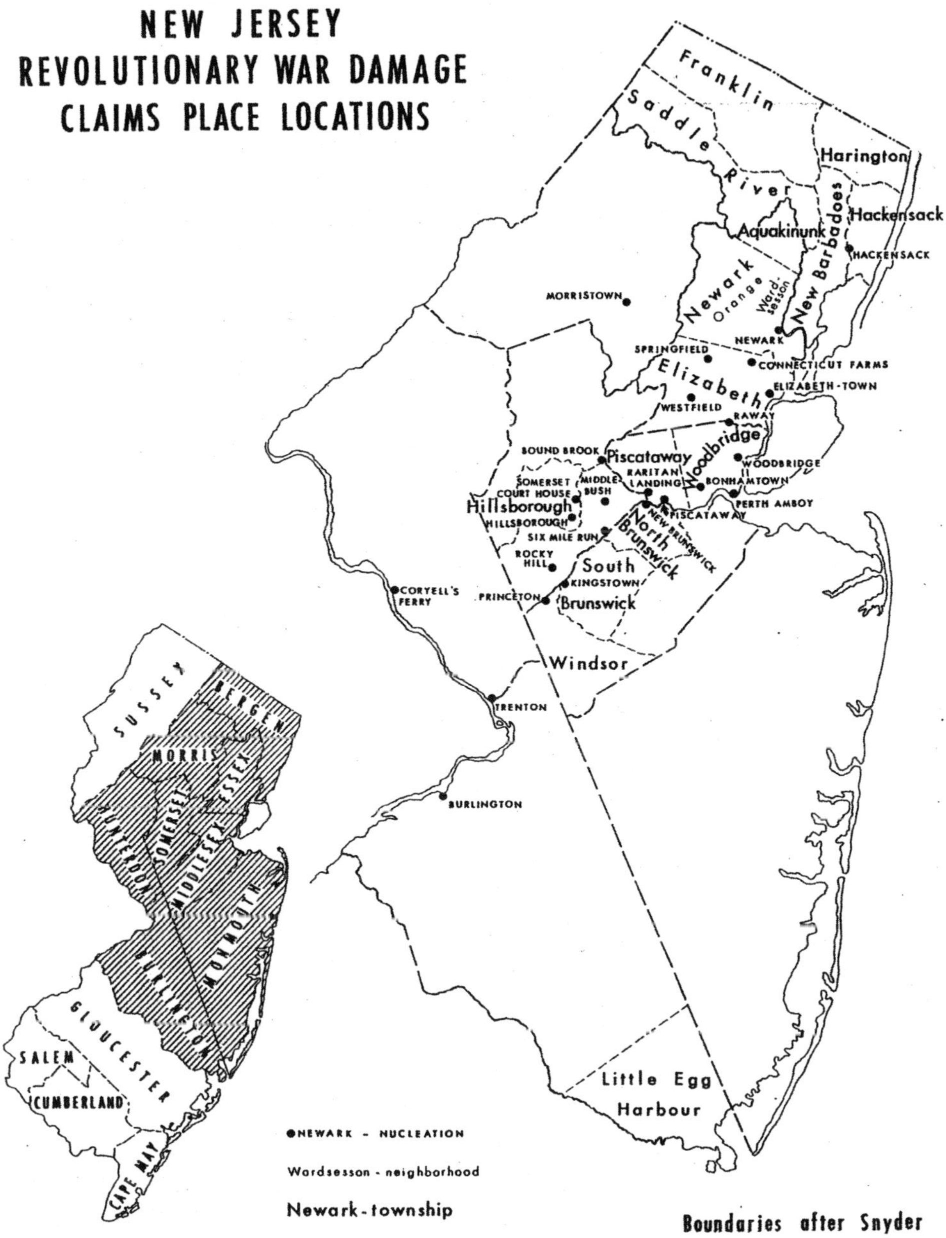
NEW JERSEY
REVOLUTIONARY WAR DAMAGE
CLAIMS PLACE LOCATIONS
Franklin
Saddle River
Harington
Hackensack
HACKENSACK
Aquakinunk
New Barbadoes
Newark
Orange
Ward-sesson
MORRISTOWN
NEWARK
SPRINGFIELD
CONNECTICUT FARMS
Elizabeth
ELIZABETH-TOWN
WESTFIELD
RAWAY
Woodbridge
WOODBRIDGE
BOUND BROOK
Piscataway
RARITAN LANDING
BONHAMTOWN
SOMERSET COURT HOUSE
MIDDLE-BUSH
Hillsborough
HILLSBOROUGH
PISCATAWAY
PERTH AMBOY
NEW BRUNSWICK
North Brunswick
SIX MILE RUN
ROCKY HILL
South Brunswick
KINGSTOWN
PRINCETON
CORYELL'S FERRY
Windsor
TRENTON
BURLINGTON
Little Egg Harbour
SUSSEX
BERGEN
MORRIS
ESSEX
SOMERSET
HUNTERDON
MIDDLESEX
MONMOUTH
BURLINGTON
GLOUCESTER
SALEM
CUMBERLAND
CAPE MAY
●NEWARK - NUCLEATION
Wordsesson - neighborhood
Newark - township
Boundaries after Snyder

Figure 3

there were *relatively* few Dutch barns in Bergen County. The damage claims by Dutch farmers there, by description and value, refer to English barns. This is a rather interesting conclusion and bears on the regionalization of Dutch culture in New Jersey and the process of acculturation.

At the time of the Revolution, New Jersey's agricultural economy was in large part oriented toward commercial grain production for export. Wheat was the most valuable grain. Again, we know the general location of New Jersey's "wheat belt" from newspaper advertisements, and we also have references to rye and Indian corn as well. We do not, however, have any data on the relative frequency of these crops from place to place. Again, the damage claims provide us with valuable information in this regard. More than half the claims from Middlesex and Somerset counties mentioned wheat damaged in the field. This corroborates the many statements about the nature of the agricultural economy of the Raritan Valley. In other counties, damages for wheat were about one-third of all claims; rye ranged from about 18 percent in Essex to almost 40 percent in Burlington. A few claims mentioned barley in Bergen and only one in Burlington. Indian corn generally was reflected in 10 percent or less of the claims except for Essex, where corn was mentioned in 30 percent of all claims. Oats, rarely mentioned in advertisements, appear to have been ubiquitous, appearing in from about 10 to 20 percent of all claims. Obviously, the high totals for rye in Burlington and corn in Essex demand further research.

The damage claims also provide an insight into relative frequencies of livestock, fowl and even bees. For example, milch cows and cattle appear to have been more common among the Dutch than among others. Oxen were a New England predilection, as mentioned by contemporary commentators. Hogs were especially numerous in Burlington County, where a well-known commercial smoking of hams for the Caribbean market took place.

With regard to fowl, chickens, referred to as "dunghill fowls," were ubiquitous. Turkeys were mentioned in more than 25 percent of Somerset claims and in about 20 percent of Burlington claims. Geese seem to have been much more important in English-settled areas (20 percent plus) than in Dutch-settled areas. Ducks were much less important, with the highest percentage, about 12 percent, in Burlington. Beekeeping was ubiquitous.

Let us now turn to fences. At first glance, fences do not seem to be a significant material culture trait to study. But in that day, livestock roamed free and crops were fenced to protect them from the animals. Also, before barbed wire was introduced, the single greatest capital investment for the farmer was fencing. Thus, we begin to realize that fences were very significant. Fences, of course, were also transitory cultural features and disappeared quickly, and their types were rarely recorded.

Luckily for the researcher, an army "travels on its stomach." Food has to be cooked and fires lit to keep warm in cold weather. New Jersey fences provided a well-seasoned and readily available supply of firewood for the soldiers of that day. With some 700 claims for damaged or destroyed fences we can make some informed statements about fencing in New Jersey at that time. These could include the following:

1. Frequency distribution of the types of wooden fencing
2. Associations of type of fencing with specific cultural groups
3. Valuations placed on the different forms of fencing and fencing materials
4. Frequency distributions of the types of wood used in fencing
5. Associations between fence type and sizes of landholdings
6. Associations between fence types and total available woodland
7. Association between fence types and rural economy

With the relatively short time available, I will concentrate on the first two—the distribution of fence types and their association with specific cultural groups (Table 1). At this point, a few words about the classification scheme and organizational framework I have used for this table are in order. Location refers to the location given in the damage claims. In some cases, location is by township, in other cases, only by county; in other cases, a particular agglomerated settlement within a township, such as New Brunswick, is indicated. In the case of Orange township of Newark, we have an ill-defined area that was later formalized by division as a township. The "N" column refers to the number of times fencing is mentioned in the claims. In some cases, one person may have claimed twice because of two separate depredations by the troops, often several years apart. This second claim would be reflected in the "N" column. In some cases, the second claim would be for another form of fencing on the property contrasting with the earlier claim.

The fence types are organized into what seem to me to be the most defensible categories. Several different forms of post-and-rail fencing are mentioned, ranging from two rails to six rails but involving mostly four and five rail types. "Rail or rails" refers to claims for "rail fence" or "fence rails" that might involve either post-and-rail or purely rail fencing. The worm fence, as it was known in

TABLE I

FENCING LISTED IN NEW JERSEY WAR DAMAGE CLAIMS, 1776-1782
FREQUENCY DISTRIBUTION BY LOCATION, TYPES

LOCATION	N	POST & RAIL	RAIL OR RAILS	WORM	PAILING	BOARD	GARDEN	"FENCE"
BERGEN COUNTY Harington Township	1	1						
Hackinsack Township	69	64						5
Saddle River Township	19	14			1			4
New Barbadoes Township	19	16						3
ESSEX COUNTY Aquakinunk Township	11	8	1					2
Newark	32	23	2		2	1		4
Orange Township of Newark	28	13	5			1		8
Connecticut Farms	2	2						
Elizabeth-Town	3	2						
Westfield	15	8	4				2	1
MIDDLESEX COUNTY (No specific location)	18	11	2	1	1	1		2
Woodbridge Township	86	46	16	15	4	4	1	1
Bonhamtown	2	1			1			
Perth Amboy	11	7			2	2		
Piscataway Township	70	19	11	29	7		1	3
Raritan Landing	24	15		1	3	3	1	1
*New Brunswick	42	18	1	2		20		1
*New Brunswick Vicinity	26	12	1	7	3			3
North Brunswick Township	2							2
South Brunswick Township	5	3		1	1			
*Kingston	6	4		1	1			
*Princeton	19	6		3	3	4		3
Windsor Township	13	4	2	2	2	1		2
SOMERSET COUNTY (No specific location)	31	12	4	2		4	1	8
Bound Brook	1	2	1					
Middlebush	9	2	1	2				4
Somerset Court House	5	1			1			3
Hillsborough	1	1						
Near Rocky Hill	1	1						
HUNTERDON COUNTY (No specific location)	16	5	2	1		8		
BURLINGTON COUNTY (No specific location)	96	10	58	8	4	8	3	5
MORRIS COUNTY (No specific location)	13	5	5					3

*Somerset County Data for these places included.

New Jersey, is what many of us would call the Virginia rail, zig-zag, or snake type. The other fence types in the table seem to have been characteristic of agglomerated rather than dispersed rural settlements.

What can we learn from the table about gross fence type distribution? First of all, it is fairly obvious that post-and-rail fences dominate Dutch Bergen and New England-settled Essex. In Middlesex County, however, where there existed diversity in the cultural origins of the population, as far north as New England-settled Woodbridge Township, worm fencing begins to appear. In Piscataway, there is more worm fencing than post-and-rail. Farther south, when "rail or rails" is combined with worm, as it probably should be in most cases, this form of fencing is again a most significant proportion of all fencing. Post-and-rail is listed in only ten claims for Burlington County, and it is probable that worm fencing actually predominated. In Morris County, it is harder to tell because of the small number of claims, but worm fencing may also have been important. Hunterdon County claims probably largely reflect damages in and near Trenton, thus, the relatively large number of board fences.

Dutch-given names and surnames can be relatively easily distinguished from those of other ethnic groups (Table 2). When a frequency distribution of the types of fences listed by Dutch claimants is constructed, their predilection for post-and-rail fencing in Bergen County is obvious. In the Raritan Valley, where the Dutch formed only one element in a rather heterogeneous population, a predilection for post-and-rail fencing can still be identified, but it is obvious that several used worm fencing as well.

The heterogeneous nature of Raritan Valley fencing has its parallel with other material culture traits as indicated elsewhere, especially insofar as house and barn types are concerned. Why may this heterogeneity have occurred insofar as culture history is concerned? We know little of fence type origins except that post-and-rail is of European origin and appears to have been current in Dutch settlements before 1650. New Englanders in New Jersey also built post-and-rail fences. In an article written many years ago, H. F. Raup asserted that the first reference to a worm fence in America was at Salem, Massachusetts, in 1685. The original reference, however, is from a manuscript in the library of the Pennsylvania Historical Society and the stream mentioned is Alloway's Creek, so that surely Salem, *New Jersey,* first settled by English Quakers in 1675, is the proper location. There is no accepted European origin for the worm fence. As with so many other material culture traits, the distribution of fence type could logically be explained by the process of diffusion from hearths in southwest and northeastern New Jersey

TABLE II

FENCING LISTED IN NEW JERSEY WAR DAMAGE CLAIMS, 1776-1782
FREQUENCY DISTRIBUTION BY LOCATION OF DAMAGE – "DUTCH" CLAIMANTS

LOCATION	N	POST & RAIL	RAIL OR RAILS	WORM	PAILING	BOARD	GARDEN	"FENCE"
BERGEN COUNTY Harington Township	1	1						
Hackinsack Township	64	60						4
Saddle River Township	19	14			1			4
New Barbadoes Township	17	14						3
ESSEX COUNTY Aquakinunk Township	10	8	1					1
Newark								
Orange Township of Newark								
Connecticut Farms								
Elizabeth-Town								
Westfield								
MIDDLESEX COUNTY (No specific location)	2	1						1
Woodbridge Township								
Bonhamtown								
Perth Amboy								
Piscataway Township	7	2		3	1			
Raritan Landing	10	5			2	1	1	1
*New Brunswick	19	8	1	1		8		1
*New Brunswick Vicinity	15	8		5	2			
North Brunswick Township	1							1
South Brunswick Township	3	1		1	1			
*Kingston	2			1	1			
*Princeton								
Windsor Township	3	2						1
SOMERSET COUNTY (No specific location)	11	5	1	1				4
Bound Brook								
Middlebush	7	2		2				3
Somerset Court House	3							3
Hillsborough	1	1						
Near Rocky Hill	1	1						
HUNTERDON COUNTY (No specific location)								
BURLINGTON COUNTY (No specific location)								
MORRIS COUNTY (No specific location)	1		1					

*Somerset County Data for these places included.

meeting and causing heterogeneity in the Raritan Valley. Wouldn't it be nice for the Delaware Valley to claim such an American basic as this fence!

In closing, let me again thank you for your kind invitation and your generosity. I hope I have provided information of some interest to you.

THIRTY

THE ORIGINS OF FEDERALISM IN THE UNITED STATES

John E. O'Connor, Ph.D., 1988

John E. O'Connor is Professor in the Federated Department History of the New Jersey Institute of Technology and Rutgers University. He received his Ph.D. from the City University of New York and is the founding editor of *Film and History.* He is also co-editor of *Hollywood's Indian, Hollywood's West,* and *Hollywood's White House* and teaches courses on the American Revolution, the American Experience, and Historical Problems Viewed through Film.

Read to the Society on May 7, 1988, in Princeton, New Jersey

At one point in the Vietnam War, the Massachusetts General Court got fed up with United States policy and decided to intervene. It nullified the federal draft. Back in 1832, when South Carolina nullified the tariff, the result was a huge national crisis, talk of civil war, and finally one of the major sectional compromises. Out of the controversy came for the first time a coherent argument for the republic as a perpetual union. Daniel Webster, Andrew Jackson, John Quincy Adams, James Madison, Edward Livingston, and others all contributed to this increasingly powerful idea, a notion scarcely even contemplated by the founding generation. From this crisis also emerged a rival vision among some South Carolina and Virginia politicians and writers, a yearning for a separate and independent southern nation. Both convictions would gain momentum until they finally collided in the secession crisis of 1860 to 1861 and the Civil War that it generated. By contrast, the Massachusetts nullification crisis of our time lasted only a few days while the Justice Department found a federal court that would declare the action unconstitutional. Massachusetts accepted this result. No doubt the legislature never intended anything more than an angry gesture against the war, and that is exactly what it accomplished.[1]

This half-comic incident would hardly matter today except that it suggests something important about government in the United States. In our federal system, most of the boundaries between national and state power are well understood. Even where they remain hazy, the nation possesses well-established mechanisms, judicial and political, for settling such problems without resort to violence. Attorney General Edwin Meese would like to revive the early Jeffersonian doctrine that each branch of the government must decide for itself what it considers constitutional and unconstitutional. As John Marshall's critics often argued, the Supreme Court cannot claim to be the final arbiter. A century and a half ago, this debate had an enormous impact on the political and legal systems of the country. Today, the effect is much less portentous. Not even the attorney general can alter quickly the institutional habits of courts and lawyers, nearly all of whom have been educated in the Marshall

[1] *Kenneth M. Stampp, "The Concept of a Perpetual Union," in his* The Imperiled Union: Essays on the Background of the Civil War *(New York: Oxford University Press, 1980), 3–36; John McCardell,* The Idea of a Southern Nation: Southern Nationalists and Southern Nationalism, 1830–1860 *(New York: Norton, 1979), esp. Chp. 2.*

tradition. Part of the historical significance of the Meese doctrine is that, so far at least, it has *not* generated a crisis.[2]

From 1789 to 1861, disputes over what we might call the federal boundary occurred often, were regularly accompanies by threats of nullification or secession, and finally did lead to civil war. What most Americans do not realize is that this pattern is much older than the Constitution. The search for an adequate federal system, defined loosely here as a reasonably consistent and mutually satisfactory division of powers between a central government and individual colonies, provinces, or states, began in the seventeenth century. Before 1787, this process went through three principal stages. Each ended in failure. The old British Empire as it took shape between the 1650s and the 1690s was really a functioning federal system without a sustaining federal ideology. The British government in effect abandoned the series of political compromises that had made it work and tried instead after 1763 to create a much more centralized empire. Colonial resistance to these demands led to war by 1775 and to a third phase in the history of North American federalism, this one dominated by the Continental Congress and the Articles of Confederation in which centralization yielded to state sovereignty. A compelling ideology of federalism took hold only with the Philadelphia Convention, the ratification struggle, the organization of the new government, the accession of North Carolina and Rhode Island to the Union, and the drafting and ratification of the Bill of Rights between 1789 and 1791. Even then, as the Civil War would demonstrate, the republic took another century to generate adequate institutional structures to sustain this new federal idea.

Today, we take for granted the kind of federal system announced from 1787 to 1791. Nobody at the time could. The federalism of the Constitution was conceptually impossible before the 1780s. To understand why, we must examine the earlier attempts to find an acceptable boundary between central and local power. Only then can we recognize 1787 as a supreme moment of political invention or innovation, a revolutionary act that permitted the Constitution to succeed after three prior arrangements had failed.

The British Empire

The improvised system of the British Empire came close to establishing a workable boundary between localism and the obvious needs of a central state. In the early years, the demands of crown and Parliament provoked frequent

---

[2] *See, for instance, Thomas Jefferson's views of unconstitutionality in his letter to Abigail Adams, Sept. 11, 1804, in Lester J. Cappon, ed.,* The Adams-Jefferson Letters: The Complete Correspondence Between Thomas Jefferson and Abigail and John Adams *(Chapel Hill: University of North Carolina Press, 1959), I, 278–80.*

resistance in the North American and West Indian colonies. By the 1750s, the settlers seemed happier with imperial arrangements than the British were.

The institutional structure of the empire took shape between 1650 and the late 1690s. The Navigation Acts, the customs service, the vice-admiralty courts, and the basic components of royal government all appeared in these years. The architects of the system, however, never thought of themselves as creating a federal division of authority. Sovereignty, they assumed, must reside in the government of England (or, after the union of the English and Scottish parliaments in 1707, the government of Great Britain), even if crown and Parliament frequently disputed their own respective spheres.

Nevertheless, the central state did limit itself in two ways. It restricted its fiscal responsibilities by insisting that each colony must pay the costs of its own internal government. Exactly what this responsibility meant varied from one colony to another. More important, it forced the crown to negotiate this policy with those embodiments of local autonomy, the colonial assemblies. Naturally, the crown preferred to keep its prerogative powers as broad as possible while settlers tried repeatedly to narrow them in keeping with eighteenth-century metropolitan practice. But in all royal colonies after the Glorious Revolution from 1688 to 1689, crown officials eventually realized that they had to work through the legitimate assemblies or see their weakness publicly exposed. Successful governors, whether through persuasion or influence, made imperial policy attractive enough to assemblymen to win majority support most of the time.[3]

The second limit was also self-imposed, but it was less a matter of policy than of the structural tendencies of the entire British political system. Parliament's interest in the colonies rarely strayed beyond its concern for imperial trade. Because colonial commerce was overwhelmingly oceanic, parliamentary statutes affecting North America nearly always took the form of regulations of seaborne traffic. The classic examples were, of course, the seventeenth-century Navigations Acts. In effect, the British Empire gave wide latitude to the individual politics of particular colonies but imposed much greater uniformity on imperial trade. If this division of responsibility seems natural and even inevitable, it should not. The Spanish Empire, for example, kept very close watch

---

[3] *For a recent study of this process, see Jack M. Sosin,* English America and Imperial Inconstancy: The Rise of Provincial Autonomy, 1696–1715 *(Lincoln: University of Nebraska Press, 1985). For a concise example of how intelligent accommodation could increase the real strength of a royal regime, see David Alan Williams, "Anglo-Virginia Politics, 1690–1735," in Alison Gilbert Olson and Richard Maxwell Brown, eds.,* Anglo-American Political Relations, *1675–1775 (New Brunswick, N.J.: Rutgers University Press, 1970), 76–91.*

on the political systems of individual colonies but lost control of their trade, of which perhaps 90 percent was smuggled by the mid-eighteenth century.[4]

When Charles II took charge of his tiny empire in 1660, England was a minor power on the fringe of the European world. A century later, especially with the defeat of France in North America and India and also on the high seas, Great Britain emerged as the greatest global colossus that mankind had yet seen. For all of the inefficiencies of the imperial system, it outperformed its rivals by a wide margin.

It did some things quite well. By the early eighteenth century, Parliament established effective British control over the commerce of the American and West Indian provinces. Colonial trade, which had been dominated by the Dutch in the 1650s, now traveled in British ships under British skippers who commanded predominantly British crews. So routine did this expectation become that when, for example, a French vessel docked at New York City in purported distress in the 1730s, the scandal entertained newspaper readers for weeks.[5] Likewise, the major colonial staple crops—sugar, tobacco, and rice—went where they were supposed to go, that is, to Britain first and then to the continent of Europe. The main exception to this pattern was authorized by Parliament, which in 1729 permitted rice growers to export directly to southern Europe. Finally, the colonists got a huge majority of their imports from or through Great Britain. Smuggling of tea, brandy, and other products did occur, but the colonial market for British goods grew more rapidly over the entire period than any other outlet. After 1740, it expanded faster than the population of the colonies, which routinely doubled every generation.[6]

---

[4] *Though dated in some respects, Oliver M. Dickerson,* The Navigation Acts and the American Revolution *(Philadelphia: University of Pennsylvania Press, 1951) remains very perceptive in the distinctions it draws on this question. The best study yet made of how one influential group of colonists moved from noncompliance to compliance between 1650 and the early eighteenth century involves West Indian sugar Planters. See Richard B. Sheridan,* Sugar and Slavery: An Economic History of the British West Indies, 1623–1775 *(Baltimore: Johns Hopkins University Press, 1974), Chps. 2-3*

[5] *For a sample of this material, see James Alexander,* A Brief Narrative of the Case and Trial of John Peter Zenger, Printer of the New York Weekly Journal, *ed. Stanley N. Katz (Cambridge, Mass.: Belknap Press, 1963), 118.*

[6] *Ralph Davis, "English Foreign Trade, 1600–1700,"* Economic History Review, *2nd ser., 7 (1954–55), 150–66; Davis, "English Foreign Trade, 1700–1774,"* Economic History Review, *2nd ser., 15 (1962–63), 285–303; John R. Pagan, "Dutch Maritime and Commercial Activity in Mid-Seventeenth-Century Virginia,"* Virginia Magazine of History and Biography, *90 (1982), 485–501. Compare also the population and import-export data in U.S. Bureau of the Census,* Historical Statistics of the United States, Colonial Times to 1970, *Bicentennial Edn. (Washington, D.C.: Government Printing Office, 1975), II, 1168, 1176–77. Note that in the Scottish series, all columns headed "Imports" should be labeled "Exports," and vice versa. Informed colonists were acutely aware of the importance of their growing commerce to British prosperity. See, for example, Benjamin Franklin,* The Interest of Great Britain Considered with Regard to her Colonies and the Acquisition of Canada and Guadeloupe *(London, 1760), in Leonard W. Labaree et al., eds.,* The Papers of Benjamin Franklin *(New Haven: Yale University Press, 1959–), IX, 47–100, esp. 99. See also, James A. Henretta,* The Evolution of American Society, 1700–1815: An Interdisciplinary Analysis *(Lexington, Mass.: D.C. Heath, 1973), Chp. 2, esp. p. 73.*

Other oceanic policies were less successful. The Molasses Act of 1733 tried to give West Indian planters monopoly prices in New England markets for what was essentially a by-product of the sugar trade, even though the British islands could not produce enough molasses to meet Yankee needs for rum and a cheap sweetener. This policy probably produced more smuggling than anything else that Britain tried before independence.[7] Trading with the enemy in time of war also generated considerable outrage, although the practice was probably no worse in American than in British waters.[8] Very likely, the illegal colonial consumption of European and East Asian imports did increase after about 1740, although the Dutch were probably more successful at sneaking their tea into Scotland and northern England than into North America.[9] The economic importance of this trade will always be difficult to measure, but in America its political significance became quite large. Boston smugglers, for example, played a major role in organizing resistance to British policies after 1763. They also brought into the politics of the pre-Revolutionary decade an animosity toward the Royal Navy that they had been acquiring at least since the 1740s.[10]

The crown also achieved considerable success in asserting basic control over the politics of individual colonies. As late as 1678, Virginia remained the only royal colony on the mainland of North America. By the reign of George I (1714–1727), royal government had clearly become the norm. Usually the first crown governor in a given province experienced a rude welcome. He brought with him a set of standardized prerogative expectations that was bound to clash with existing institutions, such as the assembly and structures of local government, both of which antedated royal control in nearly every province. Most of the early royal governors were soldiers whose short tempers exploded when they encountered systematic resistance. They soon learned that they

---

[7] *See John J. McCusker, Jr., The Rum Trade and the Balance of Payments of the Thirteen Continental Colonies, 1650–1775 (Ph.D. diss.: University of Pittsburgh, 1970), Chps. 7–10*

[8] *The single best study remains Richard Pares,* War and Trade in the West Indies, 1739–1763, *new edn. (London: Frank Cass & Co., Ltd., 1963).*

[9] *The best studies involve tea. Benjamin W. Labaree,* The Boston Tea Party *(New York: Oxford University Press, 1964), tries to estimate pre-Revolutionary tea consumption by working backwards from statistics of coffee consumption in the 1790s. This computation gives smuggled tea nearly 80 percent of the North American market, but it rests on a false assumption. One cannot compare pounds of coffee with pounds of tea for this purpose simply because tea produces several times as much beverage per ounce as coffee. The data for Great Britain are much stronger. See Hoh-cheung and Lorna M. Mui, "Smuggling and the British Tea Trade before 1784,"* American Historical Review, *74 (1968–69), 44–73.*

[10] *John W. Tyler,* Smugglers & Patriots: Boston Merchants and the Advent of the American Revolution *(Boston: Northeastern University Press, 1986) is excellent. See also John Lax and William Pencak, "The Knowles Riot and the Crisis of the 1740's in Massachusetts,"* Perspectives in American History, *10 (1976), 163–214.*

The Empire: Reform and Collapse

For what seemed to them the best of reasons, the British tried to change this system after 1763. An agenda for reform had been accumulating at the Board of Trade since at least 1748, and the passing of the direct military threat from France seemed to provide an excellent opportunity to implement changes that had been discussed in some circles for years. The exploding national debt added real urgency to these concerns. It had doubled during the war, reaching nearly $130 million. Payment of the interest alone absorbed about 60 percent of the government's annual budget. New expenses could not be avoided, particularly the cost of garrisoning Canada, Florida, and the American West with about 7,500 soldiers. Surely, reasoned the administration of George Grenville (1763–1765), the colonists would be willing to pay a portion of these burdens. The Sugar Act of 1764 and the Stamp Act of 1765 overrode colonial objections and imposed direct parliamentary taxation. At no point, however, did Britain ask the North Americans to bear all of the costs of their own defense.

Grenville was trying to meet the needs, real and pressing needs, of the whole empire. The colonists replied that Britain could not sacrifice provincial rights in the process, real rights, sanctified by more than a century of usage. Imperial policy threatened the principle of no taxation without representation and, by expanding vice-admiralty jurisdiction in unprecedented ways, it also challenged the right to trial by jury. Colonial assemblies and pamphleteers eloquently protested both the Sugar Act and the Stamp Act. Crowd action nullified the Stamp Act by compelling the distributors to resign from South Carolina to New Hampshire. Nullification of the Sugar Act proved impossible. Ideological protests did not prevent the duties from being collected.[15]

Both sides searched for arguments to explain what was happening and justify what they were doing. The British relied upon parliamentary sovereignty as the last line of defense but denied that this principle threatened colonial rights. Administration spokesmen invoked virtual representation to vindicate the new taxes. Members of Parliament, they insisted, represented the whole empire and were certainly as solicitous of the interests of North America as they were of nonvoters in the mother country. Grenville's defenders also denied that they harbored any long-term plans for undermining the viability

---

[15] *The classic account remains Edmund S. and Helen M. Morgan,* The Stamp Act Crisis: Prologue to Revolution *(Chapel Hill: University of North Carolina Press, 1953).*

of provincial governments. Defense was a paramount need that all should recognize and support.[16]

North Americans replied that virtual representation on an imperial scale was a sham. An M.P. could legitimately represent British nonvoters because he had to share the burdens that he imposed on them. But every tax inflicted on the settlers meant smaller taxes for the British themselves. The Grenville program did not reconcile imperial and colonial interests. It polarized them, as worried provincials pointed out. If the ministry desired a colonial revenue, most North Americans insisted with growing irritation, it should ask the assemblies to vote one.[17] The government resisted a system of requisitions because its deficiencies had long seemed obvious. Noncompliance by any one province had a way of spreading rapidly to others. Parliament had overcome this obstacle during the Great War for the Empire only by resorting to subsidies, first pegged at $200,000 per year, later reduced by a third. Specie-poor colonies could claim a share of this amount in direct proportion to their overall contributions to the war effort. Although the annual outlay under this policy was less than what Britain was willing to spend each year on colonial defense after 1763, the government never considered continuing this wartime emergency policy after the Peace of Paris. Given the implicit choice, the Grenville administration thought instinctively in coercive rather than voluntaristic terms.[18]

In effect, the British argued that although ultimate power had to reside with king, lords, and commons, the settlers had no cause to worry for their traditional rights. North Americans, by contrast, groped for a federal definition of the empire. They tried to find a viable boundary between the power of Parliament and the sphere of their assemblies. Most of them distinguished between Parliament's power to legislate, which they found legitimate, and Parliament's power to tax, which they condemned. This argument left some measures difficult to classify. For example, it bestowed approval on the Molasses Act of 1733, which most New England merchants loathed, but it condemned the Sugar Act

---

[16] *For the fullest contemporary statement of the administration's position, see Thomas Whately,* The Regulations Lately Made Concerning the Colonies and the Taxes Imposed upon Them, Considered *(London, 1765).*

[17] *See Edmund S. Morgan, "Colonial Ideas of Parliamentary Power, 1764-1766,"* William and Mary Quarterly, *3rd ser., 5 (1948), 311–41 (hereafter, WMQ); Bernhard Knollenberg, Origin of the American Revolution: 1759–1766 (New York: Macmillan, 1960), Chps. 13, 17–21.*

[18] *Lawrence Henry Gipson,* The British Empire before the American Revolution *(Caldwell, Idaho: Caxton Printers; and New York: Alfred A. Knopf, 1936–72), x, 38–110 provides the fullest available discussion of wartime subsidies, but Gipson never assesses the effectiveness of the policy or even considers its potential as a precedent for postwar policy.*

of 1764, which lost legitimacy by *lowering* the duties of 1733. Smaller duties meant revenue, not regulation. And even while conceding general legislative power to Parliament, some colonial spokesmen—usually without explaining exactly what they meant—excluded their "internal polity" from this sphere. As Maryland's Daniel Dulany put it, "by the powers vested in the inferior is the superior limited."[19]

Both sides rejected Benjamin Franklin's practical distinction between external and internal spheres of authority. This argument did indeed limit the principle of no taxation without consent, for it bestowed legitimacy on the Sugar Act and any other port duties that the British should decide to impose upon the settlers. Franklin did not consider this concession dangerous. Most excesses would be self-correcting. "But the sea is yours," he told the House of Commons in 1766;

> *You maintain, by your fleets, the safety of navigation in it; and keep it clear of pirates; you may have therefore a natural and equitable right to some toll or duty on merchandizes carried through that part of your dominions, towards defraying the expence you are at in ships to maintain the safety of that carriage.*

If duties became too high, he explained, both traffic and revenues would fall, and Parliament would have to rectify its mistake. Quietly, he also suggested a voluntaristic method of raising an internal revenue for defense through the organization on an imperial scale of colonial loan offices. Only those who wished would participate, and the government's income from interest payments would almost certainly exceed what the Stamp Act had promised to bring in.[20]

Not even the reforming administration of the Marquis of Rockingham (1765–1766), which did repeal the Stamp Act, was ready to accept this limitation upon the formal sovereignty of Parliament. The price of repeal became passage of the Declaratory Act, which affirmed a sweeping parliamentary

---

[19] *Daniel Dulany,* Considerations on the Propriety of Imposing Taxes in the British Colonies, for the Purpose of Raising a Revenue, by Act of Parliament *(Annapolis, 1765), in Bernard Bailyn, ed.,* Pamphlets of the American Revolution, 1750–1776 *(Cambridge, Mass.: Harvard University Press, 1965–), I, 619.*

[20] *For Franklin's "Examination" before the House of Commons, see Labaree, ed.,* Papers of Benjamin Franklin, *XIII, 124–62, esp. 144–45, 139; see also, Franklin to Joseph Galloway, October 11, 1766, ibid., 447–50. For an analysis of grassroots resistance to internal taxes, see Thomas P. Slaughter, "The Tax Man Cometh: Ideological Opposition to Internal Taxes, 1760–1790,"* WMQ, *3rd ser., 41 (1984), 566–91.*

supremacy that Rockingham hoped his government would never have to exercise.[21] Franklin, with his extensive experience on both sides of the Atlantic, understood better than any other contemporary how the empire actually worked, but he could not find a way to show either side how to legitimate the political status quo. Neither common law nor the main schools of political theory ratified his distinction between external and internal spheres, even though he correctly understood that this line defined the power axis of the empire, the boundary between what Parliament could do without active colonial consent and what could be accomplished only with the cooperation of the settlers. Although, in the early 1760s, he had quite expected to spend his retirement years in Britain, his inability to make political headway with government officials drove him into the radical colonial camp in the decade after 1765.[22]

On a large scale, Franklin's failure became that of the empire. It collapsed because its federal reality could find no theoretical legitimacy. The external-internal dichotomy kept reappearing, but neither side could adequately handle the disjunctions that were exposed by thinking of it in other terms. Parliament could indeed collect duties from colonial commerce. Through the Revenue Act of 1766, the Rockingham government again lowered the molasses duty, this time from three pence per gallon to one penny, and imposed it on both British and foreign molasses. Even though the quest for revenue thus triumphed over any pretense of regulating trade, colonial merchants found the measure far preferable to any other policy that the ministry had adopted toward molasses since 1733. Merchant compliance worried, in turn, committed colonial patriots, who finally took a stand against the Townsend Revenue Act of 1767, which, by imposing anti-mercantilist duties on direct imports from Britain that could not be legally obtained from other sources, seemed designed only to establish a precedent for general parliamentary taxation. Resistance was divisive and incomplete, and it secured only a token concession. The new ministry of Lord North (1770–1782) repealed the duties on nonremunerative items but kept the real

---

[21] *Paul Langford, The First Rockingham Administration, 1765–1766 (Oxford: Oxford University Press, 1973); P.D.G. Thomas, British Politics and the Stamp Act Crisis: The First Phase of the American Revolution, 1763–1767 (Oxford: Clarendon Press, 1975); Robert J. Chaffin, "The Declaratory Act of 1766: A Reappraisal," The Historian, 37 (1974), 5–25.*

[22] *Franklin's "Rules by Which a Great Empire May Be Reduced to a Small One" (September 1773) and his "An Edict by the King of Prussia" (September 1773) demonstrate how radical and disaffected he had become even before the final imperial crisis of 1774–1776. See Labaree, ed., Papers, XX, 389–99, 413–18.*

moneymaker, the tax on tea. This gesture broke the nonimportation agreements and exposed the gap between colonial moderates and radicals, but it also drained colonial confidence in British justice.[23]

The same fault line emerged during the crisis of 1773–1775. In response to the Boston Tea Party, the North ministry drafted and ruthlessly enforced the Boston Port Act, which closed the city to seaborne trade until the destroyed tea was paid for. This external measure was well within the capabilities of the Royal Navy. Britain could and did shut Boston down. The effort meant another political crisis, however. Publication of the act led directly to the summoning of the First Continental Congress and the organization of massive intercolonial resistance. The other important measure of 1774 was, like the earlier Stamp Act, nullified. The Massachusetts Government Act attempted to reorganize the province in several major ways, but the colonists refused to accept it and continued to function as best they could under the royal charter of 1691. This resistance led directly to war. The fighting began at Lexington and Concord when General Sir Thomas Gage marched a small army westward from Boston to enforce the Massachusetts Government Act. Only by levying war on the settlers could Parliament exercise direct power in the internal affairs of North America without the consent of the colonists. War is not government. The British Empire collapsed because neither side could explain adequately what it could and could not do.[24]

These crises were a painful experience for nearly all participants. The British never consciously tried to create a tyranny in North America. The colonists were not trying to destroy the empire. From Lord North to Samuel Adams, everyone hoped to find some arrangement that would guarantee imperial strength and provincial rights. Far more energy, intellectual and political, went into formulating plans to salvage the empire than into devising a new American union. Several dozen such plans survive, the most famous emanating from William Pitt (Earl of Chatham), Edmund Burke, David Hartley, Lord North, and Lord Drummond on the British side, and from William Smith of New York, Joseph Galloway of Pennsylvania, and Franklin on the American side. Burke's appeal was the most eloquent, but its call for a return to 1763 could have worked only by somehow also restoring the mutual trust

---

[23] *The best history of the Townsend Crisis is Merrill Jensen,* The Founding of a Nation: A History of the American Revolution, 1763–1776 *(New York: Oxford University Press, 1968), 186–372.*

[24] *David Ammerman,* In the Common Cause: American Response to the Coercive Acts of 1774 *(Charlottesville: University Press of Virginia, 1974); John Shy,* Toward Lexington: The Role of the British Army in the Coming of the American Revolution *(Princeton: Princeton University Press, 1965), esp. Chps. 8–9.*

that had vanished since then. He made no formal concessions to federalism but defended parliamentary sovereignty coupled with a promise not to use it. Chatham and Galloway drafted the most imaginative schemes, each with genuine federal elements, but neither could muster a majority on his side of the ocean. Only North's plan became law. It embodied a parliamentary promise to use requisitions instead of direct taxes, provided the colonies paid what was demanded of them. In 1764, couched as a reward for colonies with a strong war record and a punishment for those that had done little, such a policy just might have succeeded. Effective resistance would have required the most loyal colonies to rally behind the least. By 1775, North's proposal had no chance whatever. It too relied on a mutual confidence that no longer existed.[25]

As the empire disintegrated in self-destructive war, the colonists finally had to ask themselves what an adequate North American union might be. In 1775, no one knew the answer to that question.

The First American Union

North America's first federal experiment, government under the Continental Congress and later the Articles of Confederation, also failed. The British Empire collapsed because it tried to meet common needs by sacrificing provincial rights. Congress reversed these priorities. It protected local rights so absolutely that it never acquired adequate power to address general needs. This issue involves more complexities than a short paper can discuss, but several aspects of the problem do merit examination.

Why, for instance, did Congress have any power at all? It was strong enough to raise an army and fight an eight-year war, even if it could not command the resources to press the struggle efficiently. Why did people obey this improvised gathering of colonial gentlemen, most of whom did not even know one another before they all gathered in Congress?

[25] *For the major British plans, see William Cobbett, ed.,* The Parliamentary History of England from the Earliest Period to the Year 1803 *(London: Hansard, 1806–20), XVIII, 478–538 (Burke); 198–205 (Chatham); 319–22, 334–35, 352–53 (North); and 552–71 (Hartley). On the colonial side, see Robert M. Calhoon, ed., "William Smith Jr.'s Alternative to the American Revolution,"* WMQ, *3rd ser., 22 (1965), 105–18; Julian P. Boyd, ed.,* Anglo-American Union: Joseph Galloway's Plans to Preserve the British Empire *(Philadelphia: University of Pennsylvania Press, 1941); and Labaree, ed.,* Papers of Benjamin Franklin, *XXI, 365–68, 408–11, and passim. The British plan that probably attracted the most attention in Congress was that of Thomas Lundin, Lord Drummond. See Milton M. Klein, ed., "Failure of a Mission: The Drummond Peace Proposal of 1775,"* Huntington Library Quarterly, *35 (1971–1972), 343–80.*

The legitimacy of Congress derived from the struggle with Britain. America's root quarrel lay far more with Parliament than with the crown, but in 1774 royal officials saw no alternative but to enforce parliamentary measures. As the structures of royal government disintegrated under these pressures, Congress emerged as the new focus of legitimacy. Although we usually think of it as a weak legislature compared with its parliamentary predecessor and its own post-1789 successor, we probably ought to abandon this conceptualization entirely, at least for the early years of the Revolutionary War. Congress was not a legislature. It was a plural executive. It imitated, not Parliament, but the king. It inherited the role of the imperial crown. In closed sessions, it created and commanded an army and navy, established diplomatic relations with foreign states, printed money, issued requisitions, took charge of the post office, and decided questions of legitimacy within the states. All of these functions belonged to the crown before 1774. Congress did not pass laws, levy taxes, or regulate trade, the functions that Parliament had claimed within the empire. Nor did it attempt to exercise all of the powers of the imperial crown. It did not try to appoint state governors and judges, veto state laws, or hear routine judicial appeals. These regal functions devolved upon the states instead, as did the general legislative powers of Parliament.[26]

Time muddied the clarity of this distinction between executive and parliamentary roles. The need for efficiency during the war crisis from 1779 to 1781 when British armies overran most of the Deep South prompted Congress to create its own executive departments of finance, foreign affairs, and war, each under an individual minister. As this process took hold, Congress had to appear more as a weak legislature directing executive departments than as an executive body itself. But for all of its difficulties, it encountered little public criticism. The most eloquent complaints came from within, from men exasperated with the "imbecility" of a system that they could not get to work properly.[27]

Congress grew weaker for other reasons as well. In the environment of 1774–1775, when the legitimacy of each colonial government was very much in question, Congress acquired real power arbitrating these disputes or sanctioning the overthrow of an insufficiently patriot regime, as in Pennsylvania.

[26] *For this argument see Jerrilyn Greene Marston's* King and Congress: The Transfer of Political Legitimacy, *1774–76. (Princeton: Princeton University Press, 1987).*

[27] *Jennings B. Sanders,* Evolution of the Executive Departments of the Continental Congress, 1774–1789 *(Chapel Hill: University of North Carolina Press, 1935); Arnold M. Pavlovsky, " 'Between Hawk and Buzzard': Congress as Perceived by its Members, 1775–1783,"* Pennsylvania Magazine of History and Biography, *101 (1977), 349–64.*

But as the states went through their own processes of constitution making between 1776 and 1780, they acquired a kind of legitimacy that Congress did not have, and they also had antiquity on their side. They had a history. Congress was new, its powers an improvised response to revolutionary crisis and war. Even though Congress finished drafting the Articles of Confederation in November 1777, the document was not finally ratified by all of the states until March 1, 1781. By then, even its ardent backers believed that it needed structural amendment, at the very least a limited power to raise its own revenue.[28]

These Articles of Confederation and "perpetual Union" between the thirteen colonies did become the first constitution for the new American nation. But their drafting and approval by the states had never really engaged the imagination of the public. Ten years of imperial crisis had called forth dozens of plans for imperial union and conciliation. The task of confederating the thirteen colonies did nothing of the kind. One brief proposal appeared in a Pennsylvania newspaper, and three others were laid before Congress, only one of which—the John Dickinson draft—had a sizable impact. Ordinary citizens scarcely debated confederation at all, not even during the prolonged ratification phase of the Articles. Only in Congress did the question get anything like an adequate airing, and then it had to compete with the war for attention, often without much success.

Any American union would have to combine large and growing states with small, more stagnant ones. The split between the two blocs emerged right away with the meeting of the First Continental Congress in September 1774. Large states favored proportional representation according to population. Small states battled for state equality. Large state delegates were more likely than their opponents to advocate bestowing significant powers upon Congress. John Dickinson, who owned property in Pennsylvania and Delaware and served both governments at various times during this period, resolved these questions mostly on small-state terms. He yielded on representation. Although most historians have read his draft as an effort to build a strong central government, he never proposed to give Congress power to tax or regulate trade. His careful enumeration of other powers was probably an effort to avoid a general grant of legislative authority. His list of delegated

---

[28] *The process can be followed in Merrill Jensen et al., eds.,* The Documentary History of the Ratification of the Constitution *(Madison: State Historical Society of Wisconsin, 1976–), I, 78–137. The fullest narrative of the ratification struggle is still Merrill Jensen,* The Articles of Confederation: An Interpretation of the Social-Constitutional History of the American Revolution, *1774–1781 (Madison: University of Wisconsin Press, 1940).*

powers, though lengthy, was not controversial. It consisted overwhelmingly of activities that Congress had been conducting since it took charge of the war effort.[29]

If any questioned whether such a Congress would preside over a centralized or decentralized union, Thomas Burke of North Carolina ended all doubt when he carried an amendment in 1777 that became Article Two of the completed text: "Each state retains its sovereignty, freedom, and independence, and every Power, Jurisdiction and right, which is not by this confederation expressly delegated to the United States in Congress assembled." States' rights thus triumphed over national aspirations.[30]

Within Congress, the text of the Articles had evolved mostly in response to small-state demands. Yet during the ratification process, large states quickly accepted the document. Small states prevented rapid action by demanding more concessions. The last four to ratify were Georgia, New Jersey, Delaware, and Maryland. Most of their spokesmen hoped to force large states to surrender their vast western land claims to Congress. New Jersey, tightly squeezed between the ports of Philadelphia and New York City, demanded that duties on trade go to Congress, not the states.[31]

Despite its weaknesses, the Confederation accomplished a great deal. Above all, the United States won the war and negotiated an extremely favorable peace treaty. But by 1781, congressional finances were a jungle that threatened to swallow all intruders. Congress, after it stopped printing paper money in late 1779, discovered that requisitions were every bit as unreliable as Grenville had predicted in 1764–1765. The war had pushed American voluntarism to its absolute limits and beyond. In the 1780s, Congress requisitioned millions from the states but got actual payments that amounted to only a few hundred thousand dollars. Only one state, New Jersey, formally refused

---

[29] *The best recent account is Jack N. Rakove,* The Beginnings of National Politics: An Interpretive History of the Continental Congress *(New York: Alfred A. Knopf, 1979), Chps. 7–8, although the author makes Dickinson much more of a centralizer than I would. For the split between large and small states as early as September 1774, see Paul H. Smith et al., eds.,* Letters of Delegates to Congress, *1774–1789 (Washington, D.C.: Government Printing Office, 1976), I, 30–31.*

[30] *See Thomas Burke to Richard Caswell, April 29, 1777, in Smith et al., eds.,* Letters of Delegates to Congress, 1774–1789, *VI, 672.*

[31] *Compare the ratifications by New Jersey, Delaware, and Maryland, in Jensen, ed.,* Documentary History of the Ratification of the Constitution, *I, 128–37. See also Peter S. Onuf,* The Origins of the Federal Republic: Jurisdictional Controversies in the United States, 1775–1787 *(Philadelphia: University of Pennsylvania Press, 1983).*

to comply with a requisition, and a congressional committee soon talked the legislature into rescinding its vote. But the state never did comply.[32]

The desperate need for revenue prompted Congress to recommend amendment of the Articles even before ratification was complete. But both the impost plan of 1781 and a similar proposal in 1783 failed to win the required unanimous ratification. Rhode Island blocked the first, and New York the second. Even European ratification of America's victory over Britain could not dispel congressional gloom, nor could it quiet growing doubts about the viability of the young republic. Fleeing from protesting soldiers in Philadelphia, Congress moved to Princeton, New Jersey, in June 1783, where the delegates joined students, various notables, and the local inhabitants in lavish celebration of the Fourth of July. The festivities calmed few anxieties. As Charles Thomson, secretary to Congress since 1774 and more familiar with its history than any other man alive, confided to his wife Hannah two days later that he saw "a dark cloud" hovering over America. "I confess I have great apprehensions for the union of the states," he explained, "& begin to fear that America will experience internal convulsions, and that the fabrick of her liberty will be stained with the blood of her sons." This concern punctuated his writings throughout the summer. The colonies had come together only to meet a common peril from Great Britain. Peace might well destroy the union, not perpetuate it. Those who had tried hardest to make Congress and the Articles function smoothly were often the least confident of their ability to succeed.[33]

The Constitution of 1787

Both the British and the Americans had confronted the federal problem. Both had failed. Both polarized the needs of the whole and the rights of the parts. As was just becoming evident by 1787, neither could get beyond conventional eighteenth-century notions of sovereignty, which a House of Commons man had once defined as that power limited by no power other than itself. The British and the Americans had agreed in treating sovereignty as an attribute of government. It followed for both that in a system with different levels of government, one or the other must be sovereign. The formal

---

[32] *See, generally, E. James Ferguson,* The Power of the Purse: A History of American Public Finance, 1776–1790 *(Chapel Hill: University of North Carolina Press, 1961); Richard P. McCormick,* Experiment in Independence: New Jersey in the Critical Period, 1781–1789 *(New Brunswick, N.J., 1950), 233–44.*

[33] *Eugene R. Sheridan and John M. Murrin, eds.,* Congress at Princeton, Being the Letters of Charles Thomson to Hannah Thomson, June–October 1783 *(Princeton: Princeton University Press, 1985), 19. cf., pp. 29–31.*

British argument assumed that king, lords, and commons possessed sufficient power to constitute a unitary state, even if in practice crown and Parliament were willing to concede wide latitude to subordinate colonies. The Americans explicitly lodged sovereignty in their states, which in the 1770s meant the state governments. They assumed that Congress would still be able to exercise sufficient power to keep the loose union of states together, at least for purposes of war and foreign policy.[34]

Americans needed a conceptual breakthrough to get around the dilemma posed by governmental sovereignty. Two developments nudged them in this direction. The most important was the constitutional revolution occurring at the state level from 1776 to 1780. The other was Princeton in the nation's service.

The early state constitutions, such as Virginia's, were drafted by bodies that also acted as ordinary legislatures. Although colonists had spent more than a decade trying to define firm limits to parliamentary power, their immediate answer to a sovereign Parliament seemed to be thirteen of their own. As several contemporaries instantly pointed out, any body that can create a constitution can also repeal it. Despite well-intended homage to the principles of the separation of powers and the supremacy of the people over their rulers, American legislatures remained almost completely unchecked.

This pattern changed in states that experienced acute conflict over the drafting and acceptance of their constitutions, particularly in Pennsylvania, North Carolina, and Massachusetts. By the time that Massachusetts completed the adoption of its own constitution in 1780, Americans had found a way to institutionalize an idea that all had heard enunciated on many occasions but that no society had ever been able to convert into concrete and routine principles—the sovereignty of the people. The Massachusetts Constitution was drafted by a special convention that performed no legislative function. It was ratified by the people, or at least by adult males, who voted on it article by article in their town meetings. Massachusetts announced, in short, that only the people, not government at any level, will be sovereign in the United States. This claim was more than a legal fiction. Or, if legal fiction it was, it has been the most important one in American history. No one yet drew the lesson, but popular sovereignty made it possible for Americans to decide to delegate some powers to one level

[34] *On this point and many others, I am much indebted to Gordon S. Wood,* The Creation of the American Republic, 1776–1787 *(Chapel Hill: University of North Carolina Press, 1969). On sovereignty, see pp. 344–89.*

of government, others to another level, and to insist that these powers were as full and ample as any that a just government could possess.[35]

This discovery took place at the Philadelphia Convention beginning in May 1787 when graduates of the College of New Jersey displayed extraordinary initiative in drafting the new constitution. James Madison, class of 1771, set the tone and the principal line of debate as the primary author of the large-state or Virginia Plan, which his friend Governor Edmund Randolph introduced. It was countered by the small-state or New Jersey Plan, written by William Paterson, a 1763 graduate. In the struggle between the two blocs that continued well into July, Madison's classmate, Gunning Bedford of Delaware, introduced the ultimate threat. "The Large States dare not dissolve the confederation," he proclaimed in what was, perhaps, the convention's most dramatic moment. "If they do the small ones will find some foreign ally of more honor and good faith, who will take them by the hand and do them justice." The Connecticut Compromise finally broke the impasse. One of its initiators was Oliver Ellsworth, class of 1766. Altogether, ten of the fifty-five delegates at the convention had attended Princeton, easily the highest ratio of any college in the land. They were sufficiently modest, however, to accept occasional advice from other quarters.[36]

As their prolonged struggle indicates, the delegates did not have these problems solved when they came to Philadelphia. Persuasive answers emerged only after four months of debate during a hot Philadelphia summer. Among themselves, they largely recapitulated the process that had occurred over a four-year period at the state level. The Virginia Plan closely resembled a Virginia Constitution for the entire United States. Like the Virginia Constitution of 1776, it would have lodged sovereign power in a single legislature, a virtual

[35] *For a brief but lucid discussion of this transformation, see Robert R. Palmer,* The Age of the Democratic Revolution: A Political History of Europe and America, 1760–1800 *(Princeton: Princeton University Press, 1959–64), I, Chp. 8. For fuller accounts, see Willi Paul Adams,* The First American Constitutions: Republican Ideology and the Making of the State Constitutions in the Revolutionary Era, *trans. by Rita and Robert Kimber (Chapel Hill: University of North Carolina Press, 1980), and Elisha P. Douglass,* Rebels and Democrats: The Struggle for Equal Political Rights and Majority Rule during the American Revolution *(Chapel Hill: University of North Carolina Press, 1955). The constitution-making process is exceptionally well documented for Massachusetts. See Oscar and Mary F. Handlin, eds.,* The Popular Sources of Political Authority: Documents on the Massachusetts Constitution of 1780 *(Cambridge, Mass.: Belknap Press, 1966).*

[36] *James McLachlan,* Princetonians, 1748–1768: *A Biographical Dictionary (Princeton: Princeton University Press, 1976), 675; Richard A. Harrison,* Princetonians, 1769–1775: A Biographical Dictionary *(Princeton: Princeton University Press, 1981), 465: Max Farrand, ed.,* The Records of the Federal Convention of 1787, *rev. ed. (New Haven: Yale University Press, 1937), I, 492.*

Parliament for America. But the document that emerged by September resembled instead the Massachusetts Constitution of 1780, particularly in its careful separation of powers. In making explicit provision for ratification by state conventions, the delegates drew directly on the idea of the sovereignty of the people. This result stemmed from no unique enlightenment provided by the Massachusetts delegation, whose prominence at the convention did not equal that of the Virginia or Pennsylvania contingent or even Connecticut's. It arose, rather, from a generalized learning process among the delegates. Experiences and perspectives that had been local were becoming more widely shared. For the first time, an intense debate about the American union was underway, and it would spread throughout the land from Independence Hall in Philadelphia.

To reach that point, the delegates had to innovate. Advocates of both the Virginia Plan and the New Jersey Plan flirted at times with what the French would soon call counter-revolutionary behavior. Alexander Hamilton did not even disguise his preference for the British Constitution or his wish to model America's central government as closely as possible upon British practices.[37] The degree of centralization that Madison favored at first marked a sharp repudiation of the localist passions of 1776.[38] Even though Paterson claimed to be doing no more than offering minimal changes to make the Articles of Confederation viable, his specific proposals might just as well have been borrowed from George Grenville and Lord North. Article Two of the New Jersey Plan would have empowered Congress to impose "duties on all goods or merchandizes of foreign growth or manufacture" (an American equivalent of the Sugar and Townsend acts) and to raise revenue through "Stamps on paper, vellum or parchment" (a national Stamp Act). Congress would have to meet any greater needs through requisitions upon the states. If the states did not comply on schedule, Article Three empowered Congress to "devise and pass acts directing & authorizing the same" and Article Six authorized "the federal Executive" to "call forth ye power of the Confederated States . . . to enforce and compel an obedience to such Acts" (Paterson's version of North's hated Conciliatory Proposition of 1775).[39]

Supporters of each proposal undoubtedly believed that they had a good case because Congress represented, at least indirectly ("virtually"?), American citizens in a way that Parliament never had. But many people considered it

---

[37] *For the Hamilton Plan, see Farrand,* Records, *I, 282–93.*

[38] *For the Virginia Plan, see Farrand,* Records, *I, 20–23.*

[39] *For the New Jersey Plan, see Farrand,* Records, *I, 242–45.*

dangerous to give any central government the power to collect internal taxes except during a genuine emergency. Had Paterson's proposal ever gone into effect and had a small-state coalition ever pushed through a revenue package obnoxious to large states, the debate of 1765 would have revived at once.[40]

Of course neither Madison nor Paterson consciously used Grenville or North as models, but they reached similar conclusions in similar ways, by searching out what seemed to provide the most direct solution to the problems overwhelming the central government. The counter-revolutionary thrust of their proposals was situational, not premeditated, although the secrecy of the Convention's proceedings undoubtedly permitted the delegates to be franker about these sensitive questions than they would have been in a more public forum. Yet the delegates realized as they contemplated ideal ratification procedures that whatever they proposed would have to pass close public scrutiny. This necessity imposed discipline on their speculations and, in practice, assured that the sovereignty of the people had to be more than a legal fiction if the proposed new government was ever to go into effect.

Thus, a fairly conservative band of delegates found that it could avoid unworkable counter-revolutionary proposals only through revolutionary innovation. The large-state and small-state plans both led to dead ends. Only by borrowing from the revolutionary principles that had welled up from below since 1776 did the delegates have a chance of drafting a new kind of central government, potentially stronger than either of its predecessors, and yet resting on broadly shared popular convictions. The decision to create a new government and not just amend the Articles was one such step. The determination to put the government into operation as soon as nine states ratified marked another, for this proposal scrapped the "perpetual" union of the Articles, which required unanimous approval of all amendments. The delegates were willing to destroy the union in order to save it. They had no guarantee that all thirteen states would approve their dramatically new form of government, and they knew it. This act was revolutionary but nonviolent; it was not a usurpation, for it could by its nature take effect only after a thorough public debate generated a favorable vote in at least two-thirds of the states. Popular ratification also served a more practical purpose. By avoiding bicameral legislatures and many state politicians reluctant to see their power diminished, it greatly increased the chances for approval. The

[40] *See especially Slaughter, "The Tax Man Cometh."*

Constitution had to win majority assent in only thirteen conventions, not twenty-four separate houses.[41]

As the delegates scattered from Philadelphia to their states to begin the fight for ratification, they brought with them a fully articulated argument for the federalism they had just invented. It was something new in the world, and they were proud of their creation. Madison bragged:

> *Is it not the glory of the people of America, that whilst they have paid a decent regard to the opinions of former times and other nations, they have not suffered a blind veneration for antiquity, for custom, or for names, to overrule the suggestions of their own good sense, the knowledge of their own situation, and the lessons of their own experience?*

"Happy for America, happily we trust for the whole human race," he added, "they pursued a new and more noble course. They accomplished a revolution which has no parallel in the annals of human society: They reared the fabrics of government which have no model on the face of the globe." Madison had entered the Philadelphia Convention convinced that something had to be done to curb the "licentiousness" of state governments. He left persuaded that the nation could survive only by building upon and expanding the revolution in principles of government that the states had pioneered. He still hoped, along with most of his colleagues, that the Constitution would give power to more distinguished men than those who ran the states in the 1780s, but he knew that the document had to be justified in terms validated by the popular revolution within the states. *The Federalist Papers* tried to meet this need.[42]

Because the authors of the new government called themselves "Federalists," their annoyed opponents found themselves stuck with the label of "anti-Federalists," even though the adjective *federal* had always implied decentralization of power, Anti-Federalists varied considerably in the degree of their opposition to the new Constitution, but virtually all of them agreed that a government as powerful as the one now proposed would be an appalling menace to individual liberties unless the people could be protected by a formal bill of rights, such as most states, led by Virginia, had incorporated into

---

[41] *For a slightly different reading, see Forrest McDonald,* Novus Ordo Seclorum: The Intellectual Origins of the Constitution *(Lawrence: University Press of Kansas, 1985), 279–81. McDonald's book is outstanding.*

[42] *Jacob E. Cooke, ed.,* The Federalist *(Middletown, CT: Wesleyan University Press, 1961), 88–89; Wood,* Creation of the American Republic, *Chps. 12–13.*

their constitutions. After five states had ratified, this issue became absolutely critical at the Massachusetts convention. Federalists won assent by a very narrow margin only by promising to submit a bill of rights for subsequent approval at the very earliest opportunity.

Many Anti-Federalists undoubtedly hoped that by confining the new government to powers specifically delegated, they could preserve the sovereignty of their state governments as embodied in Article Two of the Articles of Confederation. But as eventually expressed in the Tenth Amendment, this expectation found, at best, ambiguous fulfillment. By reserving all undelegated powers "to the States respectively, or to the people," the Bill of Rights injected the sovereignty of the people into the equation. Arguments for the sovereignty of state governments became almost impossible. The defense of states' rights had to rest ultimately on the sovereignty of their people, many of whom came to believe that through popular ratification, they had created a new, national compact. Whenever the argument for states' rights veered toward state sovereignty, it had to be divisive. The Constitution in no sense guaranteed that the argument for an indestructible union would triumph, but it did make it possible for nationalists to build a plausible case.

As America's first grand debate on the union ran its course, a curious inversion emerged. Within the convention, large states had led the way in forging the new system, and small states had struggled to preserve something more closely resembling the Articles of Confederation. In the state ratification process, Rhode Island long remained implacably hostile and New Hampshire extremely suspicious of the new federalism, but otherwise small states ratified quickly and overwhelmingly. The Constitution seriously divided all of the large states, which presumably would be the most conspicuous beneficiaries of the new order. Federalists won an indecently quick approval in Pennsylvania before their opponents had time to organize properly. But when ratification conventions met in Massachusetts, New York, Virginia, and North Carolina, an initial majority opposed the Constitution in each case. Only the pledge of a bill of rights, beginning in Massachusetts, secured approval. Beyond any doubt, the people of the United States have the Anti-Federalists to thank for this achievement.[43]

---

[43] *Robert A. Rutland,* The Birth of the Bill of Rights, 1776–1791 *(Chapel Hill: University of North Carolina Press, 1955); Steven R. Boyd,* The Politics of Opposition: Antifederalists and the Acceptance of the Constitution *(Millwood, N.Y.: KTO Press, 1979; Herbert J. Storing,* What the Anti-Federalists Were For: The Political Thought of the Opponents of the Constitution *(Chicago: University of Chicago Press, 1981).*

The overall pattern of constitutional change remains curious in the extreme. The Articles of Confederation, as we have seen, marked a triumph for the small states within Congress, but during the ratification process, the large states accepted the document quickly while small-state beneficiaries prevented rapid approval. The Constitution reversed this alignment. As every delegate at Philadelphia understood, the new order shifted power dramatically toward the large states. Yet most small states ratified at once, while every large state hesitated to accept the benefits it was offered.

Two considerations help resolve this paradox. One is war. As long as the British provided a viable alternative to continental confederation, large states did not dare drive small states out of the union. But after 1783, small states had to ask whether they could survive on their own in the dangerous Atlantic world of the eighteenth century. Only Rhode Island, a state that owed its existence to its founders' defiant behavior and that had two viable port cities, could seriously contemplate a positive answer to this question. Other small states knew that the cession of western lands to the United States and the passage of the Northwest Ordinance by Congress in New York while the convention sat in Philadelphia had gone a long way toward soothing their deepest fears of a strong union.[44]

Large states, by contrast, could at least imagine an autonomous future. They in particular had to face directly another major consideration. The Constitution, precisely because it gave the central government direct power over individuals, correspondingly reduced the authority of all states. Big states had more prestige to lose than little states, and they knew it. Their delegates in Congress had always sought a larger voice in the affairs of the nation. Their citizens had to decide how much power could safely reside in a distant capital. Within the convention, only such small-state delegates as David Brearly and William Paterson had suggested that "all State distinctions must be abolished, the whole must be thrown into hotchpot, and when an equal division is made, then there may be fairly an equality of representation." The idea of attaching New Jersey or Delaware to a larger neighbor or two had occurred to many observers over the decades. Indeed the adamancy of the small states derived in good measure from their fears of eventual obliteration. The large states had much prouder pasts. Their delegates knew that self-annihilation was not an option that constituents at home would tolerate.[45]

---

[44] *Onuf, The Origins of the Federal Republic; Staughton Lynd, "The Compromise of 1787,"* Political Science Quarterly, *81 (1966), 225–50.*

[45] *Farrand, Records, I, 176–79.*

The American constitutional system was not just the creation of a few brilliant Federalists, although without the contributions of Madison, James Wilson, and their supporters it would never have been born at all. The completed system was a result, rather, of the first grand public debate on the union, a prolonged and searching inquiry into what the delegates of 1787 had accomplished. This controversy generated sufficient approval of the Constitution to launch the new government and guaranteed that it would soon have a bill of rights.

Although Federalists contemplated a central government of broad powers, both external and internal, the dynamics of American politics brought the Jeffersonian Republicans to power by 1801, and they shared a much more limited vision of what the national government should do. "The true theory of our constitution is surely the wisest & best, that the states are independent as to everything within themselves, & united as to everything respecting foreign nations," Jefferson declared in 1800. He continued:

> *Let the general government be reduced to foreign concerns only, and let our affairs be disentangled from those of all other nations, except as to commerce, which the merchants will manage the better, the more they are left free to manage for themselves, and our general government may be reduced to a very simple organization, & a very unexpensive one; a few plain duties to be performed by a few servants.*

In effect, Jeffersonian constitutionalism tried to apply to the United States the old internal-external dichotomy that had characterized the British Empire. One difference mattered greatly, however. Unlike Parliament, Congress did not control the sea. Not even independence could overcome that lack, as the second war with Britain would painfully demonstrate.[46]

The result was not perfect, as virtually every Federalist was ready to concede and as the Civil War would demonstrate in the blood of more than 600,000 slain soldiers. But beyond any doubt it was something new in the world, and that something has survived even until now. Few generations can boast of comparable political achievements.[47]

---

[46] *Jefferson to Gideon Granger, August 13, 1800, in Merrill D. Peterson, ed.,* Thomas Jefferson: Writings *(New York: Library of America, 1984), 1079.*

[47] *See also, John M. Murrin, "A Roof without Walls: The Dilemma of American National Identity," in Richard Beeman, Stephen Botein, and Edward C. Carter II, eds.,* Beyond Confederation: Origins of the Constitution and American National Identity *(Chapel Hill: University of North Carolina Press, 1987), 333–48.*

THIRTY-ONE

NEW JERSEY AND THE CREATION OF THE UNION

Mary R. Murrin, M.A., 1989

Mary R. Murrin is Research Associate and Director of the Grants Program at the New Jersey Historical Commission in Trenton, NJ. She holds B.A. and M.A. degrees in American history from Washington University, St. Louis, MO.

Presented at the Annual Meeting of the Society of the Cincinnati in the State of New Jersey Washington, D.C. October 7, 1989

In the mid-1770s, as colonial resistance to the British Crown stiffened, men on both sides of the Atlantic discussed what should be the proper relationship of the colonies to the mother country. Those who hoped that estrangement would not lead inexorably to divorce offered a variety of plans that tried without success to find the correct formula that would accommodate colonial rights, parliamentary power, and Crown prerogative. Benjamin Franklin, the Earl of Chatham, Richard Lord Howe, Lord North, Edmund Burke, the members of the First Continental Congress, Joseph Galloway, and many others all offered plans of constitutional conciliation. Americans and Englishmen, in and out of office, discussed the nature of the imperial connection at length.

When the colonies finally broke with Great Britain, their bill of divorcement complained of the tyrannical power of both king and Parliament. For the colonists, individual rights could be secured only by their representative assemblies. A faraway Parliament could not represent them. It was acting tyrannically when it tried to impose its will. For their part, the British asserted that Parliament *did* represent the colonies. If Americans did not have actual representation, neither did many Britons. This assertion of virtual representation did not satisfy the colonists. The Declaration of Independence both complained of the tyranny of an unrepresentative government and discussed the proper relationship of government to man.

Independence presented the former colonies with a dilemma. How could they maintain their rights and still act in concert? One might have expected a discussion of political philosophy in the debate over the plan of government devised by the former colonies. After all, Americans had devoted considerable ink and breath to the subject for the previous twelve years. That did not happen from 1776 to 1777. When faced with the need to construct their own union, the men who drafted the nation's first constitution provided their plan with no philosophical underpinnings. The Articles of Confederation were straightforward and almost mechanical. The men who drafted the plan certainly had reservations about their creation, which they freely expressed in

> *opinion be settled if Candor, Justice and the whole interests of America were attended to. . . . We shall remain weak, and distracted and divided in our Councils, our Strength will decrease, we shall be open to all the arts of the Insidious Court of Britain, and no foreign Court will attend to our applications, for Assistance, before We are confederated. What Contract will a foreign State make with Us, when We cannot agree among ourselves?*[3]

While Congress was still considering the draft Articles, several delegates, among them John Adams of Massachusetts and James Wilson of Pennsylvania, tried to establish a precedent for congressional authority over the states and their citizens. They urged Congress to approve a planned convention of the New England states. That would establish Congress's right to disapprove of other state actions in the future. In addition, they urged Congress to authorize constables and other state officials to seize deserters, thus bypassing the state governments. Finally, they suggested that Congress approve George Washington's proclamation requiring anyone who had taken an oath of allegiance to Great Britain to take one to the United States. This oath would imply national citizenship, an entirely new concept.

Other delegates found Dickinson's plan wholly unacceptable. One of these men, Edward Rutledge of South Carolina, wrote to John Jay of New York, alarmed about the subordination of the interests of individual states to the interests of the whole:

> *I have been much engaged lately upon a plan of a Confederation which Dickinson has drawn. It has the Vice of all his Productions to a considerable Degree; I mean the Vice of Refining too much. Unless it is greatly curtailed it never can pass, as it is to be submitted to Men in the respective Provinces who will not be led or rather driven into Measures which may lay the Foundation of their Ruin. If the Plan now proposed should be adopted nothing less than Ruin to some Colonies will be the Consequence of it.*

Rutledge also exhibited more than a bit of the hostility of southerners for New Englanders and of the elite for ordinary folk. Rutledge was a fan of neither clever Yankees nor unbridled democracy:

---

[3] *Smith,* Letters of Delegates, *4:571.*

> *The Idea of destroying all Provincial Distinctions and making every thing of the most minute kind bend to what they call the good of the whole, is in other Terms to say that these Colonies must be subject to the Government of the Eastern Provinces. The Force of their Arms I hold exceeding Cheap, but I confess I dread their over-ruling Influence in Council. I dread their low Cunning, and those levelling Principles, which Men without Character and without Fortune in general Possess, which are so captivating to the lower Class of Mankind. . . . I am resolved to vest the Congress with no more Power than what is absolutely necessary.*[4]

Samuel Adams (Mass.), Richard Henry Lee (Va.), and especially Thomas Burke (N.C.), all defenders of state sovereignty, blocked the Adams-Wilson proposal and substituted one that went in the opposite direction. Their language, which became Article II of the Articles of Confederation, stated that "each State retains its sovereignty, freedom and independence, and every power, jurisdiction, and right, which is not by this confederation expressly delegated to the United States, in Congress assembled."[5] The import of the Dickinson draft was reversed. Instead of the central government having sovereignty and the state government left with powers not expressly delegated, the reverse was true.

The revised Articles gave each state a single vote, apportioned expenses according to the value of land rather than population, and qualified Congress's exclusive power to make treaties. It could not infringe on an individual state's power to impose duties on foreign goods or forbid the import or export of goods. Moreover, it gave Congress no authority over western lands; the states maintained control over the vast areas of land granted in the old colonial charters. Most important, amending the Articles required the unanimous consent of all the states. The Articles constructed a weak central government and made it nearly impossible to make that government stronger.

In some ways, the Articles complemented the view of power in the state constitutions. The new state constitutions (New Jersey is an example) generally provided for a weak executive and a strong legislature. Defense of liberties lay with representative government and the former colonists had a deep-seated fear of strong executive power. Moreover, many Americans really did not think of themselves as Americans; they thought of themselves as Virginians, South Carolinians, New Yorkers, or citizens of Massachusetts.

---

[4] *Smith,* Letters of Delegates, *4:338.*

[5] *Jensen,* Documentary History, *1:55.*

Congress circulated the new plan of government to the states for ratification. Most of the states suggested changes, or commented on areas in which they thought the Articles deficient. Many delegates were afraid that amending the Articles would make ratifying the new plan impossible and the newly independent colonies would drift apart. On July 30, New Jersey's most learned delegate to Congress, John Witherspoon, made a powerful plea for the plan, despite its deficiencies:

> *If the colonies are independent states, separate and disunited, after this war, we may be sure of coming off by the worse. . . . Will they be not ready to prefer putting themselves under the protection of Great Britain, France or Holland, rather than submit to the tyranny of their neighbors, who were lately their equals?*
>
> *Perhaps it may be thought that breaking off this confederacy and leaving it unfinished after we have entered upon it, will be only postponing the duty to some future period? Alas, nothing can exceed the absurdity of that supposition. Does not all history cry out, that a common danger is the great and only effectual means of settling difficulties, and composing differences?*[6]

Despite Witherspoon's eloquence, his own state was one of the last to ratify the Articles of Confederation. When it finally did, the New Jersey assembly produced an extensive analysis of the plan's deficiencies in a Representation sent to Congress in June 1778.

New Jersey urged Congress to require all delegates to take an oath to the United States. It argued that delegates must keep the interests of *both* their individual state and the Confederation in mind; they must not agree to any measure that might injure the confederation as a whole. In addition, the legislature asserted that Congress should have the power to regulate trade and control the western lands. The boundaries of each state should be firmly fixed, and the requisition of land forces should be based on population, a policy that would require a census and a readjustment of the quota of financial aid to the central treasury every five years.

New Jersey's own new state constitution had reflected the widespread fear of a strong executive. The governor was little more than a figurehead; the legislature, in particular the assembly that initiated all money bills, had most

[6] *Smith,* Letters of Delegates, *4:585.*

of the power. Why would New Jerseyans on the one hand see their state legislature as the protector of individual liberties and on the other hand be more than willing to strengthen the power of a new central government? This strategy would surely diminish the power of an individual state.

Like other Americans, New Jerseyans saw the state assembly as the defender of individual liberties; members of that assembly and the delegates they sent to Congress had only to look at the recent past to realize how difficult the state's position would be in the new Confederation and how troublesome would be the central government's lack of power.

New Jersey had long been dominated economically by its two larger neighbors, Pennsylvania and New York. A small, thinly populated agricultural state, New Jersey had no real port and only a small merchant class. Its economic difficulties as a colony continued and grew worse under the Confederation. New York and Pennsylvania were free to levy duties on all goods, whether foreign or from the neighboring state. In effect, New Jerseyans were adding to the treasuries of their state's richer neighbors. The requisition system of congressional finance imposed, in New Jersey's eyes, an intolerable financial burden on the state's hard-pressed citizenry. New Jerseyans were already reeling from the physical destruction of the war and the effects of a collapsed currency, and the state seemed to be supplying parts of New York's and Pennsylvania's requisitions as well as its own. For New Jerseyans, increasing the powers of the central government would give small states some protection against the actions of larger states such as New York, Pennsylvania, and Virginia.

Other small states, such as Maryland, Delaware, and Rhode Island, agreed, at least in part. All three thought congress should have authority over western lands. Connecticut, Massachusetts, and Rhode Island thought the basis for requisitions should be changed or at least refigured periodically, though Massachusetts was worried about domination of larger, more populous states by the nine smaller states.

Despite expressed objections, all the states (Maryland held out until 1781) ratified the nation's first constitution as it stood. They knew ratification would be impossible with amendments; the Articles as they stood represented the small area upon which they *could* agree.

There were attempts to strengthen this admittedly imperfect document almost immediately. In 1781, Congress asked for the power to collect import duties; this impost would be used to reduce the vast debt incurred through fighting the war. Though twelve states assented, Rhode Island, which had strong shipping interests, blocked the plan, arguing that the amendment would fundamentally alter the character of the Confederation. Virginia subsequently withdrew its approval.

In March 1781, a congressional committee recommended that Congress be given coercive power over the states and citizens and the power to impose embargoes. The recommendation went nowhere. In April 1783, Congress tried again. It asked for the power to collect import duties, this time for a limited period of twenty-five years, as well as a grant of supplementary revenue for the same period from all the states. The request came with a recommendation that the expenses of government be allocated according to population, rather than valuation of land. By1786, only eight states had approved the plan. Two had rejected it (New York and Georgia), and three had taken no action at all.

In April 1784, Congress asked for a grant of temporary power to regulate trade. The British had closed West Indian ports to American shipping. The following year, in March, a congressional committee asked that any such grant be made permanent. Since it seemed evident that the states could not agree on even a temporary grant, the committee's recommendation was more an exercise in wishful thinking than anything else.

In no case were the recommendations successful. States with ports were not inclined to give up their tariffs; southern and northern states argued over both trade regulations and whether slaves should be counted as population for apportionment purposes. Most of the states were disinclined to yield sovereignty to a central government, both because they still thought of themselves more as Virginians or New Yorkers and because they were deeply suspicious of one another's intentions.

In August 1786, Congress was still dithering about the need for more power. While some members recommended calling a convention, most insisted that Congress had to propose amendments to the Articles. The futility of proposing amendments seemed evident; in the years since the ratification of the Articles, there had been several attempts to amend them. All had failed.

A congressional committee made one final attempt. It suggested seven amendments that would have given Congress the power to regulate trade, some coercive power over the states and citizens, and the power to tax. None passed; indeed, Congress seems not even to have considered them. Even though large majorities wanted an impost and smaller ones wanted Congress to regulate trade, the existing amendment process would not let the majority rule.

Though proponents of a convention did not have a majority in Congress, a recommendation for a convention came out of the Annapolis Convention, called to consider matters of trade. The parlous state of the economy and agrarian unrest lent urgency to the call for a convention. There were protests or riots in New Hampshire, Massachusetts, Pennsylvania, Virginia, South Carolina, and New Jersey. The most serious was Shays' Rebellion in Massachusetts, which frightened everyone. Moreover, New Jersey, exasperated at the failure to secure an impost, had refused to meet the latest requisition. The climate was right for a convention to restructure the union.

When Witherspoon had urged Congress to adopt the Articles in 1776, he asked:

> *What madness is it to suppose that there ever will be a time, or that circumstances will so change, as to make it even probable, that it will be done at an after season? Will not the very same difficulties that are in our way, be in the way of those who shall come after us? . . . Will they not have the same jealousies of each other, the same attachment to local prejudices, and particular interest?*[7]

Was Witherspoon shortsighted? Perhaps, though he was certainly correct about the urgency of adopting that first constitution, however imperfect. The jealousies he described clearly did not disappear. The Philadelphia convention was successful not because the delegates all became angels, but because they abandoned a form of government handcuffed by jealousies and local prejudices and started over. What they did was clearly illegal. The new Constitution required ratification by the *people* of nine states, not thirteen. The Constitution of 1787 destroyed the union in order to save it.

[7] *Smith,* Letters of Delegates, *4:586.*

THIRTY-TWO

BRIGADIER GENERAL DAVID FORMAN: SERVICE IN THE AMERICAN REVOLUTION

Lt. Col. William H. Forman, Jr., LLD., 2002

William Harper Forman, Jr. (admitted 1966) is the great-great-great-great-great-great-grandnephew of Major Thomas Marsh Forman, Aide-de-Camp to Major General Alexander. He was born in Houston, Texas, August 13, 1936, and married Olive Goodwell Roberts. He is a lieutenant colonel in the U.S. Air Force Reserve (Ret.) and was graduated from Tulane University with a B.A. in 1958 and with an LLD. in 1961 (see illustrations 19 and 20).

Paper delivered at the 219th Annual Meeting of The Society of the Cincinnati in the State of New Jersey Anderson House, Washington, D.C. October 5, 2002

Introduction

David Forman's service in the American Revolution began in defeat as a New Jersey Militia commanding officer in the campaign around New York City in 1776. His efforts on behalf of the cause of national independence ended in victory with the evacuation of British troops from the same city on November 25, 1783. After the war, he served as vice president of the Society of the Cincinnati in the State of New Jersey between 1791 and 1793.

David Forman was born at 3:00 a.m. on Sunday, November 3, 1745, near Englishtown in Monmouth County, New Jersey. His parents were Joseph Forman and the former Elizabeth Lee. His father was a shipping merchant in New York, who in later life retired from business and settled on one of his farms in Monmouth County.[1]

The Forman family of Monmouth County was descended from Robert Forman, who emigrated from Buckinghamshire, England, to Holland and then to Long Island. It was there in 1645, during the Dutch colonial period, that he and seventeen other Englishmen founded Flushing. Robert Forman died at Oyster Bay, Long Island, in 1671.[2]

Little is known of David Forman's early life and education. He attended the College of New Jersey, which is now Princeton University.[3] He married Ann Marsh on February 28, 1767. The marriage ceremony was held in Princeton at the home of Ezekiel Forman, his elder brother. Rev. William Tennent conducted the service.[4]

As hostility arose in New Jersey against the British government, a Committee of Observation was formed in Monmouth County in 1775. David Forman joined the Committee on March 6, 1775.[5]

---

1 *Charles Forman,* Three Revolutionary Soldiers *(Cleveland, Ohio: The Forman-Bassett-Hatch Co., 1902), p. 7.*

2 *Ibid., p. 27.*

3 *Ibid., p. 7.*

4 *Ibid.*

5 The Society of the Cincinnati in the State of New Jersey *(Bethlehem, Penn.: Times Publishing Company, 1960), pp. 90–91. Hereinafter, this book will be referred to as the* 1960 Blue Book.

The Campaign Around New York City, 1776

General George Washington formally took command of the Continental Army at Cambridge, Massachusetts, on July 3, 1775. Through an "open city" agreement, the British withdrew from Boston on March 17, 1776.[6]

In June of that year, a brigade of New Jersey Militia was sent to join the forces commanded by General Washington. After Joseph Reed declined the appointment to command the brigade, Nathaniel Heard became the unit's commanding general. At the age of thirty, Lieutenant Colonel Forman was promoted to the rank of colonel and appointed to command the Monmouth and Middlesex Battalion.[7]

The summer of 1776 is best remembered for the Continental Congress's adopting the Declaration of Independence on July 4th. This provided the American cause with a well-defined objective.

General Washington next moved the forces under his command to New York City. The British and Hessian expeditionary force, commanded by General Sir William Howe, landed on Long Island on August 22, 1776. The American opposition force numbered about 20,000. After a series of defeats, and in order to save the American army from destruction, General Washington issued orders to retreat across the Hudson River into New Jersey. Instead of exploiting his advantage by pursuit, General Howe ordered the troops of his command to retire to winter quarters in New York City.[8]

The Battalion commanded by Colonel Forman was sent to Monmouth County during November to suppress a British Loyalist uprising.[9]

On January 11, 1777, the Continental Congress authorized an additional regiment for the Continental Army. Organized during the spring in Monmouth County, the new unit was called Forman's Additional Continental Regiment. It consisted of four companies from southern New Jersey and Maryland.[10] The planned strength of such infantry regiments was 728 men, but the goal was seldom realized.[11] Colonel Forman commanded the regiment until it was consolidated with the Fifth New Jersey Regiment on April 1, 1779.[12] Also, on

---

[6] *Howard H. Peckham,* The War for Independence *(Chicago: University of Chicago, 1958), p. 218.*

[7] *Forman, pp. 8–9.*

[8] *Department of the Army,* American Military History, 1607–1958 *(Washington, D.C.: U.S. Government, 1959), pp. 51–57.*

[9] *Forman, p. 9.*

[10] *Robert K. Wright Jr.,* The Continental Army *(Washington, D.C.: U.S. Army, 1983), p. 321.*

[11] *Ibid., p. 47.*

[12] *Ibid., pp. 324–25.*

March 5, 1777, the New Jersey Legislature promoted Colonel Forman to the rank of Brigadier General of Militia.[13] It was a common practice at the time for the same man to hold more than one office.

The Philadelphia-Monmouth Campaign, 1777-1778

Following a comfortable winter in New York City, General Howe decided to advance on Philadelphia. He hoped that the fall of the Continental Congress's capital would end the American uprising.

General Forman, meantime, had been assigned to detached duty for intelligence purposes along the New Jersey coast. On June 10, 1777, he reported to General Washington from Sandy Hook, New Jersey, that British ships were sailing southward.[14]

In August, the British army of 14,000 began its march from the head of Chesapeake Bay to Philadelphia. Hoping to save the Continental Congress's capital, an American force of 11,000 engaged the British army at Brandywine on September 11, 1777. The American army barely escaped being trapped by a British turning maneuver. The Americans retreated, and British forces moved into Philadelphia unopposed on September 26.[15]

Nine thousand British troops were next deployed to Germantown to protect Philadelphia from the Continental Army. On October 4, 1777, the New Jersey Brigade commanded by General Forman joined a Maryland unit in forming one of the four columns that attacked the British at Germantown.[16] Despite orders, the four American columns did not converge at the appointed time. The two militia columns never engaged the British. Despite an initial advance, the two remaining American columns were thrown back and they began to retreat in disorder. The British cautiously followed them for several miles but then stopped. Once again, General Howe failed to exploit his victory by pursuing the Americans.[17]

---

[13] 1960 Blue Book, *p. 91.*

[14] *Douglas Southall Freeman,* Washington *(New York: Touchstone, 1995—abridgment by Richard Harwell), p. 340.*

[15] *Peckham, p. 69; Department of the Army, pp. 66–67.*

[16] *Forman, p. 10;* Webster's American Military Biographies *(Springfield, Mass.: G. & C. Merriam Company, 1978), p. 126.*

[17] *Peckham, pp. 71–72; Department of the Army, pp. 67–69.*

The fog of war—both internally and externally—was so great during the battle at Germantown that General Howe's dog followed the retreating Americans. He was later returned to the British under a flag of truce.[18]

American losses at Germantown included 152 killed, 521 wounded, and 400 captured. The British had 100 killed and 420 wounded.[19]

Despite his success, General Howe on October 22 wrote a letter to Lord George Germain, Secretary of State for the Colonies, requesting that he be relieved of his command.[20] He was replaced by General Sir Henry Clinton.[21]

Early in November 1777, David Forman resigned his New Jersey Militia commission as Brigadier General. The cause of his resignation is explained in a letter that he wrote to General Washington at Princeton on November 7. The legislature apparently wanted to investigate his election to the generalship, and General Forman naturally wished to be present during the proposed investigation. At the same time, he was equally desirous of attending to his military duties. He, therefore, asked the legislature to postpone the investigation for several days so that the militia's affairs would be left in good order. The request for postponement was denied. Confronted with the alternatives of having the investigation conducted in his absence or of resigning, he chose to resign. The matter was not fully explained in his letter for he told General Washington that his action would be approved when his full explanation was received. Governor William Livingston tried to persuade David Forman to withdraw his resignation, but he refused.[22]

Despite the British occupation of Philadelphia, a treaty of alliance between the Americans and French was signed at Paris on February 6, 1778.[23] American prospects were definitely improving.

British forces in Philadelphia had an obvious supply problem. Chesapeake Bay is about fifty miles southwest of the city.[24] General Clinton, therefore, issued orders for his command to return to New York City. On June 18, 1778, around 10,000 British troops began to move out of Philadelphia. A Continental force of about 13,500 men pursued them.[25]

---

[18] *Peckham, p. 72.*

[19] *Ibid., p. 73.*

[20] *Ibid., pp. 78–79.*

[21] *Ibid. p. 94; Department of the Army, pp. 79–80.*

[22] *Forman, pp. 10–11;* Webster's, *p. 126.*

[23] *Peckham, pp. 89–93.*

[24] *Ibid., p. 68.*

[25] *Department of the Army, pp. 80–81.*

On a hot, sultry June 28, the Americans launched an attack on the retreating British at Monmouth Court House. Major General Charles Lee commanded the attacking force, and General Forman was a member of his staff. Despite a successful advance, General Lee ordered the Americans to retreat.[26]

General Washington arrived, exchanged harsh words with General Lee, and ordered the retreat to stop. The Americans then rallied and fought the British to a standstill until nightfall. During the night, the British withdrew and continued their retreat to New York. General Forman's nephew, Major Thomas Marsh Forman, also served in the Battle of Monmouth.[27]

American losses at Monmouth numbered 69 killed, 161 wounded, and 131 missing—37 of whom died of heatstroke. The British had 147 dead, 170 wounded, and 64 missing.[28]

Following the battle, General Lee demanded a trial by court-martial. His request was granted.[29] During the trial, General Forman testified that he had advised General Lee to order certain military movements during the Monmouth conflict, but that his advice had been ignored.[30] Other officers joined in testifying against General Lee. As a result, he was found guilty of disobedience of lawful orders, misbehavior before the enemy, and disrespect toward a superior officer. He was sentenced to a suspension from the service for twelve months.[31] After the trial, General Lee continued to write letters abusive of General Washington. Colonel John Laurens challenged him to duel. General Lee was wounded in the duel.[32]

Shortly after the Battle of Monmouth, General Washington instructed General Forman to arrange for Colonel John Laurens to visit the French ship commanded by Admiral Count D'Estaing, then stationed off the New Jersey coast.[33] Shortly thereafter, Colonel Laurens wrote the following letter to his father:[34]

---

[26] *Forman, pp. 11–12;* Webster's, *p. 173.*

[27] *Forman, pp. 25–26.*

[28] *Peckham, p. 97.*

[29] *Department of the Army,* The Army Lawyer: A History of the Judge Advocate General's Corps, 1775–1975 *(Washington, D.C.: U.S. Government Printing Office, 1975), pp. 15–16. (Hereinafter referred to as* History of the JAG Corps.*)*

[30] *Forman, p. 12;* Webster's, *p. 126.*

[31] History of the JAG Corps, *p. 16.*

[32] Webster's, *p. 230.*

[33] *Forman, p. 12 and Freeman, pp. 404–405.*

[34] *Forman, pp. 13–14.*

18 July, 1778

My Dear Father:

I am very happy in having an opportunity of introducing to your acquaintance, General Forman, a gentleman for whom I have the highest esteem, on account of his indefatigability and great sacrifices in the public service.

You will discover at a first interview that he is a man of enlightened understanding, and will receive much satisfaction from his account of the most interesting military transactions of the present day. I must refer you to this gentleman, likewise, for a more minute relation of the obstacles which have delayed the French fleet. We were on board of the Admiral together, and he had an opportunity of being acquainted with the difficulties under which the Admiral has struggled.

Whatever civilities or services it may be in your power to offer to Gen'l Forman, will give particular pleasure to

Your most affectionate,
John Laurens.
To the Honorable Henry Laurens, Esq.,
President of Congress, Philadelphia

Intelligence Service, 1780–1782

By June 1780, General Forman organized intelligence detachments for more than fifty miles along the New Jersey coast. From these posts, he gathered information about the movements of British ships near New York. When British ships were sighted, he sent messages to General Washington.[35]

On September 14, 1780, General Forman wrote the following message from Freehold, New Jersey, to General Washington: "I am this minute informed that [British] Admiral Rodney with twelve sail of the line and four frigates are arrived off Sandy Hook from the West Indies."[36] Hoping for additional French ships at the time, General Washington realized that he had to bide his time in the face of British naval superiority.[37]

[35] *Forman, p. 441.*

[36] *Ibid.*

[37] *Forman, pp. 13–14.*

General Forman frequently rode his horse out to some high point along the coast to make observations personally. The zeal and fidelity of his work can be appreciated only by an examination of his letters to General Washington. The letters are full of the most minute details as to the movements and positions of ships in the waters adjacent to New York. As to the fidelity and intelligence with which General Forman performed his duties, it is best to let the most competent judge, General Washington himself, speak. The following letter[38] was written after the Yorktown Campaign had begun:

> *Headquarters, Head of Elk, Maryland*
> *Sept. 7, 1781*
>
> *Dear Sir:*
>
> *I have received yours of the 6th inst. I feel myself not only personally, but with respect to my Country, so much indebted to you for your exertions on all occasions, that I cannot refrain from expressing my obligations on the subject. Be assured, Sir, it shall always be retained in grateful remembrance, and every opportunity embraced to convince you of my esteem and Friendship. It is with particular pleasure I inform you that Count de Grasse with twenty sail of the Line, arrived in the Chesapeake,* . . . [He then tells of his plans.] *Should anything of an interesting Nature come to your knowledge, I wish to receive the earliest account of it, and by your returning Expresses, I will forward the news of the day, and the success of our movements.*
>
> *I am, Dear Sir, With every sentiment of esteem,*
> *Yours, &c.,*
> *G. Washington*
> *Gen. Forman.*

In the preceding July, when the arrival of Count de Grasse was expected, some of the militia cavalrymen were stationed at such distances that dispatches could travel from Monmouth to General Washington's headquarters at Dobbs Ferry in twelve or fifteen hours. After the Army started south, the letters were directed to be sent to a designated officer who re-forwarded them

[38] *Ibid.*

to General Washington. The express riders' dispatch service was discontinued in the latter part of 1781. But beginning in August 1782, and for some months thereafter, General Forman again sent information in accordance with General Washington's request as to the enemy's naval strength.[39]

The Court-Martial of Stephen Edwards

Besides sending intelligence reports, General Forman was very active in Monmouth County in suppressing the Tories and Loyalist refugees from the New Jersey coast and the desperadoes known as Pine Robbers. He was hated by the Tories who called him "Devil David." However, his friend, the Rev. Dr. John Woodhull, often remarked that General Forman was worth more to the American cause in Monmouth County than 500 men.[40]

Early in the war, Colonel George Taylor of Middletown deserted to the Tories. During the latter part of the war, a young man named Stephen Edwards left his home at Shrewsbury and joined the Loyalists in New York. He was sent by Colonel Taylor to Monmouth with written instructions to ascertain the strength of the American force there. He was arrested on a Saturday at midnight at his father's house, taken to the courthouse, and tried by court-martial on the following day. He was found guilty of spying and sentenced to death. His execution took place at 10 o'clock on the following Monday morning. General Forman was a member of the court-martial that tried, convicted, and sentenced him.[41]

Captain Joshua Huddy was another member of the court-martial. He was taken prisoner by the Tories at Toms River on April 2, 1782, and was hanged on Middletown Heights ten days later in retaliation for the death of Philip White, who had been shot in attempting to escape while being taken to jail. In addition, the Tories justified their decision to hang Captain Huddy because of his connection with the Edwards trial.[42]

General Forman took the leading part in obtaining evidence as to the facts of White's death, about which there had been false reports. He next brought the matter to the attention of General Washington upon the advice of the American Commissioners for the exchange of prisoners-of-war to whom

---

[39] *Ibid., pp. 14–16; Richard P. McCormick,* New Jersey: From Colony to State, 1609–1789 *(Newark: New Jersey Historical Society, 1981), p. 151.*

[40] *Forman, p. 15.*

[41] *Ibid., pp. 15–16; McCormick, pp.151–52.*

[42] *Forman, pp. 15–16.*

the matter had been first submitted. General Washington wrote to General Clinton demanding that those persons guilty of executing Captain Huddy be delivered to the Americans.

General Clinton complained about American cruelty to Tories in New Jersey, especially in Monmouth County. As a result, General Washington warned Governor Livingston that he would deliver to the British any New Jersey Militiamen caught violating the laws of war.[43]

Frustrated, the Americans decided to retaliate upon one of the British prisoners. A young officer, Captain Charles Asgill, was selected by the lot. But his family was influential, and his mother appealed to the French government to intercede on her son's behalf. The intervention was successful because the Continental Congress finally ordered the young man's release.[44]

Conclusion

The peace treaty between the United States and Britain was signed in Paris on September 3, 1783. On November 25, British troops in New York City boarded ships for the voyage back across the Atlantic.[45] What had begun with defeat in the campaign around New York City in 1776 ended in victory. David Forman, now at the age of thirty-eight, had witnessed that war from beginning to end.

The New Jersey Society of the Society of the Cincinnati was organized at Elizabethtown on June 11, 1783. David Forman was elected to honorary membership in the New Jersey Society on September 22. He became a hereditary member of the Society on July 4, 1787, and he served as the Society's vice president from 1791 to 1793.[46]

David and Ann Marsh Forman had eleven children—Joseph, Sarah Marsh, Elizabeth Lee, Ann, David Lee, Augustine (a daughter), Emma, Eliza, Malvina, Rivine, and Alfred. Six of the children died before his decease.[47]

The affection that his children had for him was great. Because of his wife's extremely delicate health, he often took their care upon himself. He and

[43] Dictionary of American Biography, *Vol. III, edited by Allen Johnson and Dumas Malone (New York: Scribner's, 1959), p. 154.*

[44] *Forman, pp. 15–16; McCormick, pp. 151–52.*

[45] *Peckham, p. 220.*

[46] 1960 Blue Book, *pp. 90–91.*

[47] *Forman, p. 16.*

his family also attended the Old Tennent Church in Monmouth.[48] During this time, David Forman served as judge of the Court of Common Pleas in Monmouth County.[49]

In February 1794, David Forman and his family moved to Chestertown, Maryland. On September 10, 1796, he left Chestertown to visit Natchez, Mississippi, where he owned a large landed estate. While there, during March 1797, he had a stroke. This resulted in the paralysis of his left side.[50]

By August, his health and strength had improved considerably. He traveled down the Mississippi to New Orleans, then under Spanish domination. While en route to New York, the vessel on which he was traveling was seized by a British privateer, and he was taken to the Bahaman Islands. The grave anxiety and disappointment was too much for him in his weakened condition; for on September 12, 1797, at 2 o'clock in the afternoon, David Forman died at the age of fifty-two.[51]

David Forman served the new nation as a soldier. His career of public service brings to mind the ideals of the Society of the Cincinnati. Those ideals are contained in the Society's motto—*omnia reliquit sevare rempublicam*—translated, "he left all to serve the Republic."

The Continental Army under General Washington's command escaped destruction when it crossed the Hudson River into New Jersey in 1776. The Army stayed intact throughout the war as did the nation's cause of independence. As General Washington wrote in his "Farewell Orders to the Armies of the United States," that cause remained alive because of a "patriotic band of Brothers."[52] David Forman was a member of that band.

---

48 *Ibid., p. 17.*

49 *Ibid., p. 16; Johnson and Malone, p. 524.*

50 *Forman, pp. 7–8.*

51 *Ibid., p. 8; Johnson and Malone, pp. 524–25.*

52 *McCormick, p. 155.*

∽ THIRTY-THREE ∾

THE REFUGEE WAR AND TERRORISM DURING THE AMERICAN REVOLUTION

Harry M. Ward, Ph.D., 2004

Harry M. Ward received his B.A. from William Jewell College in 1951, and his M.A. and Ph.D. in history from Columbia University. He then taught at Georgetown College and Morehead State College and is now the William Binford Vest Professor of History Emeritus at the University of Richmond, Richmond, Virginia, with a teaching specialty in Colonial and Revolutionary War History.

Read to the Society on October 2, 2004
at Anderson House, Washington, D.C.,
in the evening after the Annual Meeting

The War for American Independence was very much a civil war. Some 50,000 Americans fought on the British side. These included 15,000 men in 50 provincial corps of 312 companies raised in America; among these troops were Lt. Col. Banastre Tarleton's Legion and Lt. Col. John Graves Simcoe's Queen's Rogers. The remainder of the fighters for Great Britain were guerrillas and other irregulars such as independent Tory militia. Some of the Loyalist operatives were hardly more than outlaws, often preying indiscriminately on victims of both Tory and Whig persuasion and answering to no higher authority. Much of the fighting for the British cause was accomplished by the American refugees. Had the British government from the beginning of the war fully recruited and supported all refugee troops, the outcome of the war may have been drastically different.

I would like to focus on the refugee-irregulars. They and their rebel counterparts were motivated not only to capture resources from the enemy and to assist in military operations, but also to settle old scores, wreaking vengeance and inflicting punishment, which served as examples of the peril of being allied with the wrong side.

British regular forces were primarily responsible for the destruction of urban centers, chiefly Falmouth, Maine; Norfolk and Richmond, Virginia; and villages, such as Camden, South Carolina; and Springfield and Connecticut Farms, New Jersey. Major James Weymess's dragoons demolished plantations in a seventy- by fifteen-mile stretch between Georgetown and Cheraw, South Carolina. However, most of the indiscriminate desolation in large areas was the result of the Refugee War. Substantial irregular warfare existed in Westchester and Dutchess counties, New York; both sides of Long Island Sound; Bergen, Essex, and Monmouth counties, New Jersey; the New Jersey–New York Highlands; Chesapeake Bay and its inlets in Maryland and Virginia; and throughout the Carolinas and Georgia. A French chaplain, Abbe Claude Robin, traveling along the Hudson River, north of New York City, observed:

> *The sorrowful vestiges of war and desolation—the houses plundered, ruined, abandoned or burnt. These Americans . . . are here transformed into monsters implacable, bloody and ravenous, party rage has kindled a spirit of hatred between them; they attack and rob each other by turns,*

> *destroy dwelling houses, or establish themselves therein by driving out those who had before dispossessed others.*

General Nathanael Greene, shortly after assuming command of the Southern army, in December 1780, complained that in South Carolina:

> *The Whigs and Tories pursue one another with the most relentless Fury killing and destroying each other wherever they meet. Indeed a great Part of this Country is already laid Waste & in the utmost Danger of becoming a desert.*

General Anthony Wayne, from Ebenezer, Georgia, wrote in January 1782 that most of the countryside was "a perfect desert." In November 1783, a Presbyterian minister, John Simpson, traveling in southeastern South Carolina, found that "all was desolation. . . . Every field, every plantation, showed marks of ruin and devastation. Not a person was to be met in the roads." What we usually forget about the American Revolution was the large-scale evacuation of whole families from many areas.

We may note some of the most significant groups of refugee militants who were quite effective in spreading terror among the citizenry. The Corps of Loyalist Westchester Refugees, sometimes simply dubbed Cowboys, headed by Lt. Col. James DeLancy, relentlessly raided in what came to be called the Neutral Ground above New York City. DeLancy's Cowboys, as did most of the other embodied refuge irregulars, served without pay and lived off their plunder. It is estimated that DeLancy's 500-man unit was so successful that it supplied one-third of the provisions going to the British army in New York City.

Whaleboat marauders, both Tory and Whig, in hit-and-run tactics preyed upon the farms and homes on Long Island, New York, and the opposite Connecticut shore.

New Jersey played a major role in the refugee war, with British forces nearby or at least stationed in the New York City vicinity, where Tory raiders might find succor and refuge. Five thousand New Jersey men left their homes to serve in a military capacity against the American patriots. Some of these joined regular units. Fifteen hundred of the refugees were formed into three regiments of the New Jersey Volunteers, commanded by the state's former attorney general, Brigadier General Cortlandt Skinner. Although registered as a British unit, the Volunteers received very little support from the British military command, and generally they chose and attacked their targets at will. Until1781, most of the

New Jersey Volunteers were stationed in a place much like a maroon community, Refugeetown on Sandy Hook; other Volunteers made camp on Staten Island, and for a while at a post on Newark Bay. The Volunteers frequently made raids up and down the New Jersey shore; they were especially effective in stealth attacks from across the Hudson River. Sometimes the Volunteers pushed into the interior, engaging small bands of rebel armed forces, interrupting supplies and the mails, and foraging for provisions for the British army. Most famous of the New Jersey Volunteers was Lt. James Moody, who was driven from his home in Sussex County and had an extraordinary career as raider and spy behind American lines.

Private bands of refugee raiders, coming from New Jersey, lower New York and New England, and Long Island were placed, on December 28, 1780, under the umbrella of the Board of Associated Loyalists, headed by New Jersey's last royal governor, William Franklin. The Associated Loyalists met their expenses from rebel plunder. The three main groups were DeLancy's Westchester Loyalist crops; a force based at Lloyd's Neck, between Oyster Bay and Huntington, Long Island; and units having a toehold on the New Jersey shore. The Associated Loyalists, only generally advised by British authorities, went much their own way in harassing rebel militia and Continentals in hit-and-run assaults and in conducting privateering raids on shoreline commerce. The Associated Loyalists acquired a reputation of terrorizing victims whom they robbed. African Americans joined the Associated Loyalist forces. Many of the 11,000 slaves in New Jersey, who formed 8 percent of the state's population, went over to British lines. Most notable of the black leaders of Associated Loyalists was a former slave named Titus, whose master had been John Corlis of Colts Neck, near Shrewsbury in Monmouth County. Dubbed "Colonel Tye," an honorary title bestowed by the British, with a large band of both black and white followers, Col. Tye conducted hit-and-run raids along the New Jersey coast from 1779 to 1780. Tye, mortally wounded in September 1780, was succeeded in command by Stephen Bleuke, a freeborn black from Barbados. The Board of Associated Loyalists was disbanded by the British in December 1780, but most of its membership continued depredations until near the end of the war.

A different kind of refugee irregulars were the individual robber bands that plagued the New York Highlands, chiefly in Orange and Dutchess counties, and the Pine Barrens region of New Jersey, a ninety- by thirty-mile belt from upper Monmouth County southward to Gloucester and Camden counties. Local militia and vigilantes, such as the Monmouth Association for

Retaliation, played an important role in rounding up these villains, most of whom were merely cutthroat plunderers.

Much of the Refugee War may be deemed shore piracy. Broad ranged and quite successful throughout the war were the Chesapeake Bay picaroons. With a large number of Tories residing on the Eastern Shore and in Tidewater Maryland and Virginia, the picaroons had the advantage of local support. Operating from barges, really flat-bottomed whaleboats with crew of about thirty hands, mostly African Americans, the picaroons had great maneuverability in hit-and-run raids against plantations, warehouses, and various watercrafts. Joseph Wheland became the most successful and durable of the picaroon leaders. Groups of picaroons fought several significant battles with local militia. Wheland and his followers continued on raids long after the surrender at Yorktown, such as his destruction of the town of Benedict, Maryland, on the Patuxent River in February 1783.

Many Loyalists throughout the Carolinas and Georgia joined forces with the British, much like their counterparts in the North, serving in bands in the plundering and destruction of property, all too frequently with little regard of the allegiance of victims. Some of the Loyalist refugees conducted partisan warfare as members of irregular bands unaffiliated with the British command and other groups only loosely tied to British authority. In spring 1778, some 600 residents of western South Carolina, plundering on their way, trekked to East Florida, where they were formed into ranger troops.

Most successful of the military refuges in the South were forces led by Thomas Brown, Robert and William Cunningham (the latter known as "Bloody Bill"), and David Fanning. The most famous of the outlaw type of Southern Loyalist irregulars was Daniel McGirth, who throughout the war serially raided the Georgia–lower South Carolina countryside, specializing in stealing cattle that he brought into British- and then Spanish-controlled East Florida. Even after the war, he persisted in his bandit ways.

Inciting terrorism was frequently the intention of the various assaults inflicted by the contenders in the Refugee War. Although the term *terrorism* did not gain popular usage until the Jacobin excesses of the French Revolution, it can be applied retrospectively to certain violence during the Revolutionary War. Generally, *terrorism* means the use of violence for political ends, especially in a civil war or during guerrilla warfare. In dictionary parlance, the word is defined as that which induces terror, which in turn is referred to as a feeling, instance, or cause of intense fear; to terrorize is to dominate or coerce by intimidation. In fact, history is replete with instances of terrorism; one can cite the wanton cruelties of many invading armies or bands or, more narrowly construed, the awful murders by groups such as the Order of Assassins in the Middle East during the eleventh century. Modern terrorism owes much to the criminal anarchism appearing in the nineteenth century, which advocated violent overthrow of government by any means. The fear of retaliation prevented the regular American and British armies from indulging in terrorism during the Revolution. Of course, there were exceptions of inflicted cruelty on opponents, more by omission than commission, not the least being the deadly confinement of American prisoners of war aboard British prison ships in New York harbor, an experience, however, kept out of the public's eye.

Today we think of terrorism as aiming at violence as much toward innocent citizens as targeted individuals to compel action from a third party. Although during the Revolution, much harm was committed upon persons indiscriminately, the victim usually was considered culpable in some way or had something worth taking.

Many incidents of small-scale terrorist actions resulted from a situation created by word of mouth that so-and-so (a local Tory or rebel) had valuables in the form of money or other personal property. Striking at a victim or victims spread terror through a whole neighborhood. Often with blackened faces or other disguises, the villains, in quasi-military bands or simply as banditti, made their dreadful excursions late at night. A Long Island, New York, housewife, Mrs. Lydia Post, commented that "robbers come over from the near shore in boats, and keep us in constant alarm. They belong to no party, and spare none; freebooters, cowardly midnight assassins, incendiaries, indiscriminate, bold, and daring."

Similarities between terrorist acts in the American Revolution and those of the modern era include unwarranted massacres, kidnappings, wayfaring on the roads, torture, and summary executions.

Several examples of massacres committed by one side or the other during the Refugee War may be noted. At the Waxhaws, South Carolina, on May 29, 1780, Lt. Col. Banastre Tarleton and his British Legion of Loyalist cavalry surprised Colonel Abraham Buford and his Virginia troops, butchering more than 200 soldiers out of a force of 350, giving no quarter to those attempting to surrender. In kind, Colonel Henry Lee's cavalry murdered nearly 300 of the 400 Tory militia led by Colonel John Pyle in northern North Carolina on February 15, 1781. On the way to join the British army, Pyle mistook Lee's troops for Tarleton's Legion, and Pyle's men lined up along the side of the road for inspection were slaughtered.

Bloody Bill Cunningham's Tory refugee militia, who ranked among the most notorious killers in the south, slaughtered two dozen rebel militiamen when they sought to surrender at Cloud's Creek in the Ninety-sixth District of South Carolina on November 7, 1780, and a few days later reenacted the event a few miles distant at Hayes Station when another two dozen militiamen, coming out of a burning house and asking for quarter, were killed.

To cite another example of mass murder, in the North, on October 27, 1782, the outlaw refugee gang led by John Bacon massacred most all of the twenty-five men under Captain Andrew Steelman while they slept in camp on Long Beach Island at Barnegut Bay, New Jersey.

Of the activities of the militant refugees, kidnapping certainly has been replicated by modern terrorists. Of course, during the Revolution, abduction was simply for a ransom or the purpose of delivering persons of military importance to the British command, thereby meriting a reward to the kidnappers. Lt. James Moody of the Loyalist New Jersey Volunteers and his small band gained notoriety by their huge success in kidnapping American militia officers. Because of his sheer mastery in rescuing Tory prisoners in American custody, Moody has been referred to as the "Scarlet Pimpernel of the American Revolution." Another dashing refugee operative, Wiert C. Banta, carried off similar exploits, not the least being the kidnapping of the American Mustermaster General and his deputy and seizing the army's muster rolls at Washington's encampment in Orange County, New York. Abduction of high military officers was especially a priority. Another example was the kidnapping from his home of General Gold Selleck Silliman of the Connecticut militia; he was later exchanged for a Tory justice of the New York Supreme Court, Thomas Jones. Jones had been captured at his Long Island residence by rebel raiders. Refugee bands had mixed success in attempting to abduct state governors. They failed to snatch New Jersey's governor William Livingston, who was frequently on the move and a step ahead of his would-be abductors. Richard Stockton, a signer of the Declaration of Independence from New Jersey, was not so fortunate; he was seized in November 1776 and suffered a harsh imprisonment. Governor Thomas Burke of North Carolina and his council were nabbed by the daring refugee chieftan, David Fanning, in a raid on Hillsborough on September 12, 1781. Burke eventually escaped and returned to the governorship. In fall 1777, John McKinly, president of Delaware, was seized. At the time, Caesar Rodney, a member of Congress from Delaware, complained that "seldom a day passes" that someone was "taken off" by "the enemy and refugees." Congress, on February 28, 1778, resolved that any Loyalists joining together for the purpose of kidnapping any "loyal citizens, officers, and soldiers" and taking them behind British lines should face the death penalty. Of course, rebel irregulars and even George Washington himself were always on the lookout for opportunities to abduct prominent Loyalists and high-ranking British officers. Rhode Island militiamen abducted General Richard Prescott from the British garrison at Newport in July 1777, and, of course, there is the famous incident of several militiamen along the Hudson River seizing a passerby, the adjutant general of the British army, Major John Andre.

Indeed, one of the most pervasive forms of terror during the Revolution that parallels situations in parts of today's world was the fear of being attacked while traveling the roads. Particularly in the South, but also a problem in banditti-infested regions in the North, the peril was two-fold. Tory and rebel militiamen alike poised along roadways to accost passersby, and highwaymen found easy access and ready escape by darting in and out of woods lining roads. General Nathanael Greene, in December 1780, observed that in lower North Carolina and upper South Carolina persons "are frequently murdered as they ride along the road," and in this "extent of Country great numbers of Tories are way laying the roads."

Citizens living in areas most prone to robberies and marauding had well-justified fears of torture. To extract information, particularly as to location of valuables, refugee and rebel banditti alike employed devices such as sprinkling hot ashes on the body, hanging a person until unconscious, hanging by the thumbs, ducking in a closed water sack, placing hot coals in cupped hands, whipping, tar and feathering, or, as in the Cloud Creek section of South Carolina, cutting off the hands of a captured rebel officer. A typical report of distress in North Carolina, coming in a petition of May 1782 from residents of the Salisbury district, though likely with some exaggeration, cited the "misbehavior" of rebel and Tory militia, such as putting persons

> *to Death in the most torturing manner; many have been the cruel and barbarous methods. . . . Women and Children have been tortured, hung up and strangled, cut down, and hung up again, sometimes branded with brands or other hot irons in order to extort Confessions from them. . . . and after torturing them, and practicing every kind* of *Cruelty . . . go off triumphantly, after first having plundered and rob'd the poor man's house* of *every Article they could lay their hands on, and sometimes set the house on fire. (Wayne E. Lee,* Crowds and Soldiers in Revolutionary North Carolina, *University Press of Florida, 2001, p. 179)*

An example of a horrible ordeal, not too atypical, was the attack of a Tory robber band in July 1782 on Henry Reynolds and his family at their farmhouse in Orange County, New York. The villains were remnants of the Claudius Smith gang, whose leaders had been executed several years before. Intent on gaining plunder and wreaking revenge on Reynolds as a leading Whig who had been instrumental in bringing about the fate of the earlier gang members, the villains hanged Reynolds several times, with his twelve-year-old daughter, Phebe, cutting him down alive in each instance. Phebe herself was stabbed many times, and her younger brother knocked unconscious. Reynolds's wife, pregnant and ready to give birth, had to witness the whole proceedings. Before the intruders left, they set fire to the house. American rebels could be just as brutal. Militiamen, seeking revenge for the murder of patriots by Tory refugees at Piney Bottom, in Cumberland County, North Carolina, were ordered to split open the heads of their captives with a sword.

American revolutionaries were accustomed to a large degree of inhumanity. Soldiers in Washington's army were fiercely whipped about every day and more infrequently hanged, often for what today would seem minor infractions. Civilian authorities meted out brutal punishments for lower-class citizens, and executions were exceedingly popular. Some 20,000 spectators witnessed the hanging of Sergeant Thomas Hickey in New York City in July 1776. The noose also became a favorite means of revenge and retaliation during the bloody partisan warfare in the South from 1780 to 1782. As one author notes, "the principle seems to have been that one atrocity deserved another" (Richard Maxwell Brown, *Strain of Violence: Historical Studies of American Vigilantism,* Oxford University Press, 1977, p. 78).

Lt. Col. Thomas Brown of the King's Rangers allegedly hanged thirteen rebel prisoners at one time and allowed Indian allies to behead four more. Rebel military leaders could be just as cruel. Patriot militia hanged nine prisoners after the battle of King's Mountain in October 1780, and Lt. Col. Lighthorse Henry Lee had four prisoners hanged from the fence-gate of Mrs. Rebecca Motte, near the military post on the Congaree River on May 12, 1781. "Bull Dog" Benjamin Cleveland of the North Carolina militia frequently hanged captive Tories.

The Refugee War in the North, however, exhibited more restraint than its counterpart in the South because the irregulars operated under the noses of nearby major armies and in substantially settled areas. Near the end of the war in April 1782, a band of Associated Loyalists summarily hanged a rebel militia captain, Joshua Huddy, near Sandy Hook, New Jersey, allegedly for the murder of a Loyalist refugee, Philip White, by patriot militia. The affair so incensed General Washington that he singled out a British officer to be executed in retaliation; fortunately, with intervention of the French government and reconsideration, the reprisal was not carried out.

The Refugee War floundered on British policy of waging a limited war in America. From 1779 on, full British victory depended on the success of armed Loyalists. With the countryside controlled, or at least challenged, by American forces, many British-leaning citizens were too intimidated to take up arms, and when they did, they did not have the expected assistance from British military units; with the divide-and-conquer strategy of the patriot effort in the South, British military power dwindled to the point of extinction, lastly holding only to several seaports.

The restoration of local government and opening of the courts in southern New York, the Carolinas, and Georgia ended the anarchy that made it possible for freebooting refugees and rebels to operate on a broad scale.

The Refugee War had particular impact: it helped prolong the conflict, and the collapse of participation of the refugees in turn brought on the outcome. Its excessive brutality affected the American psyche. Judge Aedanus Burke, in a charge to a South Carolina jury on June 10, 1783, stated his fear that citizens "from the habit of putting their enemies to death, have reconciled their minds to the killing of each other" and that "man by custom may be so brutalized as to relish human blood." The later resort to vigilantism and today's proneness toward violence are legacies of the turmoil of America's first Civil War. In today's life, American violence confronts worldwide terrorism.

In the course of this talk, I have briefly sketched military activity and brutality affecting Loyalist refugees along the Atlantic seaboard. If we include the Loyalists who wound up as refugees at Niagara and other locations in Canada and fought for the British side as rangers along the northeastern frontier, the whole scope of the Refugee War is greatly enlarged. Sir John Johnson's "Royal Greens" engaged in raids and the battles in the Schoharie and Mohawk river valleys. Colonel John Butler and his son, Captain Walter Butler, joined their Tory rangers with Iroquois Indians to devastate the New York–Pennsylvania frontier, including the Wyoming Valley, Pennsylvania, massacre of July 3–4, 1778, and the Cherry Valley massacre in New York on November 11, 1778. And if we were to pause and consider the Indian country per se, we find that many of the Native Americans who fought against the patriot cause were themselves refugees—Iroquois tribes, Delawares and Shawnees of the Ohio country, and the Cherokees. The Iroquois routed by the Sullivan expedition of 1779 fled to Canada and from there resumed hostilities. The Ohio

Indians, as they fought rebel forces, retreated deeper into the northern Indian territory. Among the displaced Native Americans from the Cherokee wars of 1776 to1777, the Chickamauga Cherokees, led by Dragging Canoe, finally relocated in southern Tennessee from where they continued fighting frontier Americans throughout the remainder of the war. If we look at the Refugee War on the frontier, we find the most unmitigated examples of terror ever committed in the annals of mankind: from local militia's hacking to death of peaceful Indian men, women, and children to the Indian's burning captives alive and an ingenious variety of mutilations or the combination thereof. The hideous, excruciating tortures of Lieutenant Thomas Boyd by the Seneca Indians in September 1779 and Colonel William Crawford by Delawares in June 1782 are stark examples. One historian writes that the killings of captives on the frontier were noteworthy "because of their excessive and senseless cruelty" and "they were sadly typical of Indian-rebel frontier fighting during the last years of the Revolution. Each atrocity committed had to be avenged in kind, until blind hatred of the other race seemed the only motivation left for making war" (Robert A. Hecht, *Continents in Collision: The Impact of Europe on the North American Indian Societies,* University Press of America, 1980, p. 118).

We like to celebrate the glory that was the Revolutionary War. In reality, however, it was a dirty, nasty war that brought terror to the lives of many Americans. Gloria Emerson, writing in a book review for the *Nation,* September 18, 1995, called attention to the fact that when historians write about war, they seek to describe "the noise of weaponry," but in so doing they fail to convey the meaning of war. She believes that one should examine the full paths of war, for "in the detail is the horror."

THIRTY-FOUR

NEW JERSEY MEN IN THE CONTINENTAL ARTILLERY

William B. Brown III, 2006

William Brown III was born February 10, 1932, in Camden, New Jersey, and lived in Haddonfield, New Jersey, before graduating from the Peddie School in 1951. In 1955, he received an A.B. (geology and geography) degree from Bucknell University, Lewisburg, Pennsylvania, and took additional geology courses at the University of Pennsylvania in Philadelphia. In 1957, he was employed as an exploration geologist/micropaleontologist by Amerada Petroleum Corporation in Houston, Texas, examining well cuttings from Libya and British Somaliland. Brown then worked for independent oil and gas exploration companies in the Appalachian Basin, locating the largest natural gas well in New York State in 1965 and for ten years was a contributing editor for *Producers Monthly Magazine*, Bradford, Pennsylvania. From 1978 until 1988, he worked for the State of New Jersey, DEP, Division of Water Resources as the section chief responsible for closing 400 landfills. In 1989, he formed Brown/Cameron Associates, an environmental, oil, and gas consulting company drilling several oil wells in Oklahoma (see illustration 21).

Delivered at the Spring Meeting of
The Society of the Cincinnati in the
State of New Jersey
At the Nassau Inn in Princeton, N.J.
April 22, 2006

A little-known chapter of the American Revolution is the contribution of New Jersey men to Washington's army. What follows is an abridged version of data obtained from primary sources in Woodbury, Trenton, and Newark, New Jersey; Washington, D.C.; New York City; and Boston, Massachusetts. The purpose of this paper is to identify these patriots and make known their labors in the cause of freedom.

On February 13, 1776, the Provincial Congress of New Jersey authorized the establishment of two artillery companies: the Western Company commanded by Captain Samuel Hugg of Gloucester County, and the Eastern Company commanded by Captain Frederick Frelinghuysen of Somerset County (Captain Frelinghuysen resigned his commission on April 20, 1776. He was replaced by Captain Daniel Neil, who was killed in the Battle of Princeton on January 3, 1777). Each company was to have four officers and sixty men with enlistments of one year. They were known as New Jersey State Troops.

Temporary barracks were built for Captain Hugg's men at Elsinboro in Salem County. On June 29, 1776, Hugg and his men were ordered to march to New Brunswick. By December 1776, before the Battle of Trenton, the two new artillery companies were assigned to Washington's main army, then in Bucks County, Pennsylvania. General Stryker, writing one hundred years later, mentioned their role in the Battles of Trenton and Princeton and quoted Thomas Rodney of Delaware, "It was only with the greatest care and labor the horses and the artillery could be ferried over the river." Captain Hugg's battery marched toward Trenton under the command of Major General Sullivan by the River Road. Captain Alexander Hamilton and Lieutenant James Monroe also took part in the battle that night.

When the New Jersey men's enlistments were up early in 1777, they were given the choice to either sign up with the Continental Army or stay in state service. Virtually all chose to reenlist in federal service. Captain Hugg, however, did not elect to serve in the Continental Army. The men who did sign up for Continental service were credited with the starting date of January 1, 1777.

Captain Hugg's place was taken by Captain-Lieutenant Joseph Dayton until July 1, 1777, when he resigned. On September 1, 1777, a muster roll of this company was taken which referred to it as "the Late Capt. Samuel Huggs

Company of Artillery under the Command of Brig. Gen. Henry Knox." From 1777 until 1780, these men served in the Fourth Pennsylvania Battalion of the Continental Artillery commanded by Colonel Thomas Proctor. On September 1, 1777, the company was placed under the command of Thomas Randall of Massachusetts (who was taken prisoner at the Battle of Germantown, October 4, 1777, exchanged in December 1777, and resigned his commission May 1, 1779). On January 1, 1778, Captain Randall's company was transferred to the Second Battalion of Artillery commanded by Colonel John Lamb, where they stayed until the end of the war, serving under captains Isaiah Wool and Thomas T. Bliss.

In addition to being in the battles at Trenton and Princeton, they were at the battles of Brandywine, Germantown, Short Hills, Springfield, Monmouth, and Yorktown. Their unit served until they were disbanded at West Point in 1783.

A chart regarding the organizational arrangement follows. Attention is called to a rank that does not exist in the present United States Army, *matross*. Matrosses were the privates of the artillery who did the physical work involved in transporting and firing field pieces. Many matrosses were by trade house carpenters, utilizing their skills in reading angles to plot trajectories. Because of the effort required to place cannons, they were generally larger men than those who served in the other branches of the army. The following chart is based on an Act of Congress, dated May 27, 1778, of a battalion or regiment showing their number of men and their monthly wages in Continental dollars.

	INFANTRY		**ARTILLERY**	
Rank	**Number**	**Pay ($)**	**Number**	**Pay ($)**
Colonel	1	75	1	100
Lt. Colonel	1	60	1	75
Major	1	50	1	62 ½
Captain	6	40	12	50
Capt.-Lt.	1	26 ⅔	12	33 ⅓

	INFANTRY		ARTILLERY	
Rank	**Number**	**Pay ($)**	**Number**	**Pay ($)**
First Lt.	8	26 ⅔	12	33 ⅓
Second Lt.	9	20	36	33 ⅓
Sergeant	27	10	72	10
Bombardier	—	—	72	9
Corporal	27	7 ⅓	72	9
Gunner	—	—	72	8 ⅔
Drummer	18	7 ⅓	24	8 ⅔
Matross	—	—	336	8 ⅓
Private	477	6 ⅔		

The military records of ninety of these men were assembled from several sources, notably the Department of Defense records in the New Jersey State Archives, Trenton, New Jersey, and the National Archives, Washington, D.C. The civil records were primarily from the New Jersey State Archives.

I have listed these artillerymen by name, rank, and the location of their New Jersey home. Rather than reading the entire list of these patriots, each of you will be able to follow my remarks by checking your handout, which lists the men in alphabetical order.

Of the ninety men, I have identified, thirteen were officers and seventy-seven enlisted men. At least three of the officers are represented in the New Jersey Society of the Cincinnati: (1) Captain-Lieutenant Seth Bowen is represented by James Hampton Magruder. In the *History of Gloucester: Salem and Cumberland Counties* by Cushing and Sheppard, written in 1883, mention is made of Seth Bowen's grandson, Herman Burgin who, "now represents Lieut. Seth Bowen, who died without male issue, in the New Jersey Society of the Cincinnati.

(2) First Lieutenant Eli Elmer is represented in the New Jersey Society of the Cincinnati by George Eugene Diament III. First Lieutenant Elmer was at the siege of Yorktown and surrender of Cornwallis. In 1787, he was a member of the New Jersey Convention, which ratified the Constitution of the United States. In 1788 and 1789, he was a member of the New Jersey Assembly and in 1795, became a member of the New Jersey Senate. At his death in 1802, he held the position of colonel in the New Jersey Militia. (3) First Lieutenant Chilion Ford is represented in the New Jersey Society of the Cincinnati by Tenney Shepard Ford Jr. His gravestone in the Morristown Presbyterian Cemetery records that he died on October 19, 1800, aged 42 years and nine months. Other officers including Captain-Lieutenant Franklin Davenport and Captain John Doughty later became brigadier generals in the New Jersey Militia. Among the enlisted men, William Pennington who attained the rank of sergeant, became Governor of New Jersey. A matross who served the entire war was John Brown—my third great grandfather.

NAME	RANK	HOME	REMARKS
Ackley, Bezeliel	Matross	Chatham, Essex	Deserted 9-26-1781
Adams, McCalery	Matross	West Jersey	Sick in Hospital 1777
Albertson, Levi	Matross	West Jersey	Died 4-16-1777
Barber, John	Matross	Salem County	
Barnet, George	Matross	West Jersey	Deserted 5-1-1777
Barret, William	Corporal	West Jersey	
Bennet, Joseph	Bombardier	Cumberland County	
Booten, John	Matross	West Jersey	Deserted 5-1-1777
Bowen, Seth	Lt.	Cumberland County	
Brida, John	Matross	West Jersey	Died 2-7-1777
Bright, James	Corporal	Greenwich, Gloucester	
Brown, John	Matross	Deptford, Gloucester	Died 1-2-1827
Brown, William	Matross	West Jersey	Died 1-19-1777
Bunn, Barnes	Matross	Woodbridge, Middlesex	Wounded & Discharged
Cahill, David	Matross	West Jersey	Sick in Hospital 9-1-1777
Cahill, John	Matross	Waterford, Gloucester	Received pension

NAME	RANK	HOME	REMARKS
Cann, John	Sergeant	Salem County	
Carlile, John	Sergeant	West Jersey	
Carter, Steven	Matross	Chatham, Essex	
Casey, James	Matross	Springfield, Burlington	
Cattel, Jonas	-	Deptford, Gloucester	
Christian, Michael	Matross	West Jersey	Sick in Hospital 9-1-1777
Cole, Benjamin	Matross	Elizabethtown, Essex	Deserted 9-26-1781
Cole, Samuel	-	West Jersey	
Collier, Richard	Matross	West Jersey	
Crisp, John	Matross	West Jersey	Died 2-7-1777
Cristy, Mattias	Bombardier	Elizabethtown, Essex	Deserted 9-26-1781
Cross, Andrew	-	West Jersey	
Davenport, Franklin	Capt.-Lt.	Gloucester County	Became Brig. General
Dayton, Ephraim	Sergeant	Fairfield, Cumberland	Died 2-20-1810
Dayton, Joseph	Capt.-Lt.	West Jersey	Resigned 7-1-1777
Dill, Nicholas	Matross	West Jersey	
Diskill, Nathaniel	Matross	West Jersey	
Doughty, John	Capt.	Morristown	Became Brig. General
Drew, Lawrence	Matross	West Jersey	Sick 9-1-1777
Dugan, Matthew	Sergeant	West Jersey	Wounded 1-1-1777
Dunwoody, James	Matross	West Jersey	Deserted 1-4-1777
Elmer, Eli	Lt.	Bridgeton, Cumberland	Captain in Militia
Flint, Joseph	Matross	West Jersey	
Ford, Chilion	Lt.	Morristown	Died in 1800
Frelinghuysen, Fred	Capt.	Somerset County	Resigned 4-20-1776
Garrison, Jonah	Matross	West Jersey	
Green, Thomas	Matross	Penns Neck, Salem	Deserted 4-2-1777
Haines, Benjamin	Matross	West Jersey	
Haines, Judiah	Matross	West Jersey	
Heath, Thomas	Matross	West Jersey	

NAME	RANK	HOME	REMARKS
Hodge, Barnet	Matross	West Jersey	Died 1-20-1777
Hugg, Joseph	Matross	Greenwich, Gloucester	Deserted 9-26-1781
Hugg, Samuel	Capt.	Gloucester County	Resigned 5-1777
Husted, Richard	Matross	West Jersey	
Inskeep, John	Matross	West Jersey	
Johnson, William	Bombardier	West Jersey	
Kinsey, John	Matross	Woodbridge	Died 10-22-1802
Kitchell, Matthew	Gunner	Morristown	
Langley, Thomas	Matross	West Jersey	
Lawrence, Daniel	Matross	West Jersey	
LeGrange, Thomas	Matross	Pittsgrove, Salem	
Lummis, Joseph	Drummer	West Jersey	
Lummis, Parvon	Matross	West Jersey	
Magee, Thomas	Matross	West Jersey	
McFarland, Thomas	Matross	Somerset County	
McGinnis, Arthur	Matross	West Jersey	
McKim, Thomas	Matross	West Jersey	Died 5-18-1777
Moore, David	Lt.	Deerfield, Cumberland	
Moore, Eliphalet	Matross	Woodbridge, Middlesex	Died 6-14-1828
Moore, John	Matross	West Jersey	Deserted 1-1777
Parvin, Matthew	Sergeant	Cumberland County	
Peck, Andrew	Gunner	Upper Alloway, Salem	
Pennington, Willaim	Lt.	Newark, Essex	Elected Governor of NJ
Peters, Philip	Matross	Gloucester County	
Pettitt, Jabez	Matross	Hardwick, Sussex	
Price, Elijah	Matross	West Jersey	Alive in 1821
Price, Nathaniel	Matross	West Jersey	Alive in 1821
Rawlins, William	Matross	Gloucester County	Deserted 4-2-1777
Reves, Joseph	Bombardier	West Jersey	

NAME	RANK	HOME	REMARKS
Robinson, John	Matross	Gloucester County	
Roe, Michael	Matross	Essex County	Deserted 5-28-1779
Roe, Richard	Matross	East Jersey	
Ryley, Job	Matross	West Jersey	
Sayres, Richard	Matross	West Jersey	
Sharp, Levi	Matross	Evesham, Burlington	
Skill, Elisha	Matross	East Jersey	
Smith, Thomas	Corporal	West Jersey	
Sparks, George	Matross	Waterford, Gloucester	
Stone, James	Matross	Newton, Gloucester	Deserted 3-1-1777
Telford, John	Matross	West Jersey	
Tunison, Garret	Sergeant	Raritan, Somerset	Died 8-31-1837
Westcott, John	Lt.	West Jersey	Died 11-25-1813
Wiles, John	Matross	West Jersey	
Whittal, Benjamin	Lt.	West Jersey	

THIRTY-FIVE

A Revolution and Its Soldiers

Bruce Chadwick, Ph.D., 2006

Bruce Chadwick, Ph.D., is a Professor of Writing at New Jersey City University and lecturer on history and film at Rutgers University in New Jersey. Previously, he had a long career in journalism, writing on arts and entertainment and a column on trends in American culture. Eventually he became an editor at the *New York Daily News.*

Read to the Society on October 7, 2006, at Anderson House in Washington, D.C.,in the evening after the Annual Meeting

The rising world shall sing of us a thousand years to come, and tell our children's children the wonders we have done.

—song written by a soldier in the 2d New York regiment

In October of 1781, two hundred and twenty five years ago this month, the Continental Army, under the command of George Washington, who lived across the Potomac River, just a few miles from here, defeated the British Army in a battle that effectively ended the American Revolution. It remains today one of the most stunning victories in world military history. The British had the best army and navy in the world and unlimited resources and yet they lost to an always badly fed, ill equipped, mostly untrained collection of farmers, blacksmiths, carpenters and shoemakers. And they lost to amateurs. The exalted British Army, and their hired mercenaries, such as the Hessians, was composed of battle-scarred veterans who had spent their adult lives in the service; the average age of the American soldier was just eighteen.

But the American Revolution was not simply a military victory to gain independence. Since it involved 240,000 men, nearly 40 percent of every able-bodied man in the colonies, it was a war in which all of the parents, brothers, sisters, wives, girlfriends and children of those men had a vested interest. If you add up all of those people, you wind up with a revolution not just of the American army, but the American people. They all had a high stake in the military victory and then, later, they had an even higher stake in the development and success of the nation their soldiers fought so hard to create.

All Americans can proudly tell their children's children, as the soldier in the 2d New York regiment wrote, of the wonders they had done.

Let us begin by looking at John Greenwood. He was just fifteen years old and he wanted to join the army. Following the battles of Lexington and Concord in the spring of 1775 that began the American Revolution, he walked eighty miles from his uncle's home on Cape Cod, Massachusetts, to Cambridge to enlist in the Continental Army there as a fifer in one of the new fife and drum bands established to provide music for the troops. A short time later, the young boy who went to war as a musician found himself under fire at the battle of Bunker Hill. Within a year, the youngster abandoned his fife and became an infantryman and participated in the invasion of Canada, the crossing of the Delaware and the historic surprise attack on the Hessians in Trenton.

John Greenwood left the army in a dispute of some kind after Trenton, missing the battle of Princeton, and went home. He followed the war in the newspapers and after a year could not remain on the sidelines. He did not want to rejoin the regular army, so he enlisted in a militia company in Massachusetts and fought with them for two years. Greenwood left the war again and went back to Cape Cod and worked in the fishing industry. The inability of the Americans to win the war brought him back yet once more. Still angry with the army, not interested in another stint in the militia, this time he signed on as a sailor on one of the hundreds of privateers, the merchants ships re-fitted with cannon to become part of the rather amateurish American Navy. He was promptly captured on the high seas and imprisoned in a run-down jail on an oppressively hot Caribbean island. Upon his release, he went back to Boston. Most men would have simply gone home, not Greenwood. He signed on with another privateer and was captured and imprisoned yet again. As soon as he was free, he signed on with a third privateer. He was captured and imprisoned once more. By the time the war ended, Greenwood had fought for his country for nearly eight years. He had fought in the army, the navy and the militia. He had grown from a young teenaged boy into a battle-hardened veteran. He did it, as he shouted out in a crowded tavern on one of the first nights he arrived in Boston in 1775 at the tender age of fifteen, because "I want to fight for my country."

Over the years, millions of American men and women have joined the armed forces of the United States "to fight for my country." They were all the descendants of young John Greenwood and the other 240,000 men who fought alongside George Washington in the American Revolution, an eight-year uphill struggle that, in the end, resulted in a new nation that Abraham Lincoln later proclaimed "the last hope of earth."

My recent book, *The First American Army*[1] chronicled the stories of a handful of men in the Revolution. What I tried to do with their stories was to tell the stories of all the men in the Revolution, and in telling all of their stories show that it was the bravery of the soldiers and sailors, the militia recruits, not simply the military brilliance of George Washington, that won independence for America.

---

[1] *Sourcebooks, Inc., Napierville, Illinois, 2005.*

But what I wound up doing, I like to think, was to tell the story not just of these eight men, and soldiers they represented in the first United States Army, but of America itself, an American nation that was not a nation until it had fought its revolution.

Simply put, all revolutions are started for complicated reasons but, in fact, these reasons are often as simple as they are complex and, always, involve extraordinary emotion in the hearts of all the people who fight them. Revolutions are often fought to topple unpopular governments that the people believe unfairly oppress them, to install new and better political systems and to permit a small group of radicals to seize the government and run it. They are often led by charismatic figures such as Mao on his long march, Castro riding into Havana on the back of a jeep, Lenin returning to Moscow in triumph with the Bolsheviks.

The American Revolution was very, very different. It was fought by a people determined to preserve the freedoms and rights they had worked hard to gain during more than 150 years of existence as colonies separated from England by three thousand miles of ocean. In the 1770s, the Americans honestly believed that an oppressive King George III and Parliament wanted to take away all of their rights, impose unfair high taxes, jail anyone who opposed the new policies and reduce the Americans to political slaves. The war was fought to retain the rights Americans had won over those years and to preserve the democratic governments they had established in their colonies, governments with elected assemblies and fair courts, plus forty-four newspapers whose editors had the freedom to write whatever they wanted.

That simple need to prevent England from taking away what was theirs after all those years was the root cause of the Revolution to the people. In researching *The First American Army*, I read the diaries and journals of more than one hundred soldiers. I could not find a single discussion of political theory in any of them. In each, I found the soldiers writing to loved ones back home, and to themselves, that the war was fought for liberty, for freedom, to oust the British tyrants from American soil. It may have been complex to men like John Adams and Benjamin Franklin and Thomas Jefferson, but to the ordinary men who served in the army, and to most people, it was independence to continue to do what they had done for generations—freedom.

The more journals and diaries that I read of the men of the American Revolution, the more I became simply dumbfounded at how similar these men were, in that first American conflict, to all the other men, and later women, who fought in subsequent American wars.

Their goal was simple in 1770: kick the British out of the United States and win freedom. It was simple in 1941 for my father's generation: defend freedom.

In the diaries of the men of the Revolution, the men in my book and the others I have read, there was that same simplicity. Recruiters for the army did not explain political theory or intellectual concepts about democratic government. They just told the men that they had to fight for their homes and their families against the Redcoat oppressors who would take them away from them.

I think, too, that the first American soldiers established the ideal of the gritty, ingenious American fighting man. The American soldier has become unique in the world, but not for the overwhelming resources that our government has at its command, and has had, following needed mobilizations over the years. The American soldier has always used his wits and wiles to prevail: the Christmas sneak attack across the Delaware at Christmas, 1776, the nighttime evacuation of Brooklyn earlier that year, the feigned attack on New York City and subsequent race to the bottled-up British at Yorktown to win the war. Within these campaigns, and within individual battles, the Americans always somehow managed to snatch victory from the jaws of defeat and to do it in ingenious ways.

At one point, I thought it would be really easy to write this book. After all, there were thousands of diaries kept in the Civil War and in World War I. I thought it would be simple to read through the thousands of diaries that must have been written in the Revolution and then spin them together into a book.

I could not have been more wrong. This turned out to be the hardest book of all the twenty-four I have written.

Here was my dilemma, and it is the dilemma of any historian, as the writers you have bestowed your book award on probably have told you. In this book, I needed to find a cross section of soldiers. The revolution was not the story of a company from New Jersey or one from Pennsylvania. The soldiers came from all thirteen colonies and included hundreds of slaves who won their freedom by fighting in the army. I needed men to represent the entire country. I needed men who had been in several key battles of the war. I needed people who had stayed in the army for several years. I wanted soldiers who represented life itself—married men, single men, young and old. Finding them was a difficult journey.

I had the help of the best researchers in America, the folks at the David Library of the American Revolution, at Washington's Crossing, Pennsylvania, the site where the crossing was made. They found most of the diaries I read.

I trudged to a dozen other libraries, too, and searched endless Web sites. Here's the problem. The typical soldier diary entry went like this:

> *"Monday: it rained."*
> *"Tuesday: it rained again."*
> *"Wednesday: it rained some more."*

I found men who wrote nothing at some of the major events of the war at which they were present. One of the soldiers in my book was present at the hanging of Major John Andre, who convinced Benedict Arnold to betray his country, and wrote nothing about it. Can you imagine what he could have written? Should have written? Others would jot down, "met Benjamin Franklin yesterday." And that was all. What a chance for an historian to learn what an ordinary soldier thought of the magnificent Benjamin Franklin. Several diaries I read had single line entries, like "won at Saratoga yesterday." That was it!

I went just about anywhere to find a long discussion of the war. I was certain I had struck gold when I discovered the resting place of the diary of a chaplain who served for eight long years in the war and was at Boston, the invasion of Canada and other key spots. His diary—400 handwritten pages of it—was in the Princeton Theological Seminary. I remember the joy of anticipation I had as I sat down at a reading machine and began the 400-page diary. In 400 pages, and eight long years of writing it, the chaplain said . . . absolutely nothing. Admirably, he talked a lot about God and how privileged he felt to be God's servant on earth, and complained from time to time that the soldiers cursed too much, but had nothing else to say in 400 pages. Wasted trip.

And then you had the diary notes I just loved—the great ordinary humanity of the war. Soldiers then were like soldiers now, Americans then like all of us tonight, were exactly the same. They argued with each other, despised their bosses, thought most politicians were bunglers and feuded with just about anyone they came in contact with. These feuds consumed their diaries and provided a marvelous glimpse into the typical soldier, and typical American, and sustained the knowledge that people never change. One man wrote a single line, "defeated the British at Saratoga yesterday and changed the history of the world." A single line. Then he proceeded to write four entire pages, single spaced, small, scribbling little letters, to complain bitterly that another soldier in his company had owed him a dollar for two weeks and had still not repaid him. The debtor not only had the money, our man wrote, he had paid another soldier in the company back the two dollars he had borrowed from him. But he had not paid our man back the dollar. Well, he concluded after four long pages of bitterness, that behavior was probably to be expected—the man was from Philadelphia.

But I did find the soldiers I was looking for, and if I had searched a thousand libraries I could not have come up with a braver group of men. They were married and unmarried, young and old and from a number of states. There was young John Greenwood, whom I mentioned, who, ironically, later in life became George Washington's dentist and made the only set of false teeth the President ever felt comfortable wearing. There was Jeremiah Greenman, a 17-year-old teenager from Rhode Island who, like millions of soldiers after him, joined the army to see the world. He surely did—he was a POW in Canada and later fought at the battles of Springfield and other key conflicts and earned a place in history. There was 35-year-old Sylvanus Seely, a courageous militia captain and a hopeless womanizer who spent as much time chasing his neighbors' wives as he did chasing the British. There was Lieutenant James McMichael, a newlywed and a fledgling poet, who galloped home to see his new bride every time he could fast talk his commanding officer into giving him a furlough.

There was Ebenezer Wild, from Massachusetts, who hoping to get his military feet wet in a casual skirmish somewhere—and wound up in his first fight at Saratoga. There was Elijah Fisher, who fell into the Schuylkill River at Valley Forge and was rushed to the hospital, where he nearly died because instead of simply keeping him warm and dry the doctors bled pints of blood out of him, reaffirming the popular adage about Revolutionary hospitals: if you get sick, no matter what, don't go to the hospital.

And there were the more then 5,000 black soldiers, some trained by Jeremiah Greenman, who fought bravely, convinced that the men who started the Revolution would end slavery, since they had declared that Americans did not want to be slaves to England. They were wrong. It would take another American war to end slavery.

And, among my personal heroes, there were a chaplain and a doctor who met by accident during the catastrophic retreat following the failed invasion of Canada in 1775. One healed the soldiers' bodies and the other healed their souls. And both, day after day, exemplified a marvelous humanity toward all the brave young men in uniform amid the dead and dying in the whirlwind of war.

One of the things that historians love to do—always—is to discover that at the bottom of their impressive statues, our heroes had feet of clay. Newly discovered diaries and letters often show that our most highly regarded Presidents did have flaws, that the great explorers mistreated their men, that the legendary western marshals sometimes ran away from a gunfight. I thought I might do that too in *The First American Army.* Could the winter camps have been that harsh? Did men really go for three or five days with nothing, not even a handful of bread? Were they really half naked in snowstorms, barefoot on the marches, forced to suck the juice out of leather?

In short, they did. I think that more than anything else the hardships the first American soldiers confronted, and their ability to overcome them and stay together, and win the war, is what impressed me, what amazed me, the most in my work. At Valley Forge 2,500 men died from disease and malnutrition, one sixth of the army. Again and again in the winters of the war, men went without food for days. In Morristown in that God-awful winter of 1779–1780, with its twenty-six snowstorms and six blizzards, the men ate the food usually fed to the horses; some sucked bark and all used the dirty snow as water. Some slept six in a row next to each other, clinging, in snow, for warmth. They did wrap cartridge belts around their feet for shoes. They did live in flimsy lean-to huts, battered by rain and snow and wind.

What I also discovered was that overcoming these hardships—while at the same time they knew the British soldiers were living well in heated city homes, with warm meals and plenty of ale to drink—made them different men. I don't mean that it simply toughened them. It turned all of them into very different kinds of soldiers. It was the foundation of the gritty, determined American fighting man—and woman—today, who can overcome any hardship in order to triumph. Nearly starving to death, nearly dying of disease, going four days without food, walking with straps tied around their feet for shoes and pulling coats over bare chests in snowfalls did not merely toughen them physically. It gave them a whole new dimension as fighting men, created a different army than the one that began that war, a different army than the British. They were the forerunners of all those other fighting men and women who have braved snowfalls, lack of food and clothing, blistering heat to emerge victorious in American history.

There was no better example of that than Valley Forge. Baron Von Steuben, a Prussian officer, trained the men to march, maneuver and fight as well as the Europeans that winter, following the awful hardships that put one in six men in a cemetery. The Americans had survived a brutal and lethal winter—probably the worst experience in all of American military history—and trained themselves anew for battle. They did not trudge mournfully out of Valley Forge, barely able to walk. No, they marched out proudly, in triumph, at a quick step, ready, willing and eager to take on the British, or anybody. They came away from the awful hardships of Valley Forge not as a stumbling, bungling gaggle of farmers, as the British liked to believe, but as one of the best armies in the world, in the history of the world.

They created the image of the American soldier that we have remembered so well in other wars and in other places, whether the troops storming the beaches of Pacific Islands, the men struggling ashore on D-Day, the jungle patrols in Vietnam or those engaged in tank battles in our conflicts in the Middle East.

Again, over the eight years of the conflict, there were 240,000 men in that war, nearly 40 percent of the male population of the United States. If you add to that all of their parents, wives, brothers, sisters and children, you can see that England was not fighting just an army of rebels under the command of a Virginia farmer, but an entire country. It was not just the soldiers, then, that came out of that Revolution defining this new and distinct American spirit, but everybody. The Revolution did not simply give independence to America—it defined America.

I discovered a number of surprising things in my research on the Continental Army for which the Society is kind enough to honor me tonight, as well as in my first book about the Revolution, *George Washington's War,* and in my latest work, *The General and Mrs. Washington.* The most extraordinary thing I discovered, though, was the mercurial relationship between the ordinary soldiers and George Washington.

As I mentioned, I read over one hundred diaries and journals of soldiers. In all of them, the men complained, and at great length, about their officers. They lambasted the lower ranking officers, but saved their real venom for the generals. They accused the generals of bad decision making, poor leadership, lack of sympathy for the men, no regard for their needs in food and clothing and overall bungling. In none of those diaries, though, was there a word of criticism of George Washington. Never. He was admired greatly by his troops. Why?

By all accounts, George Washington maintained an arm's length relationship with the ordinary soldiers. Oh, he did visit the hospitals and he did ride through camp and make some inquiries of the troops as to their needs, but in general he kept a distance from them, as all Commanders do, in order to keep their respect as underlings. He was certainly not one of the rebel leaders of legend and lore who swam, ate and spent leisure time with their men. He was not a soft leader whom the men like for leniency. No, he was a tough disciplinarian who had his men hanged and shot and imprisoned for infractions, the quintessential stern taskmaster. He was as tough on the Americans as the British commanders were on their troops, yet there was no great love of Howe or Clinton or Cornwallis by their men.

The answer was that the troops in that war wanted to win, but they also wanted to get home safely to their loved ones. They wanted a Commander who was always working on their behalf, in battle and in camp, a man who fought for them with Congress for their pay and supplies, who fought with farmers and merchants for them to get food and clothing, a man who was always checking to make certain that his men were taken care of the best the army and government could.

All of that would have been enough to engender their admiration. But there was more. The soldiers certainly did not expect Washington, as Commander in Chief, to put himself in danger, to ride in the line of fire with them. But he did. Time and again, at Trenton, Princeton, Monmouth, Yorktown, and in other battles, he was right there leading attacks, supervising retreats, cannon shells exploding around him and musket balls whistling past him. At Monmouth, he rode back and forth in front of his men to rally them as the British cannon thundered away and Redcoat sharpshooters fired at him—thankfully, missing. That willingness to risk his life, as he was asking the ordinary troops to risk theirs, endeared him to those men forever.

This was summed up best for me not by any diary from the 1770s, but from a conversation with one of my students at Rutgers University last year, a student who had just returned from a tour of duty in Iraq. He said that a soldier in any war wants to win the battle, of course; but win or lose that battle, he wants to get out of it safely—alive and not wounded. He wants a commander who knows how to win but knows how to lose and retreat to save his men. The soldier wants a commander who in battle does everything possible to secure the safety of his troops and, if possible, assure victory. The soldier wants a commander who takes care of him in battle but, just as importantly, off the battlefield—making certain he gets proper medical care and has proper equipment, food and clothing. That commander should not work with the defense department or the politicians, but with his troops. Soldiers know that you rarely find that kind of commander. Today's generals, my student said, never put their lives on the line with their men—the final bond. They are well in the rear—planning. George Washington put his life at risk all the time. Any soldiers who sees his Commander in Chief out there with him, in the line of fire, risking his life, has got to love that man.

At first, the heroic soldiers of the Revolution were robbed of their victory parades and celebrations. Success at Yorktown effectively ended the major fighting in the conflict, and brought about peace talks, but the war did not actually end until eighteen long months later, in 1783. By then, almost all of the soldiers had left the army and returned home. George Washington had only eight hundred troops with him when he entered New York City as the British Navy sailed away to signal the official end of the conflict. Those eight hundred troops were cheered by the populace of New York, but there was little cheering for the other 239,000 veterans of the Revolution.

Oh, there were small celebrations. Friends would hold a dinner for a man who returned to his town from the army. Perhaps there would be a few toasts at the local tavern or a final singing of the war's triumphal song, "War and Washington," and a few barbecues to honor a few men here and there when they were back on their farm or in their village shop.

There were no large parades, even in cities, because after Yorktown the war had not formally ended. Washington, in fact, suspected that the British would be on the attack again during those eighteen months. So there were no celebrations.

George Washington was feted, of course, in New York and then along the way to his resignation from the army at Annapolis, where Congress was meeting that year. Several hundred veterans turned up at the resignation, jamming their way into the hall, in their uniforms, to give one last huzzah for their commander. But then they traveled home, alone.

They returned home to an America victorious in war but struggling economically in peace. Trade with England and Europe had been severely restricted during the Revolution and all U.S. production had been cut back dramatically. The end of the war meant the end of the privateering business for sailors and thousands of them were laid off. Hence, there were few jobs. No one held a veteran's job for him, as they do now. There were no jobs for anyone. Subsequently, unemployment for the soldiers was very high. If they could work, wages were low and, as I showed in my book, employers treated them very badly. Fought for their country in the war? The war was over. There was a meager pension for them, but nothing like there is today for an army vet. There was no Veterans' Administration or V.A. hospitals where those badly injured during the Revolution could be nursed back to health—those wounded just limped through the rest of their lives. The soldiers of the first American Army had won independence and freedom for their country and, in doing so, astounded history by defeating the greatest army and navy in the world. Yet they returned to a few toasts, a pat on the back and not much else.

What happened later, though, was extraordinary.

George Washington was unanimously elected President of the United States in 1789 and rode from Mount Vernon to New York for his inauguration. His route was well publicized and everywhere he went thousands turned out to greet him, whether in large cities, small towns or tiny villages of just a few residences at a dirt highway crossroads. And the veterans came out to cheer on their old commander, many proudly wearing their old uniforms—a bit tight at the waist now.

Everywhere that he went, he honored his old troops with a wave of his hand or a nod and the people gathered on the longest parade route in American history cheered for him and they cheered for the veterans of the army, too. In the large cities Washington was greeted by hundreds of veterans—almost all in uniform. When he approached Philadelphia, hundreds of uniformed veterans met him just as he crossed a bridge into the city. There was sustained cheering all around him. The church bells of the city pealed for hours and every cannon that the city could muster thundered throughout the afternoon to celebrate the arrival of the President-elect. There were more than twenty thousand people crowded on to the parade route, nearly the entire population of the city and the surrounding area. Just imagine a parade in New York City today attended by twenty million people. There were so many people that hundreds took up perches on stoops, in windowsills and even on the tops of roofs. There was nowhere to put the hundreds of disappointed veterans. Washington immediately told the organizers to ask his men to walk behind him in the parade route, as they had walked behind him at Yorktown, Springfield and Monmouth, and proudly out of Valley Forge. They happily joined the parade and as they all walked through the streets of Philadelphia, where the Declaration of Independence was written and Congress met for all those years, the ear-splitting roars of all the residents there were for the troops as well as the President-elect—much to their delight, and his, also.

So in the end, when America celebrated the inauguration of their national hero and the Commander of the Continental Army, it finally celebrated the ordinary troops, too—the farmers and cabinetmakers and blacksmiths and grocers and dressmakers and carpenters. And with those roars on that parade route the country also celebrated all of the people who aided the revolution—those who gave the army food and clothing on credit and still had not been paid for it, the women who knitted all those soldiers' socks and shirts in a thousand sewing circles, the ministers who had turned their pulpits into recruiting stations, the farmers who drove their cattle a hundred miles in the snow to feed the troops, the bankers who loaned the army money they never got back, the thousands of city and county recruiters, the newspaper editors, the chaplains, the doctors, the hundred or more spies who had worked for the army.

In short, on that long parade from Mount Vernon to New York, and at the first President's inauguration, the country celebrated them all—and in so doing celebrated itself.

Let me conclude by telling you my favorite story of all of my research and of the Revolution itself—the story of a soldier in his mid-thirties at the Battle of Rhode Island in 1778. As the British army began to march menacingly toward the American line, the soldier loaded two musket balls, not one, into the barrel of his gun, to the surprise of the 17-year-old private standing next to him. When the boy asked him why he did that, the soldier in this first American army looked him straight in the eye, smiled and said, as all American soldiers have said in the hundreds of years since then, "They want a fight? I'll give them a fight."

Appendix

Toasts

The drinking of toasts in late eighteenth-century America was common at both public and private events. Toasts included drinking either wine or other forms of alcohol and usually came at the end of a meal. As this collection shows, the number often exceeded a dozen or more. We have no way of knowing just how much wine, rum, or beer was consumed with each toast, but the amount probably varied with the event and location. At some public events, the toasts were followed by gun, cannon, or rocket fire, occasionally after each toast. In Colonial America, they almost universally started with toasts to the health of the King, the Queen, the Prince of Wales, and the Royal family. As the Revolution approached, the words became more political, often exhorting the British government and its officials to change their policies in favor of the Colonies. Lists of toasts were sometimes printed in local newspapers and the more popular ones were repeated from city to city.[1] These post-Revolution toasts were given to an audience composed almost exclusively of former Continental Officers of the Line who were war veterans. One can almost feel the flushed feeling of victory in the words of the early toasts. Their gratitude to the allies, especially France, is palpable. Later toasts are more reflective and recognize the great economic, political, and cultural challenges facing the new Republic.

---

1 *For a full discussion of this subject refer to "The American Revolution Seen Through a Wine Glass," Richard J. Hooker,* William and Mary Quarterly, *Third Series, Volume XI, 1954, pp. 42–77.*

This collection of Toasts of the New Jersey Society of the Cincinnati, 1782–1804, is located in the Special Collections, University of Delaware Library, Newark, Delaware. What follows is a description of the collection by Anne E. Krulikowski, writing in 1999:

> *The toasts of the New Jersey Society of the Cincinnati collection contains holograph manuscripts of eight lists of toasts for the traditional Fourth of July meetings for eight years from 1782 through 1804. Only the last three are dated, although internal evidence provides a clear chronological order for the lists. The first poses a problem. The Society was not formed until May 1783 and the New Jersey Society a month later in June of that year. However, the first list contains a toast to the diplomats who are negotiating the peace treaty, signed on January 20, 1783. This does call into question whether the earliest list is, in fact, attributable to the Society of the Cincinnati. However, the sentiments of the toasts, even the order in which they appear, strongly connect the first to the later seven lists.*
>
> *Spanning the Confederation, Federal, and Jeffersonian periods, the subjects and language of the toasts reflect the republican ideals of the era. They also provide some clues as to where the society's members stood on the contemporary political issues: pro-Constitution and strongly Hamiltonian.*

—John W. Gareis, M.D., Assistant Secretary,
Society of the Cincinnati of the State of New Jersey

1782

1. The United States in Congress.
2. The Independence of America.
3. His most Christian Majesty Lewis the 16th, King of France.
4. Queen and Royal Family of France. The Dauphin of France.
5. Count Rochambeau and the French Army.
6. His Excellency Gen. Washington and the Army.
7. General Green and the Southern Army.

8 The Allied Fleets.

9. The United States of Holland and all the friendly Powers of Europe.

10. Governor and State of Jersey.

11. The Chevalier de la Luzerne.

12. The American Ministers.

13. May the swords of America continue unsheathed, until in conjunction with her Allies the basis of Independence establishes a lasting and honorable Peace.

14. Actaeon's fate to all lawgivers who wish to unkennel the hurtful passions of Men.

15. American Republicanism—Equality of right—freedom of opinions and submission to the constituted authorities.

16. The Fair daughters of Columbia—May they always meet the gallant defenders of their country with presented arms.

1783

1. The United States of America now universally acknowledged free and independent.
2. The Federal Congress. Wisdom in their deliberations, and energy in their recommendations.
3. Lewis the 16th of France under whose happy auspices this peace is obtained.
4. General Washington and the American army. May their services in the field be rewarded in the cabinet.
5. The American Commissioners at Paris—thanks to them for their noble acquisitions and decided superiority in the late negotiations.
6. The State we live in and may she enjoy that commerce by the revolution which British policy formerly debarred her from.
7. The Marquis de la Fayette, our Noble assistant in the day of trial and hazard.
8. The civil Officers of the United States with judgment and dispatch to them in the execution of their employment.

9. An increase of Republican Virtue and frugality at the expense of Monarchical luxury and extravagance.
10. Prosperity and Perfection to the Arts, Agriculture, Manufactures and Commerce of America.
11. May Nassau Hall again flourish, continue the Nursery of Statesmen as she has been of Warriors.
12. Success to Republicanism.
13. An increase to our exports and a diminution of our imports. May we never depend upon Europe for what we can have within ourselves.
14. May all the World enjoy that Freedom which we have lately acquired ourselves.
15. May the event which occasions this meeting be as permanent as it is honorable.
16. May the Independence of America be as lasting as the World.

1784

1. The United States—let their concord of happiness be perpetual.
2. Congress—may that illustrious body never want the inclination or the power to promote the happiness and glory of their country.
3. France—may that friendly kingdom never want on her throne a prince as great and as good as Lewis the sixteenth!
4. Gen'l Washington—let his well-earned fame be eternal!
5. The late army of America—may their immortal laurels flourish with those of their beloved Cincinnatus!
6. Never let the ambition of power or territory corrupt the principles, or disturb the union of the American republics.
7. *Independence* on every other power, and *submission* to our own laws!
8. The happy era that gave birth to the exertion of our own talents by exempting us from the disgraceful tutelage of another!
9. The State of New Jersey, may her sons be as distinguished for virtue and knowledge as for military prowess!
10. May New Jersey become the Attica of America and Princeton the Athens of that Attica!

11. May the Governor of New Jersey ever continue to be greater than a king by ruling in the hearts of a free people!
12. A health to the *Majesty of the people!*
13. Let the hilarity of this day be a virtuous example of the manners of a young republic!

    (The 12th may be omitted and instead of it after France drink to the following —

14. The United Netherlands—may the corruption of their manners never invite a Caesar to destroy their liberties!)

1798

1. The United States. May their sovereignty and independence be perpetual.
2. All classes of the people. May they be prosperous and happy.
3. The president. May he be supported by his constituents.
4. Gen'l Washington. May his western sun be as bright as his meridians.
5. Our Envoys extraordinary at Paris—may they continue to deserve well of their country.
6. The Army and Navy of the United States. May they be crowned with triumph.
7. Our agriculture, arts and commerce. May they grow with the squares of the years of our independence.
8. Our fellow soldiers who fell in the conflict for liberty. May they be imitated by their successors.
9. The Society of the Cincinnati. May their country be dear to them and they to their country.
10. Union and Stability to the friends of the Constitution.
11. May virtue and merit be always rewarded.
12. May candor and honesty be our governing prince.
13. May power be influenced only by justice.
14. May authority be amiable without debasing its dignity.
15. May we never seek applause from party principles, but always deserve it from public spirit.
16. The American Ladies. May they smile only on the friends of their country.

17. The youthful volunteers of America. May they never shrink from their pretensions nor disgrace their ancestors.

1799

1. The Day. May each returning Anniversary find the American people more and more convinced of the Truth and Rectitude of Washington's principles and policy.
2. The United States—Embarked on a tempestuous sea, may they not make shipwreck of their Liberty and Independence.
3. The Memory of our late beloved Chief and Father, Gen'l George Washington—Bright as day, durable as time.
4. The President of the United States.
5. Both Houses of Congress—May their rulings be purely American and their Councils be wise, dignified and impartial.
6. The Army and Navy of the United States.
7. The Militia of the United States.
8. The Memory of our late Brother officers and Soldiers.
9. Our surviving Brethren of the Cincinnati—May they continue to deserve well of their country.
10. General Pinckney, the President General of the Cincinnati.
11. Agriculture, Commerce, and Manufactures—Mutually dependent on each other, may the fostering hand of a wise policy cherish their Connection.
12. The Judiciary of the United States—Independent of party, of power and of popularity.
13. The State of New Jersey—May her citizens discover an attachment to principles and not Men.
14. The first Article in addition to and amendment of the Constitution of the United. States. The Liberty of Speech and of the Press is Essential to the Security of Freedom in a State.

1802

1. The Day and those who have not learned to dishonor it.
2. The memory of Gen'l Washington our late President—May his heroic deeds and patriotic virtues be an example for every rising generation.

3. The President of the United States.
4. The Congress—May their motives be pure and their measures wise.
5. The Constitution of the United States—Support to its real friends and confusion to Pretenders.
6. Major General Hamilton—May he continue to deserve well of his country.
7. Our Foreign Envoys—May they rival the wisdom and firmness of Marshall and Pinckney.
8. The Army and Navy—May they stand high on the scale of merit.
9. The memory of our Departed Heroes who have fallen in defense of true liberty and religion.
10. Our brethren of Cincinnati—May the Heart of each member be an altar of Patriotism.
11. The Integrity of Federalism—May the misguided be aware of their folly and no longer pin their faith on imported Patriots or apostatized Americans.
12. The American Eagle—May no Foreign Connection contaminate the brood.
13. Regulated liberty to all who dare deserve it.
14. The State of New Jersey—May candor and honesty be always her governing maxims.
15. American Republicanism—Equality of right—freedom of opinions and submission to the constituted authorities.
16. The Fair daughters of Columbia—May they always meet the gallant defenders of their country with presented arms.

Volunteers

The triumph of religion and order over infidelity and confusion—Wisdom and vigor to our government. Zeal and Patriotism to our citizens.

The liberty of the Seas, may those who violate the Rights of Nations on this Element, experience the chastisement of the insurgents.

May the temples of fame and fortune be shut to all but the supporters of order and good government.

May morals and good principles never be resigned to the tyranny of time and fashion.

May that zeal for our country which derived its birth from calamity grow up to maturity through deeds of enterprise and successful conflict.

Union of sentiment and firmness of conduct in supporting our rights as a free and independent nation.

The black hole of Calcutta to the enemies of order.

The Vice President of the United States—May our modern Philosopher be illuminated with the light that struck Saul to this Earth.

1802

1. The fourth day of July 1776.
2. The memory of Gen'l Washington our late beloved President General.
3. The President of the United States.
4. The Vice President and both houses of Congress.
5. The Constitution—May its three grand pillars be kept distinct and independent.
6. The President General and all our brethren of the Cincinnati.
7. The memory of our late Brethren in arms who fell in defense of their country or who died in the bed of peace. The Army and Navy of the United States.
8. No grades in Society but what are derived from merit.
9. Public good—May it never be made a stalking horse for Private Interest.
10. May moral and good principles be never resigned to the tyranny of time and fashion. Union of sentiment and firmness of conduct in supporting of our national rights. The fair daughters of Columbia—May their frowns repel the violent and their smiles reward the brave. All faithful servants of the public in and out of office.
11. The State of New Jersey—Oblivion to all animosity among her citizens.
12. The Science of Agriculture—May it increase rapidly for the accommodation of those who practice the Art.

13. The universal advancement of Arts and Science. The real patriots and heroes of 1776—Whose wisdom and fortitude declared and secured our Independence as a nation.
14. Actaeon's fate to all lawgivers who wish to unkennel the hurtful passions of Men.
15. American Republicanism—Equality of right—freedom of opinions and submission to the constituted authorities.
16. The Fair daughters of Columbia—May they always meet the gallant defenders of their country with presented arms.

1804

1. The day—May it be celebrated to the latest Posterity.
2. The memory of our late President General and commander in chief, George Washington—The heart of every soldier is his Mausoleum.
3. Departed Heroes who fought and bled in the late revolutionary war—May their widows and children never know distress.
4. Our brother officers—May we never forget the ties that bind us to each other.
5. The President of the United States.
6. The Vice President and both houses of Congress.
7. The heads of Departments.
8. The Army and Navy of the United States.
9. Captain Bainbridge and his unfortunate associates—May they soon be restored to their country and their friends.
10. May the dreadful Idea of war be suggested only by the Idea of public welfare.
11. The General and State governments—May the whole be as indissoluble and energetic as the parts are sovereign and free.
12. May the sword never supplant the law as the sovereign arbiter of this nation.
13. May the United States never be privileged to make war upon one another after the manner of the Baronies of old.

14. The rising generation—May they continually support the independence we celebrate.
15. The President General of the Cincinnati.
16. Rulers who blend with their civil character that of Benefactor and Friend.
17. The Daughters of America—May their virtues be rewarded with love and domestic happiness.

Volunteers

Oblivion to all animosities among good men.

Union of sentiment and firmness of conduct in supporting our right as a free independent nation.

May virtue and merit be always rewarded.

May authority be amiable without debasing its dignity.